D0857529

The Paston family in the fifteenth century

THE PASTON FAMILY IN THE FIFTEENTH CENTURY

The first phase

COLIN RICHMOND

Reader in History, University of Keele

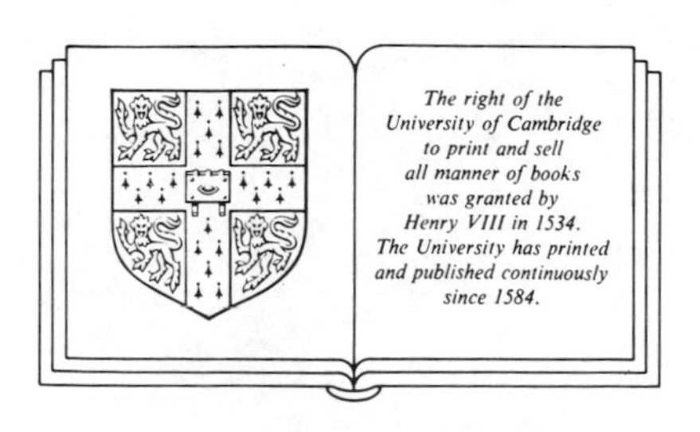
The right of the
University of Cambridge
to print and sell
all manner of books
was granted by
Henry VIII in 1534.
The University has printed
and published continuously
since 1584.

CAMBRIDGE UNIVERSITY PRESS

Cambridge
New York Port Chester
Melbourne Sydney

Published by the Press Syndicate of the University of Cambridge
The Pitt Building, Trumpington Street, Cambridge CB2 1RP
40 West 20th Street, New York, NY 10011, USA
10 Stamford Road, Oakleigh, Melbourne 3166, Australia

First published 1990

Printed in Great Britain at the University Press, Cambridge

British Library cataloguing in publication data

Richmond, Colin, 1937–
The Paston family in the fifteenth century: the first phase.
1. England. Paston (Family)
I. Title
929'.2'0942

Library of Congress cataloguing in publication data

Richmond, Colin.
The Paston family in the fifteenth century: the first phase / Colin Richmond.
p. cm.
Includes bibliographical references.
ISBN 0-521-38502-4
1. England – Social life and customs – Medieval period, 1066–1485.
2. Great Britain – History – Lancaster and York, 1399–1485. 3. Great Britain – History – Henry VII. 1485–1509. 4. Norfolk (England) – Social life and customs. 5. Paston family – Correspondence.
6. Paston letters. I. Title.
DA240.R53 1990
942 – dc 20 89-25147 CIP

ISBN 0 521 38502 4

SE

For Myrna

CONTENTS

GENEALOGICAL TABLES

PREFACE

'I found myself liking at least two tracks of "Miles in the Sky", not as jazz, but as a kind of soundtrack to some bleak pastoral such as a film of the *Paston Letters*.'[1] Philip Larkin mistakes the timeless attraction of the *Paston Letters* as surely as he does the enduring appeal of Miles Davis. From Horace Walpole's day until our own the letters have been read as much for pleasure as for profit. I find it difficult to distinguish between the two: my failure to do so has determined the nature of this book. It is written in what Ulrich Zwingli called *Geschichteswyss* – in a narrative fashion[2] – and deliberately so. It has been said[3] that analysis is a 'non-doing', that it is an alternative to action. In our society there is an analytical mania: as men, women, and children were dying on the terraces at Hillsborough so-called experts were analysing why they were. Also (it has been said) the analytical spirit obstructs enjoyment: the historian resembles the beadle of Rouen cathedral in *Madame Bovary*. My resolution was to avoid a joyless (and frustrating) examination of fifteenth-century specimens. What I resolved upon was a Shandean book: 'Could a historiographer drive on his history as a muleteer drives on his mule, straight forward . . . but the thing is, morally speaking, impossible.' Besides, there is no delight in the direct route. 'Digressions, incontestably, are the sunshine; – they are the life, the soul of reading – take them out of this book, for instance, you might as well take the book along with them.'[4] Not only a Shandean book, but one composed as if by Cide Hamete Benengeli himself:

Cide Hamete Benengeli was a very exact historian and very precise in all his details, as can be seen by his not passing over these various points, trivial and petty though they may be. He should be an example to those grave historians who give us so short

[1] *All What Jazz?* (London, 1970), p. 254. I owe this reference to Dr Ian Arthurson.
[2] Michael Baxandall, *The Limewood Sculptors of Renaissance Germany* (London, 1980), p. 186.
[3] By Marjorie Reeves, in Ann Williams (ed.) *Prophecy and Millenarianism: Essays in Honour of Marjorie Reeves* (London, 1980), p. 14.
[4] Laurence Sterne, *The Life and Opinions of Tristram Shandy Gentleman*, bk I, chs. 14, 22, and cf. the diagrams in bk VI, ch. 60.

and skimped an account of events that we scarcely taste them, and so the most substantial part of their work, out of carelessness, malice, or ignorance, remains in their ink-horns.[5]

One other explanation concerning method is necessary: 'The natural vice of historians is to claim to know about the past.'[6] The task is not the impossible one of changing one's nature; it is the almost impossible one of curbing the vicious habit of a lifetime: of obscuring the past by a presumption to knowledge of it. If to appreciate history is 'to go on reading till you can hear people talking', then I ought to have an appreciation of the Pastons: I have been listening to what they say since first encountering their letters thirty years ago. Also, it is crystal clear (to me) that there is no substitute for their own words. To try to put those words into one's own is to alter their idiom. To try to modernize even the spelling is to tamper with expression and thus with meaning. I endeavour to let the Pastons do the talking. Thus, I can say with greater conviction than most authors: 'Any shortcomings in this book are entirely mine. The truth I have taken from others.'[7]

In this first volume matters under discussion are those which preoccupy a gentry family as it is rising. The chapter headings show what these are. The book is in this respect introductory. It is also introductory in relation to the Pastons themselves, for the crux of their fifteenth-century story is the death of Sir John Fastolf in 1459. Until that date all seems in the manner of a prelude. The preliminaries are not unimportant: Judge William Paston's career from homespun to riches is what places the family in Norfolk society; his construction of a landed estate, while reminiscent of Mark 12:38–40, is both the underpinning of that place and the launching pad for the next thrust upward; the marriage he makes for his son and heir reveals not only the position he had reached but also the patron who will be the making of John Paston: Sir John Fastolf. Lastly there is Judge William's untidy death. His own late marriage to Agnes Barry meant that when he died in 1444 he left a young widow and too many young children; he dithered as to how to distribute his property among them and the resulting tensions between Agnes, John, John's sons, and the younger children were to disturb and then disrupt family harmony over the succeeding fifty years.[8] The pre-1459 phase is less well-known, less understood, less appreciated than is what follows. The book may, therefore, stand in its own right.

[5] *Don Quixote*, pt I, ch. 16. I had this reference from David Morgan.

[6] This and the following quotation are from James Campbell, *The Anglo-Saxons* (London, 1982), pp. 8, 20.

[7] Alan Ereira, *The Invergordon Mutiny* (London, 1981), p. viii.

[8] For a summary see 'The Pastons', *History and Archaeology Review*, no. 2 (Spring 1987), pp. 21–5.

There are many *Paston Letters*. They are rich and, being letters, varied in content. The writers of them, both Pastons and others, allude to (rather than recount) many stories which are incidental to the main ones. Some of these are irresistible to this historian; he may have 'reconciled himself to diminished omniscience',[9] but his desire remains that of 2 Maccabees 2:30: 'To make the subject his own, to explore its by-ways, to be meticulous about details.' In other words: there is no alternative method to the Shandean if the density of Paston life, the multiplicity of the family's concerns (trivial and otherwise), the range of their contacts (from critical to casual), and the complexity of living without knowing the future is to be described. Yet, gourmet's feast though the letters are and (paradoxically) tough to masticate – as well as digest – as they are, they still constitute the familiar 'documentary prison'.[10] It is a confinement from which I am as desperate to escape as the next historian, and in an attempt to do so, like Ralph Pendrel in *The Sense of the Past*, who 'wanted evidence of a sort for which there had never been documents enough, or for which documents mainly, however multiplied, would never *be* enough', I fairly advertently may have tried 'for an ell in order to get an inch'.[11]

Questions of context are less pressing than is the problem of density. The fifteenth century is no longer regarded as 'crepuscular', because it has been flooded with light over the last thirty years.[12] The social background has been illuminated by F.R.H. Du Boulay, the foreground (fifty years ago) by H.S. Bennett. The general economic framework James Bolton and Christopher Dyer have made clear; the particular has been clarified by R.H. Britnell.[13] The way the law worked and the ways lawyers manipulated it have been revealed by Margaret Hastings, Marjorie Blatcher, and Eric Ives. Where the all-important politics of the England of the Pastons is concerned many have carried the torch lit by K.B. McFarlane; as a specific commentary James Gairdner's introduction to the 1904 edition of the *Paston Letters* is invaluable. There is no need, therefore, to put the family into their context here. The Wars of the Roses were complex; they certainly complicated the lives of John Paston and his sons; but that is what the sequel to this volume is about.

[9] Leon Edel, *The Life of Henry James*, vol. II (Harmondsworth: Penguin, 1977), p. 417.

[10] *Ibid.*, p. 490.

[11] *Ibid.*, p. 346. I hope that my resistance has been tougher than that of Frederick Furnivall; his ability to digress reaches the risible in the following footnote (*The Fifty Earliest English Wills*, EETS, OS 78 (London, 1882), p. 129): 'Cobham Hall, Kent, 3 miles W. of Rochester, now the seat of the Earls of Darnley. – J.H. Round. (At Cobham in Surrey, on the river Mole, 19 miles S. by W. of London, I once saw a friend pull out a 4lb. perch.).'

[12] It was Professor Jacob who used the word, according to V.H.H. Green, *Bishop Reginald Pecock* (London, 1945), p. 234.

[13] 'The Pastons and their Norfolk', *The Agricultural History Review*, 36 (1988), pp. 132–44.

Finally, if it is asked why the Pastons, the answer is simple, despite all the Flaubertian reservations ('We can study files for decades, but every so often we are tempted to throw up our hands and declare that history is merely another literary genre: the past is autobiographical fiction pretending to be a parliamentary report'; 'We are dancing not on the edge of a volcano, but on the wooden seat of a latrine, and it seems to me more than a touch rotten. Soon society will go plummeting down and drown in nineteen centuries of shit'[14]). It is this and it is twofold: first, 'the history of mankind may often be summed up in the changes that have overtaken one community, one family or one man';[15] second, Kenneth Bruce McFarlane taught me that history has to be a passion as well as a discipline.

[14] Julian Barnes, *Flaubert's Parrot* (London: Picador, 1985), pp. 36, 90.

[15] Andre N. Chouraqui, *Between East and West. A History of the Jews of North Africa* (New York, 1973), p. xxii.

ACKNOWLEDGEMENTS

This book was made possible by the generosity of the Leverhulme Trust: the award of a fellowship allowed me (with the supplementary assistance of the University of Keele) to have a year's leave in order to write it. For this opportunity I am deeply grateful. 'To sum up all; there are archives at every stage to be looked into, and rolls, records, documents, and endless genealogies, which justice ever and anon calls him [the historian] back to stay the reading of: – In short, there is no end of it.'[1] At this temporary halt it is a pleasure to be able to thank all those librarians and archivists who have been so helpful, especially those at the library of the University of Keele (in particular, Martin Phillips), the British Library, the Public Record Office, the Bodleian Library, Magdalen College, and (above all) the Norfolk Record Office. There are many whose enthusiasm for this enterprise has encouraged me when mine has flagged; I am especially grateful to Margaret Aston (who read the complete text to the benefit of other readers), Barrie Dobson, David Morgan, Anthony Smith (whose work on the Pastons re-inspired mine), Diana Spelman, and Bernard Finnemore, who assisted with the chronological table and composed the index. Ralph Griffiths persuaded me to write a book on the Pastons; I hope he approves of the one I have written. Rowena Gay and Myrna Richmond worked wonders on the typewriter and at the word processor: I thank them. For kindness far beyond the dutiful my thanks go to William Davies and Jenny Potts at the Press.

The chronological table is adapted from that in Norman Davis (ed.), *Paston Letters and Papers of the Fifteenth Century*, vol. I, pp. lxiv–lxxiii. The attention of the readers is also drawn to the map at the end of that volume.

[1] *Tristram Shandy*, bk I, ch. 14.

ABBREVIATIONS

BIHR	*Bulletin of the Institute of Historical Research*
BL	British Library
Blomefield	F. Blomefield, *Topographical History of Norfolk* (5 vols., Kersfield and Lynn, 1739–75)
C	Chancery
Cal. Anc. Deeds	*Calendar of Ancient Deeds*
Cal. Charter Rolls	*Calendar of Charter Rolls*
Cal. Papal Letters	*Calendar of Papal Letters*
CCR	*Calendar of Close Rolls*
CFR	*Calendar of Fine Rolls*
CIPM	*Calendar of Inquisitions Post Mortem*
Copinger, *Manors*	W.A. Copinger, *Manors of Suffolk* (7 vols., London, 1905–11)
CP	*The Complete Peerage*, ed. V. Gibbs and others (12 vols., London, 1910–59)
CPR	*Calendar of Patent Rolls*
Davis	*Paston Letters and Papers of the Fifteenth Century*, ed. Norman Davis, vol. I (London, 1971), vol. II (London, 1976)
DKR	Deputy Keeper's Report
Ec.HR	*Economic History Review*
EETS	Early English Text Society
EHR	*English Historical Review*
Emden, *Biog. Reg. Camb.*	A.B. Emden, *A Biographical Register of the University of Cambridge to 1500* (London, 1963)
Emden, *Biog. Reg. Oxon.*	A.B. Emden, *A Biographical Register of the University of Oxford to 1500* (3 vols., Oxford, 1957–9)
Feudal Aids	*Inquisitions and Assessments relating to Feudal*

	Aids 1284–1431 (6 vols., London, 1899–1920)
Gairdner	James Gairdner, *The Paston Letters* (6 vols., Library edn, 1904)
HMC	Historical Manuscripts Commission
Hopton	C. Richmond, *John Hopton: a Fifteenth-Century Suffolk Gentleman* (Cambridge, 1981)
Magd. Coll.	Magdalen College, Oxford
NCC	Norwich Consistory Court
NRO	Norfolk Record Office
PCC	Prerogative Court of Canterbury
Pevsner	Nikolaus Pevsner, *The Buildings of England* (London, 1951–74)
PPC	*Proceedings and Ordinances of the Privy Council*, ed. Sir N.H. Nicolas (6 vols., London, 1834–7)
PRO	Public Record Office
Rot. Parl.	*Rotuli Parliamentorum* (1767–77)
SRO	Suffolk Record Office
Staffs. RO	Staffordshire Record Office
Testamenta Vetusta	ed. Sir N.H. Nicolas (2 vols., London, 1826)
Test. Ebor.	*Testamenta Eboracensia*, ed. James Raine and others, Surtees Society (London, 1836–1902)
Valor Ecclesiasticus	*Valor Ecclesiasticus* (6 vols., London, 1825–34)
VCH	*Victoria County History*
Wedgwood, *Biographies*	J.C. Wedgwood, *History of Parliament, Biographies of the Members of the Commons House 1439–1509* (London, 1936)

CHRONOLOGICAL TABLE

	FAMILY AFFAIRS	PUBLIC EVENTS
1378	William Paston I born	
1379	William Winter purchased East Beckham	
1397	William Winter died	
1399		Henry IV king
1409	Beatrice Paston died John Winter bought East Beckham	
1412	William Paston I is paid for counselling the city authorities at Norwich	
1413	William Paston I steward of courts of the Bishop of Norwich	Accession of Henry V
1414	William Paston I arbitrator concerning mayoralty of Norwich John Winter died	
1415	William Paston I a JP William Worcester born East Beckham sold to William and Joan Mariot	Henry V's first campaign in France Battle of Agincourt
1416	Geoffrey Somerton died	
1417		Henry V's second campaign in France
1419	William Paston I bought Oxnead Clement Paston I died	Surrender of Rouen
1420	William Paston I married Agnes Barry	Treaty of Troyes Battle of Baugé
1421	William Paston I serjeant-at-law John Paston I born 10 Oct.	
1422	William Paston I commissioner of assize in the south-west	Accession of Henry VI. John, Duke of Bedford Regent
1424	William Paston I in London, consulted by Norwich Corporation Walter Aslak attacks him in Norwich	Battle of Verneuil
1425	Edmund Paston I born	
1426	By this date William Paston I	

	acquired manors of Shipden and Ropers in Cromer	
1427	William Paston I buys Gresham	
1429	William Paston I justice of common pleas Elizabeth Paston born	Joan of Arc raises siege of Orleans Henry VI crowned at Westminster
1430	William Paston I acquires manors of Woodhall in Great Palgrave, Sporle, and Streethall in Cressingham	Joan of Arc captured
1431		Joan of Arc burnt Henry VI crowned in Paris
1433	William Paston commissioner to inquire into the administration of Norwich John Mautby died	
1434	William Mariot died 5 Sept. Edmund Winter seized and occupied East Beckham 20 Dec.	
1435	Mariots surrender to William Paston I all evidence of title to East Beckham 6 Jan.	Congress and Treaty of Arras Death of Bedford Sir John Fastolf governor of Anjou and Maine
1436	By this date William Paston I legal advisor to Fastolf William Paston II born	French recover Paris Siege of Calais
1437	East Beckham seized by the Crown and granted for life to Edmund Hampden	Henry VI takes on (or: does not take on) duties of government
1439		Fastolf returns to England
1440	John Paston I married Margaret Mautby by 4 Nov.	Siege of Harfleur
1441	John Mariot occupies East Beckham	
1442	Clement Paston II born William Paston I granted custody of East Beckham 22 Mar. and later leased it to Simon Gunnor and William Shepherd	
1443	William Paston I licensed to divert roads both at Paston and at Oxnead John Hauteyn claims Oxnead	
1444	John Paston III born East Beckham awarded to William Paston I 17 Mar. Agreement between William Paston I and copyhold tenants in Paston 30 Mar. William Paston I died 13 Aug.	Peace negotiations with France
1445	Agnes Paston in dispute with vicar and villagers of Paston John Mariot recovers East Beckham	Henry VI married Margaret of Anjou

1447	John Paston I a JP	Arrest and death of Humphrey, Duke of Gloucester
1448	Gresham claimed and occupied by Lord Moleyns 17 Feb. Edmund Winter died 26 Feb.	
1449	Edmund Paston I died Margaret Paston evicted from Gresham mansion by Moleyns and the mansion sacked 29 Jan. Margaret Paston fled to Norwich, Feb.	War with France reopened Rouen lost
1450	Hauteyn's claims to Oxnead abandoned John Paston I sued for trespass at Gresham by Moleyns	Duke of Suffolk impeached and murdered at sea Cade's rebellion Cherbourg lost Richard, Duke of York, returns from Ireland Crisis
1451	Agnes Paston in conflict with villagers of Paston about the wall. Amerced 6d in the manorial court of Gimmingham John Paston I regains Gresham	Gascony lost The crisis continues
1452	John Paston I complains of disturbances in Norfolk	Army under Talbot sent to Gascony Government recovers its nerve
1453	Philip Berney died 2 July	Talbot killed at Castillon and Gascony finally lost Henry VI has a nervous breakdown Edward, Prince of Wales, born
1454		York made Protector and captain of Calais Henry VI returns to active (*sic*) life at Christmas
1455	John Paston I, on Fastolf's behalf, disputes with Sir Philip Wentworth the wardship of Thomas Fastolf	First Battle of St Albans York again Protector
1456	John Paston I and William Paston II among Fastolf's feoffees Fastolf proposes to found a college at Caister	York discharged from protectorship. From Sept. the court at Coventry William Wainfleet chancellor
1457	John Paston I pays fine to decline knighthood	The French sack Sandwich
1458	Elizabeth Paston marries Robert Poynings	Warwick at Calais Magdalen College, Oxford, founded by Wainfleet
1459	William Paston III born Fastolf died 5 Nov. William Paston II and William Worcester in London about Fastolf's property	Battles of Blore Heath and Ludford York and Yorkists attainted in parliament at Coventry
1460	John Paston I buys quitclaim to	Battle of Northampton

	Huntingfield Hall, Bacton, and petitions for right to hold a manorial court	York claims the crown York killed at Battle of Wakefield
1461	John Paston II eventually elected to the Commons as knight of shire for Norfolk Duke of Norfolk (John Mowbray II) seizes Caister John Paston II in royal household Worcester on bad terms with the Pastons	Edward IV proclaimed king 4 Mar. Battle of Towton Edward crowned 28 June Duke of Norfolk died 6 Nov.
1464		Battles of Hedgeley Moor and Hexham Edward IV marries Elizabeth Woodville
1465	William Paston II a JP John Paston I in Fleet prison, June	
1466	Anthony Woodville seizes Paston property at Norwich and Caister Duke of Suffolk seizes Drayton and Hellesdon Edward IV accepts gentility of the Pastons John Paston I leaves prison Jan. John Paston I died 22 May	Richard, Earl of Warwick's relations with Edward IV deteriorating
1467	Probate of Fastolf's will granted to John Paston II and Thomas Howes	
1468	Fastolf's feoffees release Caister to John Paston II Thomas Howes declares Fastolf's will falsified	Marriage of Margaret of York to Charles the Bold of Burgundy
1469	John Paston III besieged in Caister by Duke of Norfolk and obliged to surrender Richard Calle enters East Beckham on behalf of John Paston II 3 July Mortgage of East Beckham sealed between Roger Townshed and John Paston II 6 Nov. Margery Paston married Richard Calle	Edward IV visits Norwich Battle of Edgecote Warwick captures the king
1470	John Paston II acknowledges loss of Cotton and Wickham Skeith to Alice de la Pole Agnes Paston and William Paston II initiate legal action to enforce the will of William Paston I William Paston II married Lady Anne Beaufort by this date John Paston II compromises with Wainfleet on disposal of Fastolf's	Warwick and Duke of Clarence flee to France after failed rebellion Warwick comes to terms with Margaret of Anjou, invades England with Clarence, forces Edward to flee to Burgundy and restores Henry VI

	lands, many of which pass to Magdalen College After Henry VI's restoration Norfolk releases Caister to John Paston II	
1471	John Paston II and John Paston III at Battle of Barnet on Lancastrian side Caister seized again by Norfolk in June Elizabeth Poynings married Sir George Browne	Edward IV lands at Ravenspur 14 Mar. Clarence joins him. Battle of Barnet: Warwick killed Margaret of Anjou returns, is defeated at Tewkesbury and her son, Prince Edward killed Edward IV enters London 21 May Henry VI murdered in the Tower the same night
1472	John Paston III out of favour with Duke of Norfolk, but not the Duchess William Paston II MP	Duchess of Norfolk gives birth to Anne Mowbray
1473	John Berney died 20 Jan. Walter Paston goes to Oxford	
1475		Edward IV invades France, but makes Treaty of Picquigny in return for a middle-aged pension
1476	Duke of Norfolk died 16–17 Jan. and John Paston II recovers Caister	
1477	John Paston III marries Margery Brews Clement Paston II died by Aug.	
1478	William Paston III at Eton John Paston III's son, Christopher, born	Richard, Duke of York, married Anne Mowbray Clarence liquidated
1479	William Paston II in possession of Paston with the consent of Agnes Paston, May. In Aug. Walter Paston died, Agnes Paston died, and William Paston II occupied Marlingford in defiance of John Paston II John Paston II died Nov.	
1482	William Worcester died	
1483	Sir George Browne executed for taking part in Buckingham's revolt	Edward IV died 9 Apr. Edward V and Richard of York (and Norfolk) murdered 22 June Richard, Duke of Gloucester, becomes king
1484	Margaret Paston died	
1485	John Paston III MP for Norwich, sheriff of Norfolk and Suffolk	Battle of Dadlington Richard III killed Henry Tudor takes the crown
1487	John Paston III knighted at Battle of Stoke	Battle of Stoke

1489 Settlement reached by arbitration between William Paston II and John Paston III
1496 William Paston II died
1503 John Paston III recovers East Beckham, 16 Feb.
1504 John Paston III died 28 Aug.

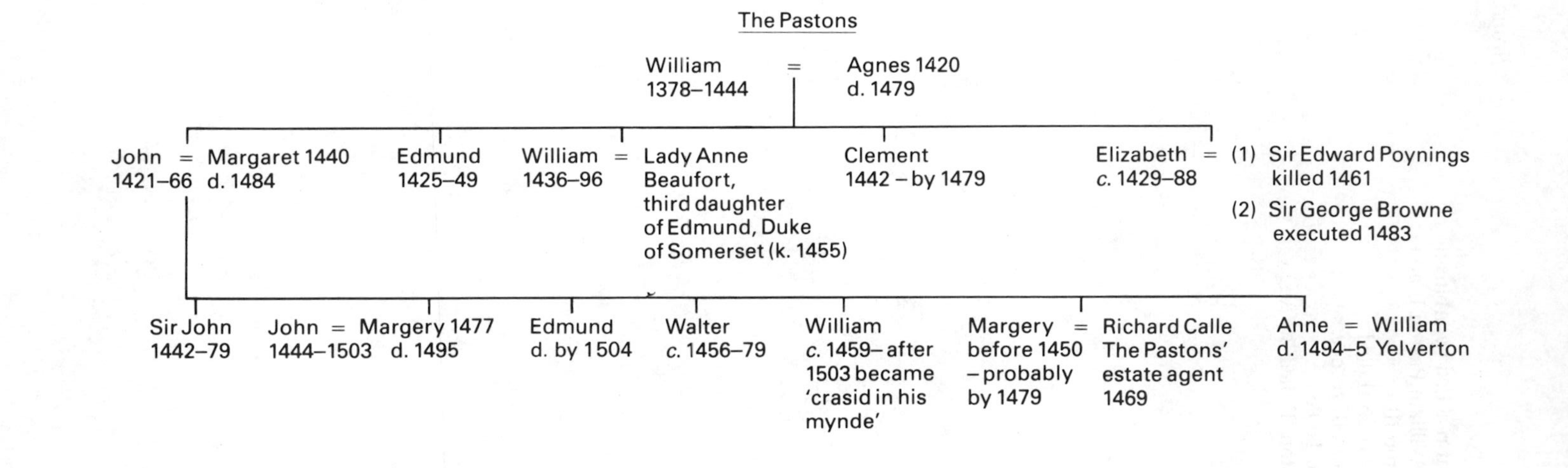
The Pastons
William 1378–1444 = Agnes 1420 d. 1479
John 1421–66 = Margaret 1440 d. 1484
Edmund 1425–49
William 1436–96 = Lady Anne Beaufort, third daughter of Edmund, Duke of Somerset (k. 1455)
Clement 1442 – by 1479
Elizabeth c. 1429–88 = (1) Sir Edward Poynings killed 1461
(2) Sir George Browne executed 1483
Sir John 1442–79
John 1444–1503 = Margery 1477 d. 1495
Edmund d. by 1504
Walter c. 1456–79
William c. 1459– after 1503 became 'crasid in his mynde'
Margery before 1450 – probably by 1479 = Richard Calle The Pastons' estate agent 1469
Anne d. 1494–5 = William Yelverton

Chapter 1

THE ORIGINS OF THE PASTONS

Sheltering from a summer storm in the porch of Gresham church on an August afternoon in 1985 – about a quarter of a mile up the hill from the moated platform of the Paston house, an oasis of shrubbery among the corn, and a couple of miles from deserted East Beckham – I shared the quiet and isolation with a Latin inscription, all that remained of a fifteenth-century memorial, which lay just over the threshold of the church itself: pray for the soul of James Catt 'generosus'.

It was a vivid hour. And James Catt's gentility (it seemed to me, proudly stated) brought vividly to mind what I am tempted to alliterate as the Pastons' predicament. Michael Sayer has written of late medieval–early modern Norfolk that its parishes 'often contained several little manors, and a parish of under 2,000 acres might support several gentle and yeoman households, by no means all manorial lords'.[1] Not being a manorial lord, particularly at Paston, was one part of Judge William's predicament; the other part was that until he was a manorial lord, and at Paston, the family, however grand he was, however many manors he bought or bargained for, might remain among that rank of gentlemen of which Michael Sayer speaks and of whom James Catt at Gresham is, or was for me that afternoon, representative. North Erpingham Hundred in 1985 still made the point; the people may have gone from the fields to leave a deserted, industrialized landscape, but the pattern of parishes and parish churches survives. The small parishes jostle one another; the church of one is just around the corner from the next: so it must have seemed on a horse. Winters, Wyndhams, Heydons, and Pastons also jostled one another in those parts, but they were

[1] M.J. Sayer, *English Nobility: the Gentry, the Heralds and the Continental Context* (Norwich, 1979), p. 12. Stalham Hall is an example of such a little manor. An estate of the abbey of St Benet's at Holm, it consisted of a handful of tenants who ought to have paid rents of about £2 and a court whose receipts were anything from 2s to £1. Arrears were a problem: at Michaelmas 1442 they stood at £9; at Michaelmas 1470 there were none; by Michaelmas 1476 they came to 28s. This property was, therefore, worth between £1 and £2 a year to its owners. In the early 1470s Walter Aslak was bailiff; one wonders how much his job was worth, as he got no fee. See Bodleian Library, Oxford, Norfolk Rolls, 92–6.

an elite: they were lords of manors. No longer merely parochial gentlemen like James Catt, they have become more than merely names to historians.[2] Getting out of the ruck may have been simpler than making a manor where there had not been one previously. I was about to say that it may have been because it was simpler to buy a manor than create one, until East Beckham came to mind: on the one hand the time and money it took the Pastons to acquire it, on the other the relative ease with which the Winters had made their manor there.[3] No case is typical. Moreover, if we are discussing social mobility (which we are), then the Pastons, like the Winters, not only had to leave the ranks of the parochial gentry: they had first to enter them. According to Judge William Paston, William Winter's father had been a husbandman; according to an anonymous and equally hostile commentator so had Judge William's.[4] Both Williams arrived at gentility by the shortest route – service: they served as lawyers to the great, in William Paston's case mainly (but not at all solely) to the Crown. They did not so much as leave James Catt behind as barely have time to notice him in passing. Yet, if William Winter's lordship in Barningham Winter was effortlessly achieved,[5] the Pastons' at Paston was not. Perhaps the reasons for the difference were straightforward: the process at Paston was more complicated – involving as it did the 'over' lordship of the Duchy of Lancaster – and William Paston died before he could complete it.

In the history of East Beckham, as we shall see, Judge William's death made all the difference: John Mariot changed sides. The departure of so overbearing a subject as Judge William altered perspectives in north-east Norfolk. It delayed for many years the progress of the Pastons towards unchallenged gentility and full 'senery' (*seigneurie*) in their native place. It gave their neighbours the courage to discuss, to taunt them with, and eventually to expose (and exploit) the skeleton in their cupboard: their sometime serfdom. John Paston was young and vulnerable in 1444. What had perhaps not been said of his father for a long time, at any rate not outside very secure walls, what his son Edmund over forty years later would write of disdainfully, with the give-away snobbery of a second-generation *arriviste*, was challenged and put to the test in John in the 1440s and

[2] How apt, therefore, to have discovered (after having written this) James Catt tangling with the Pastons (or Richard Calle at any rate) at Gresham in November 1460: Davis II, p. 223, lines 2–8. Alas, he had appeared in Gairdner (in the same letter) as James Gatte and ten years earlier: II, p. 187. [3] See below, ch. 3.

[4] William Winter's father, John, only had 20 acres: NRO, WKC 1/43/8. That, I take it, would have made him something less than the 'good pleyn husbond' William Paston's father, Clement, was with his 100–120 acres (Davis I, pp. xli–xlii).

[5] We are ignorant on this issue because William Paston ignores it in NRO, WKC 1/43/8.

afterwards: his new gentility.[6] It would take John until the mid-1460s to live down his past and to establish his lordship of Paston. These two stories are not, as they were not for John, even two sides of a coin; they are the same, but here we have to distinguish them: the lowly origins of the family *and* the making of the manor of Paston. They were linked by the writer of 'A Remembraunce of the wurshypfull Kyn and Auncetrye of Paston, borne in Paston in Gemyngham Soken'.[7] The irony is ponderous and would suggest the 'Remembraunce' was for public consumption: the writer was even less a friend of the family than Judge William had been of the Winters when he scribbled on WKC 1/43/8 a similarly unsympathetic account (though for Paston eyes only) of 'The Rise of the Winters'. Similar also, of course, because the families' origins and the manner of their departing from them were much the same. The 'Remembraunce' is central to the discussion which follows. The manor-making comes first.

The 'Remembraunce' says this of William:

> And he purchasyed myche lond in Paston, and also he purchasyd the moyte of ye vth parte of ye maner of Bakton callyd other Latymers or Stywardys or Huntyngfeld[8] qwyche moyte strechyd into Paston, and so wyth yt and wyth a nother parte of ye seyd fyve partys he hath senery in Paston but no maner place; and therby wold John Paston sone to ye seyde Wylliam make hym selfe a Lordschype there to ye Duke of Lancastrs grete hurte.

This raises as many questions as it supplies answers: for example, 'he hath senery in Paston but no maner place; and therby wold John Paston . . . make hym selfe a Lordschype there' is difficult to interpret and not only because the tenses appear confused. What are the differences between 'senery'[9] and 'Lordschype'? What is the apparent significance of the distinction 'hath senery . . . but no maner place'? Let these questions stand. Judge William's purchases of land at Paston and in its immediate neighbourhood are, so far as I am aware, undocumented, save in relation to Bromholm Priory. The

[6] Between 1487 and 1493 Edmund wrote to his elder brother John III in the context of finding a wife for John's young son William and of an impending visit of John's to London: 'Marchandys ore new jantylmen I deme wyll proferre large': Davis I, p. 642, lines 33–4.

[7] Printed and described in Davis I, pp. xli–xlii. Caroline Barron dealt with the 'Remembraunce' in 'Who were the Pastons?', *Journal of the Society of Archivists*, 4 (1972), pp. 532–5.

[8] Huntingfield or Huntingfield Hall is the name of the manor in Bacton that the Pastons got: *CCR 1454–61*, p. 290; Bodleian Library, Norfolk Charters 6; Blomefield V, p. 1402. Elizabeth, the widow of William Sywardby (for whose father or grandfather, William, see presumably Gairdner II, no. 3), was its last owner. Latimer's Blomefield (V, p. 1403) reckons a different manor, the reversion of which Judge William acquired *c.* 1428. The fifth part of Bacton certainly had its own identity; in 1436 the prior came to an agreement about it with the overlord, William de la Pole, Earl of Suffolk – the agreement that Blomefield had in front of him when he wrote: *ibid.*, p. 1406. (Might there have been here yet another matter for contention between Pastons and de la Poles?)

[9] Compare the 'seniory' of Davis II, no. 897, a document discussed below.

'Remembraunce' states that 'wher that the Pryor of Bromholm borowyd mony of the seyd William for to paie withall his Dymes,[10] ye seyd William wuld not lend it hym, but [unless] the seyd Pryor wold mortgage to ye seyd Wylliam one John Albon ye seyd Pryowris bondmanne dwellyng in Paston.' There is also a memorandum of *c.* 1430 noting that William 'recovered' a little land, pasture, and marsh in Edingthorpe, Bacton, and North Walsham from the Prior of Bromholm[11] and an indenture of 1444 of an exchange of lands and rents between the prior, Judge William, and Edmund Palmer of Witton.[12] These transactions do not look at first sight as though they are connected, but they probably all relate to William's consolidation of sufficient property to make a manor. At any rate, obtaining bond tenants was essential to the acquisition of lordship, and Judge William persisted, despite not getting his hands on John Albon ('qwyche was a styffe Cherle and a Threfty mane, and wold not obeye hyme unto ye seyd Wylliam') – the prior gave (or, presumably, sold) John and his lands to William Bernham, clerk, John Conningsby, and John Walpole in 1433 (and quitclaimed him to them in 1438).[13] On 18 May 1440 an inquisition set up for the purpose reported that no harm to the royal interest would ensue if exchange of property in Paston and Edingthorpe were to be made between the Duchy of Lancaster and William Paston. By 1443 the exchange had been effected: William gave up two free, that is, 'charterhold' tenements in Paston and Edingthorpe and received in return two unfree, that is, 'copyhold' tenements in the same townships held of the Duchy lordship of Gimingham.[14] James Gresham was drafting the terms of the letting of this

[10] The priory's indebtedness to William is evident in an account, drawn up on 5 November 1443, of what it owed him out of the manor of Huntingfield and other of its sources of income in the neighbourhood: NRO, Phillipps 537.

[11] BL Add. MS 27443, f. 89 (abstracted in Gairdner II, no. 21): $2\frac{1}{2}$ acres and 1 rod of land, 8 acres of pasture and $2\frac{1}{2}$ acres of marsh. [12] BL Add. Ch. 14571.

[13] The deed of gift is in the possession of James Stevens Cox, FSA, of St Sampson, Guernsey. I am grateful for his permission to use the xerox copy Dr Robert Dunning had made for me, as I am to Robert for bringing this small (former Bromholm) archive to my attention. In John Albon's case the writer of the 'Remembraunce' attributed another motive to William Paston: the pursuit of lordship. Still, the Pastons were stiffer than the Albons; they got their man in the end: Davis I, p. xlii.

[14] The business, seemingly a trifling one, was conducted at a high level probably because of the interest in the Duchy's revenues of Henry V's feoffees, headed at this time by Cardinal Henry Beaufort (R. Somerville, *The Duchy of Lancaster* I (London, 1953), pp. 204–6). It was Beaufort who wrote to William Phelip, Lord Bardolf, about the matter from Esher on 31 May (1440?). Lord Bardolf was not only the king's chamberlain, which is how he was addressed by Beaufort, but also chief steward of the South Parts of the Duchy of Lancaster (Somerville, *Duchy of Lancaster* I, p. 428). Beaufort's letter survives as a copy – or what appears to be a copy – in the East Beckham file; on its dorse a draft was made of William Paston's petition for custody of East Beckham, with the date of its grant (22 March 1442) added. It is NRO, WKC 1/43/21; see below p. 97. Beaufort writes that he has read the report delivered to him by Bardolf at Sheen of the enquiry he had directed Bardolf, or his deputies Oliver Gros and Richard Sedge, to make concerning the consequences of the exchange; he had then given

'custumariefeldlond copiehold' early in 1444. All the tenants, save the bloody-minded Warin Herman, had accepted Judge William's terms, so that James was able to put in his draft the day the agreement would be formally concluded, Passion Sunday, 30 March 1444.[15]

Were these, then, the first bond tenants the Pastons acquired? Later, twenty years later in 1466, they claimed otherwise:[16]

They [the Pastons] shewed divers great evidences and court rolles, how that they and their ancetors had been possessed of a court and seniory in the towne of Paston, and of many and sundry bondmen, sithen the time that no mind is to the contrary;

the report to Peter Ardern, deputy to William, Earl of Suffolk, Steward of the North Parts of the Duchy (and a lawyer retained by the Duchy: Somerville, *Duchy of Lancaster* I, pp. 425, 453); Ardern, after a thorough study of the report, had advised that the exchange should proceed, as it would 'not hurte his hignesse ner to the seid lordship of Gemyngham neyther to us of the feffement be preiudicial or harmfull, and [Beaufort continued] as fer as I can conceyve or undirstonde after my oppinyon me thynketh the same'; Paston might, therefore, sue to the king after the form of the bill Beaufort had seen and was enclosing with the letter. Beaufort, if he wrote on 31 May 1440, wrote promptly. The date of the Bardolf enquiry, 18 May 1440, is recorded in *Rotuli Parliamentorum* V, p. 59: a final provision of the act, dealing with Henry V's enfeoffment of the Duchy estates, passed in the parliament of January–March 1442, stating that the act should not be prejudicial to the exchange with William Paston. The sense of this provision, as best I understand it, is that the exchange is under way, rather than has been completed (Gairdner II, no. 42, a note of this provision, has the exchange back to front). The date of the Bardolf enquiry is also given in the warrant to the steward of the lordship and manor of Gimingham to rent to the former tenants of the copyhold properties, which were now in Judge William's hands, or any others, the 'charterhold land' formerly William Paston's 'in like fourme as the same Tenementez are now holden'. The warrant (abstracted in Gairdner II, p. 57) is dated 17 October 1443. Thus, the exchange was undoubtedly made by then. This renders the first paragraph of James Gresham's letter to Judge William of 28 January 1444 (Davis II, p. 12) most mysterious. The year might be altered, though with some wrenching of what appears to be the truth, for lines 45–9 of the letter anticipate with precision 18 March 1444 and the favourable judgement in William Yelverton's court at Norwich in the East Beckham case. We must conclude that Judge William's 'bille' of the first paragraph was some other, probably connected with what William saw as the next stage in the 'manorialization' of Paston, and possibly akin to John Paston's bill submitted to the parliament of October 1460 (Davis I, no. 57, discussed below, p. 12), virtually John's first favourable opportunity to bring this petition for a manorial court out of mothballs. Such a large request – John asked also for a grant of twenty-three messuages – would better fit the sixth, remarkable, paragraph of Gresham's letter if, that is, the 'bille' concerned here *is* the 'bille' of the first paragraph, which now, I think, it may be said to be. The paragraph is remarkable for showing Alice Chaucer's already weighty influence and her memory for business (the first no doubt a consequence of the second), as well as the 'screen' of her councillors and servants with had to be penetrated before their mistress might be reached. One last thing: the expedition and dispatch which we have noted being given to a small matter, if Beaufort's letter is of 31 May 1440, is at odds with what James Gresham reports as being done about a larger one, if the 'bille' is as we have just surmised it to be: 'the Chauncellor of the Duché . . . seid he was right well remembred of your bille, but he seid he wyst not where it was, and thanne he dede the clerk of the counseill of the Duché seke it, and atte last it was founde'. That seems more like bureaucracy as we know it. The chancellor was Walter Shirington (Somerville, *Duchy of Lancaster* I, pp. 389–90). Possibly, the 'Yn [HOLE: room for about five letters] a-nother of the counseil' of line 13 was Thomas Yonge (*ibid.*, p. 453).

[15] BL Add. MS 34888, f. 1 dorse (Davis II, no. 432, headnote). That the leasing is related to the exchange is clear from the draft's mention of the Act of Parliament. I am in Professor Ralph Griffiths' debt for his help with the Latin of this messy dorse. [16] Davis II, p. 551.

and how that Agnes Paston ... is in possession of bondholders and also of bondmen, whose ancetors have been bondmen to the ancetors of the said John Paston sithen the time that no minde is to the contrary.

Moreover, 'Also they shewed divers old deeds, some without date, insealed under autenticke seales, of divers particular purchases in the towne of Paston, reciting in the said deeds that the land was holden of the said [BLANK] Paston as of the cheife lord of the fee, and by homage, and had ward, marriage, and releife.' The original of this document in which Sir John Paston and his uncles William and Clement proclaimed their gentility does not survive. Edward IV accepted that they were 'gentlemen discended lineally of worshipfull blood sithen the Conquest';[17] whether he believed it is another matter. And whether he (or anyone else) had read their proclamation of gentility is equally doubtful: that blank before 'Paston as of the cheife lord of the fee' suggests it is a draft, or 'Briefe' as Sandford in 1674 describes it, not 'an extract from some certificate made in the King's name', which is what Gairdner believed it to be.[18] All I am suggesting is that the family's claim to have had bond tenants from time immemorial was not put to any sort of test before Edward IV accepted the family for what they said they were. His acceptance was given, I am sure, for reasons which had nothing to do with a consideration of historical evidence, authentic or faked. Thus, that the Pastons' bond tenants may only have gone back to the mid-1440s is a possibility that remains unchallenged by the king's endorsement of their claim that they went back to the mid-1340s or mid-1240s or beyond.

The 'court and seniory in the towne of Paston', which Sir John in 1466 maintained the family had had 'sithen the time that no mind is to the contrary', cannot have been any more ancient than were the bond tenants. The 'Remembraunce' asserted that Clement Paston, apart from his 120 acres at Paston, 'other Lyvelode ne maneris had he non there ne in none other place'.[19] It was Judge William, as we have seen, who began the creation of 'court and seniory' at Paston. That process may not have been complete until 1458–60, when John Paston bought the quitclaim to his manor of Bacton, called Huntingfield Hall,[20] and petitioned for the right to hold a manorial court;[21] but it was William, as the 'Remembraunce' states,

[17] *Ibid.*, p. 549. [18] *Ibid.*, p. 551, headnote; Gairdner IV, pp. 247–8. [19] Davis I, p. xlii.

[20] In spring 1458: *CCR 1454–61*, p. 290, cited by Barron, 'Who were the Pastons?', p. 533, but as *CPR*. In a somewhat misleading paragraph Dr Barron leads us to believe it was John Paston, not his father, whom the 'Remembraunce' says bought 'the moyte of the Vth parte of the maner of Bakton callyd ... Huntyngfeld'. In his roll of expenses of 1457–8 (BL Add. Ch. 17246 – a few extracts only in Gairdner III, no. 373) John records £3 spent in securing Huntingfield Hall in autumn 1457 and £1 given to Roger Pygot, a relation of Geoffrey Pygot, 'pro conclusionem securitate manerii de Huntyngfeld Halle habend' in spring 1458.

[21] Davis I, no. 57; see below p. 12.

who purchased that 'moyte [which] strechyd into Paston' and so, 'wyth yt and wyth a nother parte of the seid fyve partys', it was William who began the manor-making.

Judge William had also set about turning himself into a manorial lord in that other essential way, mentioned by the 'Remembraunce' as unfinished: 'he hath Senery in Paston but no maner place'. To the building of a parlour and a chapel at Paston William had given detailed thought, as Agnes reminded her son Edmund in London six months after her husband's death:[22]

Wetith of yowre brothere John how manie gystis [joists] wolle serve the parlour and the chapelle at Paston, and what lengthe they moste be and what brede and thykkenesse thei moste be; for yowre fadris will was, as I weene veryli, that thei schuld be ix enchis on wey and vij another weye, and pourveiithe therefore that thei mow be squarid there and sentte hedre, for here can non soche be hadde in this conttré.

Parlour and chapel were the very rooms which changed a house into a 'maner place'. It was possibly their construction and certainly other 'manorial' extensions at Paston (the great barn perhaps) which compelled William in 1443 to get (as William Winter had got at Egmere) a licence to divert the road from the south to the north of his house.[23] William and the vicar, according to Agnes, had reached agreement in Lent the following year 'and dool [boundary mark] is sette howe broode the weye schuld ben', but William's death, as we will see in other connections, altered everything: 'and nowe', continued Agnes in February 1445, 'he [the vicar] hathe pullid uppe the doolis and seithe he wolle makyn a dyche fro the cornere of his walle ryght overe the weye to the newe diche of the grete cloose'.[24] The vicar, William Pope, did not surrender his right to this disputed half acre until September 1447.[25] Opposition came not only from

[22] *Ibid.*, pp. 27–8.

[23] *CPR 1441–6*, p. 192. He was evidently building at Oxnead too, as the licence also permitted him to direct the road around the house there. (It was no doubt William who was instrumental in getting in the same year from the Archbishop of Canterbury an indulgence of a hundred days for those who contributed to the repair or new building of bridges at Oxnead: BL Stowe Ch. 608. For the larger bridge of Oxnead, see *CPR 1441–6*, p. 192.) While at Oxnead the 'splendid early brick barns with rare fifteenth-century work and some fifteenth-century embellishments' are likely to be Judge William's work, the datestones of 1581 (the one on the east end of precisely 27 February 1581), and the proud inscription 'the Bilding of this Bearne is bi Sir W Paston Knighte' on the great barn at Paston seem conclusively to demonstrate he was not responsible there. However, 'dates on buildings often record not the original construction, but some improvement or alteration', and the corbel heads on the barn's east end are certainly medieval, even if they could have been brought from somewhere else to be stuck there. The quotations are from Graham Hughes, *Barns of Rural Britain* (London, 1985), pp. 69, 70, 165.

[24] Davis I, p. 27.

[25] BL Add. Ch. 17235, abstracted as Gairdner no. 70, where this critical half acre opposite the vicarage appears as 'a piece of land, particularly described'.

the vicar; there were many at Paston who made their feelings about Agnes plain; 'Warnys wyfe' for one, 'wythe a loude vosse seyd "All the devyllys of hell drawe here sowle to hell for the weye that she hat mad."'[26] Her husband, Warin Herman (that troublesome tenant), spoke no less plainly to Agnes herself in Paston church. It is a vignette to be treasured for its setting as well as for its revelation of the terms in which a Norfolk farmer could and did speak to the *grande* or aspiringly *grande dame* of the place. Agnes described the scene to her eldest son:

On the Sonday before sent Edmond after evyn-songe Angnes Ball com to me to my closett and bad me good evyn, and Clement Spycere wyth hyr. And I acsyd hym what he wold, and he askyd me why I had stopped jn ye Kyngys wey; and I seyd to hym I stoppyd no wey butt myn owyn . . . And all that tyme Waryn Herman lenyd ovyr the parklos and lystynd whatt we seyd, and seyd that the chaunge was a rewly chaunge, for the towne was undo thereby and is the wersse by an c li. . . . And prowdly goyn forthe wyth me jn the cherche, he seyd the stoppyng of the wey xulld coste me xx nobyllys, and yet it chuld downe ageyn.[27]

This took place on a November evening in the 1450s, probably in 1451. The first destruction of the wall,[28] which in blocking the road apparently had also blocked the processional way around the church,[29] was described by Agnes:[30]

On Thurisday the wall was mad yarde hey; and a good wylle before evyn it reyned so sore that they were fayne to helle [cover] the wall and leve werke, and the water is fallyn so sore hat it standyt ondyre the wall a fote deppe to Ballys warde. And on Fryday after sakeryng on come fro cherch warde and schoffe doune all that was there-on and trad on the wall and brake sum and wente over. But I can not yet wete hoo it was.

Whoever it was, they had, after communion, perpetrated religious (and righteous) justice on the work of an anti-communal neighbour. Probably it

[26] Davis I, pp. 35–6. This was certainly (from the context) Warin Herman's wife, rather than Warin King's, though the latter was equally *engagée* as well as *enragée*: 'And Warne Kyngys wyfe, as she went over the style, she cursyd Ball and seyde that he had gevyn aweye the waye': *ibid.*, p. 35. John Ball was the village quisling in this affair. Warin Herman's wife was called Mary: 'the wyfe of Harman hathe the name of Owre Lady, whos blyssyn ye have, and myn' (Agnes to John, *ibid.*, p. 37). It was Warin's half-brother who 'was takyn wyth enemyis [while] walkyn be the se syde and [they] have hym forthe wyth hem'. Such was one of the consequences of having Henry VI on the throne: what bungling the last stages of the Hundred Years War meant for one Norfolk man. These 'enemyis' did, however, exhibit the sort of piety Henry VI was notorious for: 'and they tokyn ij pylgremys, a man and a woman, and they robbyd the woman and lete hyr gon and ledde the man to the see, and whan they knew he was a pylgreme they geffe hym money and sett hym ageyn on the lond' (Agnes to John, 11 March, probably 1450, *ibid.*, p. 32).

[27] *Ibid.*, p. 36.

[28] If Davis no. 21 does come before Davis no. 22, it was the second (at least).

[29] Agnes to John: 'I spacke thys day wyth a man of Paston syde, and he told me that a man of Paston told hym that Paston men wold nott goo presessyon ferther than the chyrche-yerde on Sent Markys Day, for he seyd the presessyon wey was stoppyd in, and seyd wyth-in chort tyme men hopyd that the wall chuld be broke doun a-geyn' (Davis, I, pp. 33–4).

[30] *Ibid.*, p. 34.

was Warin Herman, possibly Warin King, very likely it was their communally (as well as tough-) minded wives. The two men had wished to threaten Agnes with the wall's destruction through the agency of a priest, perhaps a chantry priest, possibly Agnes' chaplain, but he stayed out of trouble and it was the vicar who, after the event, reported their behaviour to Agnes:[31]

Ystyrnevyn wan I xuld goo to my bede the vycare seyde that Warne Kyng and Warne Harman be-twyxte messe and matynsse toke Ser Roberd in the vestry and bad hym sey to me verely the wall xullde doun a-gayne; and wan the vycore tolde me I wyste there-of no worde, nor yet do, be Ser Roberde, for he syth he were loth to make any stryfe.

Warin Herman was unrepentant; Agnes reported:

Warne Harmon, on the Sonday after Hallumes Day after ensong, seyd oponly in the cherche-yerde that he wyst wyll that and [if] the wall were puddoun, thou he were an hondryd myle fro Paston, he wyste well that I wolde sey he ded yt and he xuld bere the blame, seying 'Telle yte here ho so wyll, thou it xuld coste me xx nobyllys it xall be puddoun ayen.'[32]

Warin Herman's antagonism concerning the road was only part of what appears to be his general opposition to all that the Pastons were up to at Paston.[33] So far as Agnes' wall and their road were concerned Warin and the villagers may have been justly aggrieved. Agnes once more: 'And at evyn a sertyn man suppyd wyth me and tolde me that the patent grantyt to closse [enclose] but a perch on bred, and that I had clossyd more than the grant of the patent is, as men seyd.'[34] The community also pursued Agnes in the proper place: she was amerced 6d in the manorial court, probably in

[31] *Ibid.*, p. 35. [32] *Ibid.*

[33] In 1444 he dragged his feet over the exchange: see above, p. 5. He may have become nasty about it; the following is suggestive: 'Robert Hill was at Paston this wyke, and the man that duelled in Bowres place is oute there-of, and seid to Roberd he drust no lenger a-byde there-in for Waryn Herman seyth to him it is his place' (Davis I, p. 38). That was in 1451–2, as was the following, which may relate to the same matter, though is more likely to be a separate dispute. Agnes to John (*ibid.*, p. 37): 'Then he [Warin] askyd me why I had a-wey hys hey at Walsam, seyng to me he wold he had wyst it whan it was karyyd and he chuld a lettyd it; and I told hym it was myn owyn grownde, and for myn owyn I wold holde it. And he bad me take iiij acre and goo no ferthere; and thus churtly he departyd fro me jn the cherche-yerde.' There were also fishing rights at Paston – Margaret to John (*ibid.*, p. 244): 'My moder [Agnes] bad me send yow word that Waron Herman hath dayly fyshid hyre watere all this yer, and therfor she prayith yow to do ther-for whill ye be at London as ye thynk best.' Agnes and Warin were still 'fighting' each other in 1461 (*ibid.*, pp. 42–3); cf. Agnes' suit against him of Davis I, p. 34. One wonders how long neighbourly strife may have been going on when John de Paston is found witnessing a grant by Warin fitz Herman to Bromholm Priory of an acre in Paston *c.* 1200: James Stevens Cox archive, Guernsey.

[34] *Ibid.*, p. 36. Agnes goes on to describe a reported scene which I wish I could understand more completely than I do: 'And John Marchall tolde me that there was a thryfty woman come forby the watteryng and fond the wey stoppyde, and askyd hym ho had stoppyd the weye; and he seyd they that had pore to geve it, and askyd here wat was freere than gyfte. And she seyd she sey the day that Paston men wold not a sofferyd that.'

1451;[35] it might have been a shilling if Robert Edmunds and Warin King had not got it reduced.[36] The court was (of course) of the manor of Gimingham. Agnes did not pay the 6d; Warin Herman neither forgot it nor wished her to forget it: ten years later, in 1461, he was reminding the Gimingham receiver of it.[37] Warin King had not forgotten either; Agnes wrote to John:[38] 'this day Bertholomew Elys of Paston come to Norwych to me and shewyt me a rentall for the terme of Seynt Michel the yere of Kyng H. vj xxxix^ti^, and jn the ende of the seyd rentall, of Waryn Kynges hand, is wretyn "'Agnes Paston vijd. ob. Item, the same Agnes for v acre lond xxd.'" It would seem that Warin King was not going to allow Agnes to forget rent due at Gimingham. Having carried their manor of Paston out of Gimingham, the Pastons were endeavouring to sever their connection (probably their servile connection) with that lordship; one (at least) of the villagers of Paston was making it as difficult for them as he was able to.[39] We should remember: during a decade which saw a great war lost, a king lose his nerve, a queen on the rampage, bloody battles in all parts of the realm, and the throne usurped, in this corner of Norfolk conflict turned upon a wall built across a road. An amercement of 6d: is this the measure in fifteenth-century England of the class struggle? This is rhetoric, but not necessarily empty. The unpaid amercement, the new road, the modernized manor house, the advowson of the church, secured from the Prior of Bromholm in 1452,[40] were more than themselves. For the villagers, among whom until almost yesterday the Pastons had counted themselves, they represented, dare we say, oppression. Dominion, lordship, seigneurie, anyway. And yet this clutch of letters from Agnes shows us much more than the Pastons struggling to rise above,

[35] *Ibid.*, pp. 34, 35. [36] *Ibid.*, p. 35, lines 15–17.

[37] *Ibid.*, pp. 42–3, Agnes to John: 'item, I have knowlech be a trew man that whan Sharpe the reseyvore was at Gemyngham last Waryn Herman was dyvers dayes wyth hym, and put hym in mynde that the mercyment for makyng of the walle chuld be askyd ageyn and be distreynyd ther-fore'. Warin was still alive two years later: Gairdner IV, p. 70, Richard Calle's jottings.

[38] Davis I, p. 42. Warin King was at cross purposes with the Pastons as late as 1479: *Ibid.*, p. 187.

[39] At the end of this letter of 1 December 1461 (*ibid.*, p. 43) Agnes added a postscript: 'Item the seyd Bertholomew Elis seyth that the seyd reseyvore [Sharpe] wold not alowe the rent in Trunche nor the mercymentys for my sute to the curt. Gonnore wold suffyr no man to answere for me.' Apart from bringing to our attention Simon Gunnor's antipathy to the family, the mention of 'the rent in Trunche' makes more understandable Judge William's non-payment of it. It was not only that it was not asked of him (*ibid.*, p. 27), it was also that it bound him to the manor of Gimingham from which he was endeavouring to escape. The land was (presumably) the 9 acres in 'Trunchefeld' and its accompanying meadow which Agnes leased to William Palmer of Trunch for ten years in November 1446: *ibid.*, no. 16. I take it as significant that no annual rent is mentioned, only that William should pay, 'yeerly there-fore to the lordys of the fee the rentys, servys and custumys, taxes and talagys of all the holl forseyd pece duryng the terme beforeseyde'.

[40] The grant of 6 July 1452 is in the James Stevens Cox collection.

so that they may look down upon, their neighbours. It is a peculiarly brotherly (rather than otherly) struggle. It takes place in a small space, as a glance at the map reveals: church, hall, and diverted road – north of hall and church, just where Judge William Paston wanted it to be – are bunched together.[41] There is no sixteenth- or seventeenth-century distancing of great house from an impinging world, as is the case, for example, at Oxnead, Heydon, or Barningham Winter[42] and was perhaps the case even in the fifteenth century at Baconsthorpe.[43] At Paston, as Agnes' letters demonstrate, she and her opponents were forever bumping into each other in church or churchyard; moreover, whatever they all said behind her back, Warin Herman could not have been more forthright to her face that November afternoon after evensong when he accompanied her from her private pew, up the nave and out the church door. Was it not to save themselves from this sort of encounter that gentlefolk, the Pastons, indeed, at this very time, constructed chapels in their houses? Making 'space' for themselves, as they developed a new concept of themselves (in relation to others), might be another way of putting it. Meanwhile, and before modernity finally triumphed, the bickering was out in the open. Here again is Agnes in church before she and Warin Herman got up to leave:[44]

> after evyn-songe Angnes Ball com to me to my closett and bad me good evyn, and Clement Spycere wyth hyr. And I acsyed hym what he wold, and he askyd me why I had stoppyd jn the Kyngys wey; and I seyd to hym I stoppyd no wey butt myn owyn, and askyd hym why he had sold my lond to John Ball; and he s[w]ore he was nevyr a-cordyd wyth your fadyr. And I told hym if hys fadyr had do as he dede, he wold a be a-chamyd to a seyd as he seyd.
>
> And all that tyme Waryn Herman lenyd ovyr the parklos and lystynd whatt we seyd.

We should bear in mind that this was Agnes, daughter and heiress of Sir Edmund Barry; Agnes was not a trumped-up local. Is all, or any of this imaginable a hundred years later?

It is no wonder that Agnes had written as she had to Edmund in February 1445,[45] 'I sendde yow not this lettre to make you wery of Paston . . . fore in

[41] I assume that the old road is the bridle-way which runs along the churchyard wall to the south and enters the present Paston hall at the rear. Was this the way Agnes came to church? The much greater diversion of the road at Oxnead (135 perches to 32½ at Paston) is not so apparent on the map; was the old road the present public footpath which runs right through the hall and across the river to Buxton? Here, at any rate, William shifted the road well away from both church and house.

[42] Ironically (or possibly not), it was a Paston who moved the house away from church and village in 1612.

[43] John Heydon's Baconsthorpe castle was on the site of Wood Hall manor house; Baconsthorpe hall was near the church. But did John deliberately build his house a mile away from church and village? Visiting Baconsthorpe castle, one is led to wonder if the busy metropolitan lawyer did not make himself a pastoral retreat here.

[44] Davis I, p. 36.

[45] *Ibid.*, p. 27.

good feyth I dare wel seyne it was yowre fadris laste wille to have do ryght wel to that plase, and that I can schewe of good prefe, thowe men wolde seye naye.' Lording it over one's neighbours was a troublesome business. What has been brought into perspective by an explication of the manorial modifications at Paston is Agnes' oft-quoted paragraph from that same letter: 'I grete yow wel, and avyse how to thynkke onis of the daie of yowre fadris counseyle to lerne the lawe; for he seyde manie tymis that ho so ever schuld dwelle at Paston schulde have nede to conne defende hymself.' *How* they were going to 'dwelle at Paston' was the point. If as its manorial lord, then John Paston was certainly going to discover by experience his father's prediction. For the next twenty years he would have to fight to take the position there that his father was probably on the brink of winning in 1444. John's petition to parliament of 1460 for an outright grant from the Duchy of Lancaster of twenty-three copyhold messuages in Paston, Edingthorpe, and Bacton, of the right to hold a court leet with view of frankpledge for them, and of the services of the tenants, if successful would have brought fifteen years of uncertainty to a favourable close. But, opportune as the moment may have appeared, there is no evidence the petition was answered.[46] What settled the business of manorial creation, or seems to have done, is Edward IV's acceptance of the family's gentility in 1466. From then onwards Pastons were the unchallenged lords of Paston. Whether what had hindered their progress had been their attachment to the 'wrong' political groups between 1444 and 1460, or others' resistance to their rise, or both, is a matter for debate. Judge William's death (as we have indicated) seems to have been critical: John was not and was not reckoned to be by anyone the man his father had been. None the less, something else may have counted against John after 1444: the servile origins of the family. Those origins were erased by royal fiat in 1466. To the Pastons' origins we now must turn.

The royal declaration of 1466 boldly stated:[47]

> Also they shewed a great multitude of old deeds, without date and with date, wherein their ancetors were alwaies sett first in witnes and before all other gentlemen. Also they shewed how their ancetors had in old time and of late time married with worshipfull gentlemen, and proved by deeds of marriage and by other deeds how their ancetors had indowed their wives, and by descents of livelyhood and by testaments and wills of their ancetors under seale; and made open by evident proofe how they and their ancetors came linealy descended of right noble and worshipfull blood and of great lords sometime liveing in this our realme of Ingland. And also they made open proofe how they were nere of kin and blood to mony of the worshipfullest of the country, and also nere to many and sundry great estates and lords of this realme, and was openly proved and affirmed without contradiction or proofe to the contrary.

[46] *Ibid.*, no. 57 and Caroline Barron, 'Who were the Pastons?', pp. 533–4.
[47] Davis II, pp. 551–2.

We, equally boldly, retort: they never did. Indeed, the more carefully one examines and the more closely one reflects on this document the greater its fascination as the denser its tissue of lies becomes. What 'old deeds', what 'deeds of marriage', what 'testaments and wills of their ancetors under seale', what 'evident proofe', what 'open proofe'? The whole business (and what business was the declaration a product of?) can only have been 'a tongue in cheek' enterprise from beginning to end. Sir John Paston knew, as well as the unknown writer of the 'Remembraunce' knew,[48] that his great grandfather had been

> a good pleyn husbond, and lyvyd upon hys lond that he had in Paston, and kept theron a Plow all tymes in the yer, and sum tyme in Barlysell to Plowes. The seyd Clement yede att on Plowe both wynter and sommer, and he rodd to mylle on the bar horsbak wyth hys corn under hym, and brought hom mele ageyn under hym. And also he drove hys carte with dyvers cornys to Wynterton to selle, as a good husbond ought to do.

The description is reminiscent of Chaucer's ploughman, and not only in its language: there is a sense of approval to be detected here too.[49] As there ought to be; for undoubtedly Clement was an efficient and thrifty farmer, who knew more about the world than the road to Winterton market. His advantageous marriage to Beatrice Somerton and the expensive schooling of his gifted son, William, prove that. Still, plain ploughman with limited geographical horizons his will suggests he was:[50] the churches he left money to, besides Paston, were Bacton 2s, Trunch 8d, and Mundesley 6d; to Bromholm Priory he left 6s 8d. His largest bequest was probably the 6 pounds of wax towards the lights before the image of St Margaret in the chancel at Paston church. His place of burial there also suggests his modest social standing; it was to be 'inter hostium austriale eiusdem ecclesiae' and the tomb of Beatrice his wife,[51] more out of the way than James Catt at Gresham, yet inside the church none the less.

Clement died on 17 June 1419.[52] He had been one of the village elite[53] and had had a broader vision than most members of an elite. Had he held bondland, had his wife been a bondwoman? That is what the 'Remembraunce' said: 'Also he had in Paston a fyve skore or a vj skore acrys of lond

[48] Davis I, pp. xli–xlii.

[49] And reminiscent also of the delightful chapter 4 of J.A.W. Bennett's *Chaucer at Oxford and at Cambridge* (London, 1974).

[50] NRO, NCC Reg. Hyrning, f. 51b, printed in Gairdner VI, pp. 188–9.

[51] Extraordinarily, Gairdner translates 'between the north door and the tomb of his wife Beatrice'.

[52] His obit was to be celebrated at Bromholm on that day: Gairdner II, pp. 63–4. His will was dated 15 June (not given in Gairdner) and was proved on 2 October 1419.

[53] R.H. Hilton, *The English Peasantry in the Later Middle Ages* (London, 1975), chapter 2, 'The Social Structure of the Village'. In *c.* 1413 Clement and others pastured their animals on the prior of Bromholm's pasture (in North Walsham?), and fished his fishponds (Blomefield V, p. 1445): a fairly elitist act.

at the most, and myche therof bonde lond to Gemynghamhalle . . . And he weddyd Geffrey of Somerton (qwhos trew surnome ys Goneld) Sister qwhych was a bond womanne . . . And as for Geffrey Somerton he was bond also.' To Geoffrey Somerton we will have to return. There is, however, no trace of him, or Beatrice, or any member of the Paston family in the surviving Court Rolls of Gimingham which intermittently span the years 1398 to 1500: so Dr Caroline Barron discovered – 'therefore, whatever the scurrilous document [the 'Remembraunce'] may assert, the Pastons were not so bond that it was incumbent upon them to appear at the Gimingham court'.[54] This did not prevent (as Dr Barron has ingeniously been able to tell us) John Wyndham telling Agnes and Margaret Paston, 'the Pastons and alle her kyn were charles of Gemyngham'.[55] That was in a Norwich street in May 1448 in the midst of a brawl, which had broken out between the new Paston chaplain, James Gloys,[56] and John Wyndham and two of his men.[57] Tempers were high and Margaret and Agnes gave as good as they got: 'We said he lyed, knave and charl as he was.' It is surely significant that, in searching among the vocabulary of abuse, Wyndham should bring out such a specific taunt, 'charles of Gemyngham', all the more significant in that, with dagger and sword in hand and so enraged, what burst out of him is likely to have been uppermost in his mind. It was so insulting because it was true, true because it was so insulting.[58]

[54] 'Who were the Pastons?', p. 533. Nor were there any Pastons, so far as I could see, in the handful of Gimingham account rolls (1382–1410) at the Norfolk Record Office.

[55] *Ibid.* I have now checked for myself: it is indeed a deliberate hole. The only superficial oddity (as Davis indicates, I, p. 224, footnote) is that 'Gemyngham' is interlineated; the missing twelve letters, however, would exactly comprise 'charles [of Gemyngham: interlineated] and we': Add. MS 39848 f. 2.

[56] This is the first mention of their first private chaplain (Davis I, p. lxxvi). Might it mean that the chapel at Paston was finished? The Declaration of 1466 was a fiction in these respects too: 'Also they shewed divers deeds and grants before time of mind, how that their ancetors had licence to have a chaplen and have devine service within them [*sic*]' (Davis II, p. 551).

[57] James Gloys 'hadde ben in the toune and come homward by Wymondams gate'; three or four strides beyond it he was assaulted 'and defendet hym fleying in-to my moderis place'; Agnes and Margaret 'at messe in our parossh chirche' on this Friday morning, 'with the noise of this a-saut and affray' came out 'of the chirche from the sakeryng' and were insulted (Davis I, p. 224). Thus, it appears Wyndhams and Pastons were close neighbours in Norwich and hard by a church, the Pastons' parish church. Where was this? H.A. Wyndham, *A Family History: the Wyndhams of Norfolk and Somerset* (London, 1939), p. 7, reckoned that the church was St Mary Coslany and that Wyndham's house lay in the region between Dolegate and St Mary Plain. W.H. Hudson and J.C. Tingey (eds.), *The Records of the City of Norwich*, I (London, 1906), p. 287, footnote, state that the Pastons' house was on the north side of Princess Street. The Pastons acquired the advowson of St Peter Hungate only in 1458. But they already lived in the parish in 1454: NRO, Dun(A)9. I would like to picture, therefore, the vividly described scenes of Davis, no. 129 (in James Gresham's hand) as occurring on the short stretch of Princess Street between St George Tombland and St Peter Hungate, even though 'hadde ben in the toune' might suggest that James Gloys had crossed the Wensum on his way home.

[58] Davis I, p. 224, cf. Caroline Barron, 'Who were the Pastons?', p. 533. Wyndham was nothing more (nor less) than the son of a Norwich businessman anxious to establish himself

We do not only have John Wyndham's word for it. Dr Barron has set out the other evidence for the case that the Pastons had, or were believed to have had, servile blood.[59] Anthony Woodville, Lord Scales, used it as a pretext for an attempt to seize some of John Paston's property in 1465. Moreover, just as John Paston's deliberate cutting out the reference to 'charles of Gemyngham' from Margaret's letter to him describing the confrontation with Wyndham is revealing,[60] so is it that we know of Lord Scales' entry into Caister and into the Paston house at Norwich *not* from the Paston letters, but from William Worcester in the one case and the records of the city of Norwich in the other.[61] So far as the Paston letters are concerned, these events did not happen. Nor does the correspondence tell us why John Paston was in the Fleet Prison (or King's Bench[62]) – for the third time. The Norwich city records do: 'Johannis Paston quem dominus Rex pro suo nativo seisivit'.[63] This goes beyond William Worcester's reason for Anthony Woodville's occupation of Caister 'for half a [BLANK] . . . under colour of a rumour spread contrary to the truth that John Paston esq. was the . . . King's bondman although this was false'.[64] False or not, it is remarkable that John Paston should have gone to prison for six months

as a county gentleman. The occasion of the street fight is therefore of interest: Gloys kept his hat on as he walked past Wyndham standing at the gate of his house. For John Wyndham (and the Pastons) see later.

[59] Barron, 'Who were the Pastons?', p. 534.

[60] So Dr Barron was able to conclude: *ibid*., p. 533.

[61] *Ibid*., p. 534; cf. Gairdner I, pp. 225 and 339–40; Davis I, pp. xlv–xlvi.

[62] Davis I, p. 327.

[63] The entry in the first Assembly Book (f. 65) is printed in Gairdner I, pp. 339–40, as well as in Hudson and Tingey, *Records of Norwich* I, pp. 286–7. I would like to know whether kings were as prone to pursuing their villeins, or men they claimed to be their villeins, as (say) dukes were. Edward, Duke of Buckingham's vicious use of 'a practice which became increasingly common later in the century' was pointed out by Bruce McFarlane, *The Nobility of Later Medieval England* (London, 1973), pp. 51, 221, 224–6; see also, Carole Rawcliffe, *The Staffords, Earls of Stafford and Dukes of Buckingham 1394–1521* (London, 1978), pp. 60–1. For a case of 'pretended bondage used as an excuse for forcible entry' in Hampshire *c*. 1450, see A.R. Myers (ed.), *English Historical Documents* IV (London, 1969), no. 722. McFarlane's 'good example of espionage' from John Pickering's notebook of 1518–19 (*Nobility*, p. 226) should be particularly noticed here: it deals with a house in Norwich and reveals the sort of sniffing out of potentialities which must have taken place in John Paston's case.

[64] William Worcester, *Itineraries*, ed. John Harvey (London, 1969), p. 189. It is likely to have been for half a year. That he was about to descend on John Paston's property was reported on 30 July 1465: Davis II, p. 374, lines 15–19. The occupation coincides with, or rather overlapped, John Paston's imprisonment, which appears to have begun early in June (Davis I, p. 304) and to have ended some time between November 1465 (Davis II, no. 691) and February 1466 (*ibid*. no. 742), presumably nearer the later date, as Anthony Woodville seized the Norwich property at New Year 1466. August to January gives us the six months. It was a dreadful time for John. Not only Anthony Woodville took advantage of his imprisonment. The Duke of Suffolk seized Drayton and sacked Hellesdon hall, lodge, church, and village (Davis I, pp. 304, 324). William Yelverton was not only 'behind' the Duke of Suffolk at Drayton and Hellesdon, he was also, according to William Worcester (*Itineraries*, p. 189), 'behind' Anthony Woodville at Caister (and Cotton). This was part of the larger contest between Paston and Yelverton over Sir John Fastolf's lands: all these manors had been his.

because of it, and also that during this last phase of his life not only is there no mention of the charge in the Paston letters, there are (virtually) no Paston letters. Let us examine these two matters: John's imprisonment and the gap in the correspondence.

John's imprisonment, which had begun by June 1465 and ended probably sometime in February 1466:[65] was it a Woodville 'plot', like the imprisonment of Alderman Thomas Cook in 1468? Perhaps not; yet, someone is likely to have persuaded a persuadable king to imprison John Paston. It was not the king's brother-in-law, the Duke of Suffolk, who was not likely ever to have persuaded him of or to anything; it was not, surely, William Yelverton; it may have been that 'knavyssh knyght' and 'fals shrewe' Sir Miles Stapleton, a cousin of Anthony Woodville's,[66] and (as we shall see) an old antagonist of the Paston family. In July 1461 John Paston wrote to Margaret: 'And he and hys wyfe and other have blaveryd [blathered] here [London] of my kynred in hodermoder [hugger-mugger], but be that tyme we have rekned of old dayes and late dayes myn shall be found more worchepfull thanne hys and hys wyfes, or elles I woll not for hys gilt gypcer [pouch].'[67] The following month Stapleton and Gimingham court rolls are disclosed in ominous conjunction. John to Margaret:[68]

> Also if ye can be any craft get a copy of the bille that Ser Miles Stapilton hath of the corte rolles of Gemyngham, that ye fayle not but assay and do yowr devyr, for that shuld preve some men shamefully fals . . . for if Stapilton were boren in hande that he shuld be founde fals and untrewe and first founder of that mater, he wold bothe shewe the bille and where he had it.

'First founder of that mater' is suggestive. So is what John Paston II had to report to his father later in August 1461: Edward IV had the 'bille copye of the cort rolle'; when the Earl of Essex, Treasurer of England,

[65] See the last note. If it were not for John Wykes' letter (Davis II, no. 742), which reports John Paston talking to William Jenny in Westminster Hall in February 1466, I am almost prepared to consider John dying in prison: it is the only reference to him between 10 November 1465 and his death, which occurred in London (*ibid.*, p. 561; Gairdner IV, p. 227). The letter of 10 November 1465 to the gaoled John is one of the most moving of the whole collection (Davis II, no. 691: Add. MS 34889 f. 40). It is beautifully and impeccably written and is from John Wyndham. It is considerate and compassionate towards Margaret, whom once, seventeen years before, he had called a 'strong hore' to her face in the street. It has a brief postscript of great feeling: 'And how that ever ye do, hold up your manship.' This, let us remember, is from one old enemy to another, and from the man who on one occasion had been held up by James Gloys to John Paston as the watchword of cowardice: 'and he [Simon Gunnor, no less] remembred Wymdhams manhood, that iiij swyft fete were better than ij handes, and he toke his hors with the spores and rode . . . as fast as he myght rydyn' (Davis II, p. 65). We might recall also that John Wyndham was writing to 'a charle of Gemyngham', in prison because he was or was said to be – as once upon a time in a Norwich street Wyndham had said he was.

[66] Barron, 'Who were the Pastons?', p. 534.

[67] *Ibid.* Davis I, pp. 95–6. He had a de la Pole wife. Was a husbandman 'more worchepfull' than a fishmonger (as the de la Poles had once been)?

[68] Davis, I, pp. 97–8.

mevyd to hym of it he smylyd and seyd that suche a bylle there was, seyyng that ye wold an oppressyd syndrye of yowre contrémen of worchypfull men, and therefore he kepyd it styll. Never the lesse he seyd he schuld loke it uppe in haste, and ye schuld have it. Baronners undertoke to me twyes ore thryes that he schuld so a remembrid hys lord and master [the Earl of Essex] that I schuld an had it wyth-inne ij ore iij dayes. He is often tymys absent, and there-fore I have it nowthg yyt. When I kan gete it I schall send it yowe, and of the Kyngys mowth hys name that toke it hym.[69]

It is not only that Edward IV had the copy of the Gimingham court roll and that John Paston was so worried about it and about who had given it to him that is significant, it is far more that smile of the king's: it bears every resemblance to that of the Cheshire cat. Did it go on expanding until June 1465, when it disappeared and for John Paston turned into something very different? By 1465 Sir Miles Stapleton was an old man;[70] there is no mention of him in the correspondence of that time. It was probably a younger man who reminded the twenty-two year old Edward of the copy of the court roll, why not the brother of his new queen? It may be no more than circumstantial: 25 May, the coronation of Elizabeth Woodville, 11 June, John Paston in prison. Or is it far too grand a conspiracy I am postulating? It may, after all, have been prosaic William Yelverton, once a friend of Judge William Paston, but now an opponent of his son, who got John put in gaol.[71]

So much for John's imprisonment. What of the lack of letters in the final months of his life? The last letter *from* John is of 20 September 1465: to Margaret from the Fleet prison.[72] It is remarkable that we have to wait until the end for convincing evidence of John's attractiveness. For in this letter John breaks into light verse and appears, ironically when we consider where he is writing from, relaxed. He is also affectionate, closing 'be your trew and trusti husband'. He had not written to Margaret like this before;[73] he was forty-four years old.[74] Margaret's last letter to John is of 27 October

[69] *Ibid.*, p. 391. The Earl of Essex was Henry Bourgchier.

[70] He died 30 September 1466: Wedgwood, *Biographies*, p. 805.

[71] We ought after all to bear in mind William Worcester's 'Memorandum' on the whole affair: *Itineraries*, p. 189. [72] Davis I, no. 77.

[73] It is worth recalling that there are less than thirty letters of John's in the collection; only eleven are to Margaret, five of these are from prison in the summer of 1465. Once (in January 1465: *ibid.*, no. 71) he ended hurriedly in his own hand 'your own &c'. Apart from occasionally adding a few lines himself to letters written by John Pampyng, Richard Calle, or James Gresham (headnotes to Davis I, nos. 55, 56, 58, 59, 71, 72), it was not until he was imprisoned that John actually 'wrote' to Margaret (*ibid.*, nos. 73, 74). He soon returned to using John Pampyng as his scribe (*ibid.*, nos. 75, 76, 77). Even his venture into verse was set down by Pampyng; but 'be your trew and trusti husband' he did add himself: *ibid.*, p. 145, note 62. No doubt the memory of her visit to him was still sweet: 'Myn owne dere sovereyn lady, I recomaund me to yow and thank yow of the gret chere that you mad me here, to my gret cost and charge and labour' (*ibid.*, p. 140). I interpret the mode of the final phrase to be ironical–financial, not ironical–sexual.

[74] Had he been worn down, made 'werye' by the 'nede to conne defende hymselfe' at Paston? James Gairdner (I, pp. 232–3) thought so: 'We know nothing of the nature of the illness which carried him off; but three imprisonments in the course of five years, accompanied

1465.[75] Thereafter, apart from John Wyndham's courteous, helpful, even loving letter to him of 10 November 1465,[76] no letters from or to John survive. As he was not to die until 22 May 1466 in London and as he had come out of prison in mid-February 1466,[77] this hiatus is curious.[78] A six-month interval is indeed odd, when there was so much to discuss and when the letters between Margaret and John of the summer and autumn of 1465 had become so extraordinarily long and detailed. Is it sinister? I mean, was there destruction of what was regarded as incriminating correspondence? Did John or his sons or Margaret not keep, or alternatively burn, letters which did contain or might have contained references to their unfree origins: was a 'charles of Gemyngham' exercise mounted on a grand scale? Because conspiratorial, this sounds far-fetched, but I incline towards it as an explanation for a silence which otherwise is, if not baffling, hard to account for.[79] Might the great burning have been after John's death, say some time in June or July 1466? It was then that John II and his uncles, but particularly John II, one assumes, prevailed upon Edward IV to declare that the Pastons had been gentlemen since the Conquest.[80] Of course, many

with a great deal of anxiety about his newly acquired property, the intrigues of lawyers and the enmity of great men, must have exercised a depressing influence even on the stoutest heart.' It has to be said, however, that if his death was due to worries and cares, they had mainly and recently arisen through his own uncompromising attitude to the Fastolf inheritance (as to everything else): all or nothing was a stance his friends, servants, and (in the end) his wife counselled him against. John Russe (Davis II, pp. 307–8) and Richard Calle (*ibid.*, p. 311) urged on him a 'trety' and 'appuyntement' with William Yelverton. Margaret, in her last letter of 27 October 1465, joined them (I think): *ibid.*, p. 331, lines 67–9. A month or two previously she was worried, if not by John's state of health, certainly by his state of mind: *ibid.*, p. 317, lines 1–6. (Overtures *were* made to Yelverton in June 1465; he was accommodating: *ibid.*, p. 305.) Still, a verdict of death by self-infliction seems appropriate for John Paston.

[75] *Ibid.*, no. 196. John II's last is 27 September (*ibid.*, no. 235); John III's is of 2 October (*ibid.*, no. 324). [76] See above p. 16, note 65.

[77] See above p. 15, note 64. There seems no reason to doubt the assignment of John Wykes' letter to John Paston II of 17 February 1466 (Davis II, no. 742) to this year, although the sentence which is used to date it to 1466 'the Lord Lovell ys son hath weddyd my Lady Fitzhugh ys doghtere &c': which marriage occurred *before* 14 February 1466, according to *CP*, VIII, p. 225, and was of Francis, Viscount Lovel himself not his son, as Davis states in the footnote) immediately follows another ('the Earle of Arundell ys son hath weddyd the Quyne ys sustere') which retails news so old it can have been no news at all to John Paston II, for, according to *CP*, I, p. 250, Thomas Arundel married Margaret Woodville in October 1464. I am tempted to assign this letter to 1465; I wish I knew how long before 14 February 1466 Francis Lovel's wedding had taken place.

[78] James Gairdner (I, p. 232) noted the gap ('the correspondence is scanty'), but was not curious about it.

[79] Is it coincidental or evidence for my argument that two pages of the 'Paston Book of Arms' (NRO, MS Rye 38) have been cut out and that entries on the pages preceding and succeeding those cut out have been defaced? The missing pages are likely to have contained notes on the Paston descent. See, Edmund Farrer, 'A Norfolk Armory of the Fifteenth Century', *Norfolk Antiquarian Miscellany*, 8 (1887), pp. 425–6. These pages of the book were partly written by William Paston, *c.* 1454: Norman Davis and G.S. Ivy, 'MS Walter Rye 38 and its French Grammar', *Medium Aevum*, 31 (1962), pp. 110–24. [80] Davis II, nos. 896, 897.

questions, possibly too many, remain or are created; one, for example, is: why was there a weeding out for the months between May and October, yet a bonfire of everything from November to May?[81] This could be fantasy; it may simply be that there were no letters during that period;[82] yet I am reluctant to believe it: someone *did* cut out 'charles' from the phrase 'charles of Gemyngham'[83] and John *was* worried about that copy of the Gimingham court roll in August 1461.

Given John's concern, is it further evidence for the truthfulness of the 'Remembraunce' that none of the surviving Gimingham court rolls after 1398 shows Pastons as bondmen? I think not: their own letters they might have done away with, incriminating Gimingham court rolls they cannot have made disappear. Surely it is much more likely that the court roll, the copy of which Sir Miles Stapleton was showing around in 1461, was a much earlier one and that *if* it had Pastons on it they were of long ago and were not necessarily the ancestors of Clement Paston. That may be why it was the historian and genealogist, William Worcester, who was able (when the Pastons themselves were not) to condemn as false the claim that John Paston was a bondman of the Crown.[84] For, although there had been John Pastons at Paston for centuries (as there had been Warin Hermans), John in the 1460s was probably no more able to know which were his ancestors than we, which is to say not at all. Besides, he did not want to know which, if any, of these peasant farmers of the thirteenth and fourteenth centuries were his ancestors.[85] One of them, none the less, who was not a Paston John may have been aware of. Alongside thirteenth-century Pastons there appears Robert Wiston of Paston:[86] was his name the inspiration for their fictional 'first ancetor Wulstan [who] came out of France'?[87]

These men were peasants. There is no indication that they were unfree.

[81] Why, or how, did John Wyndham's letter of 10 November and Friar Mowth's of 12 May avoid destruction?

[82] Even if John, his wife, and sons did not write to each other, which given the circumstances was most unlikely, one cannot believe that John Wyndham and Friar John Mowth were John's sole correspondents in these months. Why is there nothing from Richard Calle after 10 July 1465? Apart from John Wykes in February (possibly: see note 77), no one wrote to John Paston II either, nor, it seems, to Margaret.

[83] Whoever he was, he left for future generations to read that Agnes and Margaret had been called 'strong hores'.

[84] *Itineraries*, p. 189.

[85] Various deeds: those in BL cited by Davis I, p. xl; at NRO, Phillipps 281–2, 527, 530; the College of Arms, 326/40, 326/60, 326/109, 110, and especially 112 – an interesting, because defaced, deed of 11 April 1414 (which I have not seen); it is a gift of 2 acres of land in Paston to Clement of [?Paston], says the NRA catalogue. I owe some of these references to David Morgan as well as the information that among the grantors of the 2 acres in Paston in 1414 (326/112) was Thomas Paston. There is also PRO, SC8/87/4302.

[86] Bodleian Library, MS Douce Charter 3, cf. NRO, Phillipps 109.

[87] Davis II, p. 552. This Robert Wiston appears in Blomefield's attempt at a pedigree (III, pp. 690–1) as the son and heir of 'Wystan or Wolstan de Paston, whom I take to be the lineal ancestor of Sir William Paston the Judge'.

But have we been looking in the wrong place, despite that mysterious Gimingham court roll? Among the undertenants at Bacton in 1262–3 there was a William Paston holding 15 acres for 3 shillings, one hen, and various services. Of course, among the free tenants there was also Edmund Paston.[88] Neither of these may have been the ancestor of Clement Paston. Besides, the issue is (and was) not whether dim and distant Pastons had been serfs, but that Clement Paston himself, as the 'Remembraunce' maintained, held bondland and had married a bondwoman, Beatrice, sister of Geoffrey Somerton, 'And as for Geffrey Somerton he was bond also . . . he was both a Pardoner and an Attorney; and than was a good werd [world] for he gadred many pens and halfpens, and there wyth he made a fayre Chapelle att Somerton.'[89] On the issue of Clement's bondland we cannot (for want of evidence) pronounce, but he certainly married Beatrice Somerton[90] and there is plenty of information about Geoffrey Somerton, justice of the peace[91] and member of parliament for Great Yarmouth.

Geoffrey appears with his father John de Somerton in 1373 and 1374, in the latter year as benefactors of Bromholm Priory.[92] In January 1376 he was an attorney of John Fastolf the younger, in February a mainpernor for Hugh Fastolf.[93] Two years later he sat for Yarmouth in parliament, as he did again in 1383 and twice in 1384. He was also a commissioner in Norfolk in 1381, 1382, and 1383.[94] It looks as though politics in 1386 cut him down in full flight: a justice of the peace in April, he was removed in July.[95] Thereafter, all, so far as politics (local or national) are concerned, is silence. Geoffrey does not surface again until December 1399, when he was a feoffee of Thomas, Lord Morley of Hingham.[96] Are we to suppose he was in the wilderness for thirteen years? In 1404 he was quitclaimed a manor in Winterton: Robert Mautby and William Paston were among the wit-

[88] An Extent of the Honour of Eye of that date (47 Henry III) among the Stafford Papers at the Staffs. RO, D641/1609. It is worth recalling that the manor of Huntingfield was in Bacton and Henry Windsor's words to John Paston *c.* 1458, 'Item as touchyng your awun mater of the honour of Eye or of the manoir of Bakton, and ever it come in my sight of so old tyme ye shall son have knolage' (Davis II, p. 175, lines 26–8).

[89] Davis I, p. xlii.

[90] Clement's wife, Beatrice, predeceased him (his will: Gairdner VI, p. 188; she died in 1409, according to her obit in the 'Paston Book of Arms', NRO, Rye MS 38, p. 120. The Paston–Somerton coat of arms is number 8 in the 'Paston Book of Arms': Farrer, 'Norfolk Armory', p. 429.

[91] Albeit only for a few months in 1386: *CPR 1385–89*, p. 82; *CCR 1385–89*, p. 167.

[92] *CCR 1369–74*, p. 550; *CPR 1370–74*, p. 459. Far from being of low ancestry, might they not have descended from the manorial lords of Somerton, the de Somertons? (See Blomefield V, pp. 1537–8 and *Cal. Anc. Deeds* IV, A7943; V, A11922, 11924; VI, 66293). They might well have done, save that according to the 'Remembraunce' their name was Goneld.

[93] *CPR 1374–7*, p. 211; *CFR 1368–77*, p. 336.

[94] *CPR 1381–5*, pp. 76, 79, 250, 351.

[95] See note 91, above.

[96] *CPR 1399–1401*, p. 173; cf. *CCR 1399–1402*, pp. 111, 307, 308.

nesses.[97] The last reference to him is in November 1406.[98] The 'fayre Chapelle att Somerton', which the 'Remembraunce' says he built, is in ruins and has been since Blomefield's day.[99] Geoffrey died, according to his obit in the 'Paston Book of Arms', in 1416.[100]

As the 'Remembraunce' makes clear in its nostalgia for an earlier, more expansive age (which modern historians paradoxically think of as one of economic crisis and social dislocation),[101] Geoffrey Somerton's collection of 'pens and halfpens' was crucial for 'the origins of the Pastons'. Whether he, Beatrice, and Clement were bond or not matters less – though it mattered some, as we have seen – than the money this town attorney made from the law and advanced to his brother-in-law for his nephew's education: Geoffrey had no children of his own; therefore, he promoted the career of his sister's son. Here, he was not unlike John Hody:

> Adam Hody was a bondeman to my Lorde of Awdely and heywarde of Wollavyngton, and he had 2 sonnys, John and Thomas. Thys John went to scole with a chawntery prest in Wollavyngton and fro that to Oxforde, and so he hadde lycens of the Lorde of Awdely, and was imade a prest, and after that be fortune he was a chanon yn Wellys and Chawnceler yn Wellys.
>
> Then hys brother, Thomas Hody, hadde a wyfe and 2 chelderyn, John Hody and Elysawnder Hody. And ther unchull that was the Chawnceler of Wellys fownde them to scole, and he bowzth them fre of my Lorde of Awdely that was in that tyme, and hadde ther manymysoyon. And yn the tyme of Kynge Hary syxth, John Hody was made Cheffe Juge. And Elysawnder was actyfe yn batell, and ther he was made a knyzt.[102]

There were undoubtedly many other Geoffrey Somertons and John Hodys in late medieval England, for the law and the church were the avenues to success for the less privileged. War (despite Robert Knollys or Robert Salle[103]), administration, and perhaps trade too were for the more

[97] *CCR 1402–5*, pp. 296, 383.

[98] *CFR 1405–13*, p. 55. There is also a reference to him on the back of a 'Paston Letter'; he seems to have been owing 13/4d for twenty-four years: Gairdner II, pp. 9–10.

[99] Blomefield V, p. 1538. Pevsner has an unusually studied photograph (*North East Norfolk and Norwich*, illustration 4a) and an unusually graphic description: 'the ruin stands most romantically amid the beech trees and other trees, with an oak growing inside the nave' (*ibid.*, p. 124). [100] NRO, MS Rye 38, p. 121; cf. Farrer, 'Norfolk Armory', p. 427.

[101] John Gillingham, 'Crisis or Continuity? The Structure of Royal Authority in England 1369–1422', *Das spätmittelalterliche Königtum im europäischen Vergleich*, 32 (Sigmaringen, 1987), pp. 59–80, discusses the limits to this view of 'crisis' in England.

[102] H. Maxwell-Lyte (untitled note), *Somerset and Dorset Notes and Queries*, 18 (1925), pp. 127–8, from 'a rare, apparently early sixteenth century, family history': Robert W. Dunning, 'Patronage and Promotion in the Late Medieval Church', in Ralph A. Griffiths (ed.), *Patronage, the Crown and the Provinces* (London, 1981), p. 173. It was Dr Dunning's discussion of the Hodys and his quotations from this family history which made me aware of them and it.

[103] See Froissart (in R.B. Dobson (ed.), *The Peasants' Revolt of 1381*, 2nd edn (London, 1983), pp. 262–3): 'There was a knight . . . called Sir Robert Sale. He was no gentleman born . . . but . . . for his valiantness King Edward made him knight . . . Ye be no gentleman born [said

privileged. (Presumably there was no avenue at all for the rural labourer.) None the less, although we may justifiably call Adam Hody and Clement Paston 'less privileged', Adam was no doubt as substantial a farmer as was Clement, and probably as important a member of the community at Woolavington, Dorset, as was Clement Paston at Paston, Norfolk. If yeomen were the backbone of England, husbandmen like Clement and Adam were the country's sinews. They were not franklins, but their being bondtenants did not matter; not, anyway, where the careers of their sons were concerned.

Yet Geoffrey Somerton did not do one thing John Hody did: he did not buy the manumission of William Paston. Whether it was strictly necessary or not, perhaps he ought to have done. Some of his pennies and halfpennies spent on that would have saved the Pastons pounds and shillings later.

the rebels of 1381 at Norwich] but son to a villein such as we be.' Walsingham (*ibid.*, p. 258) probably unwittingly makes his end an apt one for the sort of self-righteous, self-made man he appears to have been: 'Robert de Salle . . . did not keep his life for long amidst the rebels for he did not know how to dissimulate . . . and began to deplore and condemn their actions publicly. For which reason he was knocked on the head by a rustic who was one of his own serfs and soon died.' Or did the elitist Walsingham know what he was doing? A class traitor knocked on the head by a member of the very class he had deserted and was now exploiting is surely too poetically just to be other than fiction.

Chapter 2

LAND: ACQUISITION AND DEFENCE

What did William Paston do with the pounds his legal practice (purchased, so to speak, with Geoffrey Somerton's pennies) brought him? The short answer is that he bought land. The answer to the next question (why did he buy land?) is set out in a conversation between the Archdeacon of Barchester and Major Grantly:[1]

> 'I wonder people are so fond of land', said the major.
> 'It is a comfortable feeling to know that you stand on your own ground. Land is about the only thing that can't fly away. And then, you see, land gives so much more than the rent. It gives position and influence and political power, to say nothing about the game.'

The disadvantages of landowning in fifteenth-century England (on the other hand) are well known; they have been extensively studied:[2] collecting rents and getting dependable farmers for demesne land was more difficult than at any time between the ninth and the nineteenth centuries. That these were stiff tasks which the landlord and his agents worried about and worked at is abundantly documented in the Paston letters: we have to be selective.

Sir John Heveningham's plaintive excuse for not helping out John Paston, 'I have as moche as I may to gader myn owune lyfflode, and truli, cosyn, I can not gadere that well',[3] is perfectly illustrated for the Pastons themselves by the memorandum of 22 August 1477: 'The names of the maners of Agnes Pastons and William Paston in Norfolk, how thai shulde be taken hede to this harvest anno xvij.'[4] Against ten properties are marks in the margin, which a note at the end of the document explains: 'These maners

[1] Anthony Trollope, *The Last Chronicle of Barset* (London, 1949), p. 547.

[2] The starting point remains Christopher Dyer, 'A Redistribution of Incomes in Fifteenth-Century England?', *Past and Present*, 39 (1968), pp. 11–33. Worth adding is the success of the bond tenants of Syon Abbey's manor of Cheltenham in 1452 in reducing the annual payment of 'work silver' from just over £10 to £6 13 4d; this was after protest had led to arbitration by Ralph, Lord Sudeley (at a cost of just under £10); he had raised what the tenants had originally offered to pay by a mere ten shillings: hardly class solidarity. See Gwen Hart, *A History of Cheltenham* (Leicester, 1965), pp. 41–2.

[3] Davis II, p. 259.

[4] Davis I, no. 98.

that ar trahid take gode hede that ye be in gode suertye of them this harvest tyme.' This is understandable, as the comments on these estates, and they include Paston, Oxnead, and Marlingford, make clear: 'Sele doris and distrayne, and put in a newe fermour', or 'seall doris and distrayne and lete hym not renne in debte as other fermours did', or more usually the straightforward 'Sele doris and distrayne'. Moreover, 'Distrayne' or 'Distrayne the tenauntis' are comments on other estates and 'Gadir the rente' is less frequent than 'Aske rente' or 'Aske the ferme': presumably there was a difference. Once there is 'Aske the rente and areste Smythe.'

In 1469 Richard Calle wrote as plaintively to Sir John Paston as Sir John Heveningham had to Sir John's father:

And I take not a peny in all Suffolk nor Flegge of your lyflod, nor Boyton nor Heyneford. I take non but at Gughton, weche I am feyne to gadre it myselfe of the tenauntes for the baylyf woll not come there, at Saxthorp, Spoorle, and Sneylewell, and xxvjs. weche I had at Techewell – thes ar the places wher I have money and in non other place.[5]

There may, of course, have been particular reasons, but there always were. Distance may have been one, so far as Sir John Fastolf's Yorkshire manor of Bentley was concerned, for instance; dishonest or incompetent officials were no doubt one consequence of infrequent visitation. John Paston and Thomas Howes reported to Fastolf on 24 May 1458:[6]

Please you to wete that yerstenday I and othyr of youres were at your manere of Bentlay, whych ys ryght a fayre manere, and yn the shrewdest reule and goveraunce that ever I sawe.[7] Ye hafe had so manye officers and reulers there whych hafe caused dyvers parties kept yn your toune, to grete trouble of your tenauntes, and som for ylle wylle hafe be put owte of her landes, and your land leten by your officers to your hurt and othyr menys grete avaylle. And there ys owyng yow by som man for vj yeere, som man for vij yeere, and som lesse and more to the somme of cli. before Myghellmasse; and besyde that for Estern pay drawyth xl li. owyng. The worst mater for yow that we hafe to doo ys that there ys so grete debt lyeng uppon your tenauntes at ones to rere, but we shall do the best that we may; for we be sure of gentlemen of the contree to wayt uppon ws and to help ws yn that at nedeth.

Negligence, for example, in not having a rental, was as much a failing of the master as the servant. At Knapton the consequences were disastrous, as William discovered in 1479; had the culprit been Agnes or one of her old protagonists, Warin King? William wrote:[8]

[5] Davis II, pp. 395–6.

[6] Davis I, pp. 85–6. This letter is in William Worcester's hand. One ponders the trip north of this assorted trio. This is John Paston's *only* surviving letter to Fastolf, which is, I think, surprising. Fastolf had appointed Paston surveyor of his two Yorkshire manors of Bentley and Wighton on 1 May; the letter of attorney survives as NRO, Phillipps 612/2.

[7] 'Shrewdest' meaning 'in bad order'.

[8] Davis I, p. 187.

As for Waryn Kyng, wer I understond be zowr wrytyn that he seyth he delyverid me all evydens, I understond not that; and as for rentall I am suyr he deliverid me non. And yff so be that he can make the rentall be hart, I wold he ded make on, for it war nessessaré for me, for I understond be jow that ther was no rent gaderid this xv ar xvj yer for deffawth off a rentall, and reson yt is I had on.

At Cromer, however, Agnes had in William Reynolds a zealous officer, no doubt (as he was one of her tenants there) the bailiff: 'I have late alle youre londes everychon. I know not oon rode unlate, but alle ocupyed to youre profyghte.'[9] He had even managed to lease out John Rycheman's place despite its delapidation:

For the lockes of the dores arn pulled of and born a-waye, and the wyndowes ben broken and gone and other bordys ben nayled on in the stede of the sayd wyndowes. Also the swynsty ys doun and all the tymbyr and the thacche born a-way. Also the hedge ys broken and born a-wey quiche closed the gardeyn, querethorgh the place ys evyl apeyred to the tenaunt.

None the less, there was one major problem. Here we arrive at the sort of particular, the type of detail, which makes the Paston correspondence the critical source it is: an antidote to, as well as an enhancement of, generalization. For the new tenant of Rycheman's place was not liked by the adulterous Joan Icklingham who lived next door. While her husband, a chapman, was away Joan did things the new tenant disapproved of. William Reynolds tells it best:

On Sent Marckes Daye I entred the seid place and lete it to youre be-hove, and on the day after cam Henré Goneld and seyd my latyng schald not stond, and went and seled the dores; querfore I beseche youre graciows favore that my latyng may stond, for I have late alle youre londes everychon. I know not oon rode unlate, but alle ocupyed to youre profyghte. The tenaunt quich by youre lycens schuld have youre place to ferme by my latyng ys gretely be-hated with oon Johane the wyfe of Robert Iclyngham, chapman, quich ys voysed for a mysse governyd woman of hyr body by the most parte of owre town wel recordyth the same, and sche duellyth al by youre seyd plase. And by-cause thys seid tenaunt ys gretely ayens hire for hire ungoodly governaunce, therfor sche mad menys to on Abraham Whal, quiche ys on of hire supportores, and he hath spoke with the seyd Henré Gonelde that hy myght seke a remedy to cause this seyd tenaunt to be avodyd and kept oute youre seid place and not come ther-inne.

Of such stuff are socio-economic 'trends' too seldom made.[10]

Farmers were no easier to get than tenants. William Cotting reported to John Paston:

[9] Davis II, p. 17.

[10] More seriously, the reason for Richard Calle's difficulty in letting a farm of 40 acres of arable, an acre of meadow 'and other smale parcelles' at Boyton in 1461 ought to be stressed: 'The londe is so out of tylthe that a-nedes any man wol geve any thyng for it.' Land getting out of tilth brings us to the heart of the rent problem for landlords in a period when tenants could

Please it yow to wete that the man which I wolde have hadde to a be youre fermour at Snaillewelle hath tolde me that he will not therof, and this he makith his excuse: he seythe that he shall dwelle with his wyffes fader and fynden hym for his good as longe as he levyth, and he will no forther medill in the werde. I fele well by hym that he hath inquered of the maner, for he coude telle me well that olde Briggeman aught my maister youre fader, whom God assoile, moche good, and how that he hadde al that was ther whanne Briggeman was ded, and that this Briggeman owith yow moche good at this tyme. I answered therto, as for olde Briggeman I seide that it was his will that my maister shulde have his good, be-cause he was a bonde-man and hadde no childer; and as for this Briggeman I seide that he hath bought a faire place sithe he was youre fermour, and payed therfor. But for this I kan not turne hym. Wherfor and it like yow to sende to me a bille of the value of the maner, I shall inquere if ony other may happe to be gete and sende yow worde therof.

Evidently, where the matter was one of bargaining, as it was so preeminently in the fifteenth century, all the ploys canny rural folk could devise were part of the process – no wonder distant landlords, distant by class and culture more than by geography, were at a disadvantage: retirement by the hearthside of one's father-in-law looks to me more like the first feint in a campaign to bring down the price of the lease than the unshakeable decision it looked to William Cotting.[11]

Once a farmer had been got, there remained the problem of getting the

and did pick and choose; in the fifteenth century arable must very quickly have got out of condition. One Cheeseman had paid £4 or 66s 8d – Calle altered the figure between 5 November and 29 December 1461 – for the whole farm; we are not told how long before. In November 1461 Calle could not get more than 40s for the arable; repairs and fencing were to be at Paston's cost. In December 1461 no one would have the whole farm above 46s 8d and for no shorter a term than five or six years. This is *ibid.*, pp. 256, 261. In his November letter Richard Calle describes another unsatisfactory remedy which landlords were forced to resort to: 'And as for Spitlynges I have lete som of the lond in smale parcelles because I cowde gete no fermour for it.'

[11] *Ibid.*, pp. 81–2. William Cotting was conscientious, as his letter concerning the farm at Titchwell shows; perhaps obsessively so: 'I beseche yow of this acquitaunce and of this bagge [which he had sent the money of the farm to Margaret Paston in].' He was, none the less, a servant to treasure; his honesty and probably his religion too – he was the parson of Titchwell – shines through 'Your reparacion shall not be moche, for I do it as husbondly as I wolde for my-selfe and shall take as good heed therto as I wolde for myn owne, and so is my parte to do': *ibid.*, pp. 348–9. Religion also informs the response of another clerical observer of his local rural scene; the letter of the vicar of Quinton, Gloucestershire to the president of Magdalen College, Oxford, has been noticed by Christopher Dyer, 'Deserted Medieval Villages in the West Midlands', *Ec.HR*, 2nd series, 35 (1982), p. 29. It is a relief to discover that John Rous' was not a lone voice and reassuring to learn 'as Quinton still exists, the advice may have saved an endangered community'. Bishop William Wainfleet had evidently been of another mind: Magdalen College, Quinton 61 is an undated lease from Wainfleet to Sir Richard Beauchamp of the manor of Quinton for five years at £30 per annum. For the earlier fifteenth-century history of Quinton see *Hopton*, p. 26, note 104. For another priest concerned about the community see Davis I, p. 670, William Paston IV's only letter to his father John III, *c.* 1495: 'Also, I beseche yow that ye wol se a remedy for the comun of Snaylwel, for the bayly of Snaylwel and on of your fermors war wyth my tutor and me and sheuyed me that all the comun shuld a be takyn a-way butt for Master Cotton and the vecur of Fordan, hom I beseche yow to thank.'

farm out of him. No doubt prompt payment is not normal in any society and whatever the object of the transaction. In fifteenth-century England this perennial problem for creditors may have been aggravated by a lack of coin, what economic historians call the silver famine of the later Middle Ages; it is otherwise impossible to conceive of Humphrey, Duke of Buckingham not having the cash ready to pay John, Viscount Beaumont part of his daughter's marriage portion, even if it was 17 March.[12] Still, if there were 'cash-flow' problems beyond the control of landlords, tenants, and farmers alike, this did not mean that getting those farmers (and those tenants for that matter) to pay was not a main preoccupation of landlords. It was.[13]

In November 1452, for instance, Agnes wrote to John:[14]

> Item, as for Horwelbury I sende you a bill of all the reseytes syn the deth of youre fadere, and copy wrete on the bak how youre fader lete it to ferme to the seide Gurnay. I wulde ye shulde write Gurnay and charge him to mete wyth you from London warde, and at the lest weye lete him purveye x li., for owyth be my reknyng at Myhelmesse last passed, be-syde youre faderes dette, xviij li. xiiij s. viij d. If ye

[12] 'And like it you to knowe I perseeve by the tenor of the seid lettre, your gode desire of certein dubete that I owe unto you. In gode faith, brother, it is so with me at this tyme, I have but easy stuffe of money withinne me, for so meche as the seison of the yer is not yet growen, so that I may not plese youre seide gode brotherhode, as God knoweth my will and entent were to do, and I had it' (Gairdner II, p. 76). A rent day was to fall eight days later, but Buckingham cannot have had that in mind: he would surely have waited to reply to Beaumont if he had been anticipating revenue on the Annunciation of the Blessed Virgin Mary. For the marriage, see C. Rawcliffe, *The Staffords, Earls of Stafford and Dukes of Buckingham* 1394–1521 (Cambridge, 1978), p. 119. MS Rawcliffe's conflation of the important 'marriage account' transcribed into the sixteenth-century Great Cartulary of the Staffords (Staffs. RO, D. 1721/1/1, f. 395) ought to be corrected. Joan Stafford's marriage portion was £1,533 6s 8d. Duke Humphrey cleared £300 of this by paying for Joan's maintenance in Beaumont's household for six years (ending in August 1459) at £50 a year. A further £50 12s 5½d was the cost of the upkeep of the husband, William, Lord Bardolf, and his retinue ['et aliarum personarum in Comitiva sua'] in the ducal household at Writtle and Maxstoke between 25 July 1454 and 11 May 1459. Another £740 the duke paid in annual but decreasing instalments, beginning with 500 marks on 6 August 1452 and ending with £40 on 12 August 1459. Thus, the account correctly concluded, on 16 August 1459 Viscount Beaumont was owed £442 14s 2½d. William, Lord Bardolf, was born in 1438, Joan apparently *c.* 1427. I assume the wedding was in August 1452, and that they began living together in May or August 1459. The marriage was set aside in 1477; Joan then married Sir William Knevet of Ashwellthorpe and New Buckenham, Norfolk, a councillor of her brother Henry; William, after his release from prison in 1485, married in 1486 Elizabeth Scrope; he was said to have lost his reason in 1487: *CP* II, p. 63.

[13] Not that they, landlords, were any better payers themselves, the Pastons included. The Abbot of Langley wrote to Sir John Paston in 1463 (Davis II, p. 372) concerning 'oure ferme for Heylesdon . . . prayng your jantylnesse that I send no more therfore, for it is unpayed for the yeere a-fore the Halwemesse that my mayster Fastolff deyed, and for the same yere that he deyed in, and sythen for ij yere, and v s. unpayed of a yere, and come Myhelmesse nexte xal be a nothere yere unpayed. Thus is iiij yere unpayed and v s., and at Myhelmesse next xal be v yere and v s.' He ended with a pious warning which, I suspect, embodied only a pious hope: 'This thus kepte from Holy Chirchez good may not be without grete parelle of soule; where the parelle is God knoweth. I pray God amend it, and geve hem grace that have his goddez so to dyspose them that thei and the dede both may be oute of parelle.'

[14] Davis I, p. 38.

wolde write to him to brynege suerté bothe for youre faderys dette and myn, and pay be dayes so that the man myte leven and paye us, I wolde for-yeve him of the olde arrerages x li., and he myte be made to paye xx marc. be yere. On that condicion I wolde for-yeven him x li., and so thynketh me he shulde han cause to preye for youre fader and me, and was it leten in my faderes tyme. I fele be Roberd his wif is right loth to gon thens; she seide that sche had lever I shulde have all here gode after here day then thei schulde go out there-of.

But, willing as Agnes was to have prayers rather than money, Gurnay's wife, it seems, did have to leave. Agnes wrote to John in July 1453:[15] 'Sone, I grete yow well and send you Godys blyssyng and myn, and lete you wete that Robert Hyll cam homward by Horwelle-bery; and Gurney tellyd hym he had byn at London for mony be you. I pray for-get yt not as ye com homward, and speke sadly for j nothyr fermour.' Sir John Fastolf, on the other hand, was not willing to forgo money for prayers, and, although not absolutely uncompromising, he wrote to John Paston in a tone different from that of Agnes:[16]

[15] *Ibid.*, p. 39.

[16] Davis II, pp. 191–2. So we come to Loundhall, Saxthorpe, a property which briefly would be in John Paston's possession after Fastolf's death, before, via William Wainfleet, it came to Henry Heydon in 1472: 'Item, yt ys told me that Harry Heydon hat bowthe of the seyd lord [Wainfleet] bothe Saxthorpe and Tychewelle, and hathe takke possessyon there-in. We bette the busschysse, and have the losse and the dysworschuppe and othere men have the byrdys.' (Davis I, p. 364). Cf. HMC *Blickling MS*, pp. 55–6, and NRO, NRS 13832: an arbitration by Henry Spelman and Roger Townshend of 10 January 1473; they rejected the claim of William Gurnay, presumably of the family which had lost Loundhall earlier in the century (see chapter 3). William Gurnay had entered Saxthorpe (against the Pastons) in January 1470 (Davis I, p. 552, quoted in *Hopton*, p. 254). In May a similarly peaceable scene was enacted here by Gurnay and John Paston III. Henry Heydon, however, was waiting armed in the wings to help William, or, as the 1472 arbitration shows, to help himself. John Paston III reported to his brother (Davis I, p. 557): 'But and ye be not at London I wold avyse yow to let Townysend tak a wey wyth hym [Gurnay], for it lyeth not in my power to keep werr wyth hym; for and I had not delt ryght corteysly up-on Holy Rood Day I had drownk to myn oystyrs, for yowng Heydon had reysyd as many men as he kowd mak in harneys to have holp Gornay, but when Heydon sye that we delt so corteysly as we ded he wythdrew hys men and mad hem to go hom a-yen. Not wyth-standyng they wer redy and ned had be, and also my lord of Norffolkys men wyll be wyth hym ayenst me, I wot well as yet, tyl bettyr pesse be.' Loundhall was farmed out for £34 in 1431–2 (with an additional farm of £5 for the watermill), just after Fastolf had bought it. John Kirtling, Fastolf's receiver-general, had liveries of £23: NRO, NRS 19653, the farmer's account. In 1445 its annual value was estimated to be £23 11s 2d: Magdalen College, Fastolf Paper 69, thanks to Anthony Smith. By 1457–8, when there was a bailiff, accounting seems to have been in disarray – to judge by the state of the accounts of that year: NRO, NRS 19687. This disorderly and not properly made-up account (in a variety of hands, and with its reference to the unavailability of the bailiff's livery robe: '6/8 pro liberatura sua pro eo quod nullam habuit ex Garderoba domini hoc anno ut allocata fuit in anno precedente') might seem to bear out William Worcester's criticisms expressed to John Paston earlier in 1457 (Davis II, pp. 170–2), were it not for the account of 1450–1 (NRO, NRS 19685). This has the charge totalled in a second hand; this sum is then, presumably as a result of simple carelessness, repeated as the total of the discharge. By 1450–1 Thomas Howes was receiver-general, as he still was in 1457–8: this may be relevant. For further discussion see chapter 7. At the foot of the 1457–8 account

And cosyn, hit is so, as I am enformed, that a fermoure of myn maner in Saxthorp called John Bennes shuld come be-fore yow for to appoynte for suche dewté as he oweth to me upon his ferme. I sende to yow the bokes of his accompt, to th'entent that Spyrlyng may awayte vpon yow at his comyng and declare hym his dewté, wheche as myn receyyvoure seyth hit wole drawe to the summe of xlv li., and more money at Mihelmasse now next comyng. And the ferme is but xx li. yerly, by wheche ye may understande that he hath hadde greet favoure in his payementes, to his weel and myn greet hurt, as I reporte me to youre greet wysdom. Neverthelesse, sethe hit is so that he hath hadde this advayle upon me I wold seen now that suche dewté as shal ben dewly founde upon hym by accompt to be made at this day, that I may ther-of have payement in hande, as reson wole, or of as moche as the day is ronne of; and for the resydewe to have greable sewerté, that is to sey of xx li. growen at Mihelmasse next comyng, to have payement therof at the festes of Seynt Andrew and the Annunciacion of Oure Lady next comyng by even porcions, as in his endenture made of the seyd lees more playnly is conteyned. And this don I am content that he goo at large, and ell that Spyrlyng take a rekenyng of hym so as I may be aunswered accordyng to the statute &c.

One thing is clear, or was to Richard Calle, if a good farmer was hard to find, once found he had to be favoured:[17]

Item, William Smythe schal occupie hes ferme this yere, and Croumer; and as for the yeres aftre, I haue founde a meane that all your londes schall be letten as weele as ever they weere in that maner with helpe of on Robert Coole, weche Robert fereth hym sore of the affence weche he ded a-yenst John Herlyng; for he is informed that your maistreschip hath taken an axion a-yenst hym, and John Herlyng hath do hym lost in the hundred xl d. and he hath hym in the scheryffes turne. Wherfore that it like you to withdrawe if any axion ye have a-yenst hym, for he will abide any ij men award ther-aboute; and more-over he is the moost able man to take a ferme of lond that I knowe in your lordeschip, and he schal be a gret fermour of youre the next yere.

Thus, so precious could a 'gret fermour' be that something close to pampering him might have to be recommended; such consideration for the tenant reveals how unusually, how uniquely disadvantaged mid-fifteenth-century landowners were. One suspects that Sir John Fastolf's legalistic approach,[18] Edward, Duke of Buckingham's harsh arrogance,[19] and even

(NRO, NRS 19687) is written 'Valor huius maner £13 14s 2d', which (however it was arrived at) is a good deal less than the farm of 1431–2 or John Kirtling's liveries of £23 of that year or even of John Bennes' £20 farm of the *mid*-1450s. (John Bennes was bailiff in 1450–1; he was not in 1457–8). This fall in revenue, especially anticipated revenue, might appear to be further evidence of the truth of Worcester's strictures. Yet while there was an improvement on paper after Henry Heydon's purchase of the estate, for example a new terrier was made at Michaelmas 1472 (NRO, NRS 12402) and the accounts of 1482–3 (NRO, NRS 15856) are in the form of a carefully written booklet with covers, revenues had not picked up: in 1482–3 the charge (less arrears) was £20; liveries were £16; arrears were £8.

[17] Davis II, p. 223.

[18] K.B. McFarlane, *England in the Fifteenth Century* (London, 1989), p. 192, especially note 86; also his *The Nobility of Later Medieval England* (Oxford, 1973), pp. 49–52: 'harsh efficiency' is the keynote.

[19] C. Rawcliffe, *The Staffords*, pp. 54–65 and 164–76.

John Cornwall, Lord Fanhope's 'leefe no peny behynde'[20] got them no greater revenue in the end.

How, one wonders, did Judge William Paston treat his farmer at Paston, William Joye? The terms of their agreement of 18 September 1422 were that Joye was to cultivate for the following year Judge William's land in Paston and Edingthorpe, which he had had to farm before, as well as all other land there that had fallen to Judge William or that he had purchased, in return for half the crop and 40 shillings in money. He was also to ride and to go on errands when Judge William required him to, for which he was to receive 26s 8d, 'reasonable' meat and drink, and a gown of his own 'weryng'.[21] The animals, grain, farm tools, and domestic utensils (duly apprised by Robert Gynne and John Albon of Paston), which were handed over to William Joye, were carefully detailed in an inventory.[22]

The separation of this inventory from the leasehold agreement it was meant to accompany – the first is in the Bodleian Library, the second is now in the Norfolk Record Office – takes us back to those boxes, trunks, chests, and 'several sacks full' with which Blomefield spent a fortnight at Oxnead in 1735,[23] and thus to what is missing from the Paston letters and papers. It is the documents of estate management – accounts, *valors*, rentals, court rolls, and deeds – which are wanting, presumed burnt[24] rather than dispersed so far as accounts, *valors*, rentals, and court rolls are concerned, as few, if any have turned up. This may be a blessing. It makes impossible a discussion of what financial value to the Pastons their estates may have been, which would have been, as such discussions invariably are, drawn-out, tedious, and necessarily inconclusive. We are not bound to tackle, because if they are there they cannot be ignored, those reassuring facts and figures, which in truth flatter the urge for quantifiable certainty but only to deceive. So far, therefore, as Judge William and William Joye are concerned we will never know, or think we might know, how the one treated the other. Nor can we

[20] As he concluded in a letter to Walter French, his bailiff at Cheltenham, written from Ampthill on 22 March 1424 and attached to the Cheltenham acounts for 1–2 Henry VI: PRO SC6/852/11, cf. Hart, *History of Cheltenham*, pp. 39–40. This was lamprey country – the letter was principally concerned with the dispatch of lampreys, well-wrapped in canvas; cf. K.B. McFarlane, 'William Worcester and a Present of Lampreys', in his *England in the Fifteenth Century*, chapter 11, where the lampreys were to be sent from nearby Oxenton.

[21] NRO, Phillipps 532.

[22] Davis I, no. 11, to be associated, I think, with the agreement of 1422. The early date is confirmed by the presence of Robert Gynne, who witnessed Clement Paston's will in 1419: Gairdner VI, p. 189. John Albon, we have met before, 'a styffe Cherle and a Threfty mane' of the prior of Bromholm's, who was (according to the 'Remembraunce', Davis I, p. xlii) no friend to Judge William.

[23] Davis I, pp. xxv–xxvi.

[24] Blomefield wrote: 'or whether you will have them burnt, though I must own 'tis a pity they should; except it be those (of which there are many) that relate to nothing but family affairs only. I have placed everything so that now the good and bad are distinguished.' Oh, 'the good and bad' indeed.

estimate the revenue Judge William drew from the landed estate he put together during his lifetime, for although East Beckham escaped him, other properties did not; we know it ought to have been, for the son of Clement Paston, ample, that William ought to have said as Rose Armiger said, 'To the "likes" of me, how can that be anything but a duck of an income';[25] it is fairly certain that he did not: enough, especially to a self-made man, is very rarely enough.

What may be done, or rather, what should be attempted, is a description of what the landed estate was and an examination – cursory, limited – of how it was put together. William's last will of January 1444 is our starting point for both.[26] In disposing of his lands, William began with those which he had had from his father; those he had had with his wife we come to only later. Let us, nevertheless, notice Agnes' estates first: Marlingford, Norfolk, Stansted, Suffolk, and Orwellbury near Royston, Hertfordshire.[27] The latter was her father, Sir Edmund Barry's home. It is to be noted that William, the son of a husbandman, married not just the daughter of a knight but the daughter of a knight without sons. He may have had to wait for her; he was forty-two when they married in 1420. His father, Clement had died the previous year: is this coincidence, or would it have been too embarrassing for the successful son to have had his 'good pleyn husbond' of a father (his clothes still covered in flour from the mill) at his wedding? And how many marriage contracts were written by the groom himself? More feasibly, William may have waited until his career had begun to take irretrievable flight and until Agnes was old enough – for she was surely younger than he, surviving him as she did by thirty-five years. The lands he got with Agnes ought to stand at the head of any list of William's estate: they were the best and probably easiest bargain he had.

The property he inherited from Clement Paston (a messuage, a mill[28] and lands, tenements and rents) lay in Paston, Edingthorpe, Witton, and Mundesley. Other property in Paston and Bacton William had obtained

[25] Henry James, *The Other House* (London, 1948), p. 46.

[26] Davis I, no. 12 (incomplete); Gairdner VI, pp. 190–8 (complete).

[27] Blomefield I, p. 690 is confusing when he suggests East Tuddenham became William Paston's. It is clear William chose Orwellbury rather than East Tuddenham in 1420, on his marriage to Agnes: the contract is Gairdner II, no. 4. Sir Edmund Barry's manor in East Tuddenham went to his other daughter Alice on her marriage to Sir Thomas Bardolph of Ellough, Suffolk. In 1454 (*recte* 1434?) when Thomas and Alice quitclaimed Marlingford to William and Agnes, William and Agnes quitclaimed East Tuddenham to Thomas and Alice – as Blomefield himself says in another place (V, p. 1223). Thomas and Alice's heir, Elizabeth, married a Thomas Aslak (*ibid.*). For Holwellhall manor in East Tuddenham held by the Pastons, see below, p. 33.

[28] Could this have been the very mill Clement had once taken his corn to? (How had he acquired so seigneurial an attribute?) It was probably Wood Mill in Bacton, which Agnes leased out in 1446 (Davis I, no. 15); it was a water mill: see BL Add. Ch. 14514.

from Bromholm Priory in an exchange for lands which were of the manor of Latimers or Latimers Hall in Bacton. There was also the manor of Latimers Hall itself, or what was left of it after the exchange with Bromholm Priory.[29] Next William mentions a toft, a dovecote,[30] and lands and rents in Bacton, Paston, Edingthorpe, Witton, and Keswick which had been Hugh atte Fenn's of Yarmouth – these were presumably purchased.

Agnes when recalling William's death (probably in 1466) says,[31] 'And in owre presens all he began to reede hijs wyll, and spak fyrst of me and assynyd to me the maneris of Paston, Latymer, and Schypden and Ropers in Crowmer fore term of my lyffe, and the manerys of Merlyngforthe, Stonsted, and Horwelbury, wyche wasse myn own enheritans, and Oxned, whych wasse my jontore.' Agnes seems to have shorthandedly put together as 'the maneris of Paston [and] Latymer' all the properties in Paston, Bacton, and their vicinity, which we (following William in his will) have so far described, and one we, like William, have not, namely the manor of Huntingfield Hall in Bacton. The manor of Paston, whose 'basis' was presumably a compound of the lands of Clement Paston, Bromholm Priory, and Hugh atte Fenn (and possibly also the manor of Huntingfield Hall itself), clearly was not a manor in 1444, but was by 1466; the reversion of Latimer's Hall Judge William had acquired *c.* 1428.[32] For the manors of Shipden and Ropers in Cromer, which, indeed, *were* Cromer, there seems no evidence of how William had acquired them by July 1426, when he obtained confirmation of the charter of Edward I granting the Friday market and annual fair there.[33] They were surely valuable. As was Oxnead, Agnes' jointure and the last of this group of properties assigned to her for life by her husband, all the estates, that is, thus far described: her inheritance, her dower, her jointure. The valuation placed on this group of estates, 'per communem aestimationem', was £100 per annum.[34] We shall return to Oxnead, because something of its purchase and of the problems its purchase entailed is known.

Gresham, about which there is also more to be said, went to John Paston in 1444. He claimed that it was worth 50 marks 'clerly by yeere' before Lord

[29] Gairdner VI, pp. 190–1. According to Blomefield (V, p. 1403) William Paston had acquired the reversion of Latimers Hall from Thomas atte Fenn in 1427–8.

[30] To tenant farmers the dovecote must have been an irritating, if perfect example of the power of the lord. [31] Davis I, p. 45. [32] See note 29 above, and Gairdner VI, p. 191.

[33] *CPR 1422–9*, p. 346.

[34] Gairdner VI, p. 191. Stansted was estimated by William Paston *c.* 1480 to be 'nere up-on the value of xxli.', and Orwellbury 'is worthe an viij li.': Davis I, pp. 193, 194. At Marlingford in 1552–3 liveries were £28 (account of all the manors of Sir William Paston, 6 Edward VI – I Mary: the third item in Brian Spencer's MS, formerly Phillipps MS 3840. Blomefield's bookplate is at the front of this item. I am deeply grateful to Brian Spencer, who with characteristic kindness allowed me to carry off this MS from the London Museum.) Thus, if these three Barry manors alone were worth as much as £50–£60 per annum, the £100 valuation for *all* the estates Agnes was to hold for life – Oxnead (worth perhaps £25 per annum), Cromer, 'Paston [and] Latymer' are the others – seems too low.

Moleyns occupied it in 1448.[35] Snailwell in Cambridgeshire was valued at 40 marks per annum in William's will; the damp has denied us the surname of the John from whom William acquired it.[36] That manor was to go to Edmund Paston. William, the third son, was to have the lands which lay in central Norfolk – the manor of Holwellhall (and Beauchamp) in East Tuddenham, and other property in Wymondham, Bonwell, Colton, and Mattishall, which had belonged to Richard Doket, William Thuxton, and others.[37] Their value was reckoned to be 25 marks per annum. To Clement, the youngest son, went property of the same value: the manor of Riston and lands in East and West Somerton, Herringsby, Martham, and Winterton, and other property in Potter Heigham and distant Buckenham, all of which had been Geoffrey Somerton's' 'avunculi mei, videlicet fratris Beatricis, matris meae carissimae'.[38]

So far, therefore, we have an estate (inherited and purchased) of an annual value of about £200. There remains 'swyche land as he [William] hadde not wrytyn in hijs wyll',[39] the land which, for that reason, was to cause so much bad blood among the family. The estates Agnes goes on to mention (in her discussion of William's intentions on his deathbed) are Sporle, Swainsthorp, Palgrave, and East Beckham.[40] We shall discuss East Beckham shortly; an incompleted purchase, it was not to produce any revenue for the family for the next sixty years. One Norfolk manor Agnes forgot, or William never mentioned is Cressingham, or rather Streethall in Cressingham.[41] The manor in Great Palgrave was Woodhall; William had obtained it about 1430;[42] it was worth at least £5 a year.[43] Great Palgrave adjoined Sporle. Sporle was worth £25 a year and more;[44] William had also

[35] Davis I, p. 58. Just over 100 years later, in 1552–3, liveries were £38: Brian Spencer MS, see the previous note.

[36] Gairdner VI, p. 191. Calle's accounts on the dorse of Davis II, no. 703, p. 328, note 9, suggest it was a valuable property. Between November and Whitsun in a year *c.* 1460 he collected nearly £30 from Snailwell, mainly from John Wylly, its farmer. Not much more was collected nearly a hundred years later: liveries in 1552–3 amounted to £34 (Brian Spencer MS, see note 34).

[37] Gairdner VI, p. 192, cf. Davis I, pp. 622–3. I cannot find the manor of Holwellhall and Beauchamp in Blomefield. The manor of Oakfields in East Tuddenham was purchased by William Paston II in 1468–9, says Blomefield (V, p. 1221).

[38] Gairdner VI, p. 190, 195. This, I hope, shows that William had been the heir of the presumably childless Geoffrey Somerton.

[39] Davis I, p. 46.

[40] *Ibid.*, pp. 44, 46–7.

[41] Davis II, pp. 7, 555, 609. Blomefield III, p. 428. Calle's accounts on the dorse of Davis II, no. 703, do not help so far as Cressingham's revenue is concerned; he recorded only one payment of forty shillings. In November 1479 John Paston collected £5 10s 0d at the court there; his costs for four days while deputizing for the steward were 3s 4d (Davis I, pp. 616–17).

[42] Blomefield III, p. 447; Davis II, pp. 7, 555, 609.

[43] Or rather, Richard Calle collected £5 13s 4d there between February and July in an accounting year *c.* 1460: Davis II, no. 703, p. 328, note 9.

[44] Again this is interpreting Calle's collecting £24 13s 4d there between October and April in that same year: *ibid.*

acquired it about 1430.[45] Swainsthorp he had got ten years later;[46] there is no evidence of its worth. It would be reasonable to suppose that these estates were not the most valuable of William's purchases; that he wished his perpetual chantry to be funded out of Swainsthorp (at 4d daily for the monk who would sing for him in the Lady Chapel of Norwich Cathedral)[47] gives some support to this supposition. In all, we cannot be far wrong if we reckon William's landed income to have been something over £250 a year; it may have been closer to £300.[48]

How had he put it together?[49] By marriage – as we have seen and shall notice again; by inheritance – from his father and generous uncle; by purchase – above all (one is tempted to exaggerate) by prevailing upon widows to part with their lands, as was almost the case where Joan Mariot and East Beckham were concerned.[50] This melodramatic aspect of William's purchasing policy we shall deal with first, before discussing the better-documented cases of Oxnead and Gresham.

It is also sensible to proceed from the unknown (but suspected) to the known. At Sporle, for example, one can only suspect that the death of Agnes, widow of the childless Walter Garleck, in 1432 was critical for Judge William's acquisition of the manor.[51] More suspicious is the settlement of

[45] Blomefield III, p. 445. [46] *Ibid.*, p. 40. [47] Davis I, pp. 44–5.

[48] Using the will's valuation we have arrived at £200. For the estates not dealt with in William's will Calle's 'accounts' on the back of James Gresham's letter (Davis II, no. 703) will have to serve. For Cressingham there is the payment of £2; in a rough and ready way I will multiply that by four. For Palgrave there are two payments totalling £5 13s 4d; I shall multiply this by two. For Sporle there are three payments amounting to £24 13s 4d; to this I shall *add* £8; out of Swainsthorp it was proposed that 4d a day could be had for William's chantry. Thus tabulated we get to the nearest pound: Cressingham £8; Palgrave £11; Sporle £33; Swainsthorp £6. These sums seem absurd as well as discrepant: in 1552–3, for example, from Sporle and Palgrave, which accounted as a unit, there were liveries of £61 (Brian Spencer MS, see note 34). Still, let them stand and contribute to the £250–£300 I am ready to put forward as William's landed income.

[49] For two recent descriptions of landed estates put together by successful lawyers, both of 'obscure' origin (albeit, in both cases it was the father of each who had made the first leap upwards, a leap similar to that of William Winter, whereas Clement Paston, of course, had not leapt anywhere), see E.W. Ives, *The Common Lawyers of Pre-Reformation England: Thomas Kebell a case study* (London, 1983), pp. 23–30, 330–44; and P.J. Jefferies, 'Social Mobility in the Fourteenth Century: the Example of the Chelreys of Berkshire', *Oxoniensia*, 41 (1976), pp. 324–36. For Sir James Hobart's twenty-eight manors and from whom he bought them, see his will, PRO, Probate 11/19, f. 256ff. One of the manors he bought was Little Plumstead (*Hopton*, p. 190, note 134), a place where we shall shortly find William Paston busy. For John Sulyard's accumulation see 'The Sulyard Papers: the Rewards of a Small Family Archive', in Daniel Williams (ed.), *England in the Fifteenth Century. Proceedings of the 1986 Harlaxton Symposium* (London, 1987), pp. 199–205.

[50] This preying upon widows was probably a feature of the land market. Sir John Fastolf may have gone in for it: Gairdner II, pp. 178, 254.

[51] Blomefield III, p. 445. Agnes' will is NRO, NCC Reg. Surfleet, f. 89v, dated 19 April, proved 23 May 1432; she desired to be buried at Sporle. The manor of Streethall in Cressingham was also the Garlecks'; I presume William obtained it at the same time as he did Sporle and by the same means. These manors in the 1370s might have become – but did not – Sir Robert

Swainsthorp on William by Elizabeth, widow of Nicholas Bloomvill, and William Bloomvill, possibly their son, in 1440.[52] This was a transaction perhaps like the one for East Beckham six years before, but without the exhausting sequel, because Judge William had on this occasion got Elizabeth and William to 'put it in writing'. It was a story certainly unlike that of East Beckham, because if William was Elizabeth Bloomvill's son he was not present at her death in Norwich in 1443 to make trouble; indeed, no Bloomvills at all feature in Elizabeth's will, though Agnes Paston does – she was bequeathed 'unam parvam tabulam cum ij trostell'.[53]

Most suspicious of all (and again like East Beckham) was the property William did not get; nor was it a manor, merely 'a messuage with xix acres of lande arable, vij acres of heth, with the appurtenauncez in Plumsted the Lytill'.[54] This, it seems, was the inheritance of 'Juliane Herbard, widue, of Norwyche, doughter and heire to Henry Herbard and to Margaret his wyf, sumtyme the doughter of William Palmere of Plumsted the Lytill'.[55] What Julian alleged William did to her in order to get and keep these few acres is amazing.[56] There were two apparent similarities with the East Beckham affair. Firstly, Judge William offered as purchase payment for the land,

Swillington's in right of his wife Margaret Belers: Blomefield III, pp. 428, 445; *Hopton*, *sub* index; and especially, S.J. Payling, 'Inheritance and Local Politics in the Later Middle Ages: the Case of Ralph, Lord Cromwell, and the Heriz Inheritance', *Nottingham Medieval Studies*, 30 (1986), pp. 67–96; for the Garlecks, see Payling, pp. 73–7. 1433 might be the relevant date so far as the manor of Woodhall in neighbouring Great Palgrave is concerned: its owner, Thomas Styward of Swaffham, died that year. Nevertheless, in his will (NRO, NCC Reg. Surfleet, f. 127, dated 29 October, proved 12 November 1433) he confidently left Woodhall to his widow Cecily for life, and on her death to his son and heir Thomas, with remainders to his other sons William and Richard, and to the heirs of his daughter Katherine and her husband John Spylman (Spelman?). What happened? Was Cecily 'got at'?

[52] Blomefield III, p. 40.

[53] The will was made at Norwich. Elizabeth, calling herself or being described as 'gentilwoman', desired to be buried (as did Judge William the following year) in the lady chapel of the cathedral. She presumably lived in the parish of St Clement in Conesford, as that church and its rector, after the cathedral and its officers, she remembered first; it was the only church she left money to for repairs. There were other Norwich bequests, including 6s 8d to Julian, anchoress in Conesford, and 2 shillings to each of Julian's servants. Elizabeth was also generous to the two churches of Great Melton, and to the rector of one of them, Henry Hall, she bequeathed *inter alia* 'unum magnum morterium de marbill'. He was one of her two executors. The other was John Blakeston, the 'Boteler' of (Isobel) Lady Morley, who also (at this time, or from time to time) lived in Norwich (see 'Thomas, Lord Morley (d. 1416) and the Morleys of Hingham', *Norfolk Archaeology*, 39 (1984), p. 10, 30. Was John Blakeston the John Boteler of Isobel's household of 1463–4?). Swainsthorp church is mentioned only as one of the five churches to which the wax remaining after Elizabeth's funeral was to be given. She left 3s 4d to the guild of St John at Great Melton and a gold ring with a diamond to (the image of) the Virgin at Walsingham. The tester in the room where she slept was to be divided among the poor. Her will is NRO, NCC Reg. Doke, f. 232; it is dated 30 September 1443 and was proved 20 November 1443.

[54] Davis II, p. 510.

[55] *Ibid.*, p. 509. Herbard is, I think, Hobart. This may be a reason why Sir James Hobart purchased the manor of Little Plumstead *c.* 1500: see note 49, and Blomefield IV, p. 25.

[56] Set out in her petitions, printed in full in Davis II, pp. 509–15.

worth, according to Julian, 30s per annum and as compensation for keeping her from it for many years, six marks,[57] which, while seeming derisively fictional (or fictionally derisive) may indicate William did not offer her a fair price in the first place, something John Mariot evidently felt had been the case with regard to East Beckham in 1434. Secondly, William was careful to get into his possession all documentary evidence of title,[58] as he did in January 1435 when getting possession of the East Beckham deedbox. These pieces of sharpish practice are easy to believe. Just as credible is that William Paston

> sodeynly sent aftere the same Juliane bitwene ix and x of the clok in the nyght by a servant of the shirreves . . .[and]. . . constreyned the same Juliane to ensele hym a blank chartre upon the whiche the same William Paston wrote with his owen hondes a generall reles of the somme and land biforesaid and an acquitaunce generall of all manere accions . . .[which]. . . was enselid in the nyght by the forsaid Juliane.[59]

We can even accept that William then promptly returned her to the London prison to which he had earlier contrived to have her sent so that she would agree to his wishes.[60] But did William actually keep her 'iij yere in the pitte withynne the castell of Norwiche in grete meschef, in so moche that sche hadde nat but a pynte of mylke yn x daies and x nightes and a ferthinge loffe', and (on another, later occasion) command 'certeines persones to smyte the brayne oute of here hede'?[61] Did he go to these lengths for land worth 30s a year? Perhaps not. In 1426 he wrote self-righteously to three monks of Bromholm,

> I preythe the Holy Trinité, lord of yowr cherche and of alle the werld, delyvere me of my iij adversaries, of this cursed bysshop for Bromholm, Aslak for Sprouston, and Julian Herberd for Thornham. I have nought trespassed a-geyn noon of these iij, God knowith, and yet I am foule and noysyngly vexed with hem to my gret unease, and al

[57] *Ibid.*, p. 510, lines 12–24.

[58] *Ibid.*, pp. 512–13. The return of these was what Julian's petition 'B' was certainly all about, though I find this document at specific points hard to interpret; for instance, the latter part of the following: 'and that of youre hie goodnesse comaunde the seide William Paston to bringe bifore yow and to schewe all the evidences and munimentes whiche that the modere of youre seide pore bisechere schulde have yeve un-to the seide William Paston state, or to any man that had it bifore hym or eny man for here seide moder or eny of the seide blode fro the tyme youre seide pore bisechere modere was borne un-to this oure.' This looks suspiciously like another instance of 'old-lady nobbling' by Judge William.

[59] Davis II, p. 510, lines 35–41.

[60] *Ibid.*, p. 510, cf. p. 514. In fact, she was only out long enough to seal the charter at 'hys ynne in Fletestrete'.

[61] *Ibid.*, p. 515. From one of her incarcerations, it is worth noting, Sir Thomas Erpingham 'poursued here deliveraunce [and] comaunded here to be atte the nexte cessions to be justefied there'. If William's mistreatment of one of his social inferiors was only half as gross as Julian complained it was, Erpingham might well have been scandalized by the young lawyer's inhumanity. Sir Thomas was also 'a myghty and a gret supportour' of Walter Aslak in his struggle with William Paston: Davis I, p. 9.

for my lordes and frendes matieres and nought for myn owyn. I wot not whether it were best in any sermon or other audience in yowr cherche or elles-where to declare ought of this matiere in stoppyng of the noyse that renneth in this case.

Had he been slandered? Or did he want propaganda from the pulpit of his local and friendly priory, a priory which was very much in his pocket? Was Julian lying or was he: 'I have nought trespassed a-geyn noon of these iij'?[62] Julian certainly pursued him for a very long time, but she had reason to, as she maintained 'William Paston the seide Juliane of the seide mees and londes now be xl wynter hath witholden.'[63] 'Now' was *c.* 1440. Is the key to William's initial misdemeanour, though not to his later and continuing atrocities, his youth? When he was a young man of twenty did Julian's 30s-worth of land represent an opportunity not to be overlooked? If so, it became for the mature chief justice a youthful indiscretion to be painfully regretted.

Whatever the truth of Julian Herberd's forty-year history – and if it were only half the truth it would be indictment enough of this lawman's lawlessness – it may be said to lay bare a man without sentiment. Yet, did William acquire 'Baxteres place of Honyng' because once the Gerbridges had held Honing, and his mother-in-law was a Gerbridge?[64] I doubt it. I am being far-fetched for the sake of moving from Little Plumstead to North Walsham: the other name of 'Baxteres place of Honyng' was (it seems) 'Walsham Place' or even 'the maner callid Walshams in Walsham'. The latter, Sir Roger Chamberlain of Gedding in Suffolk explained to Agnes,[65]

youre husbond soldyt to my moder upon condicion that she shuld never sel it but to youre sones John or William. And for the suerté of the seid condicion youre seid husbond, as I conseyve, ded the seid maner be charged with a gret annuyté upon the same condicion or the tyme that my seid moder toke astate, of the whech I suppose ye shall fynde sufficiant evydens if ye serge youre evydences therfor.

It appears an unusual arrangement and, to my knowledge, there is no evidence of John or William Paston holding land in North Walsham. Sir Roger Chamberlain's mother, however, takes us back to 'Baxteres place of Honyng', for in January 1437 at Honing William Paston's feoffees in the property 'delyvered to my Lady Scarlet seson in the seid place and Colbyes and Dounynges in Walsham'.[66] Though there were difficulties about that transaction[67] and there are difficulties in identifying this many-named property or group of properties, one thing seems clear: Lady Scarlet was Sir

[62] Davis I, p. 7. 'Thornham' might refer to John Thornham who appears in the case (p. 512), but 'Herberd for Thornham' remains a mystery. Moreover, what should we make of 'and al for my lordes and frendes matieres and nought for myn owyn'? [63] Davis II, p. 514.

[64] Blomefield V, p. 1422. Sir Edmund Barry's wife was Alice Gerbridge: NRO, Rye MS 38, p. 122, cf. Blomefield III, p. 692. [65] Davis II, p. 16.

[66] *Ibid.*, p. 5. For January 1437, see below, p. 39.

[67] Which John Gyn's letter to William Paston expounds but does not explain: Davis II, pp. 4–5.

Roger Chamberlain's mother. She had been at Paston on 9 January 1432.[68] It is also clear where Baxter's place was, or rather where the estate John Baxter sold John Roys was. William Paston called it straightforwardly enough 'the maner of Walsham', and on the reverse of the sheet of paper on which he did so he described its location.[69] Confident he may have been on the recto side of the paper; on the reverse none the less, he first wrote 'Baxteres place', then crossed this out, replacing it with 'Walsham place'. It and/or 'Bryanes', lay to the west of North Walsham church; there was a windmill and yet a third messuage, once Roger atte Hille's.[70] It was this miscellaneous piece of landed estate, not inconsiderable, judging from its purchase price, which John Roys bought from John Baxter for 350 marks – or did not buy, for on the basis of his not having bought it, one of John Baxter's feoffees stepped in to buy it for himself. That feoffee was William Paston.

Can we detect chicanery here? There is not in the end enough evidence to be certain.[71] On 22 October 1433 John Roys made his first payment of 100 marks and agreed to pay off the remainder at 40 marks a year in twice-yearly instalments at Christmas and Michaelmas. He did manage one year's 40 marks,[72] But that was all. Moreover, he owed John Baxter £80 – a debt of £40, which he had incurred before the purchase, and another £40 borrowed from him afterwards. Between autumn 1433 and summer 1436 Roys occupied the property; then, 'Will Paston, in the lyve of the seid John Roys, for defaute of payment entred in the seid maner with the seid crop and the vesture of this yeere ther-of than ther-upon.'[73] Did he act over-hastily? In his jottings he was at pains to note (after recording that not a penny beyond 140 marks had been paid to John Baxter or to him since John Baxter's death) that, although John Roys and his wife had appeared at Paston during the Christmas season of 1435 prepared to pay 20 marks, they

[68] Davis I, p. 15, note 12.

[69] *Ibid.*, p. 14. For what follows see *ibid.*, pp. 14–16, especially the footnotes, which in part describe William's memoranda on the verso of this draft letter. For what is missing in Davis, BL Add. MS 34889, f. 140v has to be consulted.

[70] Thus, it may be thought we are dealing with what Blomefield calls 'Bryan's and Walsham's' manor, which lay in Felmingham (Blomefield V, p. 1447: 'Of this fee in Felmingham', cf. V, p. 1415), were it not for the fact that Sir Henry Inglose disposed of it in his will of 1451. Sir Henry of Dilham Castle immediately to the south of Honing, held both North Walsham and Bryans in Felmingham: 'maneria mea de Bokenham Fery North Walsham Felmyngham vocatum Bryans . . .[etc.]': NRO, NCC Reg. Bettyns, f. 63v. I notice on the map Bryant's Heath: it lies to the east of Felmingham church, towards North Walsham.

[71] In John Gyn's letter, 'the evidences . . . that I shuld amende the defautes ther-jnne, and that that doon there shuld of Baxteres place of Honyng be taken estate to you as to other' (Davis II, p. 5) makes one ponder.

[72] Text of Davis I, no. 8, lines 16–17. The second memorandum (cancelled and then restored) records 100 marks and 20 marks: 'habet verba de manu Johannis Baxtere' (BL Add. MS 34889, f. 140v). The fourth memorandum (*ibid.*) has 140 marks paid.

[73] Davis I, no. 8, lines 13–14.

were not only in arrears: they still owed the £80. There is something like self-justification disclosed here. With John Baxter dead – which is why, I take it, Mr and Mrs Roys, clutching their 20 marks, came to Paston on a number of occasions at the turn of 1435, turning up once in January 1436 when Lady Scarlet was there (more than a coincidence, one would think, as she was to get the very property from which William in six months' time was going to eject Mr and Mrs Roys) – William took a prompt initiative.

At Michaelmas 1436 John Roys would have been no more than three instalments behind;[74] William did not even wait for him to be: he 'entred in the seid maner with the seid crop and the vesture of this yeer ther-upon'.[75] Having had 20 marks offered him the previous Christmas, he intervened before the possibility of further embarrassment should arise. He did not want the money, he (or Lady Scarlet) wanted the estate. On 6 October 1436 he paid to John Baxter's executors 'alle the sommes of moneye dew to hem by John Roys for a purchas made by him of the seid John Baxter of the maner of W . . . [paper decayed] except clj marcz'.[76] At this point John Roys died. John Baxter's executors seem now to have had second thoughts: their bargain with William Paston (such as it was) was broken,[77] and they entered into an agreement with W. Roys, no doubt John's heir, at Christmas 1436. To this William objected. Hence his draft 'to an unidentified lord' telling some of the story and asking that 'if it may be preved this mater be trewe that ye wille not be displesed thogh he desire to have his fre disposicion of the seid maner'.[78] I presume he had it and had it quickly, without the need to turn the draft into a letter which was dispatched, as Lady Scarlet took possession in January 1437.[79] Although there was trouble over that – John Baxter's executors, or one of them at any rate,[80] refusing to release to Judge

[74] Thus:
100 marks paid October 1433
40 marks paid for Christmas 1433 and Michaelmas 1434
20 marks owing for Christmas 1434
20 marks owing for Michaelmas 1435
20 marks offered (and rejected) Christmas 1435
20 marks *due* at Michaelmas 1436.

[75] He was careful to say that John's heirs should receive £10 for the value of the crop of 1436: Davis I, no. 8, lines 24–7. [76] Davis I, p. 15, note 12.

[77] Hence the cancellation of the third memorandum; the 151 marks I do not understand (*ibid.*).

[78] That is, Davis I, no. 8, which might therefore be dated early 1437 and *might be* (as it were) the verso of the memoranda of the recto. The 'crop ther-of this yeer . . . trewly bowth and in gret partye payed for' lines 4–5, while meaning the crop of 1436, does not have to mean the draft was composed in 1436.

[79] So, John Gyn's letter (Davis II, no. 425) should be February 1437. Lady Scarlet cannot have had seisin in January 1436 *unless* William entered very promptly after Christmas 1435; this the draft letter to an unidentified lord (Davis I, no. 8), with its John Roys 'hathe hadde and taken the profitz . . . by iij hool yeer beforn his deth' (lines 20–1) suggests was not the case.

[80] John Willyot (Davis II, p. 5, lines 20–1). Robert Tebald's behaviour seems more ambivalent. What was John Gyn's part in all this?

William's feoffees – William clearly got this 'maner called Walshams in Walsham', for he sold it to Sir Roger Chamberlain's mother, and she surely has to be Lady Scarlet.

What may be thought a detour caused by jottings on the back of a document has been essential, if only for a single result: the observation of William Paston with a troubled conscience. It is going too far to see him as vulnerable, but twinges have been observed. So I believe, and so we ought to expect: no man is a monolith. We might also consider the roundabout journey to have been necessary for our recognition of the fact that Walsham place or Bryan's manor or Baxter's place in Honing[81] was almost as valuable an estate as East Beckham: worth £10 a year, its purchase price was 350 marks.[82] It may have cost William Paston less; it certainly cost him less than East Beckham ultimately cost the Pastons. One wonders what he may have sold it for. The terms under which he disposed of it suggest that he was not altogether relinquishing it, but we know no more. Two impressions gained from the Walsham place, the East Beckham, and the Julian Herberd affairs might not be wide of the mark: namely, that William went roving up and down Norfolk after land, and that he, weighty man that he was, imposed himself on others. Nevertheless, it should be remembered that land did come seeking him, and that his troubles were not either all of his own making or all on his own behalf: others could and did impose on him.

Walker Aslak, I think we might accept, was one. The whole truth of their dispute is lost to us,[83] but there is no reason to doubt that it concerned, as

[81] The thought arises that two distinct properties are involved. I dismiss it: the manor of Honing, like the manor of Little Plumstead, came to the Boys family on the marriage of Sir Roger Boys to Sibyl, daughter and heir of Sir Robert and Catherine Ilney. Catherine died in 1417; among her feoffees was none other than John Drew, rector of Harpley (Blomefield IV, pp. 25 and 1421–2); one of her executors was John Thornham (for whom, perhaps, see above, note 62); she wished to be buried in the chancel of Little Plumstead church, to which church she made many bequests: her will is NRO, NCC Reg. Hyrning, f. 31, dated 5 April, proved 9 July 1417. Sir Roger Boys died in 1422. He left a rent of 5 shillings to maintain three lights for forty years before the image of the Holy Trinity on the south side of the high altar in the chancel of Honing church, but he wished to be buried in the choir of Ingham church, 'infra hostium eiusdem cori': his will is NRO, NCC Reg. Hyrning, f. 96v, dated 22 February, proved 19 July 1422. He was survived by Sibyl and two sons, Thomas and Robert. Thomas died in 1432 (his will, NRO, NCC Reg. Surfleet, f. 82, dated 8 January, proved 23 January 1432); Robert died in 1450 (his will, NRO, NCC Reg. Aleyn, f. 46, dated 10 August 1439, proved 6 November 1450). Sibyl was an executor of both her sons. She was still active in 1451, off to London to complain to the king about Richard Southwell's occupation of her 'manere of Hale' (Davis I, p. 241). Possibly her robust health was due to drinking ale: it was she who advised Judge William about the 'newe leyd hennes ey [egg]' for making 'faire holsom drynk of ale' (Davis I, p. 14).

[82] Davis I, p. 15, lines 20–1 and note 12. East Beckham, worth 20 marks a year, cost 450 marks in 1415. In both cases the purchase price was twenty years plus 50 marks. How formal a practice may that have been?

[83] For what remains, see Davis I, pp. 7–12; Davis II, pp. 505–7; and Edward Powell, 'Arbitration and the Law in England in the Late Middle Ages', *TRHS*, 5th series, 33 (1983), pp. 61–2.

William said, 'a sute that he [Walter Aslak] made ageyn the seid Priour [of Norwich] of a voweson of the chyrche of Sprouston . . . wher-to the seyd Walter hath nothyr title suffisaunt ne right in no maner wyse', and that William became embroiled 'for as moche as the seyd William was wyth the Priour of Norwich of counseill in hese trẹwe defence ageyn the entent of the seyd Walter'.[84] The advowson of Sprowston church had been acquired by Norwich Priory as recently as 1361; John Aslak of Bromholm did not get the manor of Sprowston until thirty years after that.[85] Walter, probably John's son, was a soldier[86] who exerted influence in East Anglia[87] as well as in Normandy. Such a dispute, up to and including the somewhat unsubtle, certainly brutal, perhaps soldierly threats to William of 'deth, betyng, and dismembryng of hys persone by certeyns servauntz of the Lordes Fitz-wauter'[88] was all in the way of business: it was what a lawyer had to expect. However self-pityingly William might express himself to the monks at Bromholm,[89] English lawyers in the fifteenth century were not and had no right to be immune – as Nicholas Radford for one discovered. Besides, in the 1420s, when Walter Aslak was offering to do to him just what was to be done to Nicholas Radford in Devon in the 1450s, William was not yet a judge. They, by the fifteenth century, seem to have been untouchable.

Thus, when William Wotton begins a letter to William Paston 'Onowre reverense and worchepys as to my moste reverent and worchepful and most trosté mayster', we know he is addressing a judge and that he wants something. The main thing he wanted, and he left his request until the end of his letter, was (of course) the judge's aid: 'And I prey yow heyleche for to schewe me good maysterchepe in reverense of God lyche as I have grete nede of yowre helpe that ye wel wowche save in the weye of charyté for to settyn me and myn undyr yowre governaunse in-to servyse of yow.' But also he wanted to sell him land. With this letter he sent his wife to offer William 'certeyn lond qweche that lyit in Lytyl Palgrave felde with parcel of a folde with othyr partenaunse'. It was (of course) bait, as was the lease of 'certeyne londe and pasture qweche the Priowre of Castelacre hathe in ferme, tyl messombyr', which he went on to dangle before the judge.[90] We have returned to our beginning – the beginning of this chapter and to the

[84] Davis I, p. 12. His retainer from the priory was, according to a hostile source, £2: Davis II, p. 509. [85] Blomefield V, pp. 1375–6.

[86] See Robert Massey, 'The Land Settlement in Lancastrian Normandy', in A.J. Pollard (ed.), *Property and Politics* (London, 1984), p. 76. [87] PRO, CI/9/347.

[88] Davis I, p. 11, lines 144–5. [89] *Ibid.*, p. 7 and above.

[90] Davis II, pp. 14–15. Thomas Cannon was another would-be seller of land in Little Palgrave and for the same reasons, only it was John Paston in 1455 to whom he wrote, 'beschechyng yow of your good masterchep that ye wyl be myn good master yf any man wyl put me to ony wronge, lyke wyse as ye have ben, for al myn hol trost is in yow. I have lond lyinge in Lytyl Pagrave and in Lytyl Donham that is clepyd Strangys, the qweche lond I desyre for to selle yow be-forne any other man and ye wyl desyryt' (Davis II, p. 115).

Archdeacon of Plumstead: land was so much more than economics.[91] Unless it is also a law of economics that to those who have, more shall be offered.

That there was land on offer in this way (or any other) and that William Paston, Sir John Fastolf, and so many others (merchants and businessmen as well as lawyers and warriors) had no difficulty in finding land to purchase, suggests the impression Bruce McFarlane left us with (or which we derived from him) is incorrect: namely, that the land market in late medieval England was 'tight'.[92] Most property moved by marriage; but much moved through death and through, as McFarlane would have said, infertility. Plenty was on the move too because of debt, or because of offers which could not be refused,[93] or because of testators' need of good works and the hope of salvation: executors and feoffees being the men to watch for a bargain. What was on the market may indeed have been a small proportion of the whole; it was, none the less, ample. Bruce McFarlane led us to believe it was not, and that because it was not, Sir John Fastolf was obliged to buy property with defective title;[94] Anthony Smith has demonstrated this was not so.[95] In other words, there was land with clear title on the market and there was plenty of it. East Beckham, like Fastolf's Titchwell, was exceptional; so was Gresham: only two manors out of the ten William Paston purchased caused problems for him or John Paston.[96] East Beckham we are bound to say was exceptionally exceptional: its title was not defective, William's purchase of it from Joan Mariot was. Gresham we cannot delay dealing with for much longer. There is no hint of any trouble arising at Cromer, Snailwell, Sporle, Swainsthorp, Woodhall in Great Palgrave, Streethall in Cressingham, or Holwellhall in East Tuddenham. And at Oxnead the trouble, which we must now turn to, was slight enough barely to count.

The trouble came from a descendant of the Hauteyns. According to Blomefield, the manor and advowson of Oxnead were sold by John Hauteyn

[91] A good example is Davis II, no. 872: report by William Burgeys of advice by William Paston. Quite what Reginald Rous' aims were in his sale of Swafield Hall to William Burgeys is not clear, but that they were not economic is. William lived, died, and was buried there: Blomefield V, p. 1440.

[92] I am thinking of his *The Nobility of Later Medieval England*, p. 53.

[93] London businessmen and civil servants buying in London's *contado* ought to be studied. For a beginning in Essex see Marjorie Keniston McIntosh, *Autonomy and Community. The Royal Manor of Havering 1200–1500* (London, 1986), pp. 223–8 and references, especially to her own, earlier work on the Cooke family; and J.G. O'Leary, *The Book of Dagenham. A History* (London, 1964), pp. 56–8.

[94] *England in the Fifteenth Century*, p. 193.

[95] 'Litigation and Politics: Sir John Fastolf's Defence of his English Property', in A.J. Pollard (ed.), *Property and Politics* (London, 1984), *passim*, but particularly pp. 59–60.

[96] Cf. Dr Smith on Fastolf: 'these five major disputes, four of which gave rise to litigation, concerned only a fifth of all the properties Fastolf bought in England with the profits of his service in France. There were another twenty acquisitions which caused him very little, or no, discernible trouble' ('Litigation and Politics', p. 59).

to Sir Robert Salle (that peasant's son butchered by the peasant rebels of 1381) in the 1360s. Of John Hauteyn's two brothers, says Blomefield, one, Henry, duly released his rights, but the other, Robert, did not and Robert Salle 'was much disturbed in suits about it'.[97] There is no sign of this on the Oxnead Cartulary Roll, a Paston document of *c.* 1437, the date of the last deed copied onto it.[98] The deeds on this roll show that William Hauteyn of Oxnead granted manor and advowson to his brother John, the rector, on 22 August 1360. Early in 1361 John conveyed the estate to Robert Salle. Henry Hauteyn quitclaimed to Salle in June 1364; Walter Hauteyn did so in December 1369. Sir Robert Salle settled Oxnead on himself and Frances, his wife, their heirs and, failing these, his right heirs in May 1372. After her husband's murder in June 1381, by means of a final concord of November of that year, the manor was confirmed to the childless Frances and her heirs. 'And her heirs' is contrary to the settlement of 1372; it also contradicts what Blomefield, using Sir Robert Salle's will, tells us, which is indeed the case, that Sir Robert required Oxnead to go to Frances for life and on her death to be sold, the money so raised to be disposed of in works of piety.[99]

Here we come up against a familiar discrepancy, to be encountered in the small histories of East Beckham and Loundhall in Saxthorpe, as well as in the larger histories of the deathbeds of William Paston and Sir John Fastolf. Frances was soon remarried, to Sir William Clopton; Margery, daughter of William Hauteyn, quitclaimed Oxnead to them in June 1383. Frances was not married a second time for long. Her nephew and heir, Sir William Trussell, quitclaimed to Sir William Clopton at Easter 1385, and did so again on 6 December 1416, three days after he had granted the reversion of the estate to William Clopton esquire of Long Melford.[100] Sir William Clopton duly confirmed this grant of the reversion six days later, on 12 December 1416. By what right was Sir William Clopton enjoying Oxnead for life?

[97] Blomefield III, p. 689.

[98] NRO, Phillipps 433 or 533 (Box 578x2). I expect this was made in the early 1440s when the Pastons were challenged at Oxnead by John Hauteyn. What happened to the originals? In 1449 John Paston needed an exemplification of one of the deeds copied on the roll, a final concord of 1328, and seems to have numbered this Oxnead no. 84; thus, he must have had nos. 1–83 somewhere, presumably in the box of Davis I, p. 514, lines 1–2. No. 84 is now College of Arms, MS 326/105. There are less than forty deeds on the Cartulary Roll, all of them misdated by a year in the left-hand margin in a much later hand.

[99] Blomefield III, p. 689, NRO, NCC Reg. Heydon, f. 189v. The will was made at Oxnead on 8 September 1380; John, the rector, and John Haughuyll, Sir Robert's chaplain, were the witnesses; it was proved at Norwich on 3 July 1381. Almost everything was left to Frances, including his house in the parish of St Michael, Coslany, Norwich, called 'Godesmannes place'. She was his principal executor. His two other urban properties, at Lowestoft and Calais, were to be sold at once; Frances was to distribute the proceeds – presumably among the poor, though he omits to say so. He was moderately generous to his sister, nephew, and niece; each had a gift of money. He was not, judging by his will, particularly wealthy: war was not as profitable as the law. Frances' fellow executors were William Danby 'Lord Latimer', and Laurence Trussell. No surprises, therefore, except perhaps that he specified no place of burial, simply that it be done 'christianly'.

[100] Cf. *CCR 1413–19*, pp. 372–3.

What right had Sir William Trussell in the estate? It looks as if Sir Robert Salle's warrior soul was having to soldier on through purgatory unaided. Yet, the Cloptons did not hold on to Oxnead. Although the widow Claricia Hauteyn[101] released her rights to William Clopton in January 1417, William Paston, the foremost of William Clopton's feoffees of the previous year, was charging ahead with his preparations for ownership. In September 1417 Sir William Trussell quitclaimed to him, in August 1418 William Clopton and the rest of his feoffees did the same. Evidently the Cloptons had changed their minds. Sir William Clopton died in summer 1419;[102] William Paston on 5 September conveyed his manor of Oxnead (and the advowson) to his feoffees. In 1420, on his marriage to Agnes Barry, he made Oxnead her jointure.[103]

Had it cost him 749 marks? This is the sum Blomefield says William Clopton paid Sir William Trussell for it.[104] It is a suspiciously unround figure. If, nevertheless, we work on the assumption of twenty years' annual value plus 50 marks, as the way in which a purchase price was arrived at,[105] then Oxnead had an annual value of 35 marks, or (let us say) about £25, which seems 'alright'.[106]

Trouble began in the early 1440s, when the Carmelite friar, or ex-friar, John Hauteyn claimed the manor, 'the which his fader whas possessid of and his auncetres fro Kyng Edward the Thred on-to Colbys tyme, and that he had fownd a tayll there-of in the Kynges bokes'.[107] Whereas he was lying about recent history, he spoke truthfully of the distant past: his father, Hamon Hauteyn of Swaffham Market (where John was born in 1399[108]) never owned Oxnead, but his ancestors had until 1361, about the time when, according to Blomefield, Sir John Colby killed Roger Hauteyn.[109]

[101] According to Gairdner II, p. 54, she had been the wife of Hamon Hauteyn. She remarried the blind Peter Fysch, and after his death William Punyant of Aylsham, with whom by 1443 she had lived for twenty-two years.

[102] Though writs of *dce* were not issued until 8 and 20 November: *CFR 1413–22*, p. 275.

[103] Gairdner II, no. 4: the marriage agreement of 24 March. The actual deed of 1 September 1420 by which William's feoffees conveyed the estate to him and Agnes is BL Add. Ch. 14806. I have omitted to note whether it is endorsed with a number; it was copied on the Cartulary Roll. Nor have I looked at the BL original of the depositions 'against John Hawteyn' (Gairdner II, no. 46), endorsed 'Hauteyn, Oxned'.

[104] Blomefield III, p. 689.

[105] See above, note 82.

[106] Thus, or possibly thus, in terms of revenue, a fourth of what Agnes was to enjoy after William's death, viz. the manor of Oxnead, and lands and tenements which had been Sir Robert Salle's, Sir William Clopton's, and Frances' (Gairdner VI, pp. 190–1, cf. Davis I, p. 22). In 1552–3 liveries from Oxnead were £35: Brian Spencer MS (see note 34).

[107] Davis II, p. 522.

[108] Gairdner II, pp. 53–4.

[109] Blomefield III, p. 689. As Blomefield implies that the murder came *after* William Hauteyn had enfeoffed his clerical brother John ('so that it [Oxnead] never came to Roger son of . . . William . . . that said Roger being killed at Ingworth by Sir John de Colby'); as, according to Blomefield, Sir John Colby's sister had been married into the Hauteyn family; and as Sir

Ultimately, that is at law, it is unlikely the Pastons had anything to fear from John Hauteyn – 'I wote well ye have on collaterall rellesse wyth a warente of on of the wyffys of Hauteyn of all the holl maner', Edmund wrote to his elder brother[110] – but in the political state of East Anglia in the 1440s they had cause to be apprehensive about everything. John Hauteyn may have petitioned the Chancellor of England that 'youre seid besecher can gete no counsell of men of court to be with hym in the seid maters by-cause that the seid W.P. was one of the Kynges justices, and John P., son and heire to the seid W.P., is al-so a mon of court',[111] but he had, or boasted in Norwich that

John *did* quitclaim Oxnead to Sir Robert Salle (on the feast of St Petronilla (31 May) 1364: Oxnead Cartulary Roll, NRO, Phillipps 433 or 533), Roger's murder looks more like a consequence than a cause of the Hauteyns' disposal of Oxnead. There has to be a sad story here of a family (or families) in disarray.

[110] Davis I, p. 147. Presumably Edmund is referring to Claricia Hauteyn's quitclaim to William Clopton of January 1417, subsequently copied onto the Oxnead Cartulary Roll.

[111] Davis II, p. 520. One of the men he asked John Stafford to 'assign . . . to be of counsell with youre seid besecher in the seid maters' was Thomas Littleton. Thomas was at the outset of his distinguished career in the late 1440s. There are a number of similarities between him and William Paston, aside from their both being justices of Common Pleas, which are worth pausing for. Thomas made an even better marriage than did William: not simply to an heiress, but to an heiress who was also a wealthy widow, Joan Burley, whose previous husband had been Sir Philip Chetwynd. She (and he) kept the Chetwynd heirs out of their inheritance for sixty-one years. Thomas was, as one might expect, as keen as was Judge William to get his hands on title deeds: in 1459 he sued his mother-in-law, Margaret Burley, for two chests full. He also took advantage of others' troubles to enlarge his landed estate. Sir William Peyto, in order to pay his ransom in France, mortgaged three manors to Thomas in 1451; Humphrey Stafford of Grafton was forced to sell him another three in 1465. For all this see Ian Rowney, 'The Staffordshire Political Community 1440–1500', unpublished PhD thesis, Keele University, 1981, pp. 278–9, 290–1. Of gentle birth, at least on his mother's side, for it was her name he took, Thomas was as devoted to his (and her) home, Frankley in Worcestershire, as William Paston was to Paston, particularly to his private chapel. It was called the Trinity Chapel, and he was licensed to hear mass there in January 1444, the very time when William was building his chapel at Paston. In his will Thomas requested that his 'gode litle masse boke', a set of vestments 'with thapparell', which had been his mother's, and a 'gilte chaleis', which also had been his mother's, should be used in the chapel; they were to be kept in 'a fine cofer and a bigge to be made with a fine lock and a keye therto putt inne . . . and that myn heire lorde of my manoir of Frankeley for the tyme being have the keping and the rente of the saide keye bi him silf or by other true and faithfull persone so that the saide masseboke vestmentes apparell and chaleis be surely kepte as he woll aunswer to the blissid trinite.' Nothing of Frankley Hall survives. (The fifteenth-century Pillaton Hall near Penkridge in Staffordshire his second son Richard acquired by marriage.) Thomas had a special devotion to Saint Christopher, 'the which our saide lorde Jhesu Criste bore on his shuldres', under whose image in Worcester Cathedral he desired to be buried. Was this because he was a traveller? William Paston mentioned no books in his will; Thomas Littleton bequeathed a number. They are noticed in the *Dictionary of National Biography* article, where, however, there is one significant error which ought to be corrected: 'a boke of myne whereinne is conteigned the constitucions provinciall and de gestes romanorum and other treties thereinne' was not bequeathed to the monastery of Halesowen but to Halesowen parish church, where 'in the moost convenient place withinne the same church it be laide and bounden with a cheyne of Iron att my cost so that all prestes and other may se and rede it whenne it pleasith thaim'. Thomas' will of 1481 is PRO Probate 11/7, fs. 23v–25.

he had, an ally more powerful than mere men 'of court'. 'He seyd pleynly in this toun that he xal have Oxnede, and that he hath my lord of Suffolkys good lordschip and he wol ben his good lord in that matere.' By this time, spring 1449, the Pastons had been made painfully aware of the licence Suffolk's political dominance had allowed to rogues and ruffians. Margaret, in her letter to John, continued: 'There was a persone warnyd my moder wyth-in this to days that sche xuld ben ware, for thei seyd pleynly sche was lyk to ben servyd as ye were servyd at Gressam wyth-in rytgh schort tym.'[112]

It was the turn politics were taking, rather had taken, which raised the spectre of disinheritance for some men in East Anglia – as Dr Smith has written:[113]

> The political background to Fastolf's litigation is evident in the origins of the disputes which troubled him most. These disputes all began in the 1440s when Fastolf, and those magnates (most notably the dukes of Gloucester, York, and Norfolk) who regarded him with favour, were excluded from political influence by a faction which the duke of Suffolk dominated. Indeed, with the exception of that regarding Hickling, which began in 1444, these disputes erupted between 1447 and 1449, when Suffolk's power was at its height.

At its most extremely stated, its most starkly formulated, which it was in 1399 and 1483, the equation was, as it had always been: a bad king = disinheritance. Titles did not have to be defective – as Bolingbroke and the princes in the Tower discovered – for men (and boys – let alone women[114]) to be dispossessed by tyrants, whether those tyrants were kings, or dukes, courtiers, civil servants, their cronies and hangers-on. 'Tuddenham and Heydon' had become for East Anglian landed society in 1449 what 'Bushy, Bagot, and Green' had been for the English landed establishment fifty years previously, and 'the Cat, the Rat, and the Dog (under an Hog)' were to be for the landed classes of the Home Counties twenty-five years later. So the friar became a threat. There was a small scene in the gateway at Oxnead,[115] there was a case to be brought in the courts,[116] but politics

[112] Davis I, p. 234. That was in April; cf. James Gresham in March (Davis II, p. 31): 'And my maistrese your modir bad me write to yow she hath verrey knowelage by a trewe and trusty man, whos name she shall tell yow by mouthe atte your next metyng, that ther was purposed a gret meyné of a wondir gaderyng of shipmen a-bowte Covehithe for to have come to Oxened and putte me owt there in a wers wyse thanne ye were put owt at Gresham.' [113] *Property and Politics*, p. 63; cf. *Hopton*, p. 184.

[114] For example, the Countess of Warwick in 1474. [115] Davis II, p. 522.

[116] *Ibid.*, pp. 38, 40. There is a note of confidence in these letters of James Gresham's of July 1450, as there ought to have been by then, politically speaking; 'Sotyll and other of your counseill thynk the lawe is on oure syde' is a strikingly positive statement from a young member of a profession not prone to making them. (For Henry Sotell's youth and maturity see *Hopton*, pp. 183ff.) The case had evidently begun by Easter term 1449 when John Paston got an exemplification of a final concord of 1328, viz. College of Arms MS 326/105. Also, a new enfeoffment of Oxnead was made on 19 September 1449: College of Arms MS 326/106.

taking another turn, sharp and violent in spring 1450, the threat diminished and the friar disappeared. Thereafter the 'box wyth ij ore iij bondellis wyth evydence off Oxenhed and Hauteyn' ('upon the presse at the ferther ende' in 1479) was not needed.[117]

At Gresham Robert Hungerford, Lord Moleyns, was a bigger man and a greater threat for a longer time. There was a deeper sigh of relief when it was realized that the end of the Duke of Suffolk had been the end of him too. For not only was Robert Hungerford bigger and bolder and better connected than John Hauteyn, who was a figure from the past, whereas Hungerford was very much out of the present, but also his claim to Gresham had more 'go' in it than had the friar's to Oxnead (whatever the legal merits of each) and, as a consequence of both these causes, he entered the manor and occupied the Pastons' manor house.

The interest of the Moleyns family in Gresham went back a long way: it had begun in the mid-fourteenth century as fraudulently as it was to end in the mid-fifteenth. After Sir Edmund Bacon's death in 1336 or 1337, there was a good deal of scuffling to lay hands on his estates (as well as on his widow).[118] William Moleyns, son of John Moleyns, 'the King's yeoman', married Edmund's daughter, Margery, and made an unsuccessful attempt to deprive John Burghersh, the grandson of Edmund's other daughter and heir, Margaret, of his share of the inheritance.[119] The coup having failed, Sir Edmund Bacon's lands were divided between Moleyns and Burghersh; Gresham fell to Margery Moleyns, who died in 1399.[120] She, according to

[117] Davis I, p. 514.

[118] John de Dalton 'raped' and married her: *CIPM Edward III*, X, p. 77. For this reference and for many more which follow I am indebted to Terry Simmons, 'Paston v. Moleyns: the Case of Gresham', unpublished BA dissertation, Keele University, 1980. For the Moleynses of the fourteenth century, see *CP*, IX, pp. 36ff.

[119] *CIPM Edward III*, X, pp. 77–8 (the government was obliged to make an example of him: pp. 262–7); *CCR 1349–1354*, p. 450; H.A. Napier, *Historical Notices of the Parishes of Swyncombe and Ewelme* (London, 1858), pp. 21–4. This seems to have been an 'inside job': royal officers making a raid on a royal ward. Margery Poynings was Sir Edmund Bacon's second wife and the mother of Margery who married William Moleyns (*CIPM Edward III*, XI, pp. 11, 13); for the escheator Michael Poynings' marriage to William Moleyns' elder brother John's widow, see *CCR 1369–74*, pp. 47, 60, 175. Their father, the elder John Moleyns, was a thoroughly bad lot: *CP*, IX, p. 39 and especially Natalie Fryde, 'A Medieval Robber Baron: Sir John Moleyns of Stoke Poges, Buckinghamshire', in R.F. Hunnisett and J.B. Post (eds.), *Legal Records Edited in Memory of C.A.F. Meekings* (London, 1978), pp. 198–221.

[120] That Gresham itself was divided (Blomefield IV, p. 319; Gairdner I, pp. 41–2) appears not to have been the case. Gresham does not feature among John Burghersh's estates at his death in 1391 (*CIPM Richard II*, XVI, pp. 450–1); it does among those of Sir William Moleyns, held in right of his wife, on his death in 1381 (*CIPM Richard II*, XV, p. 160). Thomas Chaucer, who married Burghersh's daughter, Maud, and thus came into possession of the old Bacon estate of Ewelme in Oxfordshire, later bought Gresham; it is his brief ownership at that stage which possibly has confused the issue.

the later testimony of Richard Wyot, one of her executors,[121] left the manor to Sir Philip Vache and Elizabeth, his wife, for their lives;[122] the executors were to sell the reversion, giving first option to her grandson, Sir William Moleyns.[123] In fact, she had granted Gresham to Sir Philip Vache on 29 May 1399 for nine years after her death.[124] Although Sir Philip died nine years after Margery did, in 1408, it was only after the death of Elizabeth Vache in 1414 that Sir William Moleyns, said Richard Wyot, agreed to purchase Gresham for 920 marks.[125] He held the estate for two years; then Richard Wyot, who was telling this story in 1427, re-entered, because the terms of payment had not been met.[126]

To overcome what was patently unsatisfactory to all parties, a new arrangement was made. Largely by means of Sir William Moleyns' wife, Margery, 'who was very farsighted', it was agreed that their son, William, when he came of age should marry Katherine, daughter of Thomas Fauconer, mercer, alderman, and mayor of London.[127] Gresham, which Thomas Fauconer was to purchase from Richard Wyot and which Sir William Moleyns was to hold meanwhile, would be the couple's jointure when (or if, as Fauconer had his doubts) they married.[128] Clearly, part of the deal whereby this London merchant got a Buckinghamshire knight's son for

[121] BL Add. MS 27443, f. 84 (abstracted in Gairdner II, no. 16). I am deeply grateful to Professor Ralph Griffiths for his prompt aid with the Latin of this document.

[122] The relationship between an influential king's knight, who was a friend of Geoffrey Chaucer's, and a woman who, according to Thomas Walsingham, was banished from the court in 1388 as 'useless' (*CP*, IX, p. 40; Anthony Goodman, *The Loyalist Conspiracy* (London, 1971), p. 42) would be worth exploring.

[123] The son of her son Richard, who had died in 1384: *CIPM Richard II*, XVI, p. 51. Not Robert as in Gairdner II, no. 16. [124] BL Add. Ch. 14677.

[125] *Not* 420 marks as in Gairdner II, no. 16. John Paston was no doubt exaggerating when he claimed Gresham was worth 50 marks a year before Lord Moleyns occupied it (Davis I, p. 58). That being so, twenty years plus 50 marks (see note 82) as the means of arriving at the purchase price might not be too wide of the mark.

[126] All William Moleyns had paid had been 20 marks, I presume the 'deposit' or earnest of payment. The account of William Wyot, steward of Sir William Moleyns' household, for 1401–2 (PRO, E101/512/17) shows Moleyns to be a knight whose landed income was about £340 per annum, though he pleaded at the Exchequer in 1406 that it was £100 less than that: PRO, E 159/182, Adhuc Recorda Hillary 7 Henry IV, m. 15d. In 1414 his debts were pardoned: *CPR 1413–16*, p. 156. William Wyot's account reveals that Moleyns was paying Isabel (probably his aunt rather than his sister), married to Sir Robert Morley (d. 1403), son of Thomas, Lord Morley (d. 1416), an annual pension of £10. The pension of his wife Margery was of the same sum. He was also involved in a limited financial transaction with Sir Philip Vache.

[127] For Thomas Fauconer see S. Thrupp, *The Merchant Class of Medieval London* (London, 1948), p. 339; J.S. Roskell, *The Commons in the Parliament of 1422* (London, 1954), p. 179; Caroline M. Barron, 'Richard Whittington: the Man behind the Myth', in A.E.J. Hollaender and William Kellaway (eds.), *Studies in London History presented to Philip Edmund Jones*, (London, 1969), pp. 217, 221–2, 225. There are two East Anglian connections: Fauconer originally hailed from Honing (see also BL Harley Ch. 45 D28) and another daughter of his, Thomasin, married John Hopton's abrasive adversary Sir John Gra (*Hopton*, pp. 18–19). Her 'blue-stocking' will is discussed below. [128] BL Add. MS 27443, f. 84.

his daughter was for him to buy the land the father of the bridegroom was to settle on the young couple: for Thomas Fauconer seeing his daughter 'right' meant reaching deeply into the bag on his belt. This is exactly what Edmund Paston meant when, many years later, he wrote to his brother that for his nephew, 'Marchandys ore new jantylmen I deme wyll proferre large . . . Well I woott yf ye depart to London ye shall have proferes large.'[129] The marriage was contracted and the arrangements for Katherine's jointure were made in spring 1417. On 20 May Sir William Moleyns settled his manor of Brill in Buckinghamshire on William Moleyns and Katherine his wife and their heirs;[130] the group of feoffees for Brill – it included Thomas Fauconer, Richard and William Wyot,[131] and Dick Whittington – was the same as for Gresham when that estate was settled on Sir William Moleyns on 27 May.[132] Brill, I take it, was Thomas Fauconer's security that Gresham would become his daughter's jointure when she and William were old enough to consummate their marriage; at that point, I assume, Brill and Gresham would have changed places.

Sir William Moleyns was surely the one who had second thoughts: on 1 May 1423 at Ewelme he married his seventeen-year-old son to the Cornish heiress Anne Whalesborough.[133] Why had he changed his mind? Were rural manors more attractive than cosmopolitan money, which now, perhaps, he needed less? Was snobbery victorious over greed, or did Anne Whalesborough satisfy both? Katherine, at any rate, was left in the lurch. Or was she? On 27 January 1427 she publicly declared in the Consistory Court of London

> that howe that hit be me beynge not fuly at that tyme of the age of faure yere at the instaunce, mediacion and informacion of the saide Thomas Faukener my fadir I not havyng at that tyme yeres of discrecion nether of age laufulle to make contracte of spousaill or matrymonye, made a contracte pretense of matrymonye with William Moleyns the sone of sir William Moleyns knyght at that tyme beyng within age also

[129] Davis I, p. 642. [130] *CPR 1416–22*, p. 105.

[131] William Wyot had been one of the young William Moleyns' godfathers at his baptism at Stoke Poges on 8 December 1405 (*CP*, IX, p. 42). Sir William Moleyns appears to have been particularly generous to the steward of his household: *CCR 1413–19*, pp. 437, 442, 443, 444. William was probably the brother of the much more successful Richard Wyot esquire, justice of the peace, sheriff, and many times knight of the shire for Buckinghamshire (Roskell, *The Commons*, p. 59). Richard was friendly with many of those who feature in this or other stories: Thomas Chaucer, Philip Vache, Thomas Clanvowe, Edmund Hampden (*CPR 1396–9*, p. 553; *CCR 1405–9*, pp. 71, 354; *CPR 1408–13*, p. 59; *CCR 1429–35*, p. 336). A lawyer, he was particularly close to Thomas Chaucer, with whom he sat in at least three parliaments. It is relevant to his role in the Gresham story that in 1414 he was appointed by Archbishop Chichele to administer the goods of Elizabeth, the widow of Sir Philip Vache; she had died intestate: E.F. Jacob (ed.), *The Register of Henry Chichele* (London, 1947), II, p. 2. Richard died in 1431. I am grateful to Carole Rawcliffe of the History of Parliament Trust for sending me a copy of her biography of Richard Wyot.

[132] College of Arms MS 326/52. [133] *CP*, IX, p. 42.

to make any contracte of spousaill or matrimonye. I the saide Katerine nowe at this tyme beynge as I am of age able to consent in to matrimonye or spousaill beynge also within the tyme that I may consent or dissent to the saide pretense contracte, dissent expressely and contrarie and reclayme the forsaide pretense contracte ymade within age as hit is aforsaide with the forsaide William, and in no maner wyse ratefie nor afferme hit as for matrimonye or any other bonde that myght as touchyng that case bynde me to the saide William Moleyns by wey of wedloke, but fully refuse hit and by the leve of God fully disgre me of hit as for any matrimonye lawfulle, the which myght in that case in any wyse bynde me to be the wyfe of the saide William Moleyns, and to that entent I wolle that this my protestacion be notyfied to alle men that I am fre as touchyng the saide William Moleyns for the cause aboven saide by the leve of God to take me an husbonde aftir the lawe of God to my plesyng, and the forsaide William Moleyns as for me I holde free to take hym an other woman to wyfe aftir his desire lawfull, and I swere here by alle the sayntes evangeles by me here bodely touchied that this forsaide protestacion, declaracion, dissent amd reclamacion by me made procedeth of myn awyn fre wille and not constreynede and princypally for the cause a boven saide trewe to my knawlaghe.[134]

Despite that last sentence, we are bound to ask: who put this fourteen-year-old girl up to it in January 1427? And: why then? The second question is more important than the first, even if the same man (I am sure) ensured that this particular child marriage which had not happened should be stated not to have done so in the proper place, and chose the time for it to be done: Thomas Chaucer. Richard Wyot was perhaps a keener ally than Thomas Fauconer, who had withdrawn from this unseemly affair eighteen months previously. It is time to set down the sequence of events which cluster thickly about Katherine's declaration of 27 January 1427. They may not explain everything, but they suggest a good deal.

As we have seen, the still under-age William Moleyns married Anne Whalesborough on 1 May 1423.[135] His father Sir William Moleyns died 8 June 1425.[136] On 29 June 1425 Thomas Fauconer and his co-feoffees

[134] Jacob (ed.), *The Register of Henry Chichele*, IV, p. 90. This reference I certainly owe to Mr Terry Simmons. Such a public disavowal was the required form: R.H. Helmholz, *Marriage Litigation in Medieval England* (London, 1974), p. 98.

[135] The legality of this marriage would surely have been doubtful, at any rate for the next three and a half years, as would have been the legitimacy of Eleanor Moleyns, born at Stoke Poges on 11 June 1426 (*CP*, IX, p. 42). Anne Whalesborough, after her husband's death at Orleans in 1429, married Edmund Hampden, who crossed William Paston's path at East Beckham in the 1430s. She survived until 1487 – another of these long-lived ladies who saw the Wars of the Roses come and go and four kings depart. In her will she styled herself Anne Moleyns, sometime (that was sixty years previously) wife of Sir William Moleyns, 'callyd that tyme lord Molence'. She left her daughter Eleanor Moleyns a standing cup of silver, the better of her two girdles 'harnesed' with gold, and many other things; her other daughter, Frideswide, was to have the other girdle. There were a number of bequests to Hampdens. Robert Chambre, her chaplain, was to pray for her at Oxford, at a salary of 10 marks per annum, for as long as it could be paid by her executors (of whom he was one) out of her goods not otherwise bequeathed. She was to be buried at Hampden, if she died there. Her will is PRO, Probate 11/8, f. 6v. It is dated the last day of February 1487; proof is not entered.

[136] *CP*, IX, p. 42.

granted Gresham to Thomas Chaucer, Richard Wyot, and Thomas Walsingham. These three were duly quitclaimed by the others in July 1425 and December 1426; finally, on 26 February 1427 Thomas Walsingham released to Chaucer and Wyot.[137] The next day these two granted Gresham to a group which included William Paston; undoubtedly this was the sale to him, or the immediate prelude to it.[138] All this looks fair and above board, as Richard Wyot testified, probably at this very time or shortly afterwards. If one is given cause for hesitation in accepting that it was, that cause lies in the conjunction of dates, of which there is one more that may be relevant. On 26 February 1427 William Moleyns, having proved his age, was given seisin of his father's lands. The farmer of them had been Thomas Chaucer.[139] Thomas Chaucer's intervention in this business is crucial: he arranged the final transfer and sale. Why did he intervene?

Richard Wyot's deposition of 1427 says that when, as Thomas Fauconer had anticipated (and armed himself against), the marriage did not take effect, Thomas Fauconer entered Gresham, which he was entitled to do under the terms of the settlement he had ensured was made in 1417. Richard Wyot still had received nothing. At this point Thomas Chaucer, a kinsman of Margery Moleyns, *née* Bacon, appeared. He pointed out to Fauconer Richard's right to the manor, 'of which he would soon hear, if he did not wish to behave reasonably and reach agreement with Richard'; Fauconer said he was obliged to Chaucer and asked what he could suggest as reasonable. Long discussion ensued. Eventually Fauconer agreed to sell to Chaucer and Wyot 'for a great sum within the value'. If, however, Wyot was to get the cash required to undertake the provisions of Margery Moleyns' will, to pay Thomas Fauconer, and for other costs which seem to have included those of Thomas Chaucer, 'who cannot be made displeased', a speedy sale of Gresham was necessary. Thomas Chaucer duly produced the buyer who, no doubt, had been eagerly waiting in the wings: William Paston.[140] Was it kinship which impelled Thomas Chaucer to take an interest? It was not a close relationship: Margery Moleyns, who had died in

137 College of Arms MS 326/53.

138 M.M. Crow and C.C. Olson, *Chaucer Life Records* (London, 1966), p. 543; *Times Literary Supplement*, 3 August 1933. The deed is in the Harvard University Library. In 1449 John Paston claimed the family had been 'pecybily poscessyd of the maner of Gresham . . . xx yere and more til xvij Februarij [1448]': Davis I, p. 51.

139 *CCR 1422–9*, pp. 217, 287. He was shortly to have the guardianship and marriage of the sole heiress, William Moleyns' young daughter, Eleanor. Her mother and grandmother were brushed aside in what looks like a 'fix' between Chaucer and the Treasurer, Walter, Lord Hungerford: *CPR 1429–36*, p. 156; M.B. Ruud, *Thomas Chaucer* (University of Minnesota Studies in Language and Literature, no. 9, 1926), p. 12 citing Nicolas, *PPC IV*, pp. 98–99. Eleanor was duly married to Walter's grandson Robert, who thus became the Lord Moleyns who claimed and occupied Gresham in 1448.

140 BL Add. MS 27443, f. 84.

1399, was his wife's great aunt. However, he knew her, he knew her grandson, he knew Richard Wyot; their local, Chiltern world was this great man's too. Thomas, therefore, may have developed a paternal, an avuncular stance towards the younger William Moleyns (as he did towards another neighbour, the young Thomas Stonor).[141] Nevertheless, in 1425 he stepped in not to help the Moleyns family but Richard Wyot. And it was another friend, William Paston, who got Gresham.

Nor can we readily discern that William got other than a property with clear title. Thomas Fauconer had been bought out and, the Fauconer–Moleyns marriage not having come off, the Moleyns family had no right to the estate – clearly Thomas Chaucer, their patron, thought they had none. What they did have was an attachment, of no ultimate legal use,[142] but a spur to action if time and occasion were propitious. Robert Hungerford in 1448 is not altogether a convincing example of the authenticity of such attachment, yet it would be wrong to deny the force of 'family' possession before 1399 and again between 1417 and 1425. Moreover, William Moleyns soon after 1399 had begun to pay for what he might very well have considered ought to have come to him by inheritance. Why did his grandmother not leave Gresham directly to him in 1399? As she had just bought his marriage,[143] it may be she was in debt to the influential man who had seen that she had been able to, Sir Philip Vache. The grant of Gresham to him was, it seems likely, a repayment of that debt. Moreover, because the grant was for nine years, she clearly saw Gresham's alienation as temporary, no more than an unwelcome interruption in ownership, but necessary for the family's independence and survival. We are face to face, I think, with this family's reluctance to give up what once it had held, in this case recently and in this case too with not even the intention of letting go what it held. If possession is nine parts of the law, atavistic commitment has

[141] Is his having Eleanor Moleyns brought back at his own cost from Orleans after her father's death not the action of a protector? (See note 139.) The best introduction to Thomas Chaucer is J.S. Roskell, 'Thomas Chaucer of Ewelme', in the third volume of Professor Roskell's collected papers, *Parliament and Politics in Late Medieval England* (London, 1983), pp. 151–91.

[142] In 1449 Margaret Paston wrote to John: 'Barow told me that ther ware no better evydens in Inglond than the Lord Moleynys hathe of the maner of Gressam. I told hym I sopposyd that thei were seche evydens as Willyam Hasard seyd that yowr were: he seyd the sellys of hem were not yett kold. I seyd I sopposyd his lordys evydens were seche. I seyd I wost wele, as for yowr evydens, ther mytgh no man have non better than ye have, and I seyd the selys of hem were to hundred yere elder than he is.' In the same letter Margaret added later: 'It is told me as for Gressam the Lord Moleynys xuld not cleym it now nother be tayl nere be evydens, but be infefment of on of his anseteris qhiche dyid sesynnyd.' Was this ancestor Margery, who died in 1399?

[143] For 700 marks in 1398; he was born in 1378: *CP*, IX, p. 41.

to be the tenth.[144] Or (after all), in 1448 at Gresham are we faced with no more than predatory calculation? At Robert Hungerford, Lord Moleyns' descent on and occupation of John Paston's principal estate we have arrived.

For the Pastons there were four phases to the Gresham affair: 1448, loss; 1449, eviction; 1450, revival; 1451, recovery. The trouble, so far as we know, came out of a clear sky. Lord Moleyns[145] entered the manor on 17 February 1448.[146] A time of competitive rent-collecting ensued.[147] John Paston got nowhere with Lord Moleyns himself, though he went to Salisbury to see him, while William Wainfleet's efforts as an arbitrator in the summer proved equally fruitless.[148] In the autumn John decided on a different strategy: confrontation at Gresham. As John himself expressed it, 'non answere had but delays, which causyd your seid besechere the vj day of Octobre last past to inhabite hym in a mansion with-in the seid town'.[149] This 'mansion' was probably the castle built by Sir Edmund Bacon;[150] it had a round tower at each corner and in appearance may have been like Nunney in Somerset.[151]

It was in fact Margaret who went there, to defend, as it were, her own, for Gresham was her jointure; in a famous letter to her husband she asked him to get her crossbows and pole-axes (as well as almonds and sugar) and described the military preparedness of the Moleyns faction – no bows for them but handguns:

[144] Worth recalling here is William, Duke of Suffolk and Alice his widow's extreme reluctance to part with his birthplace, the Suffolk manor of Cotton, sold (because of the urgent need to pay William's ransom) to Sir John Fastolf. Alice duly recovered Cotton in what one cannot help feeling was a determined act of piety to her husband: see chapter 7.

[145] Sir Robert Hungerford was summoned to the 1445 parliament as Lord Moleyns. His creation was more artificial than most, even in that decade of manufactured creations: J. Enoch Powell and Keith Wallis, *The House of Lords in the Middle Ages* (London, 1968), p. 476. [146] Davis I, p. 51. [147] *Ibid.*, pp. 223, 225.

[148] *Ibid.*, pp. 52–3; Davis II, pp. 519–20. John, after much else had happened, described this period with feeling: Davis I, p. 57, lines 21–45. One passage is worth reciting here: 'Also byfore this tyme I have agreed to put it in ij juges so thei wolde determyne by our evydences the right, moevyng nother partie to yeve other by ony mene, but only the right determyned, he to be fully recompensed that hath right; wherto he wold not agree, but alle tymes wolde that thoe juges shulde entrete the parties as they myght be drawe to, by offre and profre to my conceyte as men bye hors.'

[149] Davis I, p. 52; cf. Davis I, p. 229, Margaret speaking of John: 'I seyd to hym that ye had sweyd to my Lord Moleynys dyvers tymys for the maner of Gressm syth ye wer dissesyd, and ye cowd never gete no resonabyl answere of hym, and ther-fore ye entred ayen as ye hopid that was for the best.'

[150] Licence to crenellate 1318: *CPR 1317–21*, p. 224.

[151] Sir John drew a plan of it in a letter to his brother of 28 September 1471: Davis I, p. 442, note 6. Gairdner V, p. 112, reproduces the drawing. See also Pevsner, *North East Norfolk*, p. 155.

Partryche and his felaschep arn sore aferyd that ye wold entren ayen up-on hem, and they have made grete ordynawnce wyth-jnne the hwse, as it is told me. They have made barris to barre the dorys crosse-wyse, and they han made wyketis on every quarter of the haws to schete owte atte, both wyth bowys and wyth hand gunnys; and tho holys that ben made forre hand gunnyss they ben scarse kne hey fro the plawnchere [floor], and of seche holis ben made fyve. There can non man schete owt at them wyth no handbowys.[152]

Among Partridge's fellowship were those other antagonists of John Paston, Simon Gunnor and John Mariot – they were both eager to boast of what was in store for Margaret.[153] In the midst of a scene regarded in some quarters as 'typical' of fifteenth-century England, it is refreshing to discover a man who loathed violence. Philip Berney[154] was timid, and his timidity led him into tale-telling. James Gloys' amused account was evidently one he did not want Margaret to read,[155] but it ought to be required reading for all students of history and human psychology.[156]

Forthermore, if it plese yow to here of my Master Berney, he was at Gresham with my mastres on the Tuysday next after Halwemasday, the same day that we dystreynyd Jamys Rokkysson; and I had mette a litill a-fore with Partrych, and he thrett me and sayd that we shuld not long kepe the dystresse, and there-fore my mastres dede vs don on owre jakkys and owre salettys. My Master Berney cam in and the parson of Oxened with hym, and sey vs in owre jakkys; and he wexe as pale as any herd and wold right fayn a ben thens. So my mastres dede hym dyne . . . Whan thei had etyn he had mych hast to a be thens, so my mastres desyryd and prayd hym that he wold come a-geyn or aght long, and so with mych prayng he be-hest here if he so myth. And Herry Collys stode there by-syde and seyd to my felachep, 'What shuld my master do here?' quod he. 'Lete yowre master send after his kynnysmen at Mautby, for thei have nowt that thei mown lese.' And so thei redyn here wey. And with-in a sevenyyt after my Master Berney sent Davy to my mastres and prayd my mastres that she wold hold his master excusyd, for he had hurt his owyn hors that he rode up-on, and he dede Davy sadillyn an-oder hors, and he stode by and mad water whill he sadyllyd hym; and as Davy shuld a kyrt the horse he slenkyd be-hynd and toke his master on the hepe suyche a stroke that never man may trust hym after, and brake his hepe. And he had sent Herry Collys to Norwhich for medycynys, so he must ryde hom the same nyyt for his master had no man at home. So my mastres was rygth sory and wend that it had be trowth, but I know wele that it was not so. It happyd that I rod the next day to Norwhich, and I rood in to my mastres yowre moder, and she ded aske me after my Master Berney. And I told here how he was hurt, and she askyd the parson of Oxened if he were hurt and he seyd nay, for Davy lay with hym the same nyyt a-fore and told hym that he was heyll and mery and prayd hym that he wold be with hym the Sonday next after; and so Davy lay the same nyyt after that he had told my mastres the tale with the parson of Oxened.

[152] Davis I, p. 226. Edmund Paston bought bows, bow-strings, arrows, and gleaves for Margaret: Davis II, pp. 27–8 and 331 (lines 28–30).

[153] Davis I, p. 226; Davis II, pp. 29, 30.

[154] For Philip Berney, see chapter 5.

[155] Davis II, p. 29, lines 53–4.

[156] *Ibid.*, p. 28.

Still, it was the men of violence who, for the moment, had their way. The threat that Margaret 'shuld be plukkyd out of here howse'[157] was fulfilled on 29 January 1449[158] and the second phase of the contest began.

It was, according to John's petition to the parliament of 1449, not simply an eviction; it was also a demolition. Lord Moleyns' men, with

pannys with fier and teynes brennyng here-in, long cromes to draw doun housis, ladderes, pikoys with which thei myned down the walles, and long trees with which thei broke up yates and dores and so came in-to the seid mansion, the wiff of your seid besechere at that tyme beyng ther-in, and xij persones with here, the which persones thei dreve oute of the seid mansion and myned down the walle of the chambre where-in the wiff of your seid besechere was, and bare here oute at the yates and cutte a-sondre the postes of the howses and lete them falle, and broke up all the chambres and coferes with-in the seid mansion, and rifelyd and in maner of robery bare a-wey all the stuffe, aray, and mony that your seyd besechere and his servauntes had there, on-to the valew of cc li.[159]

No doubt the story lost nothing in the telling,[160] but the mansion at Gresham was badly enough damaged (if it is the one we think it is) never to have been repaired. Also men were hurt.[161]

In the following weeks Walter Barow esquire and his fellow Wiltshire-men, who had been drafted in for the job,[162] overawed the community at Gresham in the fashion the evil rancher's hired desperadoes dominate the town in a Western. Threats of broken limbs and dispossession were used to get men to complain in the courts against Paston supporters,[163] distraint was the penalty for the loyal tenant who had not paid his rent to the Moleyns' collectors,[164] and search was made for Paston activists in a manner we can vividly picture: 'And som of them yedyn in-to Bekkys and Purrys hwsys, bothen in the hallys and the bernys, and askyd qher thei were; and thei were answeryd that they were owth, and thei seydyn ayen

[157] *Ibid.*, p. 30.

[158] The date is given in PRO, KB9/262, a copy of which was kindly given to me by Mrs Marjory Rowling of Sevenoaks; KB9/262 is the report of the Earl of Oxford, a justice of the peace, in response to a royal directive of 1 March 1449 to enquire into this particular case of peace-breaking. Edmund Paston had ridden from Gresham to the Earl of Oxford, presumably after the assault on Margaret: Davis II, p. 331, lines 37–8.

[159] Davis I, pp. 51–3, cf. John's petition to the chancellor of 1450: Davis I, pp. 55–6.

[160] Certainly where the value of the contents of the house was concerned. Margaret, in reporting a later conversation with her removers, told John (Davis I, p. 230): 'Thei seyd I myt an had of hem at Gressam qhat I hadde desyryd of hem, and had as moche as I desyrd. I seyd nay, if I mytgh an had my desyre I xuld nother a departid owth of the place nere from the stuff that was ther-in. Thei seyd as for the stuff, it was but esy. I seyd ye wold not a goven the stuff that was in the place qhan thei com jn for a c li. Thei seyd the stuff that thei sey there was skars wurth xx li.' Was a multiplier of two or ten the norm for legal statements of damage?

[161] Davis I, p. 230, line 94.

[162] PRO, KB9/262.

[163] Davis I, p. 227.

[164] *Ibid.*, p. 228, lines 16–19.

that they xuld meten wyth hem another tym.'[165] The worst of these desperadoes were not at Gresham; they were (so to speak) back at the ranch. Or so Margaret thought. She warned John:

I here seyn that ye and jon of Damme ben sore thrett alway, and seyn thow ye ben at London ye xul ben met wyth there as wele as thow ye were here; and ther-for I pray you hertyly be ware hw ye walk there and have a gode felaschep wyth you qhan ye xul walk owtgh. The Lord Moleyns hathe a cumpany of brothell [good-for-nothings] wyth hym that rekk not qhat they don, and seche are most for to drede. Thei that ben at Gressam seyn that they have not don so moche hurt to you as thei were commawndyd to don.[166]

Such is often the way: the better guys are sent to do the dirtier work. Walter Barow was perhaps one of them, though Margaret, who had fled only so far as the house next door, that is John Damme's house at Sustead, could not make up her mind about this plausible fellow who arranged to meet her. Their encounter and exchange are a scene from the same Western:

And he seyd he xuld com forby this plase on huntyng after non, and ther xuld nomore com wyth hym but Hegon and on of his owyn men, and than he wold bryng seche an answere as xuld plese me. And after none they com hydder and sent in to me to weten if thei mytgh speken wyth me, and praing that thei mytgh speken wyth me; and they abedyn styl wyth-owtgh the yatys, and I kam owth to hem and spak wyth hem wyth-owt, and prayid hem that they wold hold me exkusyd that I browth hem not in to the plase. I seyd in as meche as thei were nott welewyllyng to the godeman of the plase I wold not take it up-on me to bryng hem in to the jantylwoman. They seyd I dede the best, and than we welk forthe and desyryd an answere of hem for that I hadde sent to hem fore. Thei sayd to me thei had browtgh me seche an answere as thei hopyd xuld plese me, and told me how thei had comownd wyth all her felaschep of seche materis as I had sent to hem fore, and that thei durst under-take that there xud no man ben hurt of hem thatt were rehersyd, nere noman that longyth to you nother, for hem nere non of here felaschep; and that they inswryd me be here trowthis. Nevere lese I trest not to here promese in as meche as I fend hem on-trew in other thyngs.[167]

Almost nothing is missing as the wronged woman confronts the smooth-talking horsemen at the gate of the friendly neighbour's home. Barow had much to say, most of it in these circumstances formulaic: he would rather not have done what he had had to do, he was sorry that he had done it. His apologetic tone, counterfeit or not, enabled Margaret to raise the wrongs done to him – why was one who had suffered as he had inflicting similar suffering on others? For he, too, had been wronged; once he had been an independent homesteader; dispossessed, now he was a hired man. Their shared sense of injury led them to discuss the real villain of the piece – the rotten ranch hand, the corrupt foreman, the no-good lawyer. In this

[165] *Ibid.*, p. 228. For these and other misdeeds of Lord Moleyns' men at Gresham at this time see also John's petition to parliament: *ibid.*, p. 52. [166] *Ibid.*, pp. 229–30.

[167] *Ibid.*, pp. 228–9.

instance it was the latter, and undoubtedly he was John Heydon. This was the conversation:[168]

Barow swor to me be his trowth that he had lever than xl s. and xl that his lord had not commawndyd hym to com to Gressam, and he seyd he was rytgh sory hidderward in as meche as he had knowleche of yw be-fore; he was rytgh sory of that that was don. I seyd to hym that he xuld have compascion on you and other that were dissesyd of her lyvelode, in as meche as he had ben dissesyd hym-selfe; and he seyd he was so, and told that he had sewyd to my lord of Suffolk dyvers tymys, and wold don tyl he may gete his gode ayen. I seyd to hym that ye had sewyd to my Lord Moleyns dyvers tymys for the maner of Gressam syth ye wer dissesyd, and ye cowd never gete no resonabyl answere of hym, and ther-fore ye entred ayen as ye hopid that was for the best. And he seyd he xuld never blame my lord of Suffolk for the entré in his lyvelode, for he seyd my seyd lord was sett ther-up-on be the informacion of a fals schrew. And I seyd to hym in lyke wyse is the mater be-twyx the Lord Moleyns and you: I told hym I wost wele he sett never ther-up-on be no tytyl of rytgh that he hadde to the maner of Gressam, but only be the informacion of a fals schrew. I rehersyd no name, but me thowt be hem that thei wost ho I ment.

At the end of the scene Barow delivered the lines movie buffs have been anticipating:[169] 'Barow sayd to me if he com to London qhil ye were there he woll drynk wyth yow, for any angyr that was be-twyx yow. He seyd he dede but as a servaunt, and as he was commawndyd to don.' As if a drink in the saloon would make all wrongs right. No, Barow was neither to be believed, nor to be trusted. Margaret (like any Western fan) knew him for what he was. She was frightened. She warned John[170] and fled the friendly neighbour's house.[171] No hero had ridden in to rescue her and save the townsfolk. Though John Paston had not lost his nerve, he certainly had not the resources for revenge. Resistance had collapsed. 'Here dare noman seyn a gode wurd for you in this cuntré, Godde amend it.'[172]

Margaret's precipitate flight from Sustead to Norwich was in February 1449. In March Lord Moleyns wrote to *his* tenants at Gresham. He thanked them for their support and reassured them that the rents they were paying to Partridge would not be paid in vain, but an iron fist is discernible at the end of his letter:

[168] *Ibid.*, p. 229. Heydon is named by John Paston in his petition to the chancellor of 1450: *ibid.*, p. 55; for his involvement, see also *ibid.*, pp. 233–4. [169] *Ibid.*, pp. 231–2.

[170] 'I pray you hertyly, at the reverens of God, be ware of the Lord Moleynys and his men, thow thei speke never so fayr to you trost hem not, ne ete not nere drynk wyth hem, for thei ben so fals it is not for to trost in hem': *ibid.*, p. 232.

[171] It was the threat of kidnapping which unwomaned her: *ibid.*, p. 231. Was it also uncertainty about her husband's care for her? 'It was done me to wete that dyverys of the Lord Moleynys men saydyn jf thei myt gete me they xuld stele me and kepe me wyth-jnne the kastell, and than they seyd thei wold that ye xuld feche me owth. An thei seydyn it xuld ben but a lytyll hert-brennyng to you. And after that I herd these tydyngs I kowd no rest have in myn hert tyl I was here, [Norwich] . . . I wol ben rytgh sory to dwel so nere Gressam as I dede tyl the mater were fully determynyd be-twix the Lord Moleynis and you.'

[172] Margaret to John: *ibid.*, p. 230, lines 117–18.

And as hertly as I can I thanke yowe of the gud wyl ye have had and have toward me; and as to the tytyll of rigth that I have to the lordship of Gressam schal with-in short tyme be knoweyn, and be the lawe so determynyd that ye schal all be glad that hath ought me youre gud wyll ther-in.[173]

As John's petition to parliament in 1449 got no favourable response, the year was a disaster. Oxnead threatened, East Beckham lost, and now Gresham gone. At last Margaret, having been told them, began to grasp the political realities. Had they not been staring her husband in the face for years? She wrote to him,[174]

And the seyd sexteyn and other folkys that ben yowre ryth willerys have kownselyd me that I xuld kownsell you to maken other menys than ye have made to other folkys that wold spede yowr materys better than they have don thatt ye have soken to ther-of be-for this tym. Sondery folkys have seyd to me that they thynk veryly but if ye have my lord of Suffolkys godelorchyp qhyll the werd is as itt is ye kan never leven jn pese wyth owth ye have his godelordschep. Therfor I pray you wyth all myn herth that ye wyll don yowre part to have hys godelordschep and his love jn ese of all the materis that ye have to don, and jn esyng of myn hert also.

John had been pinning his hopes on Thomas Daniel, a lazy patron[175] and perhaps by 1449 a broken reed.[176] Even if that were not the case, the advice was: go to the top. In 1449 the Duke of Suffolk was the top. If John did follow Margaret's promptings, his discovery of the political realities had been so delayed that it came at a date when they were on the point of changing: through 360 degrees.[177] 1449 was a very bad year for John Paston; but bad as it had been and bleak as his prospects were, it was no time to be clambering on the Duke of Suffolk's crowded bandwagon, for that was abruptly to cease rolling the following spring. The fall and murder of Suffolk

[173] Davis II, p. 521. Margaret reported the letter to John on 2 April: Davis I, pp. 233–4. It was, evidently, simple enough to obtain the letter itself, or, as it was a 'circular' signed by Lord Moleyns, one of them. [174] Davis I, p. 236.

[175] *Ibid.*: 'And I have spokyn wyth the sexteyn and seyd to hym as ye bad me that I xuld don, and he axid me ryt feythfully hw ye sped jn yowr materys. I told him that ye haddyn fayre be-hestys, and I seyd I hopyd that ye xuld don rytgh well ther-jn; and he seyd he supposyd that D. wold don for you, but he seyd he was no hasty laborere jn non mater. He seyd be hys feyth he wost qhere a man was that laboryd to hym for a mater ryth a long tym, and alwey he be-hestyd that he wold labore itt effectualy, but qhyll he sewyd to hym he kowd never have remedy of his mater; and than, qhan he thowh that he xuld no remedy have to sew to hym, he spak wyth Fynys that is now Speker of the Parlment, and prayid hym that he wold don for hym jn his mater, and yaf hym a reward, and wyth-jnne ryth schort tym after his mater was sped.'

[176] I have in mind Edmund Paston's conversation with 'Steward, the chiffe constable', two years previously: *ibid.*, pp. 147–8. Bruce McFarlane considered that it was 'Suffolk's "rule" . . . [which] was thought to be in jeopardy' (*England in the Fifteenth Century*, p. 250, note 59). From the context it is impossible to tell, though 1447 was a year when Daniel in East Anglia might have struck local observers as all-conquering, or so a rapid perusal of Wedgwood, *Biographies*, pp. 254–5 suggests.

[177] Like Sir John Paston's cultivation of the Woodvilles in June 1469, less than a month before they temporarily toppled.

in 1450 were in fact to usher in the third phase of the Gresham story: revival.

There was no immediate relief. As late as July 1450 Lord Moleyns was still on the attack: he had sued out writs against John Paston and others for trespass at Gresham.[178] So, however, was Paston: he petitioned the chancellor for a special assize and an assize of oyer et terminer to enquire into the attack on Margaret of 29 January 1449. The chancellor wrote to Lord Moleyns in August 'that he shuld comaunde his men beyng at Gresham to departe thens, and that the profitez therof shuld be receyved by an endifferent man sauftly to be kepte til the right were determyned be-twen yow [Paston] and my Lord M.'. Moleyns replied that it would not be right for a special assize to be granted: he was preoccupied with putting down rebels in Wiltshire and could not give up the king's business to come to Norfolk. Yet, even if Paston was granted a special assize that would not perturb him,

> for he knewe his title and his evydence so good for his part that he durst weel putte it in my lord Chaunceller and in what iuge he wolde calle to hym. And where my lord Chaunceller desired hym to avoyde his men from Gresham, he trustid that my lord wolde not desire that, by-cause he hadde his possession and that it was his wyffes right, and so hym thought it a-geynst reason that he shuyld avoide utterly his possession.[179]

This was simply prevarication and, as John Paston wrote when he heard of it, was to be shown as such to the chancellor. Because Moleyns had no title, no arbitration was needed, 'no offre and profre . . . as men bye hors'; besides there were the goods purloined – Moleyns had no claim to them: 'if he were disposed to do right . . . he shulde restore that, for therefor nedith nowthir comunycacion ne trete'. Nor would a general oyer et terminer do; a special assize was what John must have – the chancellor's fears that it would stir up an already turbulent county were false. 'Dyverse men of my freendis avyse me to entre in-to the maner of Gresham by force of my writte of restitucion', wrote John, but he would not do that because the estate had become so run down it was worth less than half it had been. No, he concluded, 'for whiche hurt and for othir hurtis by this special assise I trust to have remedye'.[180] As the autumn of 1450 opened John had rediscovered his vigorous sense of purpose. It was not to be deflated by the intervention of the king himself, or perhaps by those who were managing Henry VI in this time of crisis. On 18 September Henry wrote under his signet to John Paston asking him to desist from legal action against Lord Moleyns and his 'servauntes, welwillers, or tenauntes' for the time being, because Moleyns could not attend the session of the justices of oyer et terminer in East Anglia while he was about the royal

[178] Davis II, p. 39. [179] *Ibid.*, p. 41.
[180] Davis I, pp. 56–8: John to James Gresham, 4 September 1450.

business elsewhere.[181] Did this somewhat plaintive missive turn out to be an ultimate deterrent?

Richard, Duke of York's return from Ireland and his subsequent journey into East Anglia in October (before Parliament met on 6 November), while putting heart into the 'anti-Suffolk movement', did not cancel out the king's request. There was exhilaration and bustle in Norfolk that autumn as indictments of the Duke of Suffolk's anti-social followers were being prepared for the visit of the commissioners of oyer et terminer in December.[182] Yet, in the end, less came of it all than had been hoped: Thomas Tuddenham and John Heydon escaped the deserts Sir John Fastolf and his friends regarded as just. By Easter 1451 it was becoming clear that in the battle of county against court the county's victory was to be limited. So was it also in the subsidiary engagement of Paston against Moleyns. A note was made of their dispute, under the inappropriate heading of 'Maters sterid to hurt of bothe parties', on the dorse of a memorandum of cases to be put before the commissioners, a memorandum John Paston helped to draft.[183] Also, Lord Moleyns was reported as 'right wroth' when he was told that he and his men were indicted for felony, and as having 'hadde langage of yow [John Paston] in the Kynges presence' on his return from Wiltshire to London early in November,[184] but that indictment[185] merely bagged his men, who were imprisoned at Norwich.[186] He, it seems, was not caught. Thus, the royal letter of 18 September was, at least partially, effective. None the less, though Lord Moleyns might be above the law, he was not able, or allowed, to keep what he had taken illegally: John Paston re-entered Gresham unopposed. He had done so by March 1451, and did so probably early in the New Year. The last phase of the story has been reached: recovery.

The title we have given it shows that it was a successful last phase for the Pastons. Apart from recovering possession of Gresham, however, the

[181] Davis II, p. 45: 'ye wol respite as for any thing attempting ayeinst hym as for any matiers that ye haue to do or seye ayeinst hym or any othre of his servauntes, welwillers, or tenauntes by-cause of hym, unto tyme he shal mowe be present to ansuere there-unto.'

[182] For this exciting period, see R.L. Storey, *The End of the House of Lancaster* (London, 1966), pp. 56–7; R.A. Griffiths, *The Reign of Henry VI* (London, 1981), pp. 588–91. Particularly valuable is Dr Anthony Smith's 'Aspects of the Career of Sir John Fastolf, 1380–1459', unpublished Oxford D.Phil. thesis, 1982, p. 142ff. For 'the county community against . . . exploitation by courtiers who masqueraded as agents of dynamic central government' in the later sixteenth century see chapter 12 of A. Hassell Smith, *County and Court: Government and Politics in Norfolk, 1558–1603* (London, 1974). The quotation is from p. 276; the later chapters of this important book aid a reading of the 'crisis' in East Anglia of 1450–1.

[183] Davis II, pp. 525–8.

[184] *Ibid.*, pp. 52, 56.

[185] Viz. PRO, KB9/262.

[186] Davis II, pp. 49, 53.

principal issue (of title) was not resolved, nor was the secondary one of the damage committed by Moleyns' men in January 1449. It was an inconsequential phase, and as such lasted until Lord Moleyns, fighting in France in 1452 or 1453, was captured and imprisoned. He returned to England only in 1459; then other, larger, political issues engaged his attention: he fought for the Lancastrian government and was eventually taken and beheaded in 1464.[187] In other words, what 'resolved' the Gresham crisis was Lord Moleyns' involvement in foreign and domestic war after 1452 and his misfortunes in both. Just as England's political crisis of 1450 remained a crisis for another decade until resolved by the extreme but only course – that is, the removal of the cause of the crisis, the king – so the end of the Gresham affair came only with the removal of the cause of it, Lord Moleyns and (it needs to be recorded) the regime which permitted him to commit the outrage his seizure of Gresham was.

All this was in the distant future in March 1451. Gresham had been recovered; its recovery was precarious: Lord Moleyns was expected to re-enter.[188] He did not. Simon Gunnor and Moleyns' other Norfolk supporters were wrong; the world did not 'turne sumwhat after there entent'.[189] Nor did it behave as John Paston wished it to. Although in May at Walsingham the justices of oyer et terminer were ready to hear the case against Lord Moleyns and his men for the damage done by them at Gresham in and after January 1449,[190] royal intervention,[191] pressure on and bribery of the sheriff,[192] probably the hostility of Thomas, Lord Scales, one of the

[187] After 1464 the Hungerfords were never in a political position to mount another attack on Gresham. [188] Davis I, pp. 239, 240; II, pp. 64, 68.

[189] Davis I, p. 240.

[190] Some of his men had been in prison in Norwich (as we have noted) since the previous autumn: Davis II, p. 53.

[191] This time the government requested not delay but acquittal (*ibid.*, pp. 71, 73). The sheriff observed the proprieties: 'he seyde that he sent yow [Paston] the letter that the Kyng sent hym'; while Paston was predictably dismissive: 'and ye seyde a man shuld gete seche on for a noble.' The scandal surely lay in the nature of the government which issued such a directive not in the directive itself. No one would have minded a letter like that from, say, Henry V, but then Henry V would not have written one in such circumstances: an unruly lord breaking *his* peace.

[192] This is a justly renowned passage: *ibid.*, pp. 72–4; Margaret Hastings, *The Court of Common Pleas in the Fifteenth Century* (London, 1947; reprinted 1971), pp. 226–7. John Jermy or Jermyn was the lightweight sheriff: *Hopton*, p. 249, note 353. The letter Jermyn said he had received from the Duke of Norfolk 'for to shew favour in these indytementes [to Lord Moleyns]', John Osbern did not believe in: 'I suppose he had no wrytyng fro my lord of Norffolk as he seyde': Davis II, p. 73 line 21, p. 74 line 58. There is also doubt about the bribery: did he get Lord Moleyns' 20 nobles (p. 74 lines 45–7)? None the less, he was bribable, by Paston, for example, on anything, 'excepte for the aquitell of the Lord Molyns men': pp. 73–4, lines 16–17 and lines 41–57.

justices,[193] prevented justice being done: Moleyns and his men got off.[194] It was said that he was willing to go to arbitration for the goods seized in January 1449.[195] Nothing came of this. John Paston may have been no more responsive to the idea of compromise in June 1451 than he had been in September 1450,[196] for, although William Lomnor advised him to respond, because otherwise 'his [Moleyns'] men shulle justifie, wheropon your title myght be hurte',[197] it was surely the wisest course not to budge from his absolute right; having given an inch he might have found himself giving an ell. Not that he was not tempted, once while he was lacing his boots.[198] The matter did not drop: in April 1452 John Clopton of Long Melford wrote to John Paston:[199] 'Sir, the Kyng hath sent unto me by Howard to be frendly to the Lord Moleyns. Not-with-stondyng myn service shall be redy at your comawndement in that matere er any othir, by the grace of God, who preserve you body and sowle.' Lord Moleyns, however, made no attempt to dispossess John before he departed for Gascony in 1452; after his capture there he was unable to. Gresham was saved, just as Titchwell was, by 'the fortunes of the wars'.[200] Hence, the news of English defeat at Castillon and of Sir Edward Hull's death and Robert, Lord Moleyns' capture at the battle is likely to have been received by Sir John Fastolf and John Paston with a mixture of regret and relief.

The Gresham story has a happy ending – of sorts. The mansion there had

[193] Though William Lomnor writes in neutral fashion of Lord Scales (Davis II, p. 72, lines 5–7), William Wayte's letters of January 1451 show that Thomas had become an Establishment Man, for which he was murdered by *le peuple* in 1460: Davis II, pp. 60–8. Appropriately, his household comprised some 'strong thefes'; they were probably old soldiers too: Davis II, p. 69. John Paston had known Scales would be partial: 'And as for commyssioners in myn &c., . . . I can thynke them indifferent j-now in the matier except my Lord Scales, whos wyff is aunte to the Ladye Moleyns' (Davis I, p. 57); he was right: she was a Whalesborough (*CP*, XI, p. 507). It is interesting that John thought such kinship might matter.

[194] Davis II, p. 75; cf. p. 72, lines 11–12. Or better: got away with it, for perhaps it did not come to a trial and a test of William Lomnor's confidence – 'and ther is no jentelman wolde aquite his men for no goode, &c.'

[195] *Ibid.*, pp. 71, 72, 74–5.

[196] Davis I, p. 57.

[197] Davis II, p. 72.

[198] 'Please it your maistership to wete that, as touchyng Blake of the Kyngges hous, I spak with hym and he told me that if the Lord Moleyns wold take suyche appoyntement as ye agreed to, that he shuld lete me wete theof on Satirday after noon, as I tolde yow whanne ye dyd on your botes, &c. And sith that tyme I her no word of hym: James Gresham to John (*ibid.*, pp. 74–5).

[199] *Ibid.*, pp. 79–80. Howard's involvement came through his wife Catherine, daughter of Sir William Moleyns (d. 1425), and another aunt of Eleanor Moleyns. It is ironic that her funeral expenses are among the Paston papers: Gairdner IV, pp. 211–13. How far Paston animosities toward Heydon and Howard began in the late 1440s because of their stance in the Gresham affair – a searing experience, I would suggest, whereas East Beckham was no more than was to be expected – is worth pondering. Certainly, Gresham helped turn John Paston into a 'Yorkist'.

[200] For Titchwell, see the classic paper of P.S. Lewis, 'Sir John Fastolf's Lawsuit over Titchwell 1448–55', collected in his *Essays in Later Medieval French History* (London, 1985), pp. 215–34, esp. pp. 232–4.

been rifled; there was no compensation for that. Nor was there for the loss of the mansion itself. While it may have been old-fashioned, its damage beyond repair meant the family had one asset the less. Still, outweighing all this was that a valuable property worth 50 marks a year had been hung on to. Just. In Sir John Paston's 'sqare trussyng coffre' in the 1470s, alongside the 'bagge wyth evydence off Est Bekkham' reposed 'A bondell off Gresham, Moleyns'.[201] Reposed is the right word. The bundle did not have to be disturbed until its contents were used to relate the story of Gresham's acquisition and defence; they were not again required for that defence itself. Some of the documents in the bundle will have been used in this chapter, which is a suitable reflection on which to end it.

[201] Davis I, p. 444.

Chapter 3

EAST BECKHAM

To understand the Paston purchase of East Beckham it is necessary to go back fifty years, from the 1430s to the 1370s. A family's grip upon property it regarded as its own was tenacious; that is a familiar theme in this study of the Pastons. The tenacity in this instance is that of their neighbours in North Erpingham Hundred, the Winters of Town Barningham. It was William Winter who purchased East Beckham in 1379; and with him the story begins.

His origins were obscure, not as shamefully base as the Pastons' probable descent from a bondwoman, but, if Judge William Paston's hostile jottings are to be believed, William Winter's father was no more than a 20-acre man. Clement, William Paston's father, according to the account of one of *their* opponents,[1] was 'a good pleyn husbond' with 100 or 120 acres. Whatever the social consequences of the difference between 20 and 120 acres, that the fathers of these two successful lawyers were Norfolk farmers[2] gives their family histories and the story of their competition for East Beckham a poignancy they would certainly not otherwise have: distance reduces difference.

William Paston's jottings are on one side of a sheet of paper whose other side lists in shorthand form the transactions which carried East Beckham from Sir Roger Beckham to the Winters and from that family to William Mariot of Cromer between 1379 and 1425.[3] His abbreviated Latin notes follow even more abbreviated English extracts from what is said to be William Winter's last will of 1397 (complicated and controversial), and are surrounded by yet other scribblings concerning the holding of courts and

[1] Davis I, p. xli.

[2] The constant replenishment of the Norfolk gentry from the Norfolk yeomanry in the sixteenth and seventeenth centuries has been closely examined by M.J. Sayer, 'Norfolk Visitation Families: a Short Social Structure', *Norfolk Archaeology*, 36 (1975), esp. pp. 176–8: 'The predominant feature was the great rise from the yeomanry in each generation replenishing extinctions and removals.' The overall number of gentry families remained stable between *c.* 1300 and *c.* 1600 at around 400–50: the same writer in *English Nobility: the Gentry, the Heralds and the Continental Context* (Norwich: 1979), p. 12.

[3] For Judge William's habits as regards 'scribbling paper' see Davis I, nos. 2, 6, and headnotes.

the freight charges of shipping cloth, soap, figs, and raisins from London to Cromer. This much-folded (and seemingly much-consulted) sheet carries the name East Beckham in three different places, possibly in three different hands; to look at it and then to decipher it is to be made more aware of a concern for an estate which seems, though this may only be the impression of a commentator from a different culture, obsessional. Obsession or simply preoccupation, 'EB' – 'EB notat manerium de Est Bekham' as some contemporary consultant has written sideways and helpfully in the margin of this bewildering sheet – 'EB' in the 1430s and 1440s was as critical to the Pastons as Caister was to be for them in the 1460s and 1470s. Such is the measure of its importance: to them and therefore to us.

This cluttered East Beckham sheet comes from what was clearly the complementary bundle to the roll of letters concerning East Beckham now in the British Library and described by Norman Davis.[4] East Beckham generated a great deal of paper: it appears that some time after Judge William's death in 1444 (perhaps even forty years after)[5] the relevant papers were divided into two groups: copies of correspondence on the one hand, and on the other copies of legal or official documents.[6] The division was not consistent. The British Library 'Letter File' contains the copy of a lease of East Beckham of 1442;[7] the 'Business File' though it contains no letters,[8] does include a lengthy and properly written-up narrative (as viewed from the Paston angle) of the knotty legal, financial, and what we are justified in terming the political history of East Beckham from 1415 to 1445,[9] which might have usefully gone into the other file, or into both files for that matter. Indeed, from the puzzled and exasperated user's standpoint over 500 years later, one file put together chronologically would have been better altogether. One way in which it would have been straightforwardly better, is that there would not have been two files to get separated, for the 'Business File' is in the Norfolk Record Office. Yet both files had been in W. Ketton-Cremer's collection at Felbrigg Hall; he gave the 'Letter File' to the British Library; the 'Business File' lay unnoticed.[10] When asked by Professor

[4] *Ibid.*, p. 18. [5] *Ibid.*

[6] Or indeed three groups, for some of the original East Beckham deeds, now in the British Library, are numbered in what I take to be a fifteenth-century hand (Stowe Charter 177, numbered 39; Add. Ch. 14523, numbered 29; Add. Ch. 14525 numbered 15), while another is in a different hand (Add. Ch. 19325, numbered 11). I may not have recorded the numbers on others, for example those from the Phillipps Collection.

[7] Davis I, pp. 18–19.

[8] Save one: the copy of a letter from Cardinal Beaufort to William, Lord Bardolf, on the back of which has been drafted Judge William's petition for the custody of East Beckham: WKC 1/43/21. The recto of this important document has been encountered in chapter 1.

[9] WKC 1/43/4.

[10] HMC, *Twelfth Report*, appendix ix (1891), pp. 179–182 describes only the letters.

Norman Davis if he still had any Paston material, he replied negatively – a small tragedy repeating exactly that of the greater one of James Gairdner, George Frere, and the original Paston letters of John Fenn's third and fourth printed volumes.[11] The 'Business File' came to the Norfolk Record Office only on W. Ketton-Cremer's death.

The bundle at Norwich contains twenty-one items. Other, supplementary but crucial East Beckham material is to be found in adjacent Ketton-Cremer files,[12] in the British Library, the Bodleian Library, the Public Record Office, and the Phillipps Collection (now in the Norfolk Record Office). Nevertheless, the East Beckham story begins with the aide-memoire (or 'scribbling paper') of Judge William Paston's at Norwich: WKC 1/43/8. It is certainly the most difficult to decipher of any of these documents, probably it was the most ephemeral of them, undoubtedly it is the most absorbing, possibly it is the most important. But, can we believe it?

William notes that the father of William Winter lived at Little Barningham and had a messuage and 20 acres there: that was all he had, there or anywhere. Moreover, his name was John Haylstone;[13] it was William who changed to Winter.[14] William Winter's first step up in the world, according to these notes, was the filching of an inheritance from a butcher, the rightful son and heir of a relative of William's called Ode; significantly (unless Judge William was concocting a person out of a place), in Saxthorpe, next door to Little Barningham, the Winters held a tenement called Ode's: William's son, Edmund, sold it to Sir John Fastolf in 1429.[15]

The next step, the one which, so Judge William seems to be implying, was the making of William Winter, was his being the executor of the Countess of Suffolk ('Comitisse Suff'). Did Judge William mean to write the Countess of Stafford ('Comitisse Staff')? He goes on to state that by this means William Winter 'got his hands' on the Stafford manor of Barningham – the alternative name for Little Barningham. William has written 'Stafford Bernyngham' over a cancelled 'Sheryngham'; both were Stafford estates, but the former had been acquired by Ralph, first Earl Stafford, by his marriage to Margaret Audley, a Clare heiress, in 1334, whereas the latter

[11] Davis I, p. xxviii; Gairdner I, pp. 8–9. [12] NRO, WKC, 1/44, 1/45.

[13] Can we believe Judge William when he writes that William Winter changed his name because he considered the old word for Winter was Hailstone (Haylstone)?

[14] This name changing is of interest, bearing in mind that it was said of Geoffrey (of) Somerton, Judge William's influential and helpful uncle, attorney, member of parliament, and apparently bondman, that his 'trew surnome ys Goneld': Davis I, p. xlii. The two men, sometime William Haylstone and Geoffrey Goneld, were on a commission together in the autumn of 1390: *CIPM 7–15 Richard II*, p. 351.

[15] HMC, *Marquess of Lothian at Blickling Hall* (1905), p. 54. This collection is now at NRO. The sale of 13 May (not 12 May as in HMC, *Blickling Hall*, p. 54) 1429 is NRO, NRS 13768; letters of attorney of 14 May are NRO, NRS 17794.

only came to the family between 1390 and 1403 as part of the Basset inheritance.[16] It was an understandable mistake – a slip readily made; it was soon rectified, yet as he was inserting 'Stafford Bernyngham', he did not go half a dozen words back to alter 'Suff' to 'Staff'; perhaps he had not noticed he had made that error. Error it looks to be. Might William also have confused the earl with his wife? Margaret Audley died in 1347, the earl in 1372. Although the earlier date would suit a William Winter at the outset of a career,[17] the later one seems more suitable, if only because Judge William goes on to state that Winter's executorship was also how Roger Taylor got to be farmer of Stafford Barningham, and a Roger Taylor is indeed to be found at Barningham Northwood in 1373.[18] Moreover, Roger Taylor of Little Barningham, nephew of William Winter of Town Barningham, quitclaimed Town Barningham and other property to the new feoffees of John Winter, William's son, in 1412.[19] There may have been more than one Roger Taylor, but Judge William writes as if those using his jottings will know *this* Roger Taylor.[20] Roger was named as an executor in his uncle's testament of 1397[21] and was a feoffee of his cousin, John Winter, in 1408–9.[22]

William Winter was also an executor of a lady grander even than Margaret, Countess of Stafford – Mary de St Pol, widow of Aymer de Valence, Earl of Pembroke; he died in 1324, she in 1377.[23] One of the manors Mary de St Pol had held in dower was at Saxthorpe, where, as we have seen, was Ode's tenement, that estate William Winter, according to Judge William, had cheated Ode's son, the butcher, out of.[24] In 1410 John

[16] C. Rawcliffe, *The Staffords, Earls of Stafford and Dukes of Buckingham 1394–1521* (London, 1978), pp. 8–10, 12, 191–2; Blomefield III, pp. 580–1. The Earl of Stafford was in possession of Little Barningham in 1401–2: *Feudal Aids* III, p. 617. Perhaps for Little or Stafford Barningham in WKC 1/43/8 we ought to read Barningham Northwood, where in 1401–2 John Winter, William's son, held two properties: *Feudal Aids* III, p. 615.

[17] He was reported as being over sixty in 1383: *CPR 1381–5*, p. 327. A man, even a rising young man, is not, in his twenties, an influential executor of a countess.

[18] Blomefield IV, p. 295. Now called simply Barningham North.

[19] *CCR 1409–13*, pp. 225–6.

[20] As John Paston would have done, for Roger Taylor of Stafford Barningham had been a feoffee of John's wife's father, John Mautby, and grandfather, Robert Mautby: Davis I, p. 16. For Roger Taylor of Little Barningham see also, *Cal. Anc. Deeds* V, no. 11058.

[21] NRO, NCC Reg. Harsyk, f. 241. [22] *CCR 1405–9*, p. 522; *CCR 1409–13*, p. 226.

[23] See her will, printed in Hilary Jenkinson, 'Mary de Sancto Paulo, foundress of Pembroke College, Cambridge', *Archaeologia*, 66 (1914–15), p. 434; and see also *CIPM 48–51 Edward III*, p. 331.

[24] Edmund Winter sold Ode's tenement to Sir John Fastolf in 1429: (HMC, *Blickling Hall*, p. 54; viz. NRO, NRS 13768 and 17794). Included in this sale was other property in Saxthorpe and its neighbourhood, which Edmund had bought in 1422 from Thomas Barker of Barningham, son and heir of John Barker of Saxthorpe: NRO, NRS 13769 is Thomas Barker's grant of April 1422 and NRO, NRS 19740 is Robert Taylor of Little Barningham's quitclaim of his Barker property to Edmund Winter of May 1422. (This, presumably, is John Paston I's ex-Fastolf 'yard . . . yn Saxthorp callid Barkerz' of Davis II, p. 275.)

Winter, William's son, acquired a life interest in the manor of Loundhall in Saxthorpe.[25] There were two manors in Saxthorpe; Mickelhall was the

[25] HMC, *Blickling Hall*, p. 53. I am very grateful to Dr Anthony Smith for his help with the Winter manor of Loundhall, a manor Sir John Fastolf bought from Sir William Oldhall in 1428 for £446 13s 4d (HMC, *Blickling Hall*, p. 54; viz. NRO, NRS 13767. Its annual value was stated in 1445 to be £23 11s 2d: Magdalen College, Oxford, Fastolf Paper 69, valor of 1444–5). Loundhall had been sold to Oldhall in 1426 (NRO, NRS 19722; cf. HMC, *Blickling Hall*, pp. 53–4) by the feoffees of John Gurney (d. 1408) in order to pay his debts and those of his widow Alice *and* to perform his will, especially with regard to his wish for the setting up of a chantry of three chaplains (Magd. Coll., Misc. Charters 26, 182, transcriptions and photocopies of which Dr Smith was good enough to make for me). John Drew, parson of Harpley, Norfolk, was prominent among these feoffees; he will be found below (p. 82) selling East Beckham in similar circumstances. Both sets of circumstances involved John Winter. Let us explain the Loundhall set here.

John Gurney esquire of Harpley and West Barsham was in a Norfolk Lancastrian group, whose pivotal figure was Sir Thomas Erpingham and two of whose other 'members' were Sir Robert Berney and John Winter. The relevant question here is: why were John Winter and his wife Eleanor granted a life interest in Loundhall by John Gurney's feoffees in Whit week 1410 (HMC, *Blickling Hall*, p. 53; viz. NRO, NRS 13778, 19736, 19737)? This was about eighteen months after John Gurney's death. The writ of *dce* to the escheator of Norfolk is dated 16 February 1409 (*CFR 1405–13*, p. 123. A note added to NRO, NRS 19732 states 'Johannes Gurney obiit anno ix H.quarti et Johannes Drew super(vix)it'). Alice, John's widow, enfeoffed John Drew *and* John Winter in Loundhall as early as 22 January 1409 (NRO, NRS 19734, omitted from HMC, *Blickling Hall*, p. 53). John Drew and Thomas Tasburgh, John Gurney's surviving feoffees (of whom John Winter himself was another; see below), put a new group of feoffees in possession on 27 April 1409 (NRO, NRS 17789; HMC, *Blickling Hall*, p. 53 wrongly refers to Roger Drew); Alice quitclaimed her right to these on 10 June 1409 (NRO, NRS 13766; cf. HMC, *Blickling Hall*, p. 53). John Winter, Alice, and John Drew had already made an arrangement for the 'sale' of Loundhall on 23 January 1409 – the day after Alice had enfeoffed the other two – in order to pay the debts of John Gurney; these amounted to £866, double what Sir John Fastolf was later to pay for the manor (Magd. Coll., Misc. Chs. 26. What is noted in HMC, *Blickling Hall*, p. 53 (under 1412), is probably the other part of this indenture, but I could not find it among the Saxthorpe deeds of that collection at NRO). How did Sir John Fastolf get, or why did he keep Misc. Chs. 26 *and* 182, for the second document also concerns John Gurney's debts? Misc. 182 is also part of an indenture. It states that the debts of John Gurney which John Drew had paid had been summed in an account made at Norwich in February 1410, when to repay him Alice assigned him certain manors for seven years. These cannot have included Loundhall, for it had finally been made over to John Winter and Eleanor for their lives in Whit week 1410.

We return to our question: why? Did John Winter, who had been a feoffee of John Gurney's in May 1390, when Gurney had acquired Loundhall by exchange with William Dautre (HMC, *Blickling Hall*, p. 52; viz. NRO, NRS 13754), undertake to the feoffees to provide from the manor the necessary revenues for his friend's chantry? He had undertaken to his own father's feoffees to do exactly that – to maintain three priests for a year at Town Barningham out of the revenues of East Beckham to pray for his father's soul – in the previous year, 1409. This was not coincidental: both transactions, almost, if not quite identical, were going forward at the same time; the same men were involved in both: John Winter himself, John Drew, Sir Robert Berney, Sir Roger Drury, Edmund Oldhall, and the clerics Robert Winter and William Howlyn. Such identity (of idea and personnel) makes one wonder – about one's own capacity to differentiate, for example. If the idea was John Winter's, it seems to have been a bad one: he cannot have fulfilled either undertaking before his death in 1414, for East Beckham was sold by William Winter's feoffees in 1415, Loundhall by John Drew and his fellow feoffees in 1426, that is after Eleanor's death. The manor had been quitclaimed to her by one group of feoffees on 27 March 1415 (NRO, NRS

other: it was the manor Mary de St Pol had held.[26] Might she have helped William make his first mark at Saxthorpe? Might Judge William have been thinking of William Winter as *her* executor? Perhaps he should have

19739) and she had enfeoffed John Drew and another group, who made the sale in 1426, on 22 July 1415 (NRO, NRS 19722). Thus the Loundhall circumstances appear to be the following: John Drew and Alice Gurney, having made an arrangement for its 'sale' to John Winter in January 1409, released the manor in April 1409 to a group of feoffees; these put John Winter and his wife, Eleanor, in possession for their lives in Whit week 1410. After John Winter's death in 1414, John Drew (and others) were enfeoffed by Eleanor in 1415; she continued to hold the manor until her death in 1426, while continuing to accumulate debts to John Drew (Magd. Coll. Misc. Ch. 182 records these in detail). After her death, John Drew sold Loundhall.

That there was such an overlap of personnel among feoffees and executors is no surprise, bearing in mind the closeness of the Lancastrian group John Winter and John Gurney were part of. The knights Simon Felbrigg, Thomas Erpingham, and Robert Berney were the big names; but John Drew, parson of Harpley, who went on to make the two final sales in 1415 and 1426, looks like the prime mover in these two earlier and remarkably similar matters of business of 1409–10, which attempted to combine the welfare of souls with the maintenance of the landed interest of the Winters. According to Blomefield (IV, p. 560), John Drew was also rector of Northwold, Norfolk, and Therfield, Hertfordshire. Judge William Paston was connected with the latter place and church through his wife Agnes Barry. Does this make the coincidence (between the two matters of business) more or less perplexing?

John Drew's will of 1426 (NRO, NRS Reg. Hyrnyng, fs. 150–1 is a slightly better copy than the identical Reg. Surfleet, fs. 6–7) reveals no sinister connections. It does, however, reveal an interesting and perhaps unlooked-for association: among the souls of the benefactors for whose benefit the residue of his goods was to be disposed of were 'specialiter' those of 'domini mei domini Roberti Knolles militis ac domine Constancie consortis sue'. John had been a principal feoffee of Sir Robert's (Blomefield III, p. 848; Edward Hasted, *The History and Topographical Survey of the County of Kent* (Canterbury, 1782), II, pp. 574–5). This great and hugely successful soldier of obscure Cheshire origin, who died in 1407, had settled down at Sculthorpe in Norfolk (Blomefield III, p. 847; Michael J. Bennett, *Community, Class and Careerism: Cheshire and Lancashire Society in the Age of Sir Gawain and the Green Knight* (Cambridge, 1983), pp. 182, 188 and *sub* index). At Sculthorpe church John Drew requested a sung mass of the Virgin 'antequam corpus meum discesserit' – Blomefield (III, p. 848 cf IV, p. 560) asserts that Knolles built 'for the most part' Sculthorpe and Harpley churches. It was in Harpley church, where (according to Blomefield III, p. 847; cf. IV, p. 560) Knolles' arms were on the screen, that John desired his body to be buried, 'inter duas columpnas proprias pulpito'. Was it a pulpit from which he had preached (but not, one can be sure, anti-war sermons) to his patron? St Laurence's church, Harpley, was (according to Pevsner, *North West and South Norfolk*, pp. 187–8) 'mainly built when John de Gurney was patron and rector (1294–1332)'; however, 'the Perp additions are considerable'; these included the benches ('with charming pierced, quatrefoiled backs', says Pevsner). One would like to connect them with John Drew – for his listeners to sit on. That is possibly a conceit: John does not leave anything to the church in his will save some of the torches and candles which were to burn about his body at his funeral. (He might well, of course, have given the benches during his lifetime.) On the day of his funeral there was to be no bell-ringing, 'nisi cum magna campana', but his executors were to arrange a feast ('faciant unum pascum') for clergy and laity alike. He calls the two supervisors of his will, 'meum carissimum amicum'. Altogether it is an engaging document, no doubt of an engaging man. Drawn up on 9 December 1426, it was proved on 15 January 1427. As John was also a feoffee of another soldier, Sir Henry Inglose (*Cal. Anc. Deeds* V, no. 10450), he probably knew yet another, Sir John Fastolf. For Fastolf and Inglose, see chapter 7.

[26] Blomefield III, p. 703. She bought the advowson of Saxthorpe and settled it on Pembroke College: Blomefield III, p. 704.

cancelled Stafford Barningham as well as Sheryngham and at the third attempt substituted Saxthorpe. Certainly William Winter made himself useful to the great. He was also a feoffee of Bishop Henry Despencer, an executor of Philippa, Countess of March, and of Robert Ufford, an association with the family of the Earls of Suffolk which Judge William may have had on his mind when composing his memorandum.[27] The great, as Judge William indicated, were as useful to William Winter as he was to them. The greatest of them, Mary de St Pol, Winter remembered when making his testament in 1397: to her foundation of Poor Clares at Denny in Cambridgeshire he bequeathed the French books he had had from her.[28]

This useful man of business had been successful. If Judge William is to be believed, he had manoeuvred his way out of obscurity. He must, none the less, have been more than simply skilled at sharp practice: that might have got him to be sheriff of Norfolk and Suffolk in 1380 and 1393; it cannot alone have been what appealed to such a grand old lady as Mary de St Pol. But of William Winter's appealing qualities (unlike his winning ways) we are ignorant. Only the external superficialities survive. Like other self-made men, like Judge William Paston, for instance, William Winter bought land, acquired a big house and made it bigger, married into East Anglian 'society', and found for his eldest son a local heiress.

First, the land. He purchased the Norfolk manors of Wighton and Egmere,[29] and (as he disposed of it in his last will) Bodham. There was also, of course, East Beckham. Town Barningham is the mystery, if Judge William is correct in implying that William Winter's father, John, had no more than 20 acres in Little Barningham. The manor of Town Barningham was certainly William's; he left it to his eldest son, and though he lived (and wrote his testament) at Egmere, it was in the chancel of Town Barningham church that he wished to be buried.[30] Unmistakably, it was his chief estate. Was it his patrimony? Did Judge William exaggerate the lowliness of his beginnings? He was invariably called of Town Barningham; but that is what he could have made himself, lord of that place, creating there, as Judge William did at Paston, a manor, which, with its court's lordship over men, denoted an *arriviste*'s entry into gentility.

Secondly, the house: this was at Egmere near Walsingham. Just as at Paston fifty years later, the extensions to the manor house at Egmere

[27] *CCR 1374–7*, pp. 354–6; *Testamenta Vetusta*, p. 101; *CCR 1381–5*, p. 90.

[28] NRO, NCC Reg. Harsyk, fs. 240–1. Denny in the later fourteenth century, with more than forty nuns, had in Norman Scarfe's words 'high religious tone': *The Shell Guide to Cambridgeshire* (London, 1983), p. 195. For William Winter's connection with Denny see p. 82, note 73 below.

[29] Blomefield IV, p. 298.

[30] NRO, NCC Reg. Harsyk, fs. 240–341. He presented the rector to the church there in 1370: Blomefield IV, p. 300. He also bequeathed to the church 'duo magna porttsoria [?] mea'.

necessitated the rerouting of a public road at the redeveloper's expense: privacy like status, had to be paid for.[31]

Thirdly, the marriage: William Winter's first wife, so Judge William notes,[32] was Matilda, the sister of Sir Robert Berney. There is no reason to doubt Judge William: William had been an executor of Matilda's father, John Berney, in 1374;[33] William named Sir Robert Berney as supervisor of his testament in 1397;[34] and Sir Robert was a feoffee of William's son and heir, John.[35] In fact, there was both before and after the Lancastrian usurpation of 1399 a close association between Sir Robert Berney, the Winters, and Sir Thomas Erpingham (another supervisor of William Winter's testament), and of that usurpation they and their friends were beneficiaries. Erpingham, that staunch, lifelong supporter of Lancaster, was the key to both Sir Robert Berney and John Winter's success and the careers of all three in and around 1399 are inextricably tied up with each other.[36] They were also close neighbours in north-east Norfolk, for Sir Robert Berney's house at Gunton was next door to Erpingham, which itself was only a few miles south-east of Town Barningham. The hinterland of Cromer, as we might describe it, or more accurately the hundred of North Erpingham, as they would have considered this, their part of the world, was where Judge William Paston a few years afterwards wanted also to make his local mark, as for that matter a little later did John Heydon at Baconsthorpe and John Wyndham at Felbrigg. Plumb in the centre of this small region and that hundred lay two of Judge William's purchases, challengeable purchases at that, Gresham and East Beckham. That there was tension between these self-assertive, self-made men of the law jostling to buy into local society is hardly surprising; it is the narrowness, the closeness of the little world which they sought to dominate, which is: more or less a single hundred. By the time these tensions had arisen towards the middle of the century, Erpingham had departed, the Berneys had declined, and Edmund Winter was fighting (with diminished resources) what turned out to be a last-ditch, losing battle for East Beckham. None the less, when we come to explore the battlefield of North Erpingham Hundred in mid-century two things should be borne in mind. One, that fifty years before it had been otherwise – social harmony, or the nearest that gentlemen could get to that

[31] The inquisition *ad quod dampnum* was held by the eschcator at Walsingham on 19 June 1936: PRO C143/426/1. For Paston see Gairdner I, pp. 36–7.

[32] We have returned here to the dorse of NRO, WKC 1/43/8.

[33] I must acknowledge at this point the value of Trevor John's unpublished Nottingham MA thesis of 1959, 'The Parliamentary Representation of Norfolk and Suffolk 1377–1422'; in this instance p. 169.

[34] NRO, NCC Reg. Harsyk, f. 241.

[35] For example, *CCR 1409–13*, pp. 225–6.

[36] See Trevor John, 'Sir Thomas Erpingham, East Anglian Society and the Dynastic Revolution of 1399', *Norfolk Archaeology*, 35 (1970), pp. 96–108, esp. 102–3.

state, reigned; two (and on the other hand), everything is always changing or has just done so or is about to: Sir Thomas Erpingham dies without male heirs; William Winter fatally disperses his estate among his sons; Sir Simon Felbrigg, who has no sons at all, decides that his country seat shall be sold; a clever boy of humble, local family makes good and becomes a far from humble chief justice; and Henry V dies, leaving an infant son who grows into an incompetent king. Which is all perhaps saying no more than that the closest possible attention has to be paid to detail. Detail of time and place – as well as person.

That person for the moment remains William Winter. Having allied himself to the influential, he married his eldest son, a man of law like his father, to Elizabeth, daughter and heiress of a modest local landowner, William Hethersett.[37] John gained more than a wife. The brother-in-law he acquired, John Payn, the husband of William Hethersett's other daughter, was probably as helpful to the furtherance of his career as was Sir Thomas Erpingham. John Payn was in the household of Henry Bolingbroke by 1390; with Sir Thomas he shared Henry's exile and his triumphant return in 1399;[38] twice escheator of Norfolk before that date and a commissioner of the peace for that county for the first time in March 1397, after 1399 he became a king's esquire and, even before Richard was deposed, steward of the Duchy of Cornwall. When John Payn died in 1402 John Winter was an administrator of his property. By then John Winter had moved into Henry, Prince of Wales' service; by 1403 he had become Henry's receiver-general and controller of his household. As was normal, local power followed influence at the centre: in 1408, for instance, John Winter was made steward of the Duchy of Lancaster in Norfolk and Suffolk and he was knight of the shire for Norfolk seven times between 1401 and 1414. Grants of land, offices, and wardships duly came his way.[39] How he would have fared in the great adventure embarked on in 1415 by his prince who was now king must always remain unknown: John Winter died on the last day of December 1414.[40] His death without male heirs[41] – though he had married

[37] She brought him Chippenhall Manor in Fressingfield, Suffolk (*CCR 1409–13*, pp. 234–5) and possibly an estate in Barningham Northwood itself (Blomefield IV, p. 295), where John Winter was in possession of two properties in 1401–2: *Feudal Aids* III, p. 615.

[38] Trevor John, 'Sir Thomas Erpingham', p. 103.

[39] Trevor John, 'Parliamentary Representation', pp. 711–17.

[40] His brass at Town Barningham (according to Blomefield IV, p. 300), read the last day of December M[blank].

[41] Edmund, said by Professor J.S. Roskell to be his son, in *The Commons in the Parliament of 1422* (Manchester, 1954) pp. 237–8, was, according to Judge William Paston, his brother. Judge William is right; Professor Roskell was misled by Blomefield IV, p. 298.

twice[42] – complicated the Winter family's position with regard to its lands, a position complex already as a consequence of William Winter's dispersal of those lands among his sons.

To that dispersal, as recorded on Judge William Paston's memorandum (WKC 1/43/8) by himself and another in extracts from William Winter's last will of 27 August 1397, we have now to turn; the dispersal was ultimately disastrous to the Winters, and is central to the problem of East Beckham: as Judge William well knew. What one is tempted to ponder is: was the impact on the Winters of William Winter's last will – a history Judge William had taken the trouble to become intimately acquainted with because if affected his property rights – a history he called to mind on his deathbed? Did it make him hesitate to give his younger sons more than he had already given them? Though Agnes, his widow, always maintained he intended to give them more, and they took every opportunity for over forty years to take from the main stem of the family what they believed they ought to have been given in 1444, Judge William never did embody his intention in a written instrument. John, the eldest son, was able to retain (by fair means and foul) sufficient estates to carry him and the main stem of the family through the hard times of two long-lived heiresses and (well dowered) dowagers. As it was, the going was hard; if in 1444 Judge William had been more generous to his three younger sons, as openhanded as William Winter was to three of his in 1397, the Paston family may have sunk as rapidly as it had risen, just as the Winters did. It may have been that example which stayed Judge William's hand. John Paston felt badly enough treated as it was in 1444; he was not, however, left with as little as John Winter had been in 1397.

Or was meant to have been. There are two major difficulties in interpreting William Winter's last will and its consequences for the family, drawbacks which are not to be met with in an enquiry into Judge William Paston's last will and its influence on the Pastons. Both difficulties are evidential. On the one hand, we have only the abbreviated extracts of William Winter's will on the dorse of WKC 1/43/8, abstracts only, moreover, of those parts of it which were important to Judge William because they bore on the history of East Beckham. On the other hand, there is, compared with the detail of the Paston letters, so little to reveal what happened to William Winter's estates, to his widow, sons, and daughters,

[42] For the second time in or by 1407: *CPR 1405–8*, p. 290. A widow, Eleanor survived her second husband by a little over a year, dying in March 1416: PRO, PCC Reg. Marche, f. 33, cited by Trevor John, 'Parliamentary Representation', p. 721.

what his relationship with them was and how that relationship may have changed. In the end (if we might know all) it may be that John Winter was fairly dealt with by his father, that William Winter was generous to his younger sons but no more generous than Judge William Paston was to be, and that that generosity would not have been (as it cannot have been meant to be) harmful to the senior line of the family, had it not been for John's own, probably early, death and his failure to beget sons. Even then his brother and heir, Edmund's own failure and failings (which are not known to us) may be what caused the decline of the Winters. Or, it was the interaction of all these elements. Let us begin at the beginning with what we know of William Winter's will.

In the English notes (on the dorse of WKC 1/43/8) which tell us of the will's provisions, single initial letters stand for persons and places; these are sometimes crossed out and other initial letters substituted. There are also a number of erasures and interlineations; these, like the substitutions, are by Judge William Paston to an original text which is in another hand. William has also glossed that text at head, foot, and down one side in Latin. Such is the first difficulty for an interpreter. The second is one with which William was wrestling, one which William Winter's feoffees and executors themselves no doubt had grappled with at about the time Henry Bolingbroke was toppling Richard II: a series of complex and complicatedly inter-related remainders. These two problems understood, the following is one interpreter's account of what William Winter's intentions were in 1397 and what became of them in John Winter's lifetime. There are a number of parallels with Judge William Paston's intentions in 1444 and what became of them.

First, Egmere: this was to go to William's widow, Elizabeth, for life. Elizabeth was William's second wife and, as Judge William's Latin jottings inform us, she was one Elizabeth Germayn. On her death and once her son by William Winter, also called William, had reached the age of twenty-one, the feoffees were to transfer Egmere to Henry, probably the second of William's sons by Matilda Berney. There were four remainders in tail general before the right heirs of William were reached: to William, son of Elizabeth, to the putative son with whom Elizabeth was pregnant, to Gillian her daughter, and finally to the girl Elizabeth might then be carrying. Further, and contradictorily, if both Henry and William were to die without children before they were twenty-one, Egmere was to be sold on the death of Elizabeth.

Second, East Beckham: its fate was tied to that of Egmere. In the first instance it was to go to William, Elizabeth's son, when he became twenty-one. The first remainder was in tail general to Henry; the remainders then followed the pattern laid down for Egmere. If, however, Egmere was to fall to William through the early death of Henry, East Beckham was to be sold. We are not told for what purpose, but it is clear from the terms of the feoffees' later sale of East Beckham to John Winter, that certainly a chantry and probably pious works, were what, not unexceptionally, William Winter had in mind.

These English notes then close with the comment that there is more in the will, but nothing of substance concerning East Beckham. Judge William's introductory Latin gloss, none the less, adds important information from the will bearing upon East Beckham. He notes (not without second thoughts), and crucially for our unravelling if not for his, that William Winter's sons by Matilda Berney were John, Edmund, Henry, and Robert, and, 'per aliam uxorem', William. Elsewhere on the dorse of WKC 1/43/8, that is, in his Latin notes on the origins of the Winters (with which we began), Judge William not only states that William's mother was Elizabeth Germayn but also says that to distinguish this William from his father he was called William Germayn. Robert, he continues, was parson of the church of Town Barningham, John by the last will of his father was to have the manor of Town Barningham, Edmund was to have the manor of Bodham, Henry was to get Egmere and William East Beckham. He then notes the conditions (which we have already described) under which Egmere would come to William and East Beckham would be sold, namely the premature death of Henry. He ends with the comment that this information comes from William Shepherd of West Beckham (whom we shall encounter much later on): 'hec per W Shepherd de West Bekham'.

Town Barningham does not seem enough for the eldest son; as Gresham seems too little for John Paston in 1444. In both cases, however, there are the properties not mentioned in their fathers' wills. In addition to the manor of Snailwell, which fell to John on the death of his younger brother Edmund in 1449, as Judge William's will had in that event directed that it should, and in addition also to the properties John did not release to his far younger brother William when he became eighteen, which, according to his father's will, he ought to have done, there were at least four more estates, not including the troublesome East Beckham, which he inherited on his father's death. They were not the most remunerative Paston lands – his mother had these to the value of £100 per annum – and John was supposed to find £200 for his sister Elizabeth's marriage out of them (though he never did), but when added to Gresham they made John's portion a reasonable, though certainly not a generous, one. He did not believe he had been given enough; his brother William considered he had received too much.[43]

[43] For an extended version of this paragraph and the story thereafter, see chapter 6.

Similarly, John Winter inherited Wighton, the properties in Barningham Northwood, and whatever there was in Little Barningham.[44] He also obtained a life interest in the manor of Loundhall in Saxthorpe;[45] he may not have given Bodham up to Edmund.[46] Moreover, he had, just as John Paston was to have, the estates of his heiress wife, or, in Winter's case, wives. John Paston's Mautby manors were undoubtedly worth more than John Winter's portion of the Hethersett inheritance (which Elizabeth, his daughter by Elizabeth Hethersett, quitclaimed to him and his second wife Eleanor for their lives in 1411),[47] but with Eleanor, the widow of Ivo Harteston, John Winter obtained lands of substantial value in Cambridge, Cambridgeshire, and Essex.[48] John Winter also had, or was shortly to have, an income arising from his position in Lancastrian government, a position which John Paston was never to aspire to even when Yorkists replaced Lancastrians. Not that William Winter knew this in 1397.

What he did know was that he wished so to provide for his younger sons that they should not, as Judge William Paston expressed it to Agnes his wife in 1444 when thinking of what he should leave to his younger sons, 'hold the plowe be the tayle',[49] in other words, sink below the level of gentility, dirty their hands with labour, as Judge William's own father Clement had.[50] As, of course, according to that same Judge William, William Winter's father, John Haylstone, had done too.[51] The self-made William Winter and William Paston's preoccupations on their deathbeds (as perhaps throughout their lives) were, in this regard, identical. Probably very similar too were the provisions each made for his younger sons. William Winter had no need in 1397 to do any more than he had already done for one of his four sons, Robert the priest. He had sent him to Oxford and presented him to the living of Town Barningham: 'idem Robertum fiat persona ecclesie de Townbernyngham' as Judge William succinctly noticed in his list of what these young men had been given by their father.[52] Robert was probably the third

[44] *Feudal Aids* III, p. 616. [45] See above, p. 68, note 25.

[46] He was in possession in 1401–2 (*Feudal Aids* III, p. 633). According to one of Judge William's insertions on the dorse of WKC 1/43/8, at the time of his father's death at the turn of 1397–98 (William's testament of 12 December 1397 was proved on 6 February 1398: NRO, NCC Reg. Harsyk, fs. 240–241) Edmund was seventeen years old, and came of age in the second year of Henry IV (30 September 1400 – 29 September 1401), presumably and probably in 1401.

[47] *CCR 1409–13*, pp. 234–5. This was the important manor of Chippenhall in Fressingfield, Suffolk.

[48] Trevor John, 'Parliamentary Representation', p. 710, citing *Feudal Aids* IV, pp. 411, 446. John had married Eleanor by 1407: *CPR 1405–8*, p. 290.

[49] Davis I, p. 44. [50] *Ibid.*, pp. xxli–xxlii; chapter 1, p. 13. [51] See above, p. 66.

[52] NRO, WKC 1/43/8, dorse; Emden, *Biog. Reg. Oxon.*, III, p. 2126. Blomefield (IV, p. 300), however, has William Winter's executors presenting Robert in 1407; perhaps the vacancy had to be waited for.

son. He was a BA in 1394, the same year that he became a fellow of Oriel, and an MA in 1399, when Judge William tells us Robert's brother Edmund was seventeen.[53] That is little different to the eighteen of Edmund Paston when his father, Judge William, made his last will in January 1444. Edmund Paston was to have one manor, Snailwell, Cambridgeshire, worth 40 marks per annum when he became twenty-one; Edmund Winter was to have a single manor also, Bodham, Norfolk, value unknown, probably on similar terms. There was an eleven-year gap between Edmund Paston and his next youngest brother, William, seven in January 1444. William was to have two insubstantial manors and other lands worth in all 25 marks a year when he became eighteen. Henry Winter, whose age we do not know, was to have Egmere on Elizabeth Germayn's death; that manor's annual value, with its new house, was surely more than 25 marks;[54] its value was undoubtedly much closer to the 40 marks of Snailwell, and as that relatively valuable estate went to Judge William's second son, the giving of Egmere to Henry suggests it was he who was William Winter's second son.[55] That Edmund was William Winter's fourth and last son by Matilda Berney is substantiated by his youth in 1397 and by his surviving his full brothers by such a wide margin: John, Henry, and Robert were all dead by 1416; Edmund did not die until 1448, aged (we will assume) sixty-six. The baby of Judge William's family was Clement, whose age cannot be read in the will of January 1444, but who was certainly less than seven; he may have been less than two.[56] When he became eighteen he was to have a manor and lands together worth 25 marks per annum; William Winter's youngest, William (Germayn) was to get East Beckham when he became twenty-one; it was some years afterwards valued at 20 marks per annum; the figure may have been nearer 25 marks in 1397. What I am seeking to display in this comparison is the generosity of both fathers to their younger sons, the similarity of that generosity, and hence its probable conventionality. Neither father was extravagant; William Winter, with less overall to draw upon, was probably relatively more openhanded.

[53] See above, p. 76, note 46.

[54] Its valuation at 20 marks in the licence to alienate it to Walsingham Abbey of 1425 (Blomefield V, p. 797) is surely a calculated under-assessment. In the *Valor Ecclesiasticus* III, p. 385, its value is given as £13 10s 0d, but its sheep pastures were worth £15. Were these pastures part of the Winter manor?

[55] But, in the midst of conjecture as we are, does Egmere's being the dower of Elizabeth Germayn reduce the likelihood? Not knowing the terms on which Bodham was left to Edmund is a drawback. Should more trust be put in Judge William's order of the sons (see above, p. 75)? Yet, as he first wrote John, Edmund, Henry, William, and Robert, subsequently crossing out William and inserting after Robert 'per aliam uxorem Willelmum', I am not sure that it should.

[56] Davis I, p. lviii, says born in 1442 and refers the reader to the will (no. 12); I cannot find Clement's age there; it was given, I calculate, in a passage obliterated by damp.

To his sons, but not to the widow he left; whereas to Agnes Paston, though she had substantial estates of her own, Judge William gave many important manors and lands, including Paston itself, valued in all at £100 a year.[57] Elizabeth Germayn apparently was only to have Egmere: we do not know for certain that there was not more, but it seems unlikely. The reason for the two husbands' different treatment of their wives was no doubt that they were different women, differently circumstanced. Elizabeth Germayn was William Winter's second wife; she may not have been so for very long; she came, one suspects, from a less distinguished, a less demanding family than had Matilda Berney; she was not, it seems, an heiress. Agnes Paston *née* Barry, on the other hand, was; she had also been Judge William's companion for nearly twenty-five years; moreover, despite the twenty years or thereabouts which separated them in age, appearances suggest trust, if not affection, lay between them. Again, Judge William had more to give than William Winter; to Agnes he gave munificently. All of which simply goes to show the obvious: that no two marriages are alike.

Where the two men were, at least in intention, similar was in their piety. Similar, but not the same. And here we arrive at a critical point in the history of East Beckham. Deathbeds themselves were critical, nodal points in the lives of families; as critical, more critical even, than were marriages.[58] For, whereas at the union of one landed family with another only those families' secular interests were being accommodated, at the deathbed of a member of such a family, as at anyone's deathbed, religion intruded. The dying individual's religious interest as he and his priest saw and defined it came into conflict with the family's secular interest. Even a labourer's 6d. to be given to six poor folk[59] took 6d. out of the hands of his wife and children or of his brothers and sisters or nephews and nieces. How much more, then, was lost to a man's heirs when he set aside lands or revenues from lands in order that prayers might be offered for his soul.

There is a promising theme here: it is one of tension. Tension was high at Judge William Paston's deathbed.[60] John, the eldest son and heir, was still sufficiently preoccupied (with his and the family's secular interests) that, while William lay dying he 'walkyd up and down in the chamer', while his mother 'knelyd at the beddys fote'.[61] What was worrying him were his

[57] For this and the foregoing see Judge William's will, Davis no. 12 *and* Gairdner VI, pp. 190–1, which supplies former owners of estates omitted by Davis.

[58] 'The Pastons Revisited: Marriage and the Family in Fifteenth-century England', *BIHR*, 58 (1985), p. 25.

[59] J.H. Oxley, *The Reformation in Essex* (London, 1965), p. 24.

[60] As Agnes' accounts reveal, Davis I, pp. 44–8. These were preambles to her will, written probably twenty-two years after her husband's death; she had an astounding memory, even recalling dialogue: is it the memory of an illiterate? Her vivid, almost picaresque, recollections deserve to be pondered thoroughly, as I hope they are in chapter 6.

[61] *Ibid.*, p. 48.

father's last wishes, not only that more lands should be given to John's younger brothers than William had left them in his written will, but also that out of the manor of Swainsthorpe an annuity should be paid in perpetuity for a chantry in the Lady Chapel at Norwich Cathedral where William was to be buried. At fourpence a day it would only have been £6 a year; nevertheless, as William had not put his last wishes into writing, John refused to fulfil them.[62] It was John Paston's good fortune that his dying (and dithering) father did not get his final thoughts onto paper; it was John Winter's ill-luck that his father had.

What one wonders is: did John Paston, pacing the death chamber in 1444, know of that? In other words, did he have the example of John Winter clear before him, an eldest son burdened with over-endowed younger brothers and with his father's costly desire for prayers to hasten his soul through purgatory? He should have known. After all, in 1444 his father had been struggling for ten years with Edmund Winter, the head of what remained of the Winter family, over possession of the very estate which had been pivotal in John Winter's difficulties: East Beckham. If John Paston had seen the deeds and his father's East Beckham 'scribbling paper' (or, more likely, had listened to him on the matter), he would have known that it was John Winter's failure to fulfil the obligations laid upon him for the welfare of his father's soul which gave the Pastons their claim to East Beckham. That estate's history, therefore, may well have been on his mind, particularly as his father had mentioned it in his dying days as one of the properties he wanted to take from John and add to his brother's portions.[63] It is time to return to that history.

It is also the point at which we return to WKC 1/43/8, both to its notes of deeds relating to East Beckham and to Judge William Paston's account (on the other side of the sheet) of that estate and the Winters' association with it. Most of the deeds noted in WKC 1/43/8 have survived; they are a welcome corroboration of the accuracy of Judge William's abstracts. William Winter purchased the manor of East Beckham from Sir Roger Beckham; in November 1379 he handed over what was probably the full price, rather than a last instalment, £122, and agreed to pay Sir Roger £8 a year out of the estate during Sir Roger's lifetime.[64] Sir Roger lived for a further ten years: in May 1390 William Winter enfeoffed Sir Thomas Erpingham, Sir Robert Berney, and others, and duly quitclaimed to them in April 1392 the manor of East Beckham and other lands formerly Sir Roger Beckham's.[65]

[62] *Ibid.*, pp. 44–5 and 46. Indeed, he did not fulfil some of the conditions of his father's written will and endeavoured to get his fellow executors to make additions to it in his favour (see chapter 6). [63] *Ibid.*, pp. 44, 46, 47.

[64] WKC 1/43/8; cf. BL Add. Ch. 14521; NRO, Phillipps MS 22; BL Add. Ch. 14522.

[65] WKC 1/43/8; cf. NRO, Phillipps MS 23, the quitclaim of 17 April 1392.

Judge William Paston (on the dorse of WKC 1/43/8) says further that William Winter bought from one Adam Brown in Beckham – not specifying whether East or West – a tenement called Brown's. In a less than clear passage he appears to be stating that William Winter then leased out the demesne of Brown's tenement but retained its rents of seven shillings and its court, and that this court (presumably because William owned also the manor of East Beckham) became the court of East Beckham, or (put another way) the two courts getting confused with each other became one. Judge William ends by stating that John Winter acquired ('perquisvit') all this: the manor of East Beckham, the profits of the leased demesne of Brown's, and the *manor* of Brown's. I am not sure of the exact significance of this information, nor its relevance to the Paston case for their title to East Beckham, but it does reveal what is self-evident, that court holding was important to the men who were seeking to make themselves manorial lords of a place. This (as we have seen) was what Judge William himself would attempt at Paston in the 1430s – to create a manor, to hold a court, to live in a manorial hall, to have lordship over men: this Maitlandesque language discloses the enduring continuity (despite all economic change) of the pull and power of landownership, as by the fifteenth century such landholding legitimately may be described.

Acquired, not inherited, East Beckham (according to Judge William's version of William Winter's will) was to go to the fifth son, William Germayn, the only son of the second marriage, when he reached the age of twenty-one. If, however, Egmere fell to him before that, through the death of his elder brother Henry, East Beckham was to be sold.[66] This we may presume to have happened:[67] in April 1409 East Beckham (and all the lands which had been Sir Roger Beckham's, as well as the watermill, formerly Adam Brown's[68]) were 'sold' to John Winter. Or, so I interpret the two deeds of that month. The first, dated at East Beckham 11 April 1409, is a grant by Sir Thomas Erpingham and Sir Robert Berney, feoffees and executors of William Winter, to John Winter and his feoffees, who included his brother Robert, the parson, and John Drew.[69] The second is an indenture, also dated at East Beckham 22 April 1409, whereby John Winter and his feoffees regrant to Erpingham and Berney; the terms under which John could recover East Beckham were as follows: if he paid for three chaplains at Town

[66] See above, p. 74.

[67] At any rate, Judge William Paston says in WKC 1/43/8 that William Germayn was in possession of Egmere.

[68] Can a watermill become a manor? The watermill was in Sheringham as BL Add. Ch. 14523 informs us.

[69] BL Add. Ch. 19325, with two fine seals on tags. It is noticed in WKC 1/43/8, out of sequence, but with arrows showing where it ought rightly to be.

Barningham church to pray for the souls of his father and mother for a year from the coming Michaelmas and paid to Erpingham and Berney 100 marks on 24 June 1411 and a further £51 13s 4d on 14 June 1412.[70] William Paston in his précis of this indenture adds the helpful information that these sums were to be distributed in alms for the benefit of the souls of William and Matilda Winter.[71] Does not this amount to a sale? The total sum involved bears a resemblance to that paid by William Winter to Sir Roger Beckham thirty years previously.[72] Did John Winter have possession of East Beckham? That would have been usual, yet the wording of the indenture is otherwise: *not* that the executors Erpingham and Berney shall re-enter if the conditions are unfulfilled (as would have been more normal), but that John shall re-enter when he has fulfilled the conditions.

He did not do so. After his death in December 1414, we find by a deed of 10 June 1415 (abstracted in WKC 1/43/8) Erpingham and Berney enfeoffing John Drew and others. The authority they cite for their action is the grant to them by William Winter of May 1390. Thus, either John had never possessed East Beckham or the feoffees had re-entered. Probably the former; if the latter, one fancies John's heir, his brother Edmund, would have put up a stiffer and more immediate fight for it, instead of quitclaiming to the new owners in 1416. What had occurred by then, therefore, was the loss to the Winters of one of the family estates, lost through William Winter's wish that his soul might be speeded through purgatory by prayers and good works and his son and heir's inability or unwillingness to pay the price of that wish. Or command, should we say? The only difference between John Winter and John Paston (in such circumstances forty years afterwards) was

[70] BL Stowe Ch. 177, two seals as in BL Add. Ch. 19325. The witnesses are also identical; they include John's brother Edmund, significantly (as we shall see) if he was there. He may have been, but is it likely that the others spent the two weeks after Easter at East Beckham?

[71] NRO, WKC 1/43/8. He also notes that John Mariot, whom we shall shortly encounter, had the other part of the indenture. As Stowe Ch. 177 is endorsed 'East Beckham Number 39', it is likely to be the part the Pastons had, which, given its two seals, was presumably John Winter's part.

[72] £118 6s 8d plus three chaplains for a year, as against £122 plus £8 a year, as it turned out, for about ten years. So, William Winter may have had to pay rather more than he bargained Sir Roger Beckham was going to survive for. On the other hand East Beckham's value no doubt dropped over a thirty-year period, during which land values fell more sharply than at any time in England before the 1870s. Still, East Beckham was valued at 20 marks per annum in 1415 and twenty times 20 marks gives us over £265, which is higher than any figure we have just been playing with. Which was the manor in Beckham with lands in Cromer, valued by the escheator of Norfolk at 44s a year in 1392? It had belonged either to Robert Allen of East Beckham or Geoffrey Allen of Cromer. After the death of Christina, the wife of one of them, and during the minority of their daughter, custody was granted to Edward Durdent. The escheator who valued the manor was none other than John Winter, at the outset of his public career: PRO, Ministers Accounts, SC 6/929/29; cf. *and* ct. *CFR 1391–9*, p. 53.

that William Winter had got his piety down in writing and Judge William Paston had not. Might this be a measure of the respective depths of these two lawyers' religious convictions, an indication of how they viewed the respective sinfulness of their careers? Moreover, and continuing to reflect along such lines, we should also have to endeavour to weigh the relative effectiveness of the prayers of three chaplains for a year as against those of a single monk until the Last Judgement.

As it turned out, the souls of neither got the prayers each had desired. Why the successful, and thus well-off, John Winter did not find the money to save both East Beckham and his father's soul we are unlikely ever to know. Probably he thought he could take his time (despite the deadlines in the indenture of 1409), relying on the goodwill of his friends Erpingham and Berney. I suspect too that he left in his own will instructions for the fulfilment of his father's unfulfilled one, instructions that may well have included the sale of East Beckham, the sale which, with its important religious conditions, had not taken effect in his own lifetime. Neither his will nor his testament survive. There was a testament; John Drew was an executor of it. Is it not likely, therefore, that John Drew, William Frere, parson of South Repps, Clement Herward, John Mortoft, and Ralph Picard, enfeoffed by Erpingham and Berney in June 1415, were John Winter's executors? It is they, at any rate, who made the crucial sale of East Beckham on 19 December 1415 to William Mariot of Cromer and his wife Joan.[73] The price, we are told by Joan Mariot in 1440, was 450 marks – for an estate worth 20 marks a year.[74]

Squeezed into the right-hand bottom corner of WKC 1/43/8 is Judge William's note of the next, and equally important deed in the story of East Beckham: Edmund Winter's quitclaim to William Mariot of 10 February 1416. This does not now seem to exist; as it was produced in the Court of Common Pleas by the Mariots in 1436 and the court required that it was to

[73] BL Add. Ch. 14523. Actually, only John Drew, William Frere, and Ralph Picard made the sale. NRO, WKC 1/43/8, however, notes a quitclaim to the Mariots by Clement Herward and John Mortoft of 15 October – 3 Richard II is what was first written, a later, amending hand suggests 3 Henry V, that is 15 October 1415, two months *before* the sale. Is it not more likely that the amended date is correct and that Herward and Mortoft released ('relaxaverunt' is the word written) their right to Drew, Frere, and Picard? This deed of sale returns us to Denny Abbey: included in the sale was a reversion of a meadow in Felbrigg, taken for life by Isobel, daughter of William Winter and Abbess of Denny. This also takes us back to (and makes closer) William Winter's connection with Mary de St Pol.

[74] Her petition to the king: PRO SC8/128/6390. The sum *might* be 400 marks – the document is damaged at this point, and my notes on the even more indecipherable NRO, WKC 1/43/1, which is no longer producible, have 400 marks. Such a sum would be tidier, but 450 marks is what my notes on SC8/128/6390 firmly state and 450 marks is what NRO, WKC 1/43/10 unambiguously proclaims.

be kept in the custody of the royal clerk, Robert Darcy,[75] perhaps it has disappeared (or does still survive) in the vast reaches of the archives of the state. One further and next to last document noticed in WKC 1/43/8 (with alterations and extensions in a second hand) is another release of Edmund Winter's: to John Drew, parson of Northwold (amended from Harpley), executor of John Winter, of all actions 'real and personal', dated at Town Barningham ('Bernyngham Magna') 17 October 1423. An addition to this extended entry, in Judge William's hand again, states that another such release is dated 13 February 1425.[76]

By that year Judge William Paston had become directly involved in the dispersal of the Winter estates, collected only two generations before by William Winter. On 3 March 1425 he was one of the feoffees in the manor of Egmere who received licence to alienate it to Walsingham Abbey.[77] It is clear, therefore, that he would have known the history of Egmere as well, if not better than he knew the history of East Beckham: thus, we are given further confirmation of the accuracy of his notes on WKC 1/43/8. In an inserted entry on the dorse of that document about the holders of the Egmere court, Judge William notes that by 8 January 1416 when Edmund Winter held his first court, Henry and the young William Winter as well as John Winter were dead.[78] So was Robert Winter: in 1412 a new priest had been presented to Town Barningham by his brother.[79] Edmund was not simply his brother's heir; a year after John Winter's death Edmund was the only surviving male Winter.

Edmund's career has been set out elsewhere.[80] Although he married into

[75] NRO, WKC 1/43/3, copy of the plea roll of Michaelmas term 1436. Joan Mariot mentions her readiness to produce this release, sealed with Edmund's seal of his arms, in her petition to the king of autumn 1436: PRO, SC 8/128/6390.

[76] It is the second, intervening, hand which, as well as substituting Northwold for Harpley, adding the information that John Drew was the executor of the testament of John Winter, and the date and place of dating, glosses Edmund Winter's identity: brother and heir of John Winter esquire, (who was) son and heir of William Winter esquire.

[77] The other feoffees were Sir Simon Felbrigg, William Paston's father-in-law Sir Edmund Barry, and John Woodhouse, whose widow Edmund Winter was to marry. I presume these were Edmund Winter's feoffees, not John Winter's. They made the presentation to the church there in 1422. See Blomefield V, pp. 797, 798.

[78] Elsewhere in the notes on that same side of the sheet, Judge William says that after the young William's death, the daughter of John Winter, that is, according to the context of his 'filia dicti Johanni Wynter', Edmund's aunt, the wife of one John Winterworth, occupied Egmere. Out of consideration for his father and because he had tact, Edmund, it is implied, did not challenge her: 'Et quod dictus Edmundus in consideracione patris sui non fuit versimilis essendi bonis discrecionis etc.' We cannot put dates to this, particularly if Edmund's court holding in 1416 was while his aunt was in possession. At this point, as we are about to take leave of WKC 1/43/8, I gratefully acknowledge Professor Ralph Griffiths' assistance with Judge William's Latin.

[79] Blomefield IV, p. 300.

[80] Trevor John. 'Parliamentary Representation', pp. 701–8; J.S. Roskell, *The Commons of 1422*, pp. 237–8.

land and was well connected locally, Edmund did not make the mark in Lancastrian government his elder brother had done: his public life as well as his private one – if as early as the fifteenth century such a distinction may be made of a member of the landed class – was based in Norfolk. His will suggests he was something of a bookish man as well as a farming one.[81] In the 1430s, as we shall discover later, he was quite ready and able to enter and occupy East Beckham in despite of the law and to manipulate local juries to perjure themselves to his advantage. He would appear, therefore, to be altogether the model of a provincial English gentleman.

Or, was Edmund driven to being unreasonable by the loss of most of the Winter estates in his lifetime? We coolly observe the decline of the family, cold-bloodedly measuring its rise and fall in two generations: lepidopterists pinning down a specimen. Edmund, however, was that victim; he cannot have been expected to go quietly. For his family was not suffering from the terminal complaint of the landed class, a lack of male heirs: the Winters remained at Barningham Winter for many generations.[82] Yet it was only there that they remained, not at Little Barningham or Barningham Northwood, not at Egmere, disposed of in 1425, not at East Beckham, sold in 1415, not at Wighton and Saxthorpe, not apparently even at Bodham, of which Edmund was said to be in possession in 1428.[83] He cannot have

[81] His one estate at Town Barningham and his house in Coslany, Norwich, where he made his will, 'place' him neatly. To John, his son and heir, he left all his books which were in a certain 'parva poketto', that is, psalters, primers, other works and rolls; John also got the primer which had been Edmund's mother's, that is, of course, Matilda Berney – it was seventy or eighty years old by then. Edmund's daughter Margaret (*not* his sister: Roskell and John are in error here), married to Ralph Lampet, was to have his book about King Richard 'et aliis militibus', while John Heydon, his other son-in-law, was to have 'librum meum de cronicis [cronic']'. Horses and saddles, ploughs and carts, grain and the butcher at Barningham who, as the Duke of Norfolk did, owed him money, suggest the agricultural side of his life. It is a striking coincidence to meet the word 'carnifex' in Edmund's will after encountering it in WKC 1/43/8 (see above, p. 66). At any rate, the Winters' dealings with butchers serve to remind us of their importance in the meat-eating England of the later Middle Ages. Alice, Edmund's widow, who was to have virtually everything for life, enjoyed it for no more than a few weeks. Edmund's will (NRO, NCC Reg. Wylbey, f. 147), dated 20 February 1448 (*not* 1449 as in Roskell), was proved 2 March 1448; he died 26 February 1448 according to his *IPM* (PRO, C 139/130/4); Alice's will (NRO, NCC Reg. Wylbey, f. 150), dated 15 March 1448, was proved 5 April 1448. Alice, nevertheless, desired burial beside her first husband, John Woodhouse, at Norwich 'in loco vocato le charnell', and it was his soul she requested prayers for at Reydon. Hers too was a 'local' will, though the man who was to be hired to go on pilgrimage for her soul, as well as travelling to ten holy places in Norfolk, was in addition to go to the cross at the North Door of St Paul's, London and to St Thomas' shrine at Canterbury (see also Norman P. Tanner, *The Church in Medieval Norwich 1370–1532* (Toronto, 1984) pp. 85–6.

[82] Blomefield IV, pp. 298–300.

[83] *Feudal Aids* III, pp. 573, 575. Edmund's *inquisition post mortem* (PRO C139/130/4) records only Barningham. In the end even Barningham Winter went, but that it went to the Pastons has for us, even for them perhaps, a poignancy which requires expression, if only in a footnote. Sir Edward Paston, of a cadet branch of the family, bought it around 1600; he

studied such dissolution with equanimity. When the chance came of recovering East Beckham he took it. If this meant combat with an old friend (or at any rate an earlier feoffee), so be it. In 1434 the Pastons must have appeared to Edmund as the usurpers of the Winters in North Erpingham Hundred. Irked, beyond endurance, he may have seen, as we are perhaps entitled to see, the contest for East Beckham as the family's last stand; in leading its final strategic charge, he was not going to make, let alone observe, tactical distinctions between clean and dirty.

What was the reason for the Winters' decline, for the dwindling of their estates to one? Trevor John has suggested that 'gifts to religious houses by the father [that is, John Winter, the brother] somewhat reduced the Winter inheritance'.[84] The alienation of Egmere to Walsingham Abbey in 1425 might have been as a result of a pious bequest by John Winter, but, though we lack his will and testament, there is little, indeed no evidence, to suggest John was a religious man. On the contrary, we have observed him apparently failing to put into practice the piety of his father: the sale of East Beckham to the Mariots was the consequence of that want of *pietas*. William Winter, on the other hand, was devout, at any rate more devout than his eldest son, unless that is entirely illusion created by the survival of his testament and the disappearance of John's. In his (badly damaged) testament[85] William desired burial in the chancel of St Mary's church at Town Barningham 'ante ymaginam', unless he had that image placed 'apud Walsingham' during his lifetime, in which case (so the sense of this is to be interpreted) he would still be buried in the chancel, exact spot unspecified. The monks at Walsingham were to pray for his soul, so were those of Norwich and Lynn and the friars of north Norfolk houses. So were the poor: 20 marks was to be distributed to them at his funeral and at his week's and month's mind. To each of the altars of twenty-three local churches he left 2 shillings, on condition that prayers be offered for his soul, the soul of his wife Matilda Berney, and the souls of his father and mother. Sums (ranging from £1 to 6s 8d) were also left for the repair of a dozen churches. There were other, now indecipherable, religious bequests; one of them was probably for

rebuilt the house on a new site. Who depopulated the village: Winters or Pastons? In the ruined church in the park Pastons were buried where Winters had been. On the south wall of the restored chancel the refurbished brass of a Winter, John of 1414 probably, is no distance from the marble tablet to John Paston, second son of Edward Paston esquire and Mary his wife, born 1 June 1728, died 11 May 1729. So bad is the 'verse' commemorating him, its repetition (if only in a footnote) is impossible to resist:

He just stop'd here below
On his Journey to Above
And felt the Agonies of Expiring nature
to heighten his Relish of the Joys of Heaven.

[84] 'Parliamentary Representation', p. 701 (Trevor John has Edmund as the son, not the brother, of John Winter). [85] NRO, NCC Reg. Harsyk, fs. 240–1.

the chantry of Town Barningham. We should also recall his gift of books to Denny Abbey, his daughter Isobel as abbess there – perhaps she was another of his gifts – and his connection with the devout lady who was the founder of Denny, Mary de St Pol. Might not this association, which may, so to speak, have made him, have been based on a religious empathy? Judge William Paston's contempt (in WKC 1/43/8) was for a hard man; Mary de St Pol was a hard-headed woman too, like Margaret Beaufort: hard-headed, warm-hearted – is this a credible combination, for her, for him? Thus, we arrive at a supposition: the begetter of the family's fortunes was himself responsible for their near extinction. He had, and probably thought he had, every right. Still, if his soul in the hereafter was the winner, his descendants' lives in the here and now were the poorer. This is almost a form of higher selfishness; certainly it is individuality triumphing at the expense of the collective, that is the family – exactly what we would expect of the late Middle Ages, especially of the religion of the late Middle Ages.

What the Winters lost, the Mariots gained. Was it additionally galling for Edmund to see East Beckham sold to a fisherman, even if William Mariot was a deep-sea fisherman, probably a fishing-boat owner, certainly an important citizen of Cromer?[86] As he also owned a little land further down the coast at Ormesby[87] and could find, that is presumably he could borrow, 450 marks for East Beckham, he was evidently not only successful in his profession but also a respected business man. Yet, when he died in 1434 he owed 300 marks. He died suddenly, being drowned 'be tempest of the see';[88] his indebtedness, while being no measure of the state of his fishing interests, might be of his over-reaching pretensions to landed gentility. He was not in debt for East Beckham, but may he not have been because he had bought East Beckham, though that purchase had been twenty years before his death? Twenty-eight acres and 10 shillings of rent at Ormesby were one thing, a manorial estate in the country quite another. Still, the Mariots seem to have had, as Joan Mariot claimed, twenty years peaceable possession of East Beckham. At some point during that time they made an enfeoffment of the property: John Rudde of Cromer, John Clements and John Fremyll of London were their feoffees. Judge William Paston duly recorded this on WKC 1/43/8 but without a date and with the note 'non vidi cartam inde'. As this entry is unamended probably no other member of the Paston family, household, or affinity got to see it either. It is the last item with which we are concerned on that 'scribbling paper'; in fact, it is the last item, for we have

[86] I am putting together *CPR 1413–16*, pp. 363–4 and *CPR 1416–22*, pp. 16, 87, 89, 101. As William drowned at sea, he cannot be envisaged as a man whose role in the fishing industry was purely an entrepreneurial, landlubberly one. [87] PRO, C1/11/60.

[88] PRO, SC 8/128/6390.

dealt with every other. It is, therefore, with some relief that we part company with WKC 1/43/8, and also with gratitude: it has been an invaluable scrap of paper.

There is also a single document which illuminates the history of East Beckham for the ten or so years after 5 September 1434, the day William Mariot died. It is not a scrap, it is a paper roll over three foot long; it is not scribbled notes, it is a carefully considered, clearly set out account, from the Paston point of view, of that family's title to East Beckham. It is a draft, with crossings out and interlineations, corrections and amendments, some of these, I believe, in the hand of John Paston, Judge William Paston's eldest son, for whom undoubtedly the document was drawn up. It has neither date nor address, but may safely be attributed to the very end of 1445 or the beginning of 1446 and may be less securely assumed to be intended in a final form for possibly the chancellor, probably an arbitrator or arbitrators – perhaps for the third time in this struggle between Winter and Paston, William de la Pole, Marquess of Suffolk. It is in the East Beckham bundle in the Ketton-Cremer collection at the Norfolk Record Office and is numbered WKC 1/43/4. It by no means tells the whole story of East Beckham, indeed we cannot hope to tell the whole story, but we shall depend on it for the framework of that story: the multitude of other evidence, whether Paston or other, never contradicts the narrative, only supplements and elaborates it.

William Mariot drowned at sea on 5 September 1434.[89] Burdened with more than 300 marks of debt, with two sons and two daughters to maintain and with East Beckham as her sole real estate,[90] Joan, William's widow, 'profred the same maner to selle'. According to her petition to the king of six years later,[91] Edmund Winter was among those who made her offers; she 'myght ne wolde' bargain with him, however, because of 'diverse behestes be her made to other persones'. One of these appears to have been the man who almost certainly drafted her petition of 1440: Judge William Paston. To Judge William, so the Paston version of the story in WKC 1/43/4 maintains, Joan made a firm undertaking; William Mariot's will was that on his death East Beckham should be sold by his feoffees to pay his debts and to provide each of his sons with £20 – daughters are not mentioned; his executors were to be Joan and John his (presumably eldest) son. With the assent of the feoffees, WKC 1/43/4 continues, Joan proceeded to sell the manor to Judge William Paston 'be word', promising that he should have 'the evydense and that he xuld pay no mony tyl sche be his avise had mad hym a cler astate and

[89] As Joan states in PRO, SC8/128/6390.

[90] Though PRO, C1/11/60 reveals that she did have from William Mariot a small property in Ormesby.

[91] That is PRO SC 8/128/6390.

warant hym the place cler and owt of truble'. Moreover, Joan sold Judge William East Beckham 'Cs. with In the valew therof or that ony man wold gett therfor'. There is no reason to question this; Joan, in a vulnerable position, was more than likely to be favourable to the dominating, even perhaps domineering man of law that Judge Wiliam had become by the 1430s. Like other propertied Norfolk widows, she was just what the judge, seeking by all means to build up his landed estate, was looking for.

This transaction, these negotiations, were bluntly interrupted by Edmund Winter. On Monday 20 December 1434 he seized and occupied East Beckham.[92] As Joan indicated in her petition of 1440,[93] Edmund, realizing that he was not going to be able to recover East Beckham for the Winters by buying it, not at any rate with Judge William as a competitor, determined to compel Joan to sell to him by a more overt form of coercion than that (probably) deployed by the judge. Or, as WKC 1/43/4 baldly put it, Edmund entered East Beckham out of envy towards William Paston and to deter him from going through with his purchase. For one thing is clear: no money had changed hands. Promises had been made, perhaps an understanding had been arrived at, yet the strength of these may have been slender – the only evidence for them at all is from Judge William himself or from a Joan Mariot who, by the time there are documents in her name, was tied hand and foot to Judge William, her cause having become his. John Mariot, in one of his petitions, does not mention any Mariot–Paston transactions until after Edmund Winter's entry of December 1434.[94] Thus, Edmund's occupation of East Beckham was a timely stroke. It ruptured Paston's complacency. His purchase of East Beckham was not to be a relatively simple task of separating a widow from her property, but a complicated legal contest with an opponent who, as well as being head of the family which twenty years before had owned East Beckham, had also friends in the household of the young king. Nor merely complicated; costly too. Edmund's abrupt intervention turned a quiet bit of business into a lengthy, expensive, and unpredictable battle whose outcome remained in doubt until long after Judge William's death ten years later.

The immediate consequence of Edmund's seizure of East Beckham was that Joan Mariot and Judge William, in order to recover what each may have considered to belong to him (or her) self, entered into a pact of mutual offence. Thus, Joan agreed to sell the estate to William for £40 within the price, 'wer of ther is wrytyng and seelys', and William undertook to sue for

[92] NRO, WKC 1/43/10 names John Griffin, Robert Brampton, and Thomas Saxthorp as the men who actually made the forced entry. [93] PRO, SC8/128/6390.

[94] The almost illegible NRO, WKC 1/43/1, subsequently declared too fragile for production, has reappeared.

the recovery of the manor and 'to pay for her the mony that shuld be spent therfor'. If the estate was recovered, William's costs were to 'be set on wards in partye of payment', if it was not Joan 'wold content hym a geyn theroff'.[95] This, according to John Mariot,[96] was the occasion for him and his mother to surrender all their evidences of title to William: the actual day, as a case in Common Pleas of the later 1440s reveals, was 6 January 1435 and the documents were in a deed box ('pixidis').[97] Undoubtedly it was from the deeds in this box that Judge William made the notes of WKC 1/43/8. A case (which the Pastons lost) concerning the very box that contained the evidence we are here dependent on seems a thoroughly appropriate way to begin on the tangle of legal actions which occupied Pastons, Mariots, and Edmund Winter over the ensuing ten years. The unravelling which follows may be clumsy – after such an interval it is not easy to detect where all the threads begin; it is certain that some of them will be loose ends.

The first legal move to complement his unlawful initiative, was made by Edmund Winter. He brought an action of trespass against Joan and John Mariot and an action of 'detenu of deeds' against John Mariot. Both were fairly promptly determined in his favour in summer 1436. Edmund's case was that his brother John Winter alone and unconditionally had been granted and released East Beckham by Sir Thomas Erpingham and Sir Robert Berney and that John had died in sole, unconditional possession. This, as we know from British Library Additional Charter 19325 and Stowe Charter 177, was untrue.[98] Nevertheless, Edmund maintained that John Mariot withheld the non-existent charter and release from him and on the pretext of these documents' existence charged John and Joan Mariot with trespass and damage at East Beckham on 10 December 1434, that is a conventional ten days before he had entered. At Norwich on 16 July 1436 an inquiry of twenty-four jurors, a number of them distinguished Norfolk knights and esquires, found for Edmund on both charges; John and Joan were condemned in 100 marks and £40.[99]

[95] NRO, WKC 1/43/4.

[96] NRO, WKC 1/43/1. John Mariot also stated that the remitted £40 was to be for Judge William's help, labour, damages, and costs. He stressed the importance of the indentures of agreement drawn up by William at this time, 'ensealed by his own advice and having none other counsel'.

[97] NRO, WKC 1/43/9. For Stonor deed boxes and their importance, see C.L. Kingsford (ed.), 'Supplementary Stonor Letters and Papers', *Camden Miscellany*, vol. XIII (London: Camden Society, 1923), p. vi.

[98] See above, p. 80, and as the Mariots said in their petition to the king, mentioning also Edmund's release of the estate to William Mariot, which they were willing to produce.

[99] The copies of the legal proceedings are NRO, WKC 1/43/2 and 1/43/7. On the former, in the margin beside the verdict of the jury, a note records that it was false; I think the note is in Judge William Paston's hand. The latter comprises the questions put to the jury and a list of names, a number of which are marked in a variety of ways; the names marked include Sir

These sums Judge William Paston had to pay;[100] before he did so, however, John Mariot spent some time in the Marshalsea and Joan Mariot was outlawed.[101] In autumn 1436 they petitioned, undoubtedly at Judge William's prompting and under his protection, against the miscarriage of justice which had overwhelmed them. They sued to every authority to whom they could sue: king, the king in Parliament, the chancellor.[102] They were very rude, as well they might be, about Edmund Winter. For example: if Edmund did have any title or evidence of such title to East Beckham

> he is so gret a visager and so abundant of language he wold prese to blowe it thorgh all the courtes the kyng hath . . . for a nother so gret a forswerer nor so dampnabil a slawnderer ne so shameles usuell langager visager and contryver of untrewe feyned and slawnderous tales and matieres as he is was never in his dayes of his degree in that shire.[103]

Or: Edmund obtained the false verdict of the summer 'be his grete myght and rewle of suche persones as use continuelly to passe on enquestes . . . be hym and his menes craftily embraced and procured.'[104]

This is, of course, the rhetoric of a suppliant at law. Was Edmund Winter likely to overawe men of the quality of Sir John Clifton or Sir Henry Inglose, Henry Grey or William Calthorp esquires, who were four of the jurors who

John Clifton, Sir Brian Stapleton, Sir Henry Inglose, Sir Roger Harsyk, Henry Grey esquire, William Calthorp esquire, Brian Stapleton esquire, Ralph Garneys esquire. Neither of the two John Berneys is marked; on the other hand, Sir Henry Inglose and the others who are cannot be regarded as 'hostile' to William Paston – whatever we may care to mean by 'hostile'. Possibly, they were sympathetic to Edmund Winter and to the family predicament; they are unlikely to have known the legal facts of the matter; they might not have considered them particularly relevant if they had. Proceedings in these two cases were concluded at Westminster in October: *CCR 1435–41*, p. 64; NRO, WKC 1/43/2. Edmund's sureties for his appearance there were his sons-in-law Ralph Lampet and John Heydon. This early 'opposition' of John Heydon to the Pastons should perhaps be noted, as should its origin in kinship. John Heydon in 1436 was on the threshold of his successful career.

[100] I think the financial calculations of the latter part of NRO, WKC 1/43/4 are not easy to understand in detail. As John Paston reckoned his father's costs, they amounted to just over £104 as 'payed' and just over £71 'spent' on the legal battle for East Beckham. The first sum, I am fairly sure, covers the fines of 1436, the second certainly comprises the actual expenses of litigation. [101] NRO, WKC 1/43/11.

[102] For what follows see PRO, SC8/128/6390 and SC1/44/48; SC8/198/9895; NRO, WKC 1/43/11: copy of their response to Edmund's reply to their petition in chancery. Early chancery proceedings themselves (unless I have missed them) seem not to include the papers of this case: see, however, the following note for why there may not be any. All these documents are undated, but all, save possibly SC8/198/9895, which may be a year earlier, are undoubtedly of late 1436. In SC8/198/9895 John Mariot is designated (or has called himself) a mariner, Joan Mariot is termed a brewer.

[103] WKC 1/43/11. Interestingly, this speaks of the king having seen the Mariots' original bill and having sent it to the chancellor 'by Sir Rauf Botiller'; the chancellor was 'to hear and know the mater' and to report to the king his 'good conceit therein'. It is interesting because it is an early instance of the young Henry VI's involvement in government and an example of Ralph Butler's closeness to him. It also suggests that the Mariots' petition to the king (that is, SC8/128/6390) was what initiated the proceedings before the chancellor, rather than a petition to the chancellor himself; this may be why there is apparently no record of the case in early chancery proceedings: see preceding note. [104] PRO, SC8/128/6390.

returned the incorrect verdict of 1436? It is surely more likely that their acquiescence in what they may not, anyway, have considered to be unlawful was the result of their favourable assessment of Edmund Winter's case; that is, his being one of themselves, who as the head of an established county family, was endeavouring to recover a property which once had helped give that family a place it was in danger of losing. The Mariots were mere mariners[105] and brewers, and William Paston, even if he was a judge, was a pushing *nouveau riche*, a *nouveau riche* lawyer at that.

So far, therefore, Edmund Winter appears a winner. The petitions of the latter part of 1436, none the less, represent the beginning of Judge William's counter-attack against an antagonist, who, having made a successful surprise assault in December 1434, had gone on apparently to crush his opponents in July 1436. In addition to petitioning (ineffectually as it turned out), Judge William opened his campaign at common law: Joan Mariot's feoffees, John Clement and John Rudde, brought an action of novel disseisin against Edmund Winter. In Michaelmas term 1436 they produced in court Edmund's quitclaim to William Mariot of February 1416.[106] It was, it ought to have been, the decisive document in the case. Edmund, none the less, 'be craft delayd the seyd asise ii zer and more on to the tyme that the pleyntyffys besechyd my lord of Suffolk to examyne the mater and thanne be a cord of bothe partys it was put in my seyd lord [*sic*].'[107] Probably another, if minor, cause of delay was the death of John Rudde;[108] but the major one was Edmund Winter's 'craft': on 27 July 1437 at Swaffham an inquisition held by the escheator of Norfolk, John Ropley, discovered that William Mariot was not an Englishman at all but an alien born in Friesland; and that East Beckham was held in chief of the king and that William Mariot had purchased it from John Drew and others without a royal licence.[109] As a result of this disclosure the manor was seized by the crown, and on 11 November 1437 granted for life to Edmund Hampden, esquire of the body to Henry VI. Judge William's counter-attack had been smartly dealt with and looked to have been smashed: Edmund Winter had been able to call up some very big guns indeed.[110]

William, therefore, turned to a bigger: William de la Pole, Earl of Suffolk.

[105] Though, it has to be pointed out, John could be described at various times as merchant, yeoman, franklin, *and* gentleman: *CPR 1436–41*, pp. 8 and 336; *CPR 1441–6*, p. 209; NRO, WKC 1/43/2; *CPR 1467–77*, p. 2.

[106] NRO, WKC 1/43/3, copy of the plea roll. See also above p. 82.

[107] NRO, WKC 1/43/4. [108] NRO, WKC 1/43/10.

[109] William Mariot was obviously not an alien; East Beckham was held of the Earls of Stafford.

[110] *CPR 1436–41*, pp. 99 and 245; NRO, WKC 1/42 is a copy in poor condition of the privy-seal letter to the chancellor to make out the grant to Edmund Hampden in the form of letters patent – the NRO catalogue entry is (or was) entirely wrong. For Edmund Hampden, in 1437 at the start of a staunchly Lancastrian career which was to end at Tewkesbury, see Wedgwood, *Biographies*, pp. 413–14. Big guns, but new-made ones too we might notice.

This was possibly in 1439 rather than in 1438 – 'ii zer and more' from Michaelmas 1436; from this point onwards, it needs to be stressed, it is difficult to be precise about certain dates. Judge William's submission to Suffolk, or a draft of it, survives;[111] perhaps it is to an umpire appointed by Suffolk as, otherwise unaddressed, it ends with William's prayer that he may receive 'that lawe good feyth and conscience requireth after the discrecion and reule of his good maister the Justice arbityour'. Suffolk's award was on the one hand non-committal, on the other favourable to Judge William: let the law take its course, or in John Paston's words, 'he [Suffolk] for the trewth of the mater after the examynaciyon . . . awarded that the seyd Edmund [Winter] xuld no lenger delay the seyd John Clement but sufryn the cuntrie to passyn ther up on'. This was done: 'the seyd assise was a wardyd and fond for the seyd John Clement be fors of the wyche he had jugement for to recover. This was on 10 April 1441.[112] Judgement, however, was one thing, recovery another, especially as it was not only Edmund Winter but also Edmund Hampden from whom East Beckham had to be recovered. It is at this point that Edmund Winter fades from the foreground of the scene of the struggle, and Judge William, as he was forced into bidding merely for custody of East Beckham by the inquest's decision of July 1437, becomes obliged to take a leading role. Two other events propelled him into the very frontline: Joan Mariot died and John Mariot, despite (according to John Paston in WKC 1/43/4) his mother's deathbed charge to him to stick by their agreement with Judge William, turned into the judge's principal antagonist. It is likely that Edmund Winter was the man behind John Mariot, though the Pastons never say so directly; what John Paston did say was that 'John Mariot turnyd all strawnge to the seyd William Paston and was famuliar with hem that be fore tyme were adversarijs to hym and to the seyd Paston in the seyd mater';[113] this suggests John Mariot was Edmund Winter's front man.

Thus, the death of Joan Mariot changed the complexion, if it did not alter the true nature, of the contest over East Beckham. Five years and almost half-way into that contest it becomes ostensibly a straightforward one between Judge William Paston and John Mariot. This was particularly true after 22 February 1440, when Edmund Hampden (no doubt in collusion

[111] NRO, WKC 1/43/10.

[112] NRO, WKC 1/43/4. The judgement is recorded on the dorse of the jury list accompanying the last of the series of writs, which are tied onto the copies of the plea rolls relevant to the case: NRO, WKC 1/43/6. The writ to Sir Roger Chamberlain, the sheriff, was dated 23 March 1441. The justices, William Yelverton among them, met at Hingham in Easter week. Damages were awarded of £10: surely derisory. On the list of potential jurors were a number of other Paston 'friends': Sir John Clifton, Sir Henry Inglose, Henry Grey esquire, Robert Clere esquire, Thomas Brigge of Salle. There were also William Shepherd, soon to be leasing East Beckham from Judge William, and John Grickis, for whom see *Hopton*, *sub* index.

[113] NRO, WKC 1/43/4.

with Edmund Winter) vacated his grant of East Beckham for a more profitable one elsewhere.[114] At once Joan Mariot, or rather Judge William on her behalf, petitioned the king for custody of the manor.[115] 'At once' because Joan asked for custody to be granted to her for three years from 22 February 1440 and because she was dead by the time her son occupied the property, it was claimed, on 1 March 1440.[116]

Judge William and Joan Mariot had not always been in harmony, as one of her two surviving letters to him reveals: 'prayng you at the reuerense of God to hold me excused of the lewde and on-connyng langage the whych I answerd you wyth at youre being at Crowmer.' This may have been in the early days, probably as early as the autumn of 1434, when William was discussing with her his buying East Beckham, for Joan writes apologetically of the 'temptaciones that I have hadde by that same person that I told you of' as cause of her ill-temper, and mentions what looks like a promise William made to her before her friends and neighbours at Cromer that she should lease East Beckham from him.[117] Perhaps it had been Joan's dithering as much as William's lack of urgency which had given Edmund Winter his chance. Thereafter, as together they sought unsuccessfully to shut the stable gate, they probably got on better: she could no longer hesitate between alternatives, he could not be complacent. Now, apparently early in 1440, she was dead. And apparently immediately, John Mariot showed that the Mariot–Paston partnership had been dissolved, that he had other ideas, ideas of his own, or of Edmund Winter's: John's seizure of East Beckham opened the next phase of the struggle.

Or, because the story of the struggle includes many puzzles, was it immediately that John turned his coat, was it on 1 March 1440 that he entered East Beckham, was it in the last week of February 1440 that Joan Mariot died? The answer to all three of these questions has to be no. For one reason: the date of John's seizure of East Beckham, 1 March 1440, is a legal fiction. It predates his actual occupation by twenty months. On 17 March 1445 two declarations were made and sealed, one at East (or perhaps West) Beckham, the other at Cromer, by various folk of those places, including their vicars. It is the Beckham declaration which presently concerns us.[118]

114 *CPR 1436–41*, p. 386. 115 NRO, WKC 1/43/20.

116 As NRO, WKC 1/43/4 says, 'Aftyr whos deth . . . John Mariot . . . entred in the seyd maner.'

117 Davis II, no. 428. As it is 'the first of the documents surviving in this file of letters relating to the manor of East Beckham' (it is numbered *ij*, that numbered *j* has not survived), this should put it early in the sequence. Davis II, no. 429, Joan's other letter (numbered *iij*) I would like to date 30 May 1437, that is after the case of novel disseisin had begun in Autumn 1436 but before the false inquisition of July 1437.

118 It is Bodleian Library, Oxford, Douce Charter 92 (or: volume I, f. 41). I did not notice any endorsement, unlike the other declaration (BL Add. Ch. 14525), which is endorsed 'East Beckham Number 15' and thus must have been in Paston hands. The Douce Charter, therefore, has clearly strayed; the question is when?

The subscribers to it, three of whom, including John Clement of Cromer, Joan Mariot's feoffee in the manor of East Beckham, were also subscribers to the Cromer declaration,[119] stated that after Edmund Winter's seizure of the manor Joan never came to it, that John her son entered it around All Hallowstide or Christmastime after his mother's death and that he enfeoffed Miles Stapleton esquire in it at the end of the following harvest, when Miles Stapleton 'went to the see'. We have, I think, to trust their memories, despite what seems to be a discrepancy; their final declaration was that John Mariot's enfeoffment of Stapleton was the only one they knew of *until* John Clement entered (re-entered rather) and enfeoffed John Damme and others – this we know from the relevant deeds was in June 1442, whereas Miles Stapleton finally went to sea, as one of the sea-keepers appointed by the parliament of Easter of that year, in September 1442.[120] It is the smallest of discrepancies; not to accept it as such would lead us into large ones.[121] Working backwards, therefore, from Stapleton's naval service and his enfeoffment in East Beckham in the summer of 1442, we arrive at November or December 1441 for John's occupation of that property, and some time earlier in that year as the date of Joan's death.[122] Thus, John took his time, or, at any rate, took longer than a week, to turn himself from an ally into an enemy of Judge William's. Why 1 March 1440 was a necessary fiction we will come to shortly; now we must return to Joan's deathbed in 1441. It is with this that the second of the two declarations is concerned.

What Simon Norman, vicar of Cromer, John Clement, Thomas Note (both of Cromer), and William Shepherd of Beckham said and put their seals to on

[119] I presume they went on there later, as the three, with the vicar of Cromer, were the total of subscribers to that declaration, whereas at Beckham there had been twelve, headed by the vicar of West Beckham.

[120] My unpublished Oxford DPhil. thesis, 'Royal Administration and the Keeping of the Seas, 1422–1485', 1963, pp. 213–26, esp. 224: musters taken at last on 13 September. Before going to sea Stapleton made a testament. Among his executors (another of whom was Sir John Fastolf) was Simon Gunnor of Beckham, whom we shall soon encounter playing an important part in the East Beckham affair: PRO, Probate 11/5, f. 125, dated 4 August 1442. For Stapleton see Wedgwood, *Biographies*, pp. 804–5 and above, chapter 2.

[121] There is another discrepancy: John Paston in NRO, WKC 1/43/4 states that it was *after* Judge William had sued out a writ of entry against John Mariot that John enfeoffed Miles Stapleton 'for mayntenaunce'. But the court records fairly unequivocally say that Judge William's suit against John was initiated by him in May 1443. Actually NRO, WKC 1/43/4 is ambiguous and we can, I think, reconcile these differences; it goes on to say that, notwithstanding John's enfeoffment of Stapleton, William 'suyd forth the seyd wryt'. Thus, Judge William may have acquired ('and hym toke') the writ of entry *before* John's enlistment of Stapleton to his cause, but only 'suyd' it 'forth' afterwards. That William had 'take an accion a-yens John Maryete of Crowmer' by 22 October 1442 is certain, for he says so: Davis I, p. 19.

[122] She died between April and September 1441. NRO, WKC 1/43/4 says she died after Join Clement's recovery of East Beckham, which was in April 1441 (NRO, WKC 1/43/6 and above, p. 92). She was dead when John wrote to Judge William on 9 September: Davis II, pp. 10–11 and below, p. 96.

17 March 1445 at Cromer was the following.[123] Firstly, Joan (on her deathbed) asked John Clement to make estate of East Beckham to her and John jointly; she and John would immediately re-enfeoff him and others 'as strong therin as he was to fore' so that they might perform William Mariot's will and her own, and undertake the bargain she had made with Judge William Paston. John Clement said he would think it over and return the next day; then he left – so the rest he could not have witnessed. Secondly, Joan charged John Mariot to pay his father's and her own debts out of the sale of East Beckham; he replied that the debts amounted to more than 300 marks and what would be raised from the sale to and agreement with Judge William would not be sufficient to pay them. Joan, none the less, persisted in her desire that the original agreement with Paston should be kept, saying that if from that there was not enough to pay their debts, John should sell their property in Cromer 'and so content every man as he would answer at the day of doom'. Thirdly, William Mariot, Joan's other son, intervened to point out that by his father's will he ought to have 40 marks[124] from the proceeds of the sale of East Beckham. Joan responded that only after the debts had been paid were the other conditions of the will to be performed 'as far as the money wold stretche'. Joan died on the day all this took place.[125]

This is an important testimony; it reveals the impossible situation John Mariot found himself in on his mother's death in 1441, which was not only that even a 'normal' sale of East Beckham would not have raised much more than what was required to satisfy debts of 300 marks and to allow the two sons £20 or 40 marks apiece;[126] it was also that the legal battle for the estate was consuming that unrealized money with no prospect of victory in sight. By fighting that battle and paying himself for doing so out of the purchase price, Judge William was going to get East Beckham 'cheaply', so long as he

[123] BL Add. Ch. 14525. It is cut off at the foot, but Thomas Note's name is on what has to be, I think, the beginning of a seal tag. [124] £20 has been crossed through.

[125] Here was yet another deathbed where disgruntlement and disagreement, if not disillusion, predominated, of which probably the best example in the Paston letters is not Judge William's deathbed but that of Nicholas Pickering of Filby, Norfolk: Gairdner IV, p. 178. Nicholas' last words to his eldest son William might, however, have been Judge William's: 'But on thyng I shal sey to the; if thou trouble John, thy brother, or ony of myn executores, or cleyme ony more londes or goodys that evere were myne, I shal yeve ye Goddys curse and myn, for thou hast be ever forwarde to me'.

[126] It had cost William Mariot 450 marks in 1415. In 1435 it ought to have been worth less than 20 marks a year: in 1445–6 John Paston said 16 marks (NRO, WKC 1/43/4). Edmund Hampden, however, maintained (Davis II, p. 10) it had been worth 20 marks a year to him, exactly double the value the inquisition of 1432 had set on it: *CPR 1436–41*, pp. 99, 145. It looks as though William Mariot may have had to pay about as much over a twenty-year purchase price as the Pastons may have 'paid' below it. That twenty-year purchase price, of around 380 marks, would just about have failed to pay William and Joan Mariot's debts and provide the two sons with their portions; there would have been no margin out of which to have found something for the maintenance of the two daughters.

did get it and got it before he spent more than the purchase price. John Mariot, on the other hand, was going to get much less than nothing: East Beckham would have gone, his parents' debts would remain. On John Paston's reckoning, five years later it was John Mariot who owed *him* 5 marks.[127] None the less, John Mariot wrote to Judge William on 9 September 1441 professing his readiness to continue the agreement made between William and his mother.[128] If, that is, he was sincere, for the main purpose of his writing was to ask William to send him the 'endenture of owre part that I may know varili qwat zowre trewe bargeyn is ther-in and oure ryght and titil on owr part'. It is revealing of the relationship between William and Joan Mariot that John did not already, his mother having died, have it; how one-sided the whole business had been if William had kept both parts of the indenture of agreement.[129] It is interesting, possibly significant, that neither part of that indenture appears to survive; this is the case also with regard to the agreement drawn up between William Paston and John Mariot in January 1443. Before they arrived at that, however, much was to happen.

In the first place John, whether Judge William sent him the Mariot half of the indenture or not (and not is surely most likely), did not fulfil his fair words of September: two or three months later he occupied East Beckham. He 'seyd he wold havyd and kepe it to his owyn use and that the seyd William Paston xuld never have his bargeyn', John Paston went on,[130] 'contrary to all mater before rehersyd the which mater was knolachid labouryd and purveyd be his assent'.[131] Judge William believed John Mariot had been 'avysyd' to take this course, and we may believe that Edmund Winter was the chief of those who urged him to it. Who did John seize it from? Who in November or December 1441 was in possession of East Beckham? By then Judge William ought to have been: judgement in the assize of novel disseisin, which John Clement had brought against Edmund Winter as far back as November 1436, had been given in Clement's favour

[127] NRO, WKC 1/43/4.

[128] Davis II, no. 431. My reasons for dating this 9 September 1441 (not 1443, as in Davis) are given in the text above. The letter's importance to the Pastons is shown by its survival in the original – the other East Beckham letters are much later copies on a single roll: Davis I, p. 18.

[129] This is a hard letter to get to the bottom of, but, whatever one may make of it, it is clear that John not only did not have the Mariot part of the indenture, he did not even know the terms of his mother's deal with Judge William, or said he did not. Of course, all other documents Judge William had; they were in the deed box.

[130] NRO, WKC 1/43/4.

[131] This does not tally with John Mariot's letter of 9 September. John wrote that he wanted the Mariot portion of the indenture, 'that I may know varili qwat zowre trewe bargeyn is ther-in'; it strikes me as incredible, given, for example, the scene at his mother's deathbed, that he should not have known the terms of the transactions, every detail of them indeed, as East Beckham must have dominated his as well as his mother's life over the previous six years. One of these Johns is a liar.

in April 1441.[132] We know, however, that Clement did not re-enter East Beckham until June 1442, when he handed over to Judge William's feoffees, and, his job at last done, departed from the scene. Was it Edmund Hampden who was still there at the end of 1441? Far more likely that it was Edmund Winter in Hampden's name. Here we have to return to the question of the custody of the manor, a question vexed with problems of backdating.

Apparently Hampden had relinquished East Beckham as long before as 22 February 1440, when he surrendered his grant of it in return for one of an annual £20 out of the royal lordship of Risborough, Buckinghamshire.[133] Joan, as we have observed, petitioned for custody from that date; her petition[134] is undated but has to be from before 20 April 1441, as she states in it that John Clement's assize of novel disseisin against Edmund Winter 'hangith yet undetermined'. At the foot of the petition in another hand are what I take to be the words: 'granted [grunez] Paston'. Which brings us to Judge William Paston's petition for custody of East Beckham. It dates from after 20 April 1441, as it records that John Clement 'by the seid assise recovered the seid manor a geyn the seid Edmund and other', and from after the death of Joan, for it maintains that she died owing over £100 to Judge William. The petition, therefore, must have been composed between April and September 1441, by when we know Joan was dead. It was successful (as the annotations at its foot explain) on 22 March 1442, when Judge William was granted custody of East Beckham, his grant of seven years being backdated to Edmund Hampden's surrender of 22 February 1440.[135] We have also seen that when Judge William went to law against John Mariot in 1443, Mariot's occupation of East Beckham was not dated from November or December 1441, the time of his seizure of the manor, but from 1 March 1440. Why was this? Without wanting to get so deeply into this maze that we may never emerge, an attempt to answer that question has to be made, for it is related to the earlier question of who was actually in possession of East Beckham when John Mariot seized it.

No one at the time seems to have been sufficiently interested to have

[132] NRO, WKC 1/43/6 and above, p. 92. [133] *CPR 1436–41*, p. 386.

[134] NRO, WKC 1/43/20. The schedule of the attached bill, as Joan calls it in NRO, WKC 1/43/20, and which is indeed attached to her petition, is in the name of *John* Mariot.

[135] NRO, WKC 1/43/21, an intriguing document, discussed at length in chapter 1. The petition is a first or second draft made on the dorse of what I interpret as a copy of a letter from Cardinal Beaufort to William, Lord Bardolf, concerning a different matter, though one which was of even greater importance to William Paston: the creation of a manor at Paston. Probably the letter is to be dated to the previous year, 31 May 1440, though it could possibly be of 31 May 1441. One of the two notes at the foot of the draft petition is in a second hand. NRO, WKC 1/43/17 is a copy of the privy-seal writ to the chancellor to issue the letters patent for Judge William's grant; there are jottings at the foot of this document; they appear to be calculations of the date to which the seven-year term of custody will extend. For the enrolled grant, see *CPR 1441–6*, p. 44.

recorded the answer to what for us is a critical question. It was not John Mariot, nor was it Judge William Paston. John Mariot's submission of his case to William, Earl of Suffolk, attempting in 1443 to arbitrate for a second time in this affair, is irritating in its illegibility and its woolly chronology; it mentions three events in the following order: Edmund Hampden had a bill of maintenance against Judge William Paston; John himself sued an attaint (by William's advice) against Edmund Winter; Winter's friends offered money to Joan for East Beckham 'or elles' to have rest and peace. In a final clause (the eleventh of eleven clauses, of which most later ones are unreadable) John says that William was occupying not only East Beckham, but also John's property in Cromer 'and never payed his modir ne hym peny therfor.'[136] Unhelpful as this may be, it restores to our attention the two men, of whom one at least was likely to be 'in control' of East Beckham at the end of 1441: Edmund Hampden and Edmund Winter. Of these two, I fancy, it was Winter who was collecting the rents and enjoying whatever profits there were to be had there. Edmund Hampden, if he ever had been more than a sleeping partner in the whole business, we surely have to assume had pulled out either in February 1440 or some time soon afterwards. It is, it has to be emphasized, an assumption, one of many we have made about the role of this outsider in the affair. If, therefore, it *was* Edmund Winter who was at East Beckham in November–December 1441, might not John Mariot's entry have been arranged between them: another spanner thrown into the legal machine which Judge William was trying to work to his advantage? After all, at that time, although John Clement had been given judgement against Edmund Winter in April 1441, that judgement had not been put into effect. Now yet another occupier would have to be proceeded against; here, once again, was Edmund Winter deploying the delaying tactics at which he was adept.

If we are right about Edmund Winter, then should we go on to presume he had been in possession of East Beckham continuously since December 1434? Perhaps. What, however, is the significance of the back-dating of John Mariot's possession to 1 March 1440 in the case Judge William brought against John in 1443? William claimed that from that very day until the opening of the case on 31 May 1443 John had taken the profits of the property, and he named the sums John had received in that period of three years and three months. A jury later agreed with him, while drastically reducing his figures. Was William, in fact, claiming against Edmund Winter and for the period since Edmund Hampden had departed East Beckham? Or was he simply doing no more than he could attempt at

[136] NRO, WKC 1/43/1. It is written on the reverse of a copy of a plea roll which is unconnected, so far as I can see, with East Beckham.

law, that is sue for the period he had been the (back-dated) custodian of the manor, namely, from 22 February 1440?[137] Was the jury on the other hand, by cutting his figures down to an insignificant size, doing something other than pruning William's pretensions? Was it pointing to another truth, that John Mariot had actually been in possession of East Beckham only from late in 1441?[138] Moreover, was he not in possession only for six months, from November or December 1441 until June 1442, when John Clement entered the manor? Judge William was secure enough by October 1442 to make a lease of the estate for five years to Simon Gunnor, gentleman, and William Shepherd, yeoman.[139] Was his claim against John Mariot false, therefore, at, so to speak, either end? Before irresolution develops into paranoia let us return to what we do know. Or think we know. And move from the mysteries of 1441 into the certainties of 1442.

It was a better year for Judge William Paston, the best since the struggle had begun nearly eight years previously. In March he was granted custody of East Beckham[140] and in June John Clement at last entered the manor as a consequence of the judgement of April 1441.[141] The appropriate legal transfers were made at once. On 3 June John Clement enfeoffed John Damme and others; on 4 June John Damme assigned the estate to a group headed by Sir Roger Chamberlain, a group which included James Gresham and William Cotting; Gresham and Cotting at East Beckham on the following day handed over to Judge William's feoffees proper.[142] Among these were distinguished public figures, William Ayscough, William Yelverton, and John Markham, for instance; the 'working' feoffees among them, however, as other documents make clear,[143] were Philip Berney esquire, Robert Repps, Nicholas Rake, and Robert Crane. John Mariot's response (as we have earlier observed) was to enfeoff Sir Miles Stapleton, probably in August or September 1442, 'and [to have] sent the seyd William Paston word be his wyfe that he had mad a feffamente to one that xuld better dele with hym thanne he cowd.'[144] William's counter was to sue out in the names of Philip Berney and the other 'working' feoffees, the writ of entry against John Mariot. His lease of the manor to Simon Gunnor and William Shepherd on 1 October is, no doubt, a sign of his new confidence. The brief and businesslike

[137] NRO, WKC 1/43/15. Judge William's grant is recited on this copy of the plea roll.

[138] Judge William claimed £20 in lost rents and farms, £10 as profits of the manor, and £40 in damages; the jury awarded him 15 marks, 3s 4d and £5 respectively: NRO, WKC 1/43/15.

[139] Davis I, pp. 18–19; NRO, WKC 1/43/3. [140] *CPR 1441–6*, p. 44.

[141] As, for example, Bodleian Library, Oxford, Douce Charter no. 92 clearly describes it.

[142] BL Add. Ch. 14524; among the witnesses to this were Simon Gunnor and William Shepherd, two men who, being 'on the spot', really knew what was going on and, as we shall see, were probably the main beneficiaries of what one is tempted to give capitals to by this stage, The Battle of East Beckham. And the assignment of 5 June: NRO, Phillipps MS 24. [143] NRO, WKC 1/43/4 and Davis I, no. 10, for example. [144] NRO, WKC 1/43/4.

note to his 'good frende' Philip Berney from London on 22 October also displays, I think, a man who is beginning to believe he is getting the better of things.[145] By early December, and just after he had left London for Norfolk, a letter he received from Thomas West reporting an encounter in the city with John Mariot can only have made him more sanguine. John, he was told, wanted to come to terms, 'and therfore, ser, for the love of God, wyth-in thys vacacion tyme by-twene thys and the next terme he shal be at home at Crowmer, leteth somme on a-boutes yow, a-say yf ze may drawe to some good ende'. After giving other advice, both hopeful and helpful, West ended, 'And by my trawth and he be unresonable we shall bryng hym to reson, wher he will or wyll not.'[146] And so, one way or another, they did.

On 19 January 1443 an understanding was reached and an agreement 'be writyng undyr the seid John Mariot hand' entered into. Its terms were not startlingly different from those agreed between William and Joan Mariot. William was to have East Beckham

> for asmyche as it wer worth in xxti yeer abate therof the seid xl li. and alle odyr mony spent up on the ple for the recovere of the seid maner and all money deliverd to the seid Jone Mariot and John Mariot [to leve by duryng the ple] and xxiiijli.xvs.vijd. the qwyche the seid Jone and John owth to divers persones the qwyche thei had borwyd [to leve by] and whom the seid William Paston hath content at her request.[147]

All, therefore, ought to have been well. It was not. Whether John paid heed to one of the 'many excytours [who] proker [procure] hym rather to harme and frowardnesse the contrarye to your entent', whom Thomas West mentioned in his December letter,[148] or changed his mind yet again because he reckoned, with some justice, that Judge William was getting East Beckham too cheaply,[149] is only to be guessed at. What if William had been a little more generous? But he was not; nor was he conciliatory: in May 1443 his case against John for entering the manor at the close of 1441 went ahead.[150] We do not know why William chose to pursue the case he had initiated the previous summer. Mariot cannot have been in possession – can he?[151] If William was simply being vindictive, that may have been cause

[145] Davis I, no. 10. [146] Davis II, no. 430, to be dated 7 December 1442.

[147] NRO, WKC 1/43/4. The words in square brackets have been crossed through.

[148] Davis II, p. 10.

[149] Thomas West, for example, wrote to William he had 'herd sythen youre departyng that the vicarye of Crowmer came yn yowre name to John Maryete and profered hym ccc marke and lx, and he desyred iiijc marke': *ibid.* One cannot help thinking that John was not being unreasonable; the hard, not to say harsh, bargainer was William Paston.

[150] NRO, WKC 1/43/15.

[151] On his own admission he was not later in the year: NRO, WKC 1/43/20. *But* NRO, WKC 1/43/5 states he was seized of East Beckham in 1445 and had not been dislodged by the verdict in William Yelverton's court of March 1444. NRO, WKC 1/43/4 suggests, on the one hand, that John Mariot had occupied the estate for some time since 1442–John Paston claimed reasonable recompense for the suits John Mariot had brought against him 'and for

enough for John to renege on the January agreement. Unless, of course, he had already done so and William was continuing in May a struggle which he realized was far from over. In a maze, guesswork is no guide.

None the less, it is impossible to dismiss the idea that an opportunity was missed in 1443. By the end of the year, with the case undecided,[152] William, Earl of Suffolk had been called in, or had stepped in, as arbitrator for the second time.[153] On 28 January 1444 James Gresham wrote from London to his master, Judge William; among other more important news he related an encounter with John Mariot. John had been with the Earl of Suffolk, who

> told hym that he must fynde sewerté to abyde his award, whiche he hopeth weel to parfourme, as he seith, and he supposeth that my lord shall write to yow therof; for he seith that he shall a-bide his awarde and supposeth so shall ye, and therfor hym semeth it shuld not nede to sewe forther the proces etc.

Gresham had answered that it was his business, presumably as Judge William's legal agent, 'to sewe the processe', and besides, 'if eende and accorde between yow [William] and hym take ther shall no persone be hurt by the processe'. Gresham went on to inform his master of the next date Judge William Yelverton had set for the hearing of the case, 17 March 1444.[154] Is Judge William's lack of generosity, his want of magnanimity detectable here? Uppermost in John Mariot's mind was that Judge William should not continue the case against him; there is *hauteur* in Gresham's response. There was at any rate no award;[155] but there was a verdict for Judge William Paston in Judge William Yelverton's court.

The verdict on 17 March 1444 was the jury's, but one cannot help thinking that one judge may have done all he could to help another; as

the issuys and profitys of the seid maner sith it was recoveryd be John Clement of the seid Edmund Wynter'; on the other (in the financial calculations on the slip of paper attached to it), it seems to be saying the exact opposite: that John Mariot was owed by the Pastons 90 marks as the issues of the manor. Although John Paston said the manor was only worth 16 marks a year, 90 marks is best understood as five years at 18 marks, which are the terms of the Paston lease to Gunnor and Shepherd of 1 October 1442. Does this mean that this note added at the foot of the 'financial slip' in another hand is to be dated to after October 1447, say to Michaelmas 1448, when John and Agnes Paston were suing Gunnor and Shepherd for payment (for which see below, p. 106)? Yet, why should the Pastons owe to John Mariot the 90 marks they were owed by Gunnor and Shepherd (and which they never received)? Was it because they were legally owed the 90 marks *and* legally owed it to him? Does that imply that John Mariot had recovered East Beckham in Autumn 1445, and thus that the note may be of Autumn 1450? Perhaps some totally other calculation is involved in arriving at the 90 marks. We would seem still to be in the maze.

152 Possibly, therefore, Margaret Paston's first surviving letter to her husband should be dated Trinity Sunday 1443: Davis I, no. 124 (lines 7–9).

153 John Mariot's submission to him (or a copy of it) is, as we have seen, NRO, WKC 1/43/1. By this time, according to John, Judge William was occupying East Beckham and the Mariot property in Cromer.

154 Davis II, p. 13.

155 And so it is not mentioned in John Paston's account of the affair, NRO, WKC 1/43/4.

Agnes Paston recalled many years afterwards:[156] shortly after her husband's death in August 1444,

> cam John Damme and askyd me whyche of the justicys my husbond trusted most, and sayde to me, 'Be ye not remembrid of suche a day my maister helde wyth Maryott at Norwych?' I sayd, 'Yis, for I was ther my-selfe.' He sayd to me my husbond toke a certeyn man a thyng wryten and insealed of my husbondys hande, but what was in ther-in he wyste never.

Yet, as we have seen, the jury (and perhaps the judge too) did not see absolutely eye to eye with William: they did not find John Mariot guilty on every count and they did not give William all the damages he asked for.[157] What Judge William got was East Beckham; as WKC 1/43/4 records it: 'be the weche verdyt the Jugiis consevyed that the seid John Mariot had disesyd the seyd Robert Crane and cofeffes and gaffe Jugement that they sxuld recuver, the wech Jugement was geff in trinite terme [1444]'.[158] This was some time after 11 July;[159] by 14 August Judge William Paston was dead.[160] His death, at the moment of triumph, altered everything.

On his deathbed William intended, so Agnes said, that East Beckham should go to one of his younger sons, William or Clement.[161] If insecure in almost all else, he may at least have felt the Pastons had secured the Beckhams, for Margaret Mautby had brought John Paston West Beckham (or rather, the reversion of it) when they had been married three or four years previously.[162] That marriage had been an integral part of Judge William's endeavours to thrust his family up the social ladder. Paston itself was in Tunstead Hundred, but on the very border of North Erpingham Hundred. The opportunities for William came in that neighbouring hundred; busy as he was to make himself a manorial lord in Paston, it was principally, though not solely, in North Erpingham that the family acquired landed estate. Mautby was in the Hundred of East Flegg and next door to Caister, where another self-made man at this very time was building himself a grand house, from which he was to see himself exercising a paternal lordship within that hundred.[163] Margaret Mautby was related to Sir John Fastolf; there was, therefore, more to be gained from John's marriage to her than manors. But three of these manors were in North Erpingham Hundred: Bessingham, Matlask, and West Beckham. Two others were not far distant: Briston near Saxthorpe, and the manor of Kirkhall in Salle. Judge William

[156] Davis I, p. 48. [157] See above, p. 98.

[158] After 'sxuld recuver', a second hand has completed the sentence; it might be John Paston's. The copies of the relevant plea rolls are NRO, WKC 1/43/15, 16. The other judge was Richard Newton.

[159] See, for example, NRO, WKC 1/43/13: copy of a writ to the sheriff.

[160] He died on 13 August 'at nyght . . . betwixt xj and xij of the clokk': Davis I, p. 47. NRO, WKC 1/43/4 says 14 August. [161] Davis I, p. 44, 46–7. [162] See chapter 4.

[163] Anthony Smith, 'Aspects of the Career of Sir John Fastolf, 1380–1459', unpublished Oxford DPhil. thesis, 1982, esp. pp. 21 and 221, and chapter 7 below.

had acquired Cromer and Gresham in North Erpingham Hundred and Oxnead in South Erpingham Hundred. It may be that by the fifteenth century such men as Sir John Fastolf and William Paston did not think in terms of Hundreds, but considered the scope of their lordship as more notional than that, not circumscribed by administrative boundaries. Nevertheless, a hundred does seem to me to be about the scale on which such men thought of the 'lordship' they were after, Fastolf in East Flegg, Paston in North Erpingham.

There were no challengers to Fastolf in East Flegg; the Pastons in North Erpingham were to have more than one. Edmund Winter was not the most dangerous of these. The dying William Paston may have thought the ten-year battle for East Beckham was over and that he had won for the family another manor in North Erpingham Hundred. He would have been wrong. East Beckham had not been secured, nor had Paston pride of place in North Erpingham and its vicinity yet been achieved. The death of such 'a grete man and a wyse man of the lawe' as Judge William had been rendered the family vulnerable in large matters, as well as small.[164] John Mariot (behind whom perhaps there was still Edmund Winter) was given new hope. The battle continued.

John Mariot was quick to attack. After Judge William's death he 'suyd a writ of a teynt a geyns the seyd Robert Crane and his seid cofeffeys retournable in the comowne place on the morwyn aftyr Sowlemesday that was the terme next after the deth of the seyd William Paston'. His case was as it had always been: that his father and mother had been jointly seized of East Beckham and that on his mother's death the manor descended to him as son and heir; he had been seized until he was disseised by John Clement in June 1442, as a consequence of the verdict of March 1441.[165] The death of Robert Crane seems to have halted the proceedings in this case in Easter Term 1445.[166] As a result John Mariot, apparently in possession of East

[164] Agnes wrote to Edmund (Davis I, p. 27): 'And there is a man in Truntche hyght Palmere to, that hadde of yowre fadre certein londe in Truntche on vij yere ore viij yere agoone for corn, and trwli hathe paide all the yeris; and now he hathe suffrid the corne to ben with-sette for viijs. of rentte to Gymmyngham, wich yowre fadre paide nevere. Geffreie axid Palmere why the rentte was notte axid in myn husbonddis tyme, and Palmere seyde, for he was a grete man and a wyse man of the lawe, and that was the cawse men wolde not axe hym the rentte.' [165] NRO, WKC 1/43/4.

[166] NRO, WKC 1/43/5: copies of the plea roll. I assume that it was in connection with this challenge of John Mariot's that the two declarations (about Joan's deathbed and on the early history of the affair) were made on 17 March 1445, that is, BL Add. Ch. 14525 and Bodleian Library, Douce Ch. 92, for which see above, p. 93. I suppose it is coincidental that this was exactly a year after the verdict in William Yelverton's court. Simon Gunnor's absence as a witness from these declarations is to be noted; it is not a surprise, considering what was being planned between John Mariot and him. It is less likely that the declarations were made in connection with the case of the East Beckham deed box, which came on, between William Paston's executors and John Mariot, in Trinity term 1445, as that case related to an event of January 1435: NRO, WKC 1/43/9.

Beckham,[167] changed his tactics: he sued against Simon Gunnor, William Paston's leasee of the manor, and in what was clearly a collusive as well as a counterfeit action[168] Simon's attorney appeared in court in November 1445 'and be assent suffryd the seyd John Mariot to recover'.[169] There John Paston, with so much else to occupy him in the years immediately after his father's death, left or was obliged to leave the vexatious matter of East Beckham, for the even more troublesome matter of Gresham was about to take its place. As he put it in bringing to an unsatisfactory close the story (so far), in WKC 1/43/4:

> John Paston, because that the seyd John Mariot and his counsell have so sclaundrid the parte of the seid John Paston that is trowth to be on trew and colouryd her owyn parte be sotyll menys that makit sum persones to be leve that herd never bothe partis that troweth wer ontrowth in this mater, tarijth and a bydyth tyme that his parte may be know swech as it js.

There was no disguising his defeat. John Mariot was the winner.[170]

Judge William's death had undone all. John Paston went on (in WKC 1/43/4) to draw up the elaborate balance sheet for East Beckham. It is testimony to his impotence. Neither estate nor remuneration were to be his – ever. Not until 1503 was John Paston III to enjoy the profits of East Beckham, almost seventy years after Judge William thought he had got control of that estate: this concluding part of what is beginning to look like another saga of tenacity we shall embark on in a moment. It may be worth pausing here to examine briefly the financial calculations of WKC 1/43/4 before we take leave of that document.

These calculations take as their starting point the Paston–Mariot

[167] *Ibid.* – if I have read it correctly.

[168] NRO, WKC 1/43/4. 'Simond is and alwey hath be of covyne and counseyl with the seyd John Mariot', that document states. Perhaps the 'alwey' is an exaggeration, though, as Simon appears never to have paid a penny of his five-year farm (for which see below, p. 106), it may not be. The action was a 'cui in vita', properly 'sur cui in vita', according to Jowitt's *Dictionary of English Law*.

[169] NRO, WKC 1/43/4; NRO, WKC 1/43/14, copy of the plea roll of the Michaelmas term 1445. John Paston in NRO, WKC 1/43/4 confuses November 1444 and November 1445. He puts everything into the Autumn after Judge William's death; on first sight this makes his 'morwe after Sowlemess day *last pasid*' hard to interpret when dating the whole document, as it is the only evidence within it (and without it) for a fairly accurate date. It must, however, mean after November *1445*.

[170] He also won his case against Agnes and John Paston for wrongful retention of the 'pixidis' of East Beckham deeds. Joan had handed this over to Judge William on 6 January 1435 (see above, p. 89). This case, initiated by John Mariot in Trinity term 1445, was brought to an end by a jury finding that it had not been given to William for his use and that it was improper for him to retain it. He was fined £50 and 5 marks for expenses; damages were set at 400 marks if the chest was not returned to John Mariot. A note following the recording of this verdict suggests that the Pastons did not pay: in year 28 (Henry VI) John Paston 'non dam' etc. One of those hostile jurors was Simon Gunnor; another was Edmund Buckenham. For this see NRO, WKC 1/43/9, especially the dorse.

agreement of 29 January 1443, which confirmed Joan Mariot's offer to Judge William (after Edmund Winter had occupied East Beckham in December 1434) that he might have the manor £40 'withjn the prise'. Before Edmund Winter's intervention it had only been £5. The 'prise', John Paston maintained in WKC 1/43/4, ought to be no more than 320 marks, as the 'seyd maner is not worth clerli be yer xvj mark'. The agreement also allowed to Judge William money given by him to Joan and John Mariot and to those from whom they had borrowed; this amounted, according to John Paston, to £104 8s 4d. Finally there was what William had spent on legal action; here John Paston was eloquent:

> And the expensys the qwyche the seid William Paston hath spent up on the seid pleys and in odyr plez be her assent in persute and diffence of ix or x accyions that wer sewyd atwix the seid Edmund Wyntir and hem and the seid John Clement in the live of the seyd Joone of the wyche ij wer speciall assises that indured ij yeer and half and in iche of hem wer viij speciall sescions of the Justices of those assises at Lynne and Hengham in the seid counte of Norffolk and in tweyn of the seid accyions the seid Joone and John wer condempnyd in an C.mark and xl li, wer of the seid William Paston dischargid hem drawith to the summe of lxxj li. vijs. jd.

Together these three sums (£40, £104 8s 4d and £71 7s 1d) amounted to just over 320 marks. Thus, John Mariot, it seemed, actually owed John Paston a few marks. However, William Paston had received money from others 'toward the helpyng of the seid plez'; John Mariot had a record of this and John Paston maintained he was ready to pay it, or rather to subtract it from the money laid out by his father. On the other hand, £20 was owing 'odir personys that in the lif of the seid Joone labouryd in the seid accyions for her avayll not takyng her reward be cause of the poverte of the seid Joone but grauntyd her to a byde til the ple wer determinyd to the end the wiche reward the seid Joone in her life grauntyd to pay'. Moreover, John Paston continued, there was 'his reasonable recompens after conscience demyd' for the suits brought against him by John Mariot as well as the issues of East Beckham since John Clement's recovery of it from Edmund Winter in 1442. As WKC 1/43/4 ends, the reader's impression (as John Paston intended it should be) is distinctly of the high price the Pastons had been obliged to pay for a manor which was not yet theirs, a price far in excess of 320 marks.

Accompanying WKC 1/43/4, that is folded in with it but not attached to it, is a slip of paper headed, 'This is to be abated of the price of Bekham maner.' It may be in John Paston's (early) hand. The notes down its left-hand side and at the foot are in a different hand; they certainly are later, and pose a particular problem to which we will shortly come. The main text is of the individual items comprising the lump sums of £104 8s 4d and £71 7s 1d, which (as we have seen in WKC 1/43/4) were what William Paston had spent on the Mariots and in the legal battle for East Beckham. These need not detain us. What must is the one new figure added by the second hand at the foot and the final reckoning it leads to there. The figure is 90 marks; the shorthand preceding it appears to be saying that these are (or ought to be) the issues of East Beckham for the term of the lease to Simon Gunnor and William Shepherd – which had been at 18 marks a year for five years from 1 October 1442.[171] This 90 marks is then set against what the Pastons have paid out or are allowed, that is £215 15s 5d or 323 marks 8s 10d (*sic*: actually 9d) – 3 marks 8s 9d more than the price of East Beckham. Hence (the very last line records) owed to John Mariot are 86 marks 4s 7d. This calculation is troublesome as well as curious. It is particularly puzzling in the light of John's statement in WKC 1/43/4 about the issues of the manor since John Clement's recovery: that they were 'owing' to him. Perhaps the rationalization should be: Gunnor and Shepherd owed 90 marks to John Paston for their five-year lease and he owed that 90 marks to John Mariot – because East Beckham was still his and not yet legally the Pastons'. What Mariot might then owe Paston out of the issues of East Beckham since John Clement's recovery would be a matter for negotiation on the basis of who had been in control of East Beckham between that date, June 1442, and the date of the conclusive agreement WKC 1/43/4 somewhat wistfully envisaged.

What this vexing calculation more securely indicates is a date later than 1445 or 1446 for its inclusion with the original financial statement. The 90 marks has to be related to Gunnor and Shepherd's 90 marks. For this they were sued by Agnes Paston, John Paston, William Bacton, and John Damme, William Paston's executors, probably in Michaelmas term 1448, after they had failed to pay the last instalment, due on 15 March 1448, as they had failed to pay all the others.[172] No doubt, as part of this case, an inquiry was initiated into who had occupied East Beckham since Edmund Hampden had vacated it on 22 February 1440. Well might that question be asked. To it no answer survives, possibly because the original writ to the sheriff of Norfolk was 'mys mad'.[173] By 1448 John Paston was in the thick of

[171] What it actually says is (I think): 'un[acum] rece[ptis] t[a]m[en] de exit[ibus] lxxxx marks'.

[172] NRO, WKC 1/44/3. Simon Gunnor of East Beckham was a gentleman, William Shepherd of West Beckham a yeoman.

[173] NRO, WKC 1/44/1. This intriguing document is a copy of the royal writ. On its dorse is a letter, or draft of a letter, in English, explaining why the writ is 'mys mad'. The date of the writ would seem to be Michaelmas 1448, the draft letter is later, apparently a good deal later. Professor Norman Davis thought the 'hand could be James Gloys'. It would be of value for a legal historian to decipher the letter, with its analysis of the errors of the writ, the writ's subsequent history, and what might be done with it. The letter ends 'reward hym [Crosse, probably the under sheriff] for his labore'. Professor Davis considered the letter's heading 'To James Gresham' to be in John Paston's hand. John Paston's letter to John Damme (Davis 35, the last of the file of the East Beckham letters, number *viii*) might date from this time, 1448, rather than from 1445–6, even if 1448 is the last of a series of dates I have conjectured for it. It does, however, seem to have some connection with NRO, WKC 1/43/4 – or does it?

another fight, for his manor next door to East Beckham: Gresham. Nine days before the old enemy, Edmund Winter, died on 26 February 1448,[174] a new one had arisen: on 17 February 1448 Sir Robert Hungerford, Lord Moleyns, had seized Gresham.[175] Perhaps forced to postpone, eventually to cancel, his campaign for East Beckham because of this direct and far more serious attack on a neighbouring front – almost, we might say, his centre front – John Paston, for whom sympathy is not easy to find, might this once draw it out of us. He was beset with problems. Discovering among Moleyns' allies, Simon Gunnor, John Mariot, and (to cap it all) John Winter, Edmund's son and heir, may not have been a surprise to him but must have further embittered an already hardbitten young man. He was fighting for his inheritance against a host of enemies.

On Sunday 24 November 1448, for instance, Mariot and Gunnor dined with John Partridge, who was occupying the Paston house at Gresham for Lord Moleyns and who had there 'grete junkeryes and dyneres'. After evensong, presumably in Gresham church, Simon Gunnor and Margaret Paston exchanged sharp words. A few days later Mariot offered John Damme some more 'stately langage'. It must have been salt rubbed in their wounds for the Pastons to have Mariot (and Gunnor for that matter) lording it at Gresham as well as up the road at East Beckham. Mariot and his fellowship's 'meche grette langage' may have been sweet to him, it would have been sour indeed to John and Margaret.[176] The following February Lord Moleyns himself came into Norfolk; he spent Shrovetide at 'John Wynterys plase', Town Barningham, bordering Gresham to the south.[177] When and why and how they all departed is not certain; they had gone by 1 March 1451.[178]

Simon Gunnor might have been a better friend to the Pastons than he was. His father William Gunnor's soul was one of the many – actually the last in a long list – Sir John Fastolf in his will of June 1459 wished prayers to be said for.[179] William and his wife Cecily held the manor of Isaacs at East Beckham.[180] It may have been Cecily's; she did not die until 1465, when Simon, her son and heir, inherited her lands.[181] Simon Gunnor, may not, therefore, simply have resented William Paston's 'purchase' of the Mariots' manor in East Beckham in the mid-1430s as the 'muscling in' of a bigger man than himself, he may have feared, either then or later, that his mother too might be persuaded to part with what was probably his entire

[174] His *inquisition post mortem*: PRO C139/130/4. [175] Davis I, p. 51.

[176] Davis I, p. 226; II, pp. 29–30. Gunnor was still full of 'right gret langage' in March 1451: Davis I, p. 140.

[177] Davis II, p. 228, cf. (the following year) Davis I, p. 237. That March (of 1450) the reeds cut at Gresham were 'karyid to Mariottys plase att Bekkam': *ibid.* [178] Davis II, p. 64.

[179] Gairdner III, p. 157. [180] Manor Court Roll, NRO, WKC 2/58.

[181] *CFR 1461–71*, pp. 15, 175.

inheritance. His neighbour, John Mariot, got his support perhaps because Simon saw Isaacs as the next domino to fall. By 1449 he had become bailiff of North Erpingham Hundred and was able to be officially obstructive towards the Pastons on matters other than Gresham, notably in the vividly described Roughton Court episode of 1 March 1451, after which he had to spend the night at Felbrigg Hall guarded from James Gloys' wrath by forty of Lady Felbrigg's tenants, who the following day escorted him home.[182] His opposition to John Paston continued throughout the 1450s, so much so that Friar Brackley, John's great friend, included him on his list of October 1460 of those East Anglians whom the new government ought to arrest and imprison in the Tower or Newgate.[183] Eventually it was John Paston who landed in prison, the Fleet Prison, in 1465. It is odd to find him there with Simon Gunnor on his mind. In one of the most frequently cited passages of any letter in the Paston collection, John asked Margaret to 'send me hedir ij elne of worsted for doblettes to happe me this cold wynter' (it was only 20 September). He goes on, typically, to give more precise, even pedantic instructions, 'for I wold make my doblet all worsted for worship of Norfolk rather thanne like Gonnores doblet.'[184] What should we make of this? Was Gunnor noted for his dowdy doublets?

Another glimpse, at about the same time, displays Simon as thwarted social climber rather than as the aggrieved father he at first sight appears. His daughter, Cecily, he had married to the Norfolk gentleman, Robert Mortimer, in 1458.[185] Robert was elderly: he claimed a few years later to be

[182] Davis I, p. 227; Davis II, pp. 64–8. He appears to have been bailiff of the Hundred as late as 1461: Davis I, p. 43. If he was undersheriff of Norfolk in 1450–1 another bailiff was appointed, for in James Gloys' account of the Roughton Court affair Gloys took with him to confront Gunnor 'the baly of the hundred': Davis II, p. 65.

[183] Davis II, pp. 126, 164; Gairdner III, pp. 133, 227–8.

[184] Davis I, p. 140. Margaret promised him the worsted in her reply of 27 September (*ibid.*, p. 327): 'Item, I have do spoke for yowr worstede, but ye may not have it tylle Halowmesse; and thane I am promysyd ye challe have as fyne as maye be made. Richard Calle challe bryng it up wyth hym.' When the Pastons' old enemy, John Heydon, acquired the former Garney and Fastolf manor of Loundhall in Saxthorpe from William Wainfleet in 1472 he made Simon Gunnor his steward. Simon did not take the position for the fee – it was only 5s. a year. He was still steward in 1481, but had ceased to be so the following year when he was coroner of the county: NRO, Saxthorpe, Loundhall Manorial Accounts, NRS 18322 (1474–5), 15854 (1479–80), 15855 (1480–1), 15856 (1482–3), 15857 (1484–5); Roger Virgoe, 'An Election Dispute of 1483', *BIHR*, 60 (1987), p. 41. It is a measure of the division within the Paston family (see chapter 6) that Agnes and her son William in 1479 used Simon Gunnor as an attorney in their contest with John Paston II: Bodleian Library, Norfolk Charters 6, and below, p. 198.

[185] For Robert Mortimer see, for example, Davis I, nos. 5, 42 and II, no. 880. In 1451 he was reported as one who had suffered under the Duke of Suffolk's regime, and in 1452 was one of the 'jentilmen of the shyere' outraged by the assault on John Paston at Norwich by Charles Nowell and other ruffians of the Duke of Norfolk. I take it that he was of the cadet line of the Mortimers of Attleborough: Blomefield I, p. 346.

greatly aged, impotent, and bedridden, and he died between April 1465 and April 1467.[186] It was evidently a mismatch.[187] He and Cecily became estranged. Simon, having paid out a good deal to get such a husband and his property for his daughter, found the manor of Barnham Broom, which Robert had settled on himself, Cecily, and their heirs and also had leased to Simon – for Simon had undertaken to provide food, fuel, and living accommodation for Cecily during Robert's lifetime, a strange arrangement, but then it was an unlikely marriage – discovered that Barnham Broom was being denied to him. Moreover, as Robert had granted it to others, it looked as though it would be lost to Cecily also. Robert denied the terms of the marriage agreement: he had had nothing to do with its making or sealing. John Pampying, coincidentally a gentleman servant of John Paston's , was called as a witness. Presumably his deposition was decisive. The covenant of marriage shown to him in Chancery he declared he himself had written in John Grosse's house in Norwich, he had seen Robert seal it, and he had heard him agree to all its conditions.[188] Simon appears to have specialized in leases. It was to him that Roger Townshend leased none other than East Beckham in 1476. To discover how Townshend came to be in a position to do this we must return to the Pastons and John Mariot.

John Mariot's albatross was his father's debts. If he ever paid these, he incurred others, no doubt in doing so. He was taken to court not only by William Paston.[189] In 1444 Thomas Chambre, Margaret Paston's step-father-in-law,[190] sued him for £20 he had lent John at Bromholm in 1436.[191] John was also in debt to a merchant of York and a gentleman of Aldeburgh.[192] One of his debts, of £16, was to a certain Thomas Thorndon. It was owed in 1443; it was still owing in 1467; John Paston II paid it for

[186] His will is NRO, NCC Reg. Jekkys, f. 59. It is dated 28 April 1465 and was proved 11 April 1467. He does seem to have been in reduced circumstances, probably living at John Paynett's house (in Norwich?), for John is one of his two executors, and his only bequests to individuals are to Matilda, John Paynett's wife (*inter alia*, 'a coverlyght of worsted'), to Agnes Gowle, John's servant (*inter alia*, brass candlesticks and a pewter saltcellar), and to Isabel, another servant of John's (a pair of blankets and a coverlet). And, although he left 6s 8d to the church at Barnham Broom, he desired burial wherever God disposed. His other executor was Edmund Buckenham, one of his feoffees for Barnham Broom; to him Robert left his 'prucechist ligat cum ferro et meum primarium'. And that is all his will consists of.

[187] Cecily might have been less than twenty: Simon's father William was alive in 1431; Simon's mother died in 1465; Simon first appears in the 1440s; he left Isaacs to his son and heir, Richard, some time in Henry VII's reign (according to Blomefield IV, p. 289).

[188] This case is in Early Chancery Proceedings, PRO, C1/28/248–53. Pampyng's deposition is no. 248. For him (in brief) see Davis I, p. lxxvii. John Grosse was one of Robert Mortimer's feoffees.

[189] For a debt of 25 marks in 1446: NRO, WKC 1/44/2, copy of the plea roll of the Easter term.

[190] See, for instance, Davis II, p. 6.

[191] NRO, WKC 1/43/18, copy of the plea roll. Thomas' attorney was James Gresham.

[192] *CPR 1436–41*, pp. 8, 336; *CPR 1441–6*, p. 209.

him in 1469.[193] John Mariot's burden at last became too much for him; the Pastons relieved him of it and of East Beckham.

The final negotiations opened in spring 1467;[194] they reached the decisive stage in summer 1469. Richard Calle was the negotiator. In May 1469 he wrote fairly sharply to John Paston II,[195] the gist of his courteous rebuke being to leave Mariot to him: 'I schall assay what I can doo and sende you worde; for it were ryght necessary that ye were throwh with hym for he is not trusty nor just in hes promes but leggeth many thynges and all is but forto delay the tyme.' There were other obstacles besides Mariot's hesitations: first, East Beckham had to be sued 'out of the Kynges hande';[196] secondly, James Andrew, the only surviving feoffee of John Mariot's, had to be 'brought round';[197] thirdly, an annuity to John Mariot and Elizabeth, his wife, was to be paid;[198] fourthly, there was the question of the terms under which John and Elizabeth should go on living at East Beckham; fifthly, where were the Pastons to get the money from to pay off John Mariot and to purchase East Beckham; sixthly, what were Richard Calle and Margery Paston up to; and finally, would the Duke of Norfolk capture Caister? For, as the summer of 1469 turned into autumn, this became the unlikeliest of times for the family to be completing the acquisition of East Beckham. In fact, Richard Calle was able to report on 3 July 1469,[199] his last letter before the world turned topsy-turvy later that month for Edward IV, for the Pastons, and for him, that he had 'ben at Bekham and . . . aggreed with Mariot dettours' and had formally entered the property:

And so I have taken an open astate in the maner of Bekham, accordyng to your desire. I have had moche payne to brynge Mariot and enspeciall his wyf, for be my feythe she wolde not out of the howse when that I schulde take an astate. I was entretyng of hir a our and more, and so with fayer speke I brought her out, and with money weche I toke her at that tyme made her the better willed etc.

[193] *CPR 1441–6*, p. 209; *CPR 1467–77*, p. 2; Davis II, p. 398: John Paston had 'for-gevenes of cs. of the seide xvj li, weche is to your avantage and not to Maryottes'.

[194] Davis II, pp. 380, 383.

[195] John, as was his nature and breeding, had been open-hearted. That was not to his hard-pressed land agent's liking: Davis II, p. 396, lines 47–64.

[196] Davis I, p. 396. I assume the manor had been 'legally' in royal hands since the inquisition's decision of July 1437; that verdict had not been traversed.

[197] By this time John Paston II had 'the deed weche James Andrwes sealed': Davis I, p. 396. He may have had to take him to chancery in order to get it: PRO, C1/10/219. It features among the documents transferred to Roger Townshend when East Beckham was mortgaged to him in November 1469: Davis I, p. 411.

[198] Evidently one of the first issues to be concluded in 1467, as in this letter (Davis II, p. 396) Richard Calle says that Mariot had received his annuity for the year, Michaelmas 1467 – Michaelmas 1468. It was for 10 marks: Davis I, p. 411.

[199] Davis II, p. 398. It was his last action (for some time) in Paston employment; typically, it was constructive.

Thereafter, the sky fell in. The king was captured by the Earl of Warwick after the battle of Edgecote, Caister was besieged and taken by the Duke of Norfolk, the Pastons discovered that Margery was married to Richard Calle and would not be separated from him. Margery was turned out by her mother and Richard was dismissed. By October they were together at the Benedictine nunnery of Blackbrough near King's Lynn.[200]

It was now John Paston III who had to bring the East Beckham affair to a conclusion. John Mariot's sprawling indebtedness was still causing problems.[201] In January 1470 John Heydon would not surrender a deed until he received £30 Mariot owed him and in May John Paston III wrote that he could not pay Mariot's creditors until he had collected more cash from Paston tenants.[202] Raising the money to pay those creditors and John Mariot himself was complicated. Early on in the negotiations Margaret Paston had been urged by John Paston III to contribute; her plate was to save both Mariot and East Beckham: 'And as for Beckham, I warant and ye wyll send the plate whyche ye and I comond of for to helpe to paye hys dettys and for to swe forthe for hys jugement thys terme, it shall neythyr be morgagyd nor sold.' It looks as if the Pastons' last campaign for East Beckham may have begun as a now-or-never rescue operation: John Mariot had to be bailed out or East Beckham would be lost forever.[203] Margaret certainly lent £5: Calle was repaying her part of it in May 1469.[204] Possibly Margaret's money (or her plate) helped them out at this critical stage. By autumn 1469, however, they were obliged to look beyond their own resources. The clever lawyer and sharp moneylender who saw them through was yet another East Anglian making his rapid way upward in local society: Roger Townshend. This was the first occasion of many that Townshend loaned the Pastons money; his security and price on those occasions, as on this, was a mortgage.[205] The mortgage of East Beckham

[200] Davis I, p. 549. I had missed this interesting fact, and thus omitted it from 'Pastons Revisited', pp. 31–4. The nuns made Calle their receiver in 1470 (Rev. A.H. Cooke, 'Five Compotus Rolls of Blackburgh Nunnery', *Norfolk Archaeology*, 22 (1924), p. 84).

[201] In a letter to his brother, almost certainly written in October (Davis I, no. 336), John Paston III reports at length on his dealings with John Mariot. He had not mastered the situation: 'Item, I cannot redyly tell yow what ye be endettyd for John Maryot, wher-for I send yow the copy of the byll of hys dettys closyd her-in.' Richard Calle's precipitate departure had left confusion behind it: see also John Paston II on 15 September (*ibid.*, p. 407), Margaret Paston in the last week of September (*ibid.*, p. 347), John Paston III on 5 October (*ibid.*, p. 548). Both Margaret and John Paston III reported Richard's readiness to return to Paston service: 'and as for hys servyse, then shall no man have it be-for yow and ye wyll. I her not spek of non othyr servys of no lordys that he shold be in' (*ibid.*, p. 549).

[202] *Ibid.*, pp. 552, 557. See also 'Sandyr Fastolf' and his East Beckham monetary difficulties in December 1469: *ibid.*, p. 550. They were still continuing in February 1472: *ibid.*, p. 363. He appears to have been either a tenant or a bailiff who had not discharged arrears owing to the sheriff. This suggests that at some time in the years between 1444 and 1469 the Crown was in receipt of the issues of the manor.

[203] *Ibid.*, p. 536. Unfortunately, an undated letter.

[204] Davis II, p. 395.

was sealed between him and John Paston II on 6 November 1469. In the form of an indenture of sale, it recited that John Paston II had sold to Roger Townshend, gentleman, for 100 marks the manor of East Beckham and other properties thereabouts which he had purchased from John Mariot the elder of East Beckham. Almost all of the 100 marks John had received. He had made an enfeoffment to Roger and his feoffees and had handed over the documents relating to his recent purchase. Roger stated his readiness to honour John's grant of an annuity of 10 marks to John Mariot and

[205] For an earlier and too brief discussion of this, see *Hopton*, pp. 242–3. The last sentence of note 330 is being fulfilled here. The recent discovery in the attics of East Raynham of papers relating to the first Roger Townshend will, I gather from Diana Spelman, confirm our impression of him as being as sharp in the money market as he was in the law courts. Among those papers of Lord Townshend is the Townshend Cartulary (Raynham box 49, Stibbard and Ryburgh) where on f. 31 is the contract between Thomasin Hopton and Roger Townshend for his marriage to her daughter Eleanor. It is dated 28 November 1467. Eleanor's marriage portion was 450 marks: John Hopton was to pay 400 marks at 50 marks a year (which he duly did: *Hopton*, p. 243), Thomasin 50 marks, which John was not to know of. John was also not to be told of Thomasin's provision of dresses and other clothing for Eleanor. The contract is worth giving in full. For it and this transcription I am deeply grateful to Diana Spelman.

These be the frendly communications appoynte covenantes and agrementes hadde betwen Thomesyn, the wyff of John Hopton esquier, and Roger Tonnesend the Saterday after Seynt Andrew the VII yer of Kyng Edward the IIIIth, at Wyssett in the conte of Suff, for and upon maryage be ye grace of God to be had betwen the seyd Roger and Elianor, douter of the seid Thomesyn.

Fyrst, that the seyd Roger schall have 450 marc of lawful mony of Englond to be payyd in the forme folwyng, that is to sey 50 marc at the fest of Candelmesse nexte insuyng and 50 marc at the seid feste nexte ensuyng and so forth 50 marc yerly at the seid feste unto the summe of 450 marc plenrly [plainly] payed and content. For wheche 400 marc well and truly to be payed to the seid Roger and his assigns, the seid John Hopton shall fynde sufficient suerte to the seid Roger as he thenketh resonabyl, as the seyd John ys agreabyl etc. And as the 50 marc residue, the seid Thomesyn graunteth to pay to the seid Roger and that the seid John her husbond schall not know of and the seyd Roger to her etc. upon her promysse etc.

Ferthermore the seid Thomesyn, be the ful assent of her seid husbond, graunteth to the seid Roger and Alienor londes and tenementes to the yerly value of 20 marc yerly above all charges and reprises, to have and to hold to the seid Roger and Alianor and to the issue of therto bodyes be goten after the dissese of the seid John and Thomesyn savying the revercion to the seid Thomesyn.

Also the seid Thomesyn graunteth to make the chaumber of the seid Roger worth an 100 marc of good penyworthes as schall plese the same Roger etc. And wher that the seid Thomesyn graunteth to arraye the seid Alienor in gownes, kyrtelles, tyres, beys and all other arayment as the seid Roger schall be pleased and bothe he and the seid Alienor cause to pray for the seid Thomesyn, and but the seid John Hopton schal knowe but of a chaumber and arayment etc.

And moreover that the seid John Hopton and Thomesyn schal bere porvey fynde and ordeyn all manner of costes charges and expens for of and aboute the seid mariage etc.

For the weche, the seid Roger schall cause a sufficient estate of londes and tenements to the yerly valew of 40 marc above all charges to the seid Roger and Alienor and to the issu of ther to bodyes begoten, the revercion to the heires of the seid Roger.

And ferthermor, the seid Roger is a greed that the seid Alienor schall have a jointour in tayll in sweche londs and tenementes schall be bout and purchased with the seid 450 marcs.

Elizabeth, his wife, and John's arrangement with John and Elizabeth whereby they 'shuld have her dwellyng with-in the mote of the seid manoir'. He also agreed to return the property if John paid him 100 marks before 1 November 1470.[206]

John never did. In November 1474 he redeemed Sporle, the other Paston property which had been mortgaged to Townshend, but remained in debt to him; as for East Beckham, John wrote to his mother, 'he spekyth no-thyng comfortably ther-in; what he wyll do can I nott seye'.[207] What Roger did on 23 December 1476 was to lease the estate to none other than Simon Gunnor. The lease was for seven years from the previous Michaelmas at a rent of 15½ marks a year. Simon undertook to repair the barn, stable, dovehouse, and a house called the Garner; these buildings stood outside the moat. John Mariot, perhaps by this time the younger,[208]

> shall have and occupye all the closes that aioyne next to the seid maner that ys to sei the close rown a bowt the mote the wodeclos and the North pitill with all the houses with in the mote and with owt, stondyng with in the court of the same, with the fisshyng in the mote the dovehous and clos on the westside of the chirche only excepte, and reserved to the seid Symond duryng the seid terme, so that the seid John yeld or paye to the seid Symond . . . yerely as moche mony as ony other man wele geve there fore.[209]

Yet, if it looked in the 1470s as if the manor might be slipping away from the Pastons, that a later judge of common pleas was to reap where an earlier one had expensively sown, this was not to be the final outcome. John Paston III was tenacious,[210] and from 1485 his position in East Anglian society was secure: after more than a generation of troubles a Paston once more had 'clout', could exert influence, and (possibly decisive in this matter) had a close friend who was one of the foremost men of law of the day, James Hobart.[211] Moreover, Sir Roger Townshend died in 1493; his son, also Roger, was a less formidable figure. Thus, on 6 February 1503, James

[206] Davis I, no. 246. John Paston III sent off the indenture to his brother on 1 March 1470: *ibid.*, pp. 413, 556. Perhaps it went into Sir John's 'bagge wyth evydence off Est Bekkham' in his 'sqare trussyng coffre': *ibid.*, p. 444. That Sir John kept the East Beckham title deed shows the indenture with Townshend was indeed a mortgage. At Christmas time 1469 John Paston III had gone with a man of Townshend's to take 'possessyon bothe, for lesse suspessyon': *ibid.*, p. 551.

[207] *Ibid.*, p. 477. For Sporle, soon to be mortgaged to Townshend for the second time, see *Hopton*, pp. 193 and 242.

[208] The last reference to John Mariot in the Paston letters is in a letter of John Paston III to his elder brother of 8 July 1472; it epitomizes that beleaguered man's life: 'Item, as for John Maryot, I have sent to hym for the xls., but I have non answer': Davis I, p. 576.

[209] NRO, WKC 1/45/1. This document is the last of the Ketton-Cremer collection relevant to the story.

[210] Professor Davis' reflections on the date of the East Beckham letter file suggest this: Davis I, p. 18.

[211] For James Hobart and his friendship with John Paston see *Hopton*, pp. 186–93.

Hobart, the king's attorney and another East Anglian sergeant at law, John Yaxley,[212] made an award: John Paston III was to have East Beckham; he was to pay Roger Townshend £100 for it and 'ten mark besides the seid cli. because th'arrerages have ben long in the tenauntes handes'.[213] Ten days later Roger Townshend, Robert Le Strange, and William Eyre, gentlemen, entered into an obligation to Sir John Paston to pay him £200 if Townshend did not make over the estate before the coming Whit Sunday. As the seals by Townshend, Le Strange, and Eyre have been cut off (leaving only their signatures), I take it that the condition of the obligation was fulfilled and it was in this fashion voided. John Paston III recovered East Beckham.[214]

1434–1503: a seventy-year struggle for a property worth between 10 and 20 marks per annum.[215] How much did the Pastons pay for it? Not less than 600 marks (£400) is some sort of an answer.[216] At no time was it even suggested that the manor was worth 30 marks per annum. Even if we calculate that it may have been worth 20 marks, the Pastons gave thirty

[212] For whom see *ibid.*, p. 194.

[213] Davis II, pp. 612–13. The compensation John Paston had to pay for the arrears evidently had been debated; the decision was in his favour, for Professor Davis informs us, the 'ten' is 'interlineated above xxv cancelled'. See also *Hopton*, pp. 242–3 for this award.

[214] BL Add. Ch. 17743, 16 February 1503. Clearly, Sir John kept the obligation, as he did the award: see also now the appendix to this chapter on page 115. For a little of William Eyre see *Hopton*, pp. 194–5. He lived at Great Cressingham, Norfolk, so was another East Anglian; as, of course, was Robert Le Strange of Hunstanton.

[215] In the early years of the fifteenth century it would certainly seem to have been worth 20 marks per annum: the Mariots paid 450 marks for it in 1415 (PRO, SC8/128/6390; NRO, WKC 1/43/10). Edmund Hampden also maintained it was worth that *c.* 1440 (Davis II, p. 10), even though the escheator had valued it at only 10 marks a year in 1437 (*CPR 1436–41*, p. 99): patently a deliberate undervaluation. John Paston in 1445–6 said it was 'not worth clerli be yer xvj mark' (NRO, WKC 1/43/4), which was also plainly a deliberate undervaluation, as his father had leased it to Simon Gunnor and William Shepherd in 1442 for 18 marks a year (Davis I, pp. 18–19). The rent had fallen to 15½ marks per annum when Sir Roger Townshend leased it for seven years to the same Simon Gunnor in 1476 (NRO, WKC 1/45/1). By 1503 its value was probably picking up again.

[216] John Paston I claimed £175 15s 5d had been spent by his father: NRO, WKC 1/43/4. John Paston III paid Roger Townshend £100 and 10 marks in February 1503: Davis II, pp. 612–13; BL Add. Ch. 17743. To these sums have to be added the costs of litigation after the death of Judge William in 1444, the settling of John Mariot's debts in the later 1460s, and the payment of his 10-mark annuity from 1467. As East Beckham was mortgaged to Roger Townshend for 100 marks in November 1469, that sum is some sort of measure of what the family needed to deal with John Mariot *and* his creditors. But it has to be less than a minimum measure: Richard Calle wrote to John Paston III in May 1469 that 'ye owe hym [Mariot] of his l li. but xx li and xs' (Davis II, p. 396), while Mariot's debt to John Heydon was £30 (Davis I, p. 552), and the settling of another £16 debt cost the Pastons £11 (Davis II, p. 398). The annuity was paid for at least two years from Michaelmas 1467. In May 1470 John Paston III wrote to John Paston II, 'As for John Maryot, he is payid of hys anuyté into a nobyll or xs at the most' (Davis I, p. 557). But, as John Mariot was alive in July 1472 (Davis I, p. 576), it is likely to have been paid for at least four years. If we add these sums together we get either £375 (£175 15s 5d + £100 + £6 13s 4d + £66 13s 4d + £26 13s 4d: viz. Mariot's 10-mark annuity for four years) or £400 (£175 15s 5d + £100 + £6 13s 4d + £50 + £30 + £11 + £26 13s 4d).

times its annual value for it.[217] Evidently East Beckham was worth a great deal to them, worth more to them as the century wore on: by *c.* 1470 they had invested more than cash in acquiring it. With reason: there was more, much more, to be had out of an 'investment' in land in the fifteenth century than money. William Paston knew this in 1434, just as his grandson did in 1503. To conclude, therefore, that they did not get the bargain Judge William had expected in 1434, but, quite the opposite, had had to pay too high a price for what superficially was a small and unattractive piece of real estate, is to shoot wide of the mark. The value is what someone is willing to give for it. In February 1503 John Paston III, I expect, felt relieved; he did not, I think, feel hard done by.

APPENDIX

East Beckham's history may be elaborated (it seems) *ad infinitum*. At a very late stage in the making of this book I was confronted with evidence which, while not altering the narrative, deserves inclusion here. Dr Charles Moreton's 'The Townshend Family *c.* 1450–1551', unpublished DPhil. thesis (Oxford, 1989, pp. 156–63), led me to a memoranda book of the second Roger Townshend: BL Add. MS 41139. In this (fs. 8–9) are set out the arguments against the Paston case for ownership of the manor when Sir John Paston challenged the Townshends' possession in 1499. Most of those arguments are (or appear to me to be) valid; they substantiate the account given above. In brief (and in the main) they are the following. Because Judge William did not specify a purchase price nor mention having made a down-payment for the estate no lawful bargain was made between him and the Mariots; nor did he have possession save as the farmer of the king; if he had had legal title to East Beckham he would have disposed of the estate in his will – as he did of the other lands he had purchased. After Joan Mariot's death Judge William and John Mariot agreed to accept a price set by the priors of Bromholm and St Faith's: no price was established by them. John Mariot had peaceful possession of East Beckham for twenty years, even though he was a poor man and Judge William and his son were powerful

[217] As 20 marks is undoubtedly an over-estimate and 600 marks probably an underestimate the real figure may be nearer forty than thirty times. For Bruce McFarlane's discussion of the cost of Sir John Fastolf's forays into the land market see his *England in the Fifteenth Century* (London, 1981), pp. 191–5. Purchase price and legal expenses together for Titchwell, Beighton, and Bradwell amounted 'to very nearly thirty [years purchase]': pp. 194–5. McFarlane goes on, 'on several other manors such expensive mistakes were repeated'. Dr Anthony Smith, however, has convincingly demonstrated that these three estates (and the Hickling rents also) were exceptional cases: see his 'Litigation and Politics: Sir John Fastolf's Defence of his English Property, in Tony Pollard (ed.), *Property and Politics: Essays in Later Medieval English History* (London, 1984), esp. pp. 59–61.

men. Then John Mariot sold the manor to John Paston II: would Sir John have bought it if he had known of a valid purchase made by his grandfather? Moreover, John Paston I, who held West Beckham, collected rent due from East Beckham at West Beckham; plainly, he could not have both the land and the rent.

Undoubtedly these were among the arguments Roger Townshend produced before James Hobart and John Yaxley in 1500–1: Charles Moreton, 'The Townshend Family', p. 158 (Add. Ms 41139, f. 7). John Paston III had made his challenge at Common Law in spring 1499; the previous winter he had run off some of the sheep from the flock being kept at East Beckham. All this was to bring pressure to bear on the Townshends to go to arbitration: the Pastons (as defaulting mortgagors) had no legal right to the manor. Roger Townshend struggled to prevent an award being made (by attempting a dubious deal with Sir John Wyndham over East Beckham), but after two years the settlement of February 1503 was arrived at. By that John Paston III got the property his grandfather had never owned. His brother, however, had had a clear title. Thus, the distinguished arbitrators did what Roger Townshend feared they would do: show favour where the Common Law did not (Charles Moreton, 'The Townshend Family', pp. 156–60).

Chapter 4

THREE MARRIAGES

The Pastons were made by marriages. There were three that made them: Clement's to Beatrice Goneld; William's to Agnes Barry; John's to Margaret Mautby.

The least important of the three was William's – or so it appears at this distance. Agnes was an heiress; with her William got three manors as well as a loyal wife. She lived too long – so far as the family was concerned: her £100-worth of property (her inheritance, her jointure, and her dower) was not at the disposal of the head of the family, her son John I, from 1444 to 1466, or her grandson John II from 1466 to 1479, for thirty-five years. Thank God (they may have said), she did not remarry. She also had no influential, or in other ways helpful, relatives. Sir Edmund Barry, her father, who died in 1433, seems (and possibly was) a curiously detached figure in local, that is Norfolk, society. He did not live in Norfolk but at Horwellbury near Royston in Hertfordshire.[1] He cut no figure in Hertfordshire society either; his house there, however, was handy for London. May that not be a clue to his interests? It was, for instance, at Hertford on 25 December 1396 that Edmund indented with John of Gaunt 'to serve him in peace and war' for life for a fee of £10 per annum out of the Duchy lands in Norfolk.[2] Neither the Duke's death, nor Richard II's downfall disturbed this arrangement. On 26 April 1399 he was retained by Henry IV for life, his fee (now to be taken out of the customs of Great Yarmouth) being doubled.[3] He was then twenty-

[1] Horwellbury is in the parish of Kelshall to the south west of Royston: *VCH Herts.* III, p. 242. I would like to thank Mr Peter Walne, the county archivist, for this reference: I had forgotten the *VCH*, momentarily at any rate.

[2] *CPR 1396–9*, p. 542. Perhaps his *entrée* to this most prestigious of all retinues had been through Sir Robert Barry, another, earlier retainer of John of Gaunt's (S. Armitage-Smith (ed.), *John of Gaunt's Register 1372–1376*, vol. II, Camden Society, third series, vol. xxi (London, 1911), nos. 50 and 923; E.C. Lodge and R. Somerville (eds.), *John of Gaunt's Register, 1379–1383*, Camden Society, third series, vol. lvi (London, 1937), p. 8). According to NRO, Rye MS 38, a Robert does not feature in the direct male line of the Barrys; perhaps Robert was Edmund's uncle.

[3] *CPR 1396–9*, p. 542; *CCR 1396–9*, pp. 377–8; *CPR 1399–1401*, p. 146.

two years old.[4] As he had no administrative career whatsoever, aside from a brief appearance as a Norfolk commissioner in 1419–20,[5] we must, I believe, suppose him to have been a soldier. Our supposition is strengthened by his being an esquire as late as 1413, but having become a knight by 1419.[6] His friends (and enemies) were Norfolk (or Suffolk[7]) men. He was an executor of Sir Edmund Thorp of Ashwellthorp, another Norfolk knight who had no sons, and apparently a feoffee of John Winter's, as he was among the group (which included his son-in-law, William Paston) who granted Egmere to Walsingham Abbey in 1425.[8] His father-in-law was also from Norfolk: Sir Thomas Gerbridge. Edmund was a mainpernor for him in 1402, perhaps at about the time he married Thomas' daughter and heir, Alice, and a feoffee of his in 1412.[9] Alice brought him Marlingford in Norfolk.[10] This

[4] Having been born in 1377; according to NRO Rye MS 38 (Edmund Farrer, 'A Norfolk Armory of the Fifteenth Century', *Norfolk Antiquarian Miscellany*, 8 (1887), p. 426), he was two years old at his father, John's death in 1379. Sir Thomas Barre of Ayot St Lawrence, knight of the shire for Hertfordshire in the parliaments of 1400–1, 1407, and 1411, was, it seems, no relation (*VCH Herts.*, III, p. 60). [5] *CPR 1416–22*, pp. 212, 270, 323.

[6] He appears not to have been at Agincourt, as he is not in Sir N.H. Nicolas, *History of the Battle of Agincourt* (London, 1832), nor is his name among those whose indentures for war during this period survive at the PRO.

[7] He was at odds with Peter Codon of Dunwich in 1402: *CCR 1402–5*, pp. 128, 129. In 1403 it was another Lancastrian, Sir Roger Swillington's turn to be at odds with Peter Codon: *Hopton*, p. 56, note 74.

[8] *CPR 1422–29*, pp. 270, 365; E.F. Jacob (ed.), *Chichele's Register*, II, p. 144. Thorps and Barrys were related through Hengrave sisters: Cecily who married Hugh Barry and who died in 1349: Beatrice who married Sir Robert Thorp (NRO, Rye MS 38; Farrer, 'Norfolk Armory', p. 426). For John Winter and Egmere see chapter 3 above, p. 85.

[9] *CCR 1402–5*, p. 133; *CCR 1409–13*, p. 331. By then Thomas Gerbridge had married again, Cecily, widow of Sir Thomas Gyney, with whose son Thomas Edmund had been a mainpernor in 1411 for a number of Wymondham men 'that they shall henceforward make or procure no unlawful assemblies, riots or excessive or unlawful public drinkings in Wymondham church' (*CCR 1409–13*, p. 197). Had a fund-raising event for the great west tower got out of hand, or had this been simply an anti-monastic demonstration?

[10] Blomefield I, p. 690. Sir Thomas Gerbridge, according to Blomefield, had acquired Marlingford by marriage to Elizabeth, daughter of Sir Robert Wachesham. Elizabeth, Agnes Paston's grandmother (Davies I, p. 49), died in 1402 (NRO, Rye MS 38; Farrer, 'Norfolk Armory', p. 427). Robert Wachesham (Wachysham), Thomas Gerbridge, and Edmund Barry appear in the lists of lords, knights, and esquires of Norfolk and Suffolk who died without male heirs between 1327 and 1461 in NRO, MS 7197, fs. 304–6v. Thus, Marlingford descended directly in the female line in three generations – an illustration of that lack of continuity of ownership which continues to be underestimated in studies of estates and their management. William Worcester's lists in MS 7197 (for which see K.B. McFarlane, *The Nobility of Later Medieval England* (Oxford, 1973), pp. 145–6) demonstrate that too. Here are names which have already featured, or will feature, in this story: Robert Knolles, Robert Salle, Richard Ilney, Edmund Thorp, Robert Mautby, Robert Boys, William Clippesby, Thomas Tuddenham, Richard Carbonell, Thomas, Lord Morley, Thomas, Lord Scales, Simon Felbrigg, Robert Banyard. There are 141 names for 135 years. Given McFarlane's figures for the failure of upper-class families in the male line (*Nobility*, pp. 146–7, cf. pp. 175–6), these lists display just how crucial recruitment from below was to the survival of that class (or those classes), as McFarlane pointed out. It is worth noting that to Sir Thomas Erpingham's original list of eighty-seven names of lords and knights of Norfolk

marriage (and this manor) were not the beginning of his association with the county: he already had (from his father) a manor in nearby East Tuddenham.[11] When he died in 1433 he was buried beside Alice (who had died in 1430) in the Lady Chapel of the White Friars at Norwich, where the bodies of Sir Thomas Gerbridge and his wife, Elizabeth, also lay. There, too, Agnes Paston and her son Clement were to be buried.[12]

We cannot say with certainty, therefore, that William Paston in 1420 married a local girl. This may have been a marriage made as much in London as in Norfolk. William was forty-two. He had waited to marry. Had he waited for Agnes to be eighteen? If Edmund Barry and Alice Gerbridge had married in 1402, when Edmund was twenty-five, eighteen is what Alice would have been in 1420. She was only a co-heiress: could William have made a better match? Possibly he put off marrying for too long. He was not an old man but the gap between him and Agnes was wide enough, and it was not bridged by love – she did not choose to be buried beside him in Norwich Cathedral but beside her parents in the Dominican church of that city. Once it was thought that John Lydgate's *Temple of Glass* was written to celebrate their marriage; it is no longer: there is 'no reason to reject a general association with the Pastons, but the idea that it was specially commissioned for a marriage is wholly untenable and most improper'.[13] Thus, William's hand as it drew up the marriage contract on 24 March 1420 may be presumed to have been steady and businesslike:[14] a young wife of good family and three manors was what he had earned for himself. His father would have been proud of him.

and Suffolk for 1327–1413, Worcester (according to information supplied to him by Nicholas Booking in 1463) added twenty-nine lords and knights of Norfolk *alone*, for 1377–1461, and twenty-five esquires of Norfolk *alone* for the same period – in other words, the list is not a complete one of East Anglian lords, knights, and esquires for 1327–1461.

[11] Blomefield V, p. 1223.

[12] Sir Edmund's will (NRO, NCC Reg. Surfleet, f. 125v) is dated 30 September 1433; there was no proof. His obit is recorded in NRO, Rye MS 38 as 12 October 1433; Alice's obit is also recorded there as 26 January 1430 (Farrer, 'Norfolk Armory', p. 427). For the burials, see Davis I, p. 49. Sir Edmund's will, made at Norwich, is brief and unrevealing. Most bequests were to the Carmelites and their chapel of St Mary. He also left 2 marks for the repair of Ellough church, Suffolk, and £2 to John, the rector of Marlingford. Agnes was one of his executors and William Paston was the supervisor of the will. It has every indication of having been made *at* the Carmelite priory. Ellough was a Barry estate which went to Sir Edmund's other daughter, Alice, and her husband, Sir Thomas Bardolph. After Thomas' death Alice married (according to Copinger, *Manors*, VII, p. 168) John Southwell, for whom see Wedgwood, *Biographies*, p. 783, where Ellough has become Eye.

[13] Derek Pearsall, *John Lydgate* (London, 1970), p. 108. The earlier view was put by H.N. MacCracken, 'Additional Light on *The Temple of Glass*', *Publications of the Modern Language Association of America*, 23 (1908), pp. 128–40.

[14] BL Add. Ch. 17225 (Gairdner II, p. 11) in his own hand (Davis I, p. lii, note 8). They were married before 1 September the same year, when Oxnead, Agnes' jointure, was settled on them: BL Add. Ch. 14806.

So would his uncle: Geoffrey Somerton had seen William's quality and promoted it before anyone else. The man who, so to speak, pushed the Paston boat out was not a Paston at all, but Geoffrey 'qwhos trew sernome ys Goneld'.[15] It is for this reason that Clement Paston's marriage to the well-to-do Yarmouth attorney's sister, Beatrice, is more important than William's own marriage: a greater step forward and upwards. Geoffrey presumably was childless: he left his property to William, his son by proxy. William might have applauded the response of Sir William Gascoigne, who once, on being asked for his support, replied, 'if your matter were against any man in England except my uncle I would take your part, but in this you must have me excused'.[16] Kinship counted: William Paston's uncle by marriage made him and his descendants count; it was Geoffrey Somerton who got the Pastons going on their long march to an earldom.

A stage of that march was the third of these marriages which were the making of the family in Norfolk: John's marriage to Margaret Mautby in 1440. It was a local alliance of unmistakable moment. Judge William may have been patient where his own marriage was concerned; he wasted no time when it came to marrying his son and heir. John Paston had been born at 6 a.m. on 10 October 1421.[17] Married at nineteen (to a girl of eighteen) he became a father before he was twenty-one and while still a student at Cambridge:[18] John Paston II was born before 15 April 1442.[19] The contrast with his father is startling, despite the reasons for the contrast being obvious. By 1440 William was over sixty; if he wanted to see what he had created secure, a grandson was needed; his own late marriage was catching up on him. Urgency may be read into Agnes' letter describing John and Margaret's first encounter:[20]

> Blyssyd be God, I sende yow gode tydynggys of the comyng and the brynggyn hoom of the gentylwomman that ye wetyn of fro Redham this same nyght, acordyng to poyntmen that ye made ther-for yowre-self. And as for the furste aqweyntaunce be-twhen John Paston and the syde gentilwomman, she made hym gentil chere in gyntyl wyse and seyde he was verrayly yowre son. And so I hope ther shal nede no gret treté be-twyxe hym.

Speed was part of this union: first meeting April 1440; marriage before November 1440; grandson by April 1442. Everyone was happy – not least Margaret, even while she did not know the child she was carrying was going

[15] Davis I, p. xlii.

[16] T. Stapleton (ed.), *Plumpton Correspondence* (London: Camden Society 1839), p. 121.

[17] So William Worcester learned from Agnes Paston: NRO, MS 7197, f. 319. John died on 19 June 1466, aged forty-four. His father had lived for sixty-six years. Defending property wears a man down faster than does acquiring it – as St Francis might have said.

[18] He was married by 1 November 1440: Davis I, pp. 26, 215 and II, p. 21. Margaret was said to have been twelve in July 1434: PRO, C139/67/47.

[19] Gairdner II, p. 51.

[20] Davis I, p. 26.

to be a boy:[21] 'Jon of Dam was here, and my modyr dyskevwyrd me to hym, and he seyde be hys trouth that he was not gladder of no thyng that he harde thys towlmonyth than he was ther-of. I may no lenger leve be my crafte, I am dysscevwyrd of alle men that se me.' Within eighteen months she had produced a second son. Judge William may not have lived quite long enough to see this additional security for the family come into the world.[22]

Certainly no time had been lost in drawing up the settlement of Mautby properties and the reversion of others on John Paston, who, upon the birth of John Paston II, became entitled to hold them for life.[23] For Margaret Mautby was, of course, an heiress, the sole heiress of her father, John. Her lands were not only more substantial than Agnes Barry's, they were, save for the single Suffolk manor of Fritton, all in Norfolk, concentrated in two areas strategically relevant to Judge William's interests: the two hundreds of East and West Flegg, and the hundred of North Erpingham. The Mautby manors in the latter were Bessingham, Matlask, and West Beckham, while Briston was in the adjoining hundred of Holt. It is evident that the Mautby marriage was a vital aspect of William Paston's campaign to make North Erpingham Hundred Paston territory.

Equally evident is that marriage was an easier, cheaper route to lordship than purchase. John's marriage to Margaret, therefore, was William's most astute tactic of them all. The Mautby manor of Flegghall lay in Winterton and Somerton in West Flegg, while Mautby itself lay squarely in East Flegg adjoining Sir John Fastolf's manor of Caister. Nor was Fritton in Lothingland Hundred, Suffolk, far away; Fastolf, who had rich property in that hundred, owned the manor of Caldecott Hall in Fritton. This is that part of the county where William's lands inherited from Geoffrey Somerton lay.

[21] *Ibid.*, p. 217. Perhaps 'the reyng wyth the emage of Seynt Margrete that I sent yow for a rememraunse tyl ye com hom' had an inscription on it like that on one of the fifteenth-century 'love' rings in the BM: 'Whan ye loke on this thynk on them that gave you thys' (ring no. 928). As St Margaret was the patron saint of pregnant women, John's wearing of this ring would have revealed to the observant his expectant fatherhood.

[22] Late in 1444 a correspondent reported to John Paston, 'youre sonys . . . arn heyle and mery' (Davis II, p. 25, line 55). Judge William had died in August. There is a possibility that 'youre sonys' means twins, that these were John Paston II and John Paston III. It is improbable, but possible. For one thing the anomaly of identical names has never been satisfactorily explained (unless by the boys having godfathers called John, which I think they did; for another, William Paston in his will said 'ita quod si contingat predictum Johannem Paston aliquem exitum vel heredem de corpore Margarete nunc uxoris sue procreare, quod huc' (Davis I, p. 24, lines 134–6). It is, however, more reasonable to assume that William drew up this will between (at the latest) November 1440 and April 1442, than that he did so after the John Paston who had been born in April 1442 had died and before twins called John had been born in 1444.

[23] Gairdner's abstract of the agreement of 15 April 1442 (II, no. 43) is too brief a description of Bodleian Library, Norfolk Charters a8, 740, which is a long, complicated document.

A more weighty consideration, though William may not have been making calculations at this refined level (the Mautby marriage was too good – on every level – to be other than 'grabbed with both hands'), was Mautby's proximity to Caister and Margaret's kinship to its dominating and childless owner.[24] In addition to these two concentrations there were two other manors, both in north-eastern Norfolk: Sparham and Kirkhall in Salle.

Judge William reckoned this property was worth £150 a year.[25] There is no reason to question his accuracy and no means of doing so.[26] His leaving

[24] How early was Sir John Fastolf's dilemma (what to do with his lands) seen as an opportunity? Thus Agnes to John *c.* 1452: 'Item, he [John Damme] tolde me as he herd seyn Sere John Fastolf hath sold Heylysdon to Boleyn of London, and if it be so it semeth he will selle more; wherfore I preye you, as ye will have my love and my blissyng, that ye will helpe and do youre dever that sumthyng were purchased for youre ij bretheren. I suppose that Ser John Fastolf, and he were spoke to, wolde be gladere to lete his kensemen han parte than straunge men. Asay him in my name of suych places as ye suppose is most clere' (Davis I, p. 38, lines 42–7). It was, in fact, Blickling which Fastolf sold in 1452 to Sir Geoffrey Boleyn; he did so advantageously: Anthony Smith, 'Aspects of the Career of Sir John Fastolf, 1380–1459', unpublished Oxford D.Phil. thesis, 1982, p. 32 and table 2; cf. Davis II, p. 224.

[25] NRO, Phillipps MS 534, for which see below, p. 126.

[26] For Mautby Hall in Sparham (not Sparham Hall as in n. 32 of 'Thomas Lord Morley (died 1416) and the Morleys of Hingham', *Norfolk Archaeology*, 39 (1984), p. 10) a rental of 1462 (NRO, NRS 22474/256) has rents of nearly £11 and farms of just over £10. Richard Calle's accounts of 'not after 1466' (Davis II, p. 328) record about £12 received from there between All Saints and August. Margaret settled Sparham on John III and Margery Brews in March 1477 (Davis I, p. 500). In April Sir John wrote to his brother, 'I wolde be as gladde that one gaffe yow a maner off xxli. by yeer, as if he gave it to my selffe, by my trowthe' (Davis I, p. 503). He was being disingenuous; a jointure for the couple of £20 per annum was what was being discussed by the two families – 'Item, as for Sporle xxli. by yeer . . .' (Davis I, p. 503, line 18; cf. *ibid* p. 496, lines 4–6). I think we may safely regard Sparham as worth £20 per annum. Yet (where estimating landed revenue is concerned, it is always 'yet'), in the 1450s Thomas Gnateshall, possibly Margaret's bailiff at Sparham, wrote to her: 'As for the receytys of your maner of Sparham, with costys and expencys it is xli.iijs.xid. ob' (Davis II, p. 338). If Thomas Gnateshall was Margaret's bailiff at Sparham, as his letters (Davis II, nos. 708–10) suggest, she shared him with Isobel, Lady Morley, as in 1456–7 Thomas was Lady Morley's bailiff at Foulsham (Staffs. RO, D641/3/16/1: his account for that year). He had ceased to be so by 1463 (BL Add. MS 34122A, for which see 'Thomas Lord Morley', note 31, p. 10). Thomas may have lived at Sparham or at Lyng (Davis II, no. 708, line 16; no. 709, lines 8–9); Sparham and Lyng are next door to each other, Foulsham is nearby. In one letter (Davis II, no. 710) Thomas mentions Lady Morley's Norwich house ('my ladys place . . . in the town') and her doctor: 'my lady sent to Cawnbrygg for a doctour of fesyk. If ye wyll ony thyng with hym he xal abyde this daye and to-morowe. He is ryght a konnyng man and a gentyll.' It is good to have this testimonial to Dr Thomas Reed, especially at the outset of his career, when he was still an unmarried fellow of Peterhouse; after his marriage he lived in Cambridge until his death in 1504: Emden, *Biog. Reg. Camb.*, p. 475. He attended Lady Morley in October 1463 and at Easter 1464 (BL Add. MS 34122A); although she made her will shortly after his second visit (NRO, NCC Reg. Jekkys f. 50, dated at her place in Norwich, 3 May 1464), she did not die until February 1467, which is perhaps further testimony to Dr Reed's skill. What is also worth having is Thomas, Lord Scales' letter to Thomas Gnateshall (Davis II, no. 879): it is always satisfactory to discover the mighty nodding. Richard Calle's other accounts of September 1461, which, like those of 'not after 1466', are jotted down on the dorse of a letter from a Paston servant, reveal that he collected about £12 from Matlask between November (1460) and August: BL Add. MS 34888, f. 193 dorse. (Davis, for once, is wrong (II, p. 249): Calle's accounts avoid, though they do obscure, Gloys' addressing of his

Gresham and not a great deal else to John in 1444 does not make sense, unless the Mautby inheritance was valuable.[27] None the less, good sense is not necessarily to be associated with deathbeds, in particular Judge William's. Matters of importance are rarely simple enough to be treated sensibly. Just so: neither the Mautby marriage nor the Mautby lands were as straightforward as they seem.

Margaret's father, John Mautby esquire, died on 18 February 1433.[28] Margaret was eleven years old; her wardship was first granted to Sir John Tyrell, then in 1434 to Sir John Radcliff.[29] William Paston had been a feoffee of John Mautby's father, Robert Mautby esquire, and also perhaps of John Mautby himself.[30] At some date before 1433 John Fastolf had secured John Mautby's release from imprisonment in France by chivalrously buying a French prisoner of war and exchanging him for John; he did the same for another relative, Henry Inglose esquire, and for John Mautby's father-in-law, John Berney esquire.[31] By 1436, perhaps ten years earlier, William Paston had become one of Sir John Fastolf's legal advisers.[32] If, on the one hand, Margaret was an opportunity William had every intention of not missing, on the other there appears to have been competition to be beaten off: Sir John Radcliff. Or was there no contest? Sir John Radcliff, a great soldier, second only to Richard Beauchamp, Earl of Warwick, in the length of his service and quality of his military career between 1403 and 1436, was

letter to John Paston.) I think that both these accounts of Calle's are of September 1461, and that, therefore, James Gresham's letter of 'not after 1466', which Calle used the back of in the same fashion (*ibid.*, no. 703) as he used the back of James Gloys', was written in August 1461. We should note that Kirkhall in Salle and Briston together were worth about £20 per annum in the 1470s: see below, p. 132. Mautby in the 1440s was a barley and wheat farm, producing in one year marketable barley to the value of £20 and wheat which 'was ete wyth myse so pitowsly for to se': Davis II, pp. 26–7 (cf. Davis I, p. 222).

[27] Moreover, he had to leave him Gresham because it was Margaret's jointure (Davis I, p. 24, lines 134–8; *ibid.*, p. 385, lines 70–3); for the 'not a great deal else', see chapter 6.

[28] According to his *inquisition post mortem*: PRO, C139/78/40.

[29] *CFR 1403–37*, pp. 162, 198. For the powerful Sir John Tyrell see J.S. Roskell, *The Commons in the Parliament of 1422* (London, 1954), pp. 226–9.

[30] Davis I, pp. 16–17; NRO, Bulwer of Heydon (box 143 × 4), NRS 26179.

[31] Gairdner II, p. 50; III, p. 157; Bruce MacFarlane, *England in the Fifteenth Century*, pp. 192–3. Actually, it was long before 1433: see chapter 7. The young John Fastolf clearly knew Robert Mautby well: in October 1404 Robert Mautby was the first witness to Mary Mortimer's grant of Caister to her son John Fastolf (BL Add. Ch. 14597).

[32] Anthony Smith, 'Sir John Fastolf', p. 28. According to a document printed by F. Worship, 'Account of a MS Genealogy of the Paston Family in the Possession of His Grace the Duke of Newcastle' (that is, Francis Sandford's genealogy of 1674), in *Norfolk Archaeology*, 4 (1855), pp. 17–18 (cited by Trevor John, 'The Parliamentary Representation of Norfolk and Suffolk 1377–1422', unpublished MA thesis, Nottingham, p. 505), William Paston was one of the attorneys appointed by Sir John Fastolf to pursue the executors of Henry V and Thomas, Duke of Exeter for sums owing to him for military service. The document is dated 'in civitate Teroni', 16 July 1426. The other attorneys were Sir John Radcliff, Sir Henry Inglose, John Fastolf, and John Hartling, clerk.

Fastolf's brother-in-law, the husband of his half sister, Cecily Mortimer:[33] 'their friendship seems to have been lifelong'.[34] For *his* military service Sir John Radcliff was 'paid' in grants of lucrative wardships and marriages.[35] Having married two heiresses himself,[36] he made sure of another for his son; in 1433 he was granted the custody and marriage of Elizabeth, daughter and sole heir of Walter, Lord Fitzwalter. She was three years old; Sir John's son and heir, John, by his second wife was not much older; they were duly married.[37] In 1434 Sir John Radcliff cannot have had much need of Margaret Mautby. Is it not likely, therefore, that there was a 'deal' between Paston, Fastolf, and Radcliff? Radcliff, because he was best able to, got Margaret's wardship and marriage; it was understood that William Paston should have her for his son John. Sir John Fastolf, kinsman and patron to John Mautby, friend, probably brother-in-arms to Sir John Radcliff, and employer of William Paston, was (one assumes) the intermediary.[38] Yet Margaret was not the absolute and immediate prize she at first seems. Her Mautby inheritance was much encumbered. Both her grandmother and mother were living; she also had uncles whose claims on those nine manors could not be ignored.

First, her grandmother Eleanor: what were the 'reversions' a settlement of April 1442 speaks of, which were to fall to Margaret on her death? Robert Mautby esquire died in 1418. His last will of 1 April of that year is a long and elaborate document. He gave his feoffees, William Paston being one of them, detailed instructions. The detail and elaboration were necessary: Robert left a young widow, Eleanor, five sons, four of them under age, and an unmarried daughter, Agnes. Another daughter, Eleanor, was a nun at Shouldham; she was to have £1 a year to pray for the souls of her parents.[39] The maintenance of his youthful family was Robert's chief care. What resulted from his concern was a mixture of the specific and the vague, no doubt occasioned by the wide range of unknowable, alternative futures

[33] See Fastolf's will, Gairdner III, pp. 156–7, and Trevor John, 'Parliamentary Representation', p. 488. Dr John's splendid biography of Sir John Radcliff (*ibid.*, pp. 487–511) sets the record straight on this remarkable man.

[34] Trevor John, 'Parliamentary Representation', pp. 487–8. In 1426 they were rival candidates, friendly no doubt, for election to the Order of the Garter: *ibid.*, p. 495.

[35] *Ibid.*, pp. 503–5.

[36] Cecily Mortimer, who brought him Attleborough, died in 1423. By 1428 he had married Katherine, daughter and co-heir of Sir Edward Burnell, son and heir of Hugh, Lord Burnell. Katherine, who survived him and died in the winter of 1452–3, brought him other Norfolk estates. She was buried beside him at Attleborough (*ibid.*, pp. 488, 498, 506).

[37] *CPR 1429–36*, p. 263; Trevor John, 'Parliamentary Representation', p. 504; *CP*, V, pp. 484–5. They had livery of the Fitzwalter lands in January 1445.

[38] It may be that Fastolf's intervention was not required and that the Radcliff–Paston connection, so important later, began here. For John Radcliff III and John Paston III, see a subsequent volume.

[39] He seems already to have married a third daughter, Joan, to Henry Catt of Hevingham: NRO, NRS 12351 (cf. HMC, *Lothian MS*, p. 43).

which could occur. This is how Robert endeavoured to confront those futures. Eleanor was to have West Beckham for life; it was, presumably, her jointure. She was to have Sparham as her dower, but also she was to have reasonable dower out of other (unnamed) manors. The manors of Briston, Kirkhall in Salle, and Flegghall were particularly set aside for Eleanor's maintenance of the boys, Walter, Edward, Peter, and Thomas until they became twenty-one, and for Agnes until she married. Agnes' marriage portion of £80 was to be raised, at £20 a year during the first four years after Robert's death, from the profits of the estates. John, Robert's son and heir, was to have an annuity of 20 marks and on Eleanor's death five of the nine Mautby manors were to descend to him; the other four were to go to his brothers for life when they became twenty-one: Kirkhall to Walter; West Beckham to Edward; Flegghall to Peter; Briston to Thomas. If one, two, or three of the brothers died, the manor or manors released were to accrue to survivors, eventually all four to the survivor. On the deaths of these cadets, and if Eleanor had not survived them, for if she had she was to have the four manors for her life, the estates were to revert to the senior line of John and his heirs. Finally, if Agnes died before marrying, her marriage portion was to be given as a contribution towards the repair of the (south) aisle of Mautby church.[40]

By 1422 Eleanor had remarried Thomas Chambre esquire.[41] On 12 October 1422 they and John Mautby, who probably had just married

[40] PRO, C1/72/108. As one might ponder, this is a will William Paston may have had in mind when making his own twenty-five years later. Robert was son and heir of Sir John Mautby, who died in 1403; one of Sir John's executors was Geoffrey Somerton: Blomefield, V, p. 1566; cf. NRO, NCC Reg. Harsyk, f. 299 – Sir John's actual will is NRO, Phillipps MS 531.

[41] Eleanor's Thomas Chambre undoubtedly was Thomas Chambre esquire of Spratton and Holdenby, Northamptonshire, knight of the shire for Northamptonshire on three occasions from 1422, and also sheriff of that county three times, as well as once of Norfolk and Suffolk (in 1435–6: *CFR 1430–7*, p. 252). He sat for Northamptonshire in the parliament of 1435, but was an assessor of the tax it granted in Norfolk and Suffolk (*CFR 1430–7*, p. 269). He and Eleanor lived in Northamptonshire at Wilby, from where Eleanor wrote to William Paston in November 1442 (Davis II, p. 6). Curiously, Thomas was only for a few months in 1439 a justice of the peace (for Northamptonshire: *CPR 1436–41*, p. 587). Even more curious is his second marriage. Was it to Eleanor, widow of Robert Mautby, or to Eleanor, widow of William Vaux? As that Northamptonshire lawyer died in 1405 and Thomas Chambre married Eleanor Mautby in 1422 (or between 1418 and 1422), probably Eleanor Vaux was Thomas' first wife. He had Wilby from her. For him see Roskell, *The Commons in 1422*, pp. 163–4. I do, however, wonder whether the Thomas Chambre, who 'seems to have lived the life of an obscure country squire with two manors to control, Spratton and Holdenby, until towards the end of Henry V's reign he entered on a military career in France', was the soldier. May not our Thomas Chambre's early obscurity be due to youth, even if a slightly prolonged one? On the other hand, how did such a distant and dim fellow come to marry a Norfolk widow before 12 October 1422? The marriage had been made before the parliament of that year began on 9 November. For other references to this Thomas Chambre, see *CPR 1416–22*, pp. 358, 359; *CCR 1422–9*, pp. 123, 453; *CCR 1429–35*, pp. 44, 69; *CCR 1441–7*, p. 270, unless this associate of Humphrey, Duke of Buckingham, in 1444 is a different man.

Margery, the daughter of one of his father's feoffees, John Berney of Reedham, made an agreement at Sparham. Thomas and Eleanor were to occupy all Robert's lands until the following Michaelmas, 'an hol yer turned abowte' and to occupy the houses of those manors until Midsummer after that. After Michaelmas 1423 John was to enter his inheritance, saving to Eleanor her right of dower; he was also to acquit them of the £40 Robert Mautby had left for the repair of the south aisle of Mautby church – clearly Agnes had died.[42] Among the witnesses were John's father-in-law, or father-in-law to be, John Berney, Edmund Winter, 'and other Inowe'. The reappearance of Edmund Winter reminds us of WKC 1/43/8. As there, so here: William Paston has added a crabbed note in Latin in the lower right-hand corner. Robert Mautby died on 19 April 1417, he writes (in error for 1418[43]); Eleanor, he continues, had the profit of the manors from August 1418 until Michaelmas 1428; that profit amounted to over 2,400 marks.[44] Without knowing what William Paston understood by profit, let alone how he calculated it, it is evident that the Mautby lands, worth 220 or 240 marks a year,[45] were indeed valuable, in monetary as well as topographical terms. What arrangement John Mautby made with his mother for her dower William Paston does not record; it appears to have taken them until Michaelmas 1428 to make it.[46]

After John's early death in 1433 new arrangements had to be made, as his widow Margery (and by 1435 her new husband, Ralph Garneys) required her dower. Manors were now divided, at any rate theoretically, into halves and thirds. Walter Mautby had died, but Edward, Peter, and

[42] NRO, Phillipps MS 534 (Box 578 × 2). For the aisle see also Blomefield V, pp. 1567, 1569 and Margaret's will of 1482 (actually: before 1479), Davis I, pp. 383, 387. It was the mausoleum of the Mautbys and was in ruins by Blomefield's day. Davis II, p. 6, headnote is in error about the date of Eleanor's marriage to Thomas Chambre; it is an error taken from Gairdner II, p. 52, note to number 45, which was induced by a semi-colon in Blomefield V, p. 1567. [43] William wrote '5 Henry V' when he should have written '6 Henry V'.

[44] In June and August 1426 27 shillings was handed over to her – 'Alianor Chaumber domina de Mawteby' – by the bailiff of Kirkhall in Salle. As he had preserved his part of the indenture witnessing to these two payments (and made sure it was stitched into his accounts of that year), these deliveries of cash must have been in some way unusual, if only because they were direct: NRO, NRS 2616 (Box 12C2).

[45] William's phrase is 'at the rate of twelve score marks a year making a sum of 2,400 marks and more. And owing ['Et debit'] 400 marks.' It may be that the last minim of 'xij' is crossed through, giving eleven score marks; that would make more sense of the '2,400 marks and more', as William's (mis)calculation is on the basis of eleven years, not ten.

[46] An arrears list of Eleanor's officers of Michaelmas 1431 shows that she was then, or had been, in possession of Sparham, Bessingham, Matlask, West Beckham, Kirkhall in Salle, and Briston. Arrears were not a serious problem; such as there were had been paid fairly promptly – it was shillings rather than pounds which were outstanding: NRO, NRS 12242 (Box 30 D3). Perhaps the list was drawn up *because* she had handed over to John Mautby. She certainly had given up Kirkhall: she received at Michaelmas 1431 just over half of its revenues as dower; the lord received just under half: NRO, NRS 2618 (Box 12 C2). West Beckham (we should note) was leased to William Shepherd, for whom see chapter 3.

Thomas had still to be taken care of.[47] The most significant of these agreements was that by which, on 12 May 1435, William Paston and others, including the fourteen-year-old John Paston, were granted Margery's dower portion for sixty years at 40 marks a year.[48] Evidently, the ground was being prepared for the Paston–Mautby alliance. Seven years later, on 3 October 1442, after the birth of John Paston I and the settlement of 15 April 1442, another and perhaps more complete settlement – for it included, as we shall see, an agreement between Eleanor and Margaret's two surviving Mautby uncles (Peter having died) – was drawn up which reveals what Eleanor's dower was.[49] Here were set out the reversions which Margaret was to have on her grandmother's death: a half of the manors of Mautby and Fritton; a third of the manors of Sparham, Bessingham, and Matlask; and all of West Beckham. This can only have been a paper division, as on 11 November 1442 Eleanor wrote to William Paston:[50]

Ryght worchypfull and reverent sire, I recomande me un-to yow and thank yow of yowre grete labure that ye hade to me att Sparham the laste tyme that we spakun to-gydure. And for os myche, sire, os ye hadde no leysure att that tyme ye desyreid I schyde sende to yow to London now afture this Halowmese, and there ye seyde ye schyde have betture leysure and granteid me fully that ye schowlde orden that I schowlde have laufull a-state terme of my lyfe in the departyson that was grantid be-twex yow and me to-fore soch that was there for my hosbond and for me att that tyme; prayng yow that it may be done now and deliverid to my brodure Jon Chambre or to Jon Coke owre servant, brynger of this letture. And, gode sire, that this may be done in as godely haste os ye may, os my tryste is in yow, for thei have not long leysur here for odure occupaciounis that they muste have of owreis; and allso, sire, I sende yow here be hem the dede of annuité a-seleid undure my hosbondis synet and myne that I muste pay yerely to yowre childure.

The annuity which she was to pay to John and Margaret ('yowre childure' can be no other), the fact that Sparham was hers (for her phrasing 'yowre grete labure that ye hade to me att Sparham the laste tyme that we spakun to-gydure' suggests it was at her place not his that they met),[51] and that Mautby was not (the agreement of 3 October being made there shows that), demonstrate that what Eleanor and Margaret had were not halves of this and thirds of that. We may be sure William Paston arranged a more sensible division. Almost certainly Eleanor had all of Sparham, Bessingham,

[47] College of Arms MS 326/8, dated 20 October 1434, when Margery had already remarried (I owe this reference to David Morgan); BL Add. Ch. 17738 and Stowe Charter 176, cited in Copinger, *Manors*, V, p. 29. [48] BL Add. Ch. 17739.

[49] NRO, NRS 26179 (Bulwer of Heydon, box 143 × 4). [50] Davis II, p. 6.

[51] Indeed, she and Thomas held Sparham in 1428: *Feudal Aids* III, p. 594. Undoubtedly Eleanor lived there (if only from time to time) – malt and barley were dispatched to Sparham for her household from Kirkhall in 1435: NRO, NRS 12245 (Box 30 D3), Accounts of Salle Kirkhall, 1434–5. In the accounts of 1445–6 (NRO, NRS 12252 (Box 30 D4)) what were presumably her possessions were being removed from Sparham to Kirkhall by the lord, her son Edward Mautby: Eleanor had died and Sparham had become Margaret Paston's.

Matlask, and West Beckham; certainly she had a third of Kirkhall and Briston (which accounted together).[52] Margaret had Mautby and Fritton. Margaret was not kept out for much longer. Eleanor and Thomas Chambre were alive in 1444,[53] but Eleanor (and Thomas too) were dead in 1446.[54] John and Margaret were safely in possession of Sparham in spring 1448, when Margaret wrote of the relief owing to Isobel, Lady Morley, which had been 'payd in Thomas Chawmberys tym qhon her doghter Hastyngs was weddyd'.[55]

Secondly, there was the dower of Margaret's mother, Margery, who had remarried Ralph Garneys esquire. The settlement of 15 April 1442 mentions, without being specific, the reversions which were to fall to Margaret on Margery's death, and William Paston's slightly earlier draft survives of an indenture which would embody a settlement to be made with her.[56] It does not name manors and Margery Garneys is not included in the agreement of 3 October 1442. She had not died between April and October 1442 – at her and Ralph Garneys' house at Geldeston near Beccles in 1444 Margaret gave birth to John Paston III[57] – but because since 1435 her dower had been in Paston hands and she was simply receiving an annuity of 40 marks, there was no further need to settle about reversions with her.

Thirdly, there were Margaret's Mautby uncles. Here we are better informed; it is the settlement of 3 October 1442 which informs us.[58] By that date only two uncles remained: Edward and Thomas. Peter, who features as a remainder man between Edward and Thomas in William Paston's draft indenture of 1439–40,[59] has disappeared, as much earlier had Walter, the second of the five sons of 1418. The agreement of 3 October 1442 was an indenture sealed by Robert Mautby's three surviving feoffees, Sir Simon Felbrigg, Oliver Groos esquire, and William Paston;[60] John and Margaret

[52] At the foot of the accounts of Salle Kirkhall (and Briston) the accountant gave the profit ('profectus') of the manor for the year and then recorded the sums 'pro dote' and 'pro domino' as divisions of the profit: see various accounts between 1431 and 1444 in NRO, Boxes 12 C2 and 30 D3. The sum 'pro dote', apart from that of 1431 (see above, note 46), is always a third of the 'profectus'. I presume that the lord after John Mautby's death in 1433 was, as he ought to have been, Edward Mautby.

[53] The likely date of Edward and Thomas Mautby's petition to the chancellor, PRO, C1/72/107, for which see below, p. 129.

[54] The payment 'pro dote' does not feature on the account of 1445–6 (NRO, NRS 12252 (Box 30 D4); also, what I take to be Eleanor's household property was taken from Sparham to Kirkhall (see above, n. 52); thirdly, Alan Roos, Edward Mautby's 'good frende and [later] resceivour' (Davis II, p. 359), was paid just over £1 'pro debito Elienore Chaumbyr'.

[55] Davis I, p. 221. For Paston debt collecting at Bessingham and Matlask in 1453 see *ibid.*, p. 251.

[56] *Ibid.*, no. 9, to be dated 1439–1440.

[57] *Ibid.*, pp. 219, 565; cf. Davis II, p. 25, lines 54–7.

[58] NRO, NRS 26179.

[59] Davis I, pp. 17–18. Edward's name does not appear among the remainder men (p. 17); as he was intended to seal the indenture (p. 18), it is clear his omission was a slip.

[60] Two seals, one remarkably preserved, survive. Among the witnesses were Sir Henry Inglose and Miles Stapleton.

Paston were to have one part of the indenture, Edward and Thomas Mautby headed the list of those who were to have the other part. The agreement was really two agreements, for it embodied one of 24 September 1442, less than a fortnight before, between Edward and Thomas on the one hand and Eleanor Chambre on the other. Eleanor was to spend £40 on the (south) aisle of Mautby Church – she still, it appears, had not done so; Edward and Thomas were to have for their lives the manors of Kirkhall in Salle, Briston, and Flegghall. On the deaths of Eleanor and Thomas West Beckham was also to go to Edward and Thomas for their lives before reverting to Margaret Paston; in other words, Robert Mautby's intentions were being carried out.

They were not carried out at once. Paston acquisitiveness may not have been the major cause of the delay; the deaths of Judge William and Sir Simon Felbrigg were more likely to have put off implementation. Still, John Paston might have been the dog in the manger. The Mautby inheritance was, after all, another grievance for John to ruminate on beside his father's deathbed. In August 1444 did he mull over the power of women in English landed society? He may not have expressed it in so many words, but he knew it, and felt it.[61] His own mother, his wife's mother and grandmother were all keeping him from a considerable part of what he seems to have thought ought to have been his. Not only that: he was the victim, too, of a father's generosity to his younger sons – Robert Mautby to his, and now William Paston to his. John Paston's acquisitiveness may not have been natural, it could have been forced upon him, becoming habitual. In his early twenties, having begotten the son his father must have wished for as greatly as he, he discovered, or thought he had, that his father was generous to others, but not to him. He did what he could to defeat William's intentions: at the unhappy conflict between John and his younger brothers we will arrive shortly.

He also did not rush to put into effect the October 1442 agreement where it concerned Edward and Thomas Mautby. Not that Edward and Thomas waited long to petition the chancellor to get John and Oliver Groos esquire (Robert Mautby's single surviving feoffee) to carry out the October 1442 agreement.[62] The outcome was an award by John Stafford, Archbishop of Canterbury, the chancellor, on 11 April 1446.[63] His task, no doubt, was simplified by Eleanor's death in 1445; perhaps, indeed, her death spurred him into action. We do not know the terms of the award; almost certainly, however, they were those of the agreement of October 1442.[64] Thus,

[61] Davis I, pp. 47–8.

[62] PRO, C1/72/107, with a copy of Robert Mautby's will, John's response and Edward's replication, 108–10. [63] *CCR 1441–7* pp. 386–7.

[64] After Edward Mautby's death in 1479 John Paston II reported to Margaret that his widow 'brought me iij other deedys endentyd off suche astate as was made to myn ii onclys off Sall, Wynterton &c.': Davis I, p. 513, lines 31–3.

although John and Margaret got Sparham, Bessingham, and Matlask (to add to Mautby and Fritton), John Paston never did hold Kirkhall in Salle, Briston, Flegghall, and West Beckham.[65] Margaret did, but only for the five years before her death in 1484.[66] Edward Mautby died in possession of them in 1479.

Edward and his younger brother, Thomas, had divided the estates between them. We know Edward had Kirkhall in Salle because he wrote to Margaret,[67]

> that I understand by a man and servuant of yours that I have a tenaunt, a widew, duellyng in Sall, bildyng there an house upon my ground; and she is evill entretid and thret that the hous shuld be pulled doun. Wherein I praye you that ye will send for Aleyn Roos, my good frende and resceivour, and ask counsaile what is best to do therein; and that ye will have the mater in respyte untill the tyme that this somer I comme into that contree. And I praye you, faire nece, that ye will do herein for me atte this tyme, as I shall do you service in tyme to comme, I trust to God.

We know too that he had Briston, as the small manor of Briston Mautby accounted with the manor of Salle Kirkhall. Thomas had Flegghall. In the Norfolk Record Office there is a draft letter seeking advice on an intriguing matter.[68] The writer says that Robert Mautby's youngest son, Thomas, held Flegghall for life, that Edward the 'myddlyest' son was lord after him; both were dead without issue. During Thomas' time the villeins of the manor, following a suit brought against him, presumably by them, were found to be free men. Now, the question was 'qwhethir John [Mautby] or hys issu may sese them agen or noth', as Thomas had only been lord for life. The tenants were worried. The writer asked 'that ye wille shew them the law ther in whethyr they be infraunchesyd or noth. They trost sore in yowe.' It looks as if John Paston III was threatening to turn the clock back at Flegghall. Which brother had West Beckham? If the agreement of October 1442 was the basis of division between the brothers, as one assumes it was, then it was Thomas.[69] At what point Thomas died and Edward collected together all four estates we do not know.

[65] These estates do not appear in John's *IPM*, whereas Mautby, Sparham, Bessingham, Matlask (Davis I, p. 555) and Fritton in Suffolk do (Bodleian Library, Norfolk Charters a8 744).

[66] Margaret leased Kirkhall and Briston to Thomas Brigge of Salle, gentleman, in August 1480 for seven years at £18 a year: Davis I, no. 229. In her will (*ibid.*, p. 385) Margaret left money only to the tenants of Mautby, Fritton, Bessingham, Matlask, and Sparham, which suggests it was made before 1479. Margaret's first court at Kirkhall in 1479 is noted as such in a booklet of courts of the period: NRO, NRS 2721 (Box 12 D1), f. 40v.

[67] Davis II, p. 359. Alan Roos appears in the Salle Kirkhall accounts of 1445–6, but not as the lord's receiver; that was William Styward (NRO, NRS 12252 (Box 30 D4)). Still, this letter should, I think, be regarded as of a date nearer 1450 than 1470.

[68] NRO, Phillipps MS. 536 (Box 578 × 2). It cannot be to Judge William Paston, as Professor Norman Davis tentatively suggested, for it dates from after 1479.

[69] The October 1442 settlement (NRO, NRS 26179) has Thomas ahead of Edward as Eleanor's remainderman.

Edward lived in London (and had a London wife). John Paston II knew them there in the 1470s. Margaret hoped his aunt would make him some shirts out of three yards of 'scherte clothys . . . of the fynest that is in thys towne [Norwich]' in October 1470, and in November 1472 John was hoping to board his sister Ann with his aunt 'iff my moodre will depart wyth c.s. be yere, wher-off I am not serteyn'. He concluded, in his 'hoity-toity' manner and with a heavy emphasis on *my*: 'Neverthelesse I woll purveye for hyre thoghe I sholde paye the c.s. by yeer my-selffe, and, yit she is nott my dowtre.'[70] Sir John showed his more disagreeable side most clearly after his uncle's death in spring 1479. To his mother he was blunt about his Aunt Maud: 'It is a peyne to deele wyth hyre.' He went on, 'She is in many thyngys full lyke a wyffe off London and off Londone kyndenesse, and she woll needys take advise off Londonerys, wheche I telle here can nott advyse her howghe she scholde deele weell wyth any body off worshyp.'

It is a revealing passage of snobbery: the metropolitan gent. displaying his anti-bourgeois prejudice. Maud may have been being difficult, but in trying to secure an annuity from the likes of the Pastons, being easy, as she no doubt was well aware, would not get her anything. She was understandably careful. As John reported to his mother:[71]

I was yisterdaye wyth myn oncle Mautebyes wyffe . . . to have delyveré off suche evydencys as she hathe . . . I prayed hyre to se them, and soo at the laste she grauntyd me to see them, and so yisterdaye I sawe them; and ther come iiij off her neyborys and wer ther present, whyche as I conseyvyd wer but shewyd and browte uppe for that I sholde thynke that she lakked noon helpe; and many suche soleyn toyes she hathe, and she hopyth that ye sholde depart wyth her wyth a fee off x marke or xx marke by yeer. Bott as God helpe me I thynke, contrary to her promyse made to me, she hathe laten other folkys see thos evydencys, for she knywe every dede weelle j-nowe and browte me forthe fyrst iij boxis wyth olde evydencys, I syghe never older, but as to seye that ther be any that will avayle, as God helpe me I deme nott there is nott paste x ore xij olde dedys that I wolde gyffe for a grote, and yit ther be abowte an houndred olde dedys in alle iij boxis. And than for a second corse she browte me iij other deedys endentyd off suche astate as was made to myn ij onclys off Sall, Wynterton, &c., and off them wolde she speke no worde tyll that I tolde heer that she most needys have suche; and soo she wolde graunte noo more, saff that I bare hyre soo on hande that I wost well ther were more, so at the last she seyde that she shalle delyver alle iff she have her monye.

It is a passage with a theme which recurs: 'abowte an houndred olde dedys in alle iij boxis'. Deeds and deed boxes: are they more important than people? Not for Margaret. After her eldest son's death she paid an annuity to her uncle's widow, even if it was only of 6 marks.[72] So far as we are concerned, and so far as the Pastons were, Maud was the last of the Mautbys. She might not have been: all Edward left to his son in his will was a

[70] Davis I, pp. 351, 451. [71] *Ibid.*, p. 513.
[72] NRO, NRS 2624 (Box 12 C2), Salle Kirkhall accounts of 1479–80.

bed and a crimson gown; it is unlikely he had anything more substantial to give him.[73]

What had the family gained from the Mautby marriage, the marriage which I have insisted was the more important of the two Judge William made, and in its sequel was as important as Clement Paston's to Beatrice Somerton? It had acquired land and connection. The land we can now summarize. By the time John Paston III was head of the family and held all the Mautby lands he was better off for doing so by about £150 a year. That was the long-term and far from inconsiderable financial advantage of the match made in 1440. John Paston I, John Paston II, or perhaps we should say Margaret herself, had less than this for thirty or so years after the death of Eleanor Chambre in 1445. How much less is not calculable. The three manors Edward Mautby (and Thomas Mautby) held between 1446 and 1479 were probably not valuable. Kirkhall in Salle and Briston Mautby together were worth about £20 per annum in the 1470s.[74] Flegghall was

[73] Edward's will is PCC, Probate 11/6, f. 274v, dated 15 April, proved 11 May 1479. It is short. Maud was the sole executor; Roger Grove of London, 'netmaker', was the supervisor. Edward wished to be buried before the image of the Virgin Mary in St James, Garlickhithe. He left to Maud 'a bage of gold and all the money that is come of my lyvelod due to be paied to me att this tyme'. To Maud's daughter, Joan Walson, he left 6s 8d and a russet gown, to Roger Underwood, 'my manne', a doublet. That was it.

[74] There are a number of account rolls for Salle Kirkhall and Briston at the Norfolk Record Office. Once too fragile for consultation, they have now been repaired: see Boxes 12 C2, 12 C3, 30 D3, 30 D4. NRS 26133 (Box 143 × 1) is an account for 1471–2. It is a careful production. Salle Kirkhall was a discrete estate: the bailiff received monies (to the nearest shilling) from the 'messors' of Oulton (52s), Dalling (40s), Mortoft (9s), Thrynyng (65s), Woodcroft (22s), Salle (70s), and Briston (£5). The bailiff himself accounted for the leased demesne at Salle (£5 10s) and the sale of grain (6s); his outgoings were 70s. He duly handed over to the lord 'in presencia auditorum' £20 10s and was discharged. John Dynne was steward and auditor: he had a fee of 13s 4d and a gown valued at 6s 8d. (He had been steward for at least twenty-five years: NRS 12252, accounts of 1445–6.) John Dynne was an oppressor: some years later Elizabeth Brews wrote to her son-in-law, John Paston III: 'And, son, I thank you hertely for my son William Brews, and I moste pray you for the reverens of Jesu to help hym for youre tenauntes and myne, or els John Dynne will owere-rewle them' (Davis II, p. 457). William Brews held the manor of Stinton Hall in Salle: *CIPM Henry VII*, I, pp. 438–9; Blomefield, IV, pp. 418–20. An account for Briston of 1475–6 (NRS 24692) records the profit of the 'messor' as £6 and a halfpenny. And in the 1450s Thomas Gnateshall wrote to Margaret: 'I have ben att Salle and enqueryd ther, and my Mayster Edward is clerly answeryd of xviij li. be yere and more vij or viij s., and so hath it be these iiij yere, and all the londys leton ther' (Davis II, p. 337). In 1480 Margaret leased out the two estates for seven years at £18 per annum (Davis I, no. 229). The lease appears a generous one. Although the property usually produced less than £20 annually before 1470, in 1470–1 the profit ['profectus'] of the two manors was nearly £26 (NRS 2633 (Box 12 C3)), in 1471–2 the revenue for the lord was just over £20 (as we have seen), in 1474–5 it was £23 (NRS 2634), and in 1475–6 it was £21 (NRS 2635). There is no mention of Maud Mautby's annuity in the lease of 1 August 1480; the lease was to begin at Michaelmas; on 8 September 1480 Margaret paid one of £4 to her aunt-in-law, called Mary in these accounts of 1479–80: NRO, NRS 2624 (Box 12 C2). Did she continue to pay it after the lease had begun, and out of the revenues of Salle Kirkhall? The lease would then have been less generous.

not likely to be worth a great deal more; West Beckham was probably worth a great deal less.[75] Thus, the family was around £100 a year richer during these years.

But what does that mean? They were Margaret's lands; her husband, John I, certainly enjoyed them; after 1466 John II certainly did not. His financial position was worse than his father's: Agnes continued to enjoy her husband's generosity; John II survived her by no more than three months; *his* mother survived him.[76] Moreover, John II inherited the almost hopeless cause of Fastolf's will, a financial debit rather than asset until he took the course of compromise that his father refused. Sympathy, if we are allowed to express it, should be extended to him. Condemned by his father, criticized by his mother, he it was who yet contrived (against most of the odds) to bring home a little of the Fastolf bacon, which was more than none of it – something all too probable at one, perhaps at every, stage until the last. None the less, if the Mautby marriage was neither an immediate nor a simple financial coup Margaret was an incremental catch.

She was, of course, more than money. Three of her manors were in the hundred of North Erpingham: the mysterious West Beckham, Bessingham, and Matlask. East and West Beckham, Gresham, and Matlask comprised a

[75] In 1431 its farmer, William Shepherd's arrears were 78 shillings, of which he had paid 72 shillings. If 78 shillings was only half the year's farm, the estate was not a valuable one: NRO, NRS 12242 (Box 30 D3).

[76] The tension which existed between John II and his mother in 1473 was due to John II's lack of money and his mother's initial unreadiness to lend him any. We might say his having too little and Margaret having ample was caused by the division of the family lands between them, if it were not for the fact that 'family lands' is a meaningless concept: Margaret had her lands, Sir John had his. He, after all, was no more generous to John III when he wished to marry Margaret Brews in 1477, than Margaret had been towards him in 1473. This lack of family solidarity will be explored in its due place (chapter 6). Two quotations will demonstrate the predicament of an heiress's sons and grandsons. John II wrote to his mother on 30 July 1473: 'and so my fadre, God have hys sowle, leffte me scant xl li. londe in rest, and ye leffte me as pleasythe yow, and my grauntdame at hyre pleasure. Thus maye I have lytell hope off the worlde' (Davis I, p. 466). John III wrote to his brother on 8 July 1472: 'My modyr purposeith hastyly to take estate in all hyr londys, and up-on that estate to make hyr wyll of the seyd londys: parte to geve to my yonger brethyrn for term of her lyvys and aftyr to remain to yow, pert to my syster Annys maryage tyll an c li. be payid, part for to make hyr jle at Mawtby, parte for a prest to syng for hyr and my fadyr and ther ancecstrys. And in thys angyr betwen Syr James [Gloys] and me she hathe promyseid me that my parte shall be nowght; what your shalbe I can not sey. God sped the plowghe!' (*ibid.*, p. 577). She did not do any of this: to John III, as head of the family, she left all her lands; for Edmund and his wife there was only a 5-mark annuity out of Fritton, for William 100 marks to purchase lands or 'ellys to bye a warde to be maried to him if eny such may be goten'; Anne was already married and simply had £10 'to hir propre use' (*ibid.*, pp. 387–9). James Gloys, Margaret's chaplain, may have played the divisive role Margaret's sons believed him to be playing (*ibid.*, pp. 470, 582), for after his death in autumn 1473, Margaret became more accommodating to her eldest son (*ibid.*, pp. 474, 475, 477), though not immediately (*ibid.*, p. 470, lines 9–10). She was still severe on 5 November 1473, when Elizabeth Clere was pressing her for repayment of 100 marks loaned to Margaret and given to John (Davis I, no. 209, redated by Roger Virgoe).

block of Paston property which surrounded Town Barningham on three sides, while Matlask itself cut off that manor of the Winters from their property at Little Barningham. The Mautby marriage not only brought Judge William estates in the hundred he was endeavouring to dominate, these estates were so placed that Edmund Winter must have felt thoroughly beleaguered. If there was a moment when the war against the Winters was won it was when Margaret Mautby made John Paston 'gentil chere in gentil wyse' one spring day at Paston in 1440. All in all that was a momentous encounter in the Pastons' history.

For, in addition to bringing them money and strategic manors, Margaret Mautby strengthened the Pastons' place in Norfolk society. With this alliance they arrived, or thought they had. The Mautbys were an ancient, respected family. Whereas William's own marriage was a tentative advance into local society, the marriage of John and Margaret Mautby was the culmination of William's campaign. Living to see them produce a healthy son ought to have made him a happy old man. Moreover, Margaret brought them kin as well as status. What relatives of note had they had before William married Agnes? None, once the childless Geoffrey Somerton had gone, and he was barely notable. Rye MS 38, which displays their 'quality' by blazoning their alliances, shows that if the Pastons were a family created by the law, they established themselves by these two marriages. There is a single shield of Paston impaling Somerton; there are many showing Barrys, Hengraves, Gerbridges, Mautbys, Berneys impaling each other and other distinguished families. Both Agnes and Margaret brought the Pastons what anachronistically one might call class, and more than a touch. Agnes did not, however, bring worshipful kin: Barrys, Gerbridges, Hengraves were dying or dead breeds; Agnes is an isolated figure, not least because she never remarried. Nor, of course, did Margaret. Her mother did: Ralph Garneys esquire. Margaret Berney (as once she had been) also had many Berney relatives. Margaret, therefore, came trailing relations. Friends, helpful working associates, good neighbours one needed, sustaining kin were essential too. Elizabeth Clere may have meant most to Margaret herself: the Pastons and the Cleres must, therefore, be deferred to a later exposition. Sir John Fastolf undoubtedly meant most to her husband: that relationship must soon be explored. For the moment, let us turn to the Garneys and the Berneys and what they meant to the Paston family.

Chapter 5

RELATIONS: THE GARNEYS AND THE BERNEYS

Margery Berney married Ralph Garneys within eighteen months of the death of her first husband: John Mautby died in February 1433; she and Ralph were married by October 1434.[1] Ralph was an intemperate man. Between ten and eleven o'clock in the morning of 6 February 1438 in Westminster Hall in the presence of the judges of the King's Bench and the Common Pleas and all those attending the courts there he struck in the face with his right fist Edmund Fitzwilliam, deputy of the Duke of Norfolk, Marshal of the Marshalsea of King's Bench.[2] Gilbert Debenham was not a peaceable man either.[3] In 1444 that 'able and unscrupulous villain',[4] with a number of folk from the duke's town of Bungay, smashed Ralph's

> close, mills and sluices at Elyngham by Stokton [Stockton], dragged up the sluices from their base, broke them into small pieces, dug in his soil and diverted the course of the waters running to the mills, whereby his stanks remained dry, entered his free warren at Stokton, hunted therein, fished in his several fishery at Elyngham and Gelston [Geldeston] and carried away fish and land from his soil to the value of £40 and hares, rabbits, pheasants and partridges from the said warren, and lay in wait to kill him at Elyngham and assaulted and wounded his men and servants.

There were two commissions of enquiry into this outrage, one of June 1444, when William Paston was among the commissioners, the other of September 1444. In the same month of September, virtually the same group of commissioners was required to examine a complaint of the Duke of

[1] PRO, C139/78/40; College of Arms MS 326/8.

[2] *CPR 1436–41*, p. 198. Does this mean Ralph lost a hand (the penalty for striking someone in the king's court)? Among those instructed to enquire into his lands, which had been seized for this offence, were Sir John Fastolf (one of Ralph's father's feoffees) and Sir John Radcliff. At the PRO, I (and a number of keepers) have been unable to find the inquisition noted in the fourth volume of *The Calendars of Inquisitions Post Mortem* (Record Commission, 1828), p. 304, various inquisitions of the reign of Henry VI, no. 42. The calendar entry, after recording Ralph's manors of Stockton, Redisham, and Weston, reads 'Quae Dux Norfolk intravit quia praefatus Radulphus in Magna Aula Westminster pugnabat sedentibus curiis. Anno 16.'

[3] Debenham was an associate of the duke's at this time: W.I. Haward, 'Gilbert Debenham, a Medieval Rascal in Real Life', *History*, 13 (1928–9), p. 302; Wedgwood (*Biographies*, p. 264) says he was the duke's steward.

[4] *Ibid.*, p. 300.

The Garneys Family

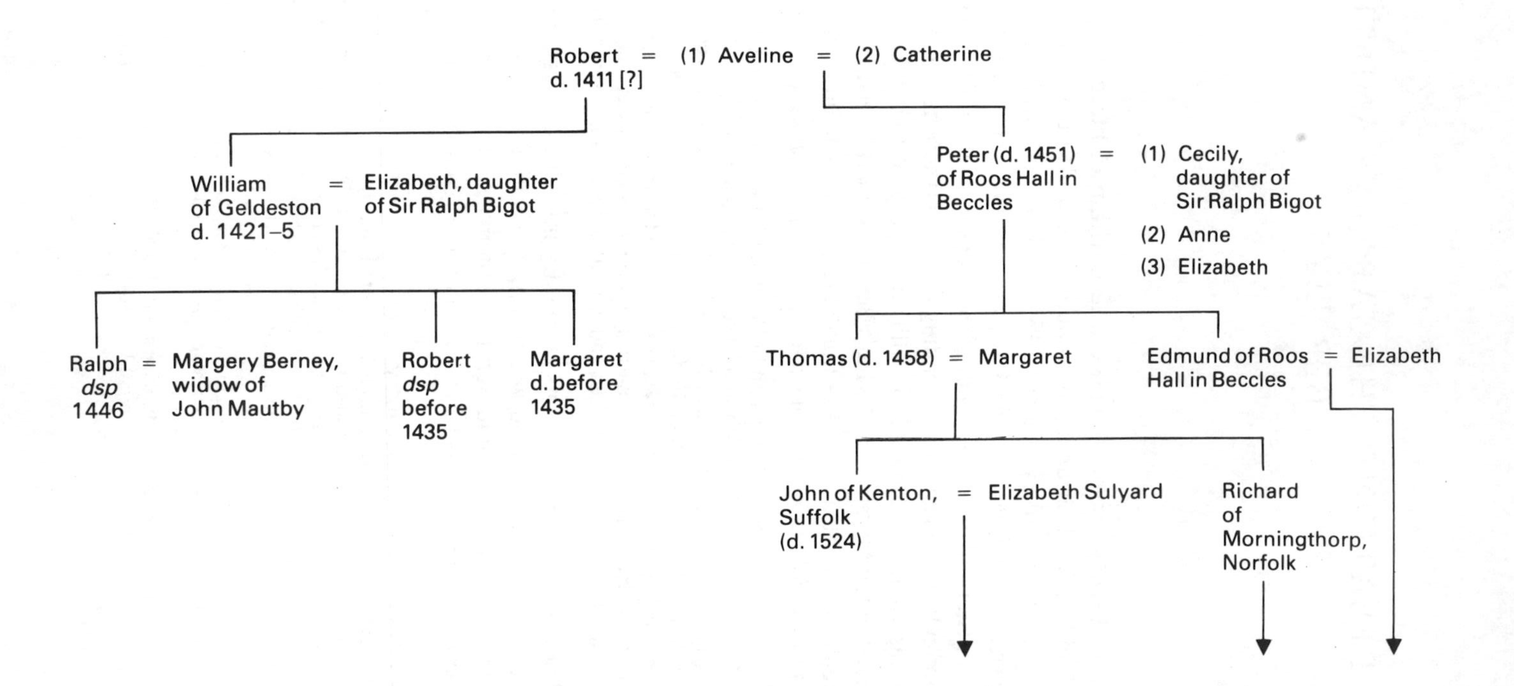

Robert d. 1411 [?] = (1) Aveline = (2) Catherine
William of Geldeston d. 1421–5 = Elizabeth, daughter of Sir Ralph Bigot
Peter (d. 1451) of Roos Hall in Beccles = (1) Cecily, daughter of Sir Ralph Bigot (2) Anne (3) Elizabeth
Ralph dsp 1446 = Margery Berney, widow of John Mautby
Robert dsp before 1435
Margaret d. before 1435
Thomas (d. 1458) = Margaret
Edmund of Roos Hall in Beccles = Elizabeth
John of Kenton, Suffolk (d. 1524) = Elizabeth Sulyard
Richard of Morningthorp, Norfolk

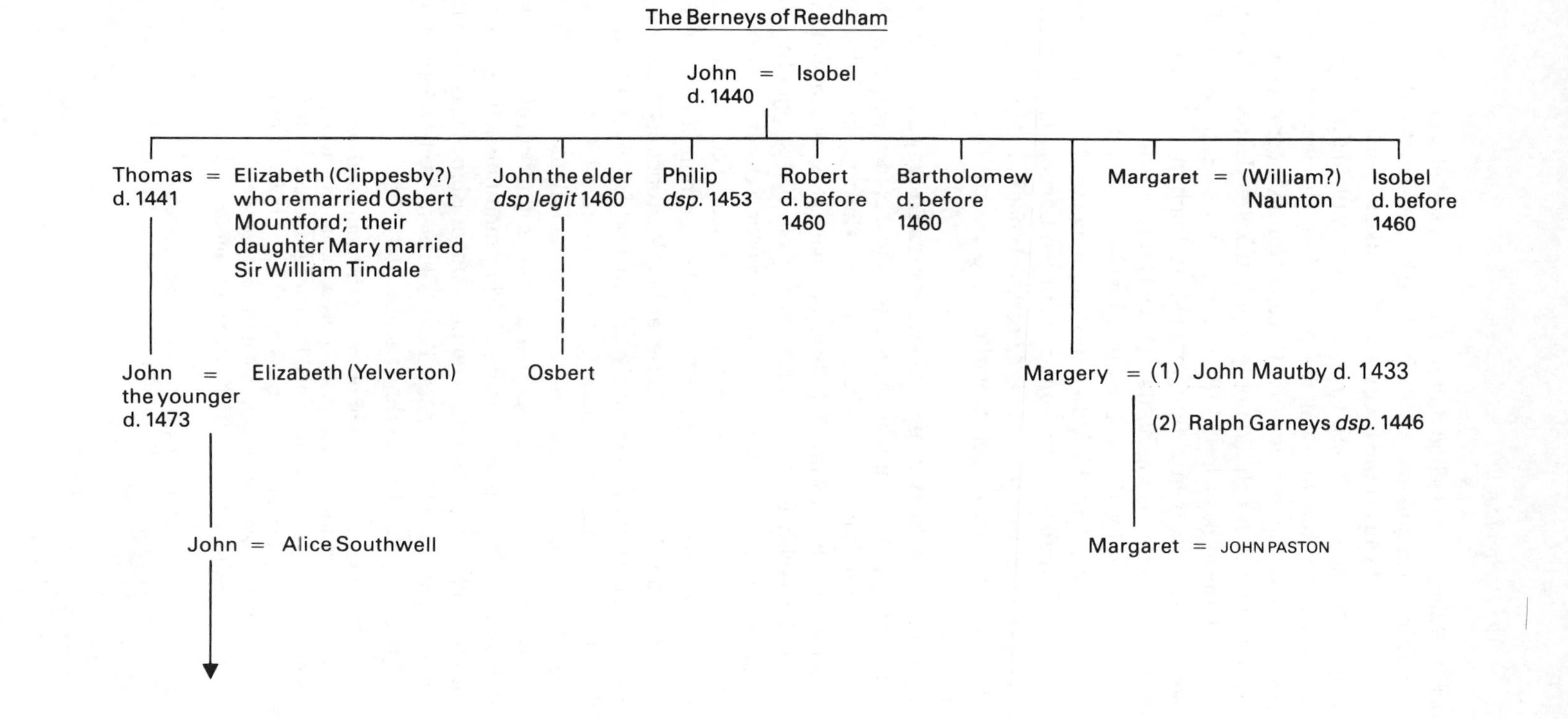

The Berneys of Reedham
John = Isobel
d. 1440
Thomas = Elizabeth (Clippesby?)
d. 1441
who remarried Osbert Mountford; their daughter Mary married Sir William Tindale
John the elder
dsp legit 1460
Philip
dsp. 1453
Robert
d. before 1460
Bartholomew
d. before 1460
Margaret = (William?) Naunton
Isobel
d. before 1460
John = Elizabeth (Yelverton)
the younger
d. 1473
Osbert
Margery = (1) John Mautby d. 1433
(2) Ralph Garneys *dsp.* 1446
John = Alice Southwell
Margaret = JOHN PASTON

Norfolk: Ralph Garneys had dug in the duke's soil at Mettingham; he had taken away earth and made a ditch which had obstructed the Mettingham brook; this had caused the flooding of the duke's meadow.[5]

How tantalizing are these references to an assault in the most public place in the Kingdom and to what we might call 'the war of the Waveney watermills'. Does John Mowbray, Duke of Norfolk's connection with both mean that he and Ralph did not 'get on'? If Ralph deliberately set upon a servant of the duke's in 1438, was the duke's setting on of Gilbert Debenham and the men of Bungay against Ralph in 1444 another act of violence in a long-lasting battle? There is one probably coincidental yet intriguing fact: Ralph Garneys' mother had been the last of the Bigots, Earls of Norfolk long before the Mowbrays and builders of Bungay Castle. One thing is sure: there was antagonism between Garneys and Mowbray. Did this propel Ralph into the de la Pole camp? What may Margaret and John Paston have learnt from her stepfather's experience? To these questions we shall return.

Violence along the Waveney valley between Bungay and Beccles was no novelty in the 1440s, nor was participation in it of members of the Garneys family. In 1406 Ralph's grandfather Robert Garneys, his father William, and uncle Peter broke into Sir Robert Ty's park at Barsham (while he was fighting the Welsh in Wales) and carried off 400 sheep. This was not rustling; Sir Robert had impounded the sheep for services due to him.[6] Peter Garneys was himself the victim of two later acts of communal anger and self-help. In 1430 the parson of Beccles led a group of fellow townsmen against him, breaking into his 'close' at Beccles, robbing and beating him.[7] Their grievance then was probably the one that led them later to 'Jeraldys Hyl', which belonged, Peter claimed, to his manor of Roos or Roses Hall in Beccles. The townsfolk of Beccles 'came to the hill and hewed, cut up and bore away broom and brakes growing there, saying openly with great cry and clamour: "This is oure Comown."' They maintained the place was part of the abbey of Bury St Edmund's manor and lordship of Beccles and got the abbey on their side. At this point Peter Garneys 'declaration' of 9 March 1449[8] becomes plaintive, perhaps deliberately so:

dan William Babyngton late 'chaumberer' of the house and now abbot . . . wyth the supportation of myghtie lordship, took an assize against Garneys, and had a panel and the country ready before Garneys had knowledge thereof, so that at the assizes he and his heirs were like to have been disinherited; he then, being of a great age and feebleness of spirit and unable to get counsel, 'offred tretees' that their titles might be examined by their 'bothers councel' and surety made to abide by the award of the

[5] *CPR 1441–6*, pp. 290, 337, 338. [6] *CPR 1405–8*, p. 230.
[7] *CPR 1429–36*, pp. 41, 124. William Paston headed the commission of oyer and terminer.
[8] *CCR 1447–54*, pp. 112–13.

abbot of Bury, so that Garneys might be warned to have counsel to declare his title; that he came to Bury to have a day assigned to have his counsel inform the abbot of his title, but he could get no longer day 'but at that same tyme'; and so, having no counsel there 'but such as were toward the hous' they threatened that they would make him lose £100 in damages and expenses; whereat being disconsolate he was ruled to take the hill and pasture to farm under his seal, against right and conscience as far as he could know; wherefore he beseeches his feoffees who were enfeoffed in trust long before his disturbance, and all other good lords, masters and friends, to help and remedy this disturbance, to which he only consented by duress and feebleness of wit and spirit.

Without doubt the feoffee of his he was most looking to for redress was William de la Pole, Duke of Suffolk.[9] Whose had been the 'myghtie lordship' which had supported William Babington? Might it have been the Duke of Norfolk's?

Peter Garneys was of 'a great age' in 1449, but his will of August and lengthy codicil of September 1451[10] display no 'feebleness of spirit'. For a man who had been a king's esquire to Henry V and who had kept his livery collar all his life,[11] he is hard to trace, harder (because he was even less active) than the surprising supervisor of his will, John Hopton esquire.[12] Although variant versions of his name (Garveys and Gerveys as well as Garneys) may have hidden some of his activity from this enquirer, Peter seems to have kept so low a public 'profile' that one begins to suspect some disability – like John Hopton's blindness. Perhaps Peter, once a soldier, to judge by his bequests of armour, had been disabled in his royal master's wars.[13] He will have known that other old soldier Sir John Fastolf, for in 1418 Peter was granted the wardship of the son of Sir Hugh Fastolf.[14] All I can discover him doing in local government in Suffolk over thirty years is being an *ad hoc* commissioner three times, the last time of array in 1436 with John Hopton.[15] Yet local grandee he most certainly was, a striking

[9] Named by him with Sir John Heveningham earlier in the declaration: *ibid*, p. 112. The Heveninghams were 'ambidextrous': the Dukes of Suffolk and the Dukes of Norfolk got their service (see *Hopton*, pp. 234–8). [10] NRO, NCC Reg. Aleyn, fs. 101v–104v.

[11] It was to be sold by his executors, not handed on to one or other of his two sons as were many other of his valuables. Was this abnormal practice? Dr Philip Morgan tells me that in 1423 Roger Jodrell bequeathed his silver collar to his third son, William: John Rylands University Library, Manchester, Jodrell Charters 35.

[12] This is the only occasion I have come across John Hopton as supervisor or executor. John was also a feoffee of Peter's: *CIPM Henry VII*, I, p. 349. This is all there is to indicate a friendship, association, acquaintance (or whatever it was) between these superficially dissimilar esquires of north-east Suffolk.

[13] He was a muster commissioner at Argentan in January 1418: T.H. Hardy (ed.), *Rotuli Normannie* (London, 1835), p. 359. In December of the following year he had licence to ship wine from Rouen to England: Calendar of Norman Rolls, *Forty-second Report of the Deputy Keeper of the Public Records* (London, 1881), p. 331.

[14] *CPR 1416–22*, pp. 134, 136; cf. *Calendar of Signet Letters 1399–1422*, nos. 821, 864.

[15] *CPR 1416–22*, p. 275; *CPR 1429–36*, pp. 137, 523.

resident of a small market town (his manor of Roos Hall lay on the western edge of Beccles), as his will demonstrates.

In the north aisle of St Michael's parish church, where he wished to be buried, his sepulchral stone had already been made ready. He was generous in his bequests to St Michael's and other local churches: to the north aisle of St Michael's, to the new towers at Endgate and Ringsfield, for repairs at Weston, Mutford, Barsham, and Worlingham. He left £5 for a thousand masses to be said by the friars of Norwich, Yarmouth, Dunwich, and Ipswich for his soul, his parents', and his wives' souls. He remembered all the neighbouring nunneries: Bungay, Flixton, Redlingfield, Bruisyard, Carrow. The Cistercian house of Sibton received £1 'pro uno vestimento albo' to celebrate the mass of the Virgin. Silver salts and goblets went to his sons Edmund and Thomas; Edmund also got the best pewter service – six of chargers, dishes, plates, and saucers. Edmund's wife, Elizabeth, was to have 'meum tabultum argentum et auratum'. Thomas' wife, Margaret, was to have his 'unycorn horn' with its golden chain. Each son was to have a fur-lined gown, and Edmund, who was to have Roos Hall, was bequeathed the contents of the rooms there, including those of the chapel and oratory; among those objects were singled out his French books ('libris galice'). His best 'Sallet' and its accompanying armour were also to go to Edmund; Thomas was to have his best pair of 'Brygaunteres'; the gild of St Michael's Church was to have other pieces of armour. There was no mention of the sword called 'Bastard' with its silver trappings left him by his brother in 1421, though it had been William Garneys' best sword.[16]

What also fits the picture (of the magnanimous old soldier at home in local society) is the identity of his first-named executor, William Oulton, parson of Beccles, for William Oulton twenty years before had led the townsmen to attack Roos Hall and assault its owner.[17] Now, one presumes, William was preparing Peter for another world: reconciliation and forgiveness were conditions of that preparation. Peter's other executors were workmanlike after a different fashion; William Jenny, Robert and John Banyard were lawyers who knew their this-worldly business; it was the Banyards who were given administration of the will when it was proved at Norwich on 5 February 1452. They had certainly done the first part of their job: what we might call the real-estate sections of Peter's will are meticulously composed. Not wishing to lose sight of Ralph Garneys, we shall simplify, which is readily done, as Peter's provisions for his properties were straightforward.

Roos Hall in Beccles went to Edmund, almost certainly Peter's second son,

[16] NRO, NCC Reg. Hyrnyng f. 136. [17] *CPR 1429–36*, pp. 41, 124.

and his heirs.[18] Thomas, who already had had Kenton in Suffolk settled on him (no doubt on his marriage), was to have the three other Suffolk manors of Redisham, Barsham, and Weston, according to the will of William Garneys, Peter's brother and Ralph's father. Kenton, where this main stem of the family[19] settled and built themselves in the early sixteenth century a fine brick house and added a modest brick south aisle to the parish church,[20] does not concern us: Peter Garneys had acquired the estate by marriage to Anne (or Elizabeth) Ramsey.[21] Redisham, Barsham, and Weston do concern us. When Peter bequeathed them to Thomas in 1451 he had enjoyed them for no longer than half a dozen years – since Ralph Garneys' death in 1446. Because Ralph had died without children, they had descended to Peter, as his brother William's will of 1421 specified.

Predictably and, as we might by this time be thinking, inevitably, nephew and uncle had fallen out over the will. On 29 January 1437, Peter, on the

[18] There was much property pertaining to the manor: a windmill, for example, tenements in Barsham and Mutford, and meadow, marsh, and woods in Endgate, Shipmeadow, Worlingham, Ilketshall, and elsewhere in and around Beccles. For the descent, thereafter, see Copinger, *Manors* VII, p. 159. It was presumably Thomas Garneys of Roos Hall (d. 1527), who was the executor of Elizabeth Morley in 1500. Not only had a Morley–Garneys connection been sustained for over a century, so had a de la Pole one: Elizabeth named her brother the Earl of Suffolk as supervisor of the will; for Elizabeth Morley, see 'Thomas, Lord Morley (d. 1416) and the Morleys of Hingham', *Norfolk Archaeology*, 39, part I (1984), p. 10 note 38; she desired to be buried in the church of the nuns of Carrow before Our Lady of Pity (NRO, NCC Reg. Cage, f. 183).

[19] According to Blomefield (III, pp. 194–5), the family successfully branched again, Thomas' second son Richard's son purchasing Boyland Hall in Morningthorp, Norfolk and settling there. Thomas Garneys died in 1458 (*CFR 1452–61*, p. 212, writ of *dce*); his widow, Margaret, who remarried Thomas Peyton esquire of Isleham, Cambridgeshire, died in 1492 in possession of Kenton (*CIPM Henry VII* I, pp. 308, 349, 352). Peter Garneys' feoffees of fifty years previously are named; they included both John Heveninghams (father and son), Thomas Brews, Robert Banyard and John Hopton, but not William, Duke of Suffolk.

[20] In 1983 the brass to Thomas' eldest son John Garneys (d. 1524) and his wife was not on the wall of what in John's will (NRO, NCC Reg. Briggs, f. 138) he calls 'my chapell on the south syde of Kenton church late by me Edified'. John's will is as long and as wordy as any of his ancestors', from among whose souls he selected those of Peter Garneys and Anne his wife, William and Robert Garneys to be prayed for daily for ninety-nine years in the chapel of his 'manor place' in Kenton which he had also 'late edified': this appears to be a family which did remember its dead – its dead of over a century past. John's wife Elizabeth was a daughter of Sir John Sulyard of Wetherden (d. 1488): 'The Sulyard Papers: the Rewards of a Small Family Archive' in Daniel Williams (ed.), *England in the Fifteenth Century. Proceedings of the 1986 Harlaxton Symposium* (London, 1987), pp. 199 ff. Was Christopher Garneys, knight porter of Calais 1526–34, he who possibly saved Mary Tudor from drowning, a younger brother of John's? For Christopher, see Muriel St Clare Byrne (ed.), *The Lisle Letters* (London, 1981), index, and *Letters and Papers*, vol. IV part III, index.

[21] Anne, according to the previous note and Copinger, *Manors*, IV, p. 295; Elizabeth, according to Blomefield III, p. 194. In his will Peter Garneys required prayers to be said in the north aisle of St Michael's church, Beccles, for ten years for the souls of both these wives, Anne and Elizabeth (NRO, NCC Reg. Aleyn, f. 102v). The soul of his first wife Cecily Bigot he did not mention; for her, to whom he was married in 1403, see below, p. 144; it looks either as if that may have been an arranged marriage which did not 'take', or that Cecily died before it might have done.

one hand, and, on the other, Ralph, Lawrence Balware, and Ralph's feoffees (who included Sir John Heveningham, William Paston, John Berney, two of John Berney's sons, as well as Edmund and Robert Wychingham[22] and John Jerningham,[23] John Fastolf of Oulton, and Robert Boys)[24] agreed to obey the arbitration of Ralph Lampet esquire, Reynold Rous, John Puttock, and John Tasburgh, with regard to 'all actions, plaints, demands and debates' about the last will of William Garneys.[25] Two of the actions were in Chancery. Ralph claimed he had been kept out of his paternal inheritance (Redisham, Barsham, and Weston) as well as his mother's estates of Stockton and Geldeston for seven years, since the deaths of his father and mother. His uncle had hung on to these properties as well as onto William's moveable

[22] Edmund Wychingham we have encountered before, busy on William Paston's behalf about Baxter's Place at Honing (chapter 2, p. 37; Davis II, p. 5). Sir John Fastolf called him cousin (Gairdner II, p. 199) as did Sir Henry Inglose, with whom Edmund was closely enough associated to be his executor (NRO, NCC Reg. Bettyns, f. 62v; Davis I, pp. 104–6, 243, 244). Edmund wrote an absorbing letter about the selection of sheriffs to John Paston I, whom he called cousin (Davis II, pp. 82–4), and John Paston I drafted an even more interesting one to Edmund's son-in-law Richard Southwell about the abduction of another of Edmund's daughters, Jane Boys, by one 'Lancasterother': Davis I, pp. 69–71, 'the master of Carbroke' (lines 44–5) was a Knight Hospitaller; the Hospitallers' house at Carbroke was next door to Edmund Wychingham's house at Woodrising. Jane's husband Robert Boys was dead by the time of her abduction (his will, NRO, NCC Reg. Aleyn, f. 46, was proved 6 November 1450); her abductor, Robert Langstrother, married her. There was trouble between them and Sibyl Boys, her first husband's mother and executor (for whom see chapter 2, p. 40), who had attempted to sell property of Robert Boys to Edmund Blake. In the reply of Robert Inglose, a feoffee of Robert Boys, to Blake's bill in Chancery, he maintained Robert Boys had said to William Bedewyll, vicar of Deopham, after making his confession, that his wife Jane and daughter Katherine should have his lands and he never altered his mind while wit and speech remained to him: PRO, CI/15/319, CI/16/606. Jane was one of Edmund's four daughters; the other three were Anne, Frances, and Elizabeth; they were unmarried in June 1451 when Sir Henry Inglose left £10 to the marriage of whichever one of them (beginning with Anne) survived to be married (NRO, NCC Reg. Bettyns, f. 62v). They all survived to be married; the £10 ought, therefore, to have gone to Anne, who married Richard Southwell: Blomefield IV, p. 442. Edmund, the second son of Nicholas Wychingham, was of Woodrising, Norfolk, one of the manors left to him by his father; Robert was Edmund's nephew, that is the son of William, Edmund's elder brother: *ibid.*, pp. 442–3. Edmund's widowed mother Joan lived with him at Woodrising; on her death in 1460 she left 13s 4d 'ad quandam tabulam de Allebaster' in the church there: her will is NRO, NCC Reg. Brosyard, f. 188.

[23] This was probably the elder John Jerningham. When the younger in 1458 wrote to his cousin Margaret Paston he was hoping to marry Blanche Wychingham: Davis II, p. 340. She was the daughter of Robert Wychingham and Agnes who remarried James Arblaster (lines 11–12; cf. Davis I, p. 329, Davis II, p. 99); James Arblaster wrote to John Paston I the engaging Davis II, no. 702, in which, as a Wychingham by marriage (so to speak), he was protecting that family's foldage rights against John Berney of Witchingham's intrusion. For the younger John Jerningham see also Davis I, pp. 269, 319. I am not sure whether it is the elder or the younger John Jerningham who died in 1474 leaving two sons, John his heir and Osbern, and three daughters, one married and two nuns, Thomasin at Denny and Barbara at Campsea: his will is NRO, NCC Reg. Hilberd, f. 34.

[24] For Robert Boys see note 22. Lawrence Balware was parson at Ralph's Stockton in Norfolk; John Berney was by this time Ralph's father-in-law.

[25] *CCR 1435–41*, pp. 109, 111.

goods. Peter's rejoinder was that he had done so in order to perform, as his brother's executor, William's will.[26] William Garneys' feoffees, led by Sir William Phelip, claimed or counter-claimed that Ralph Garneys and Lawrence Balware had deceitfully got them to make an enfeoffment to Ralph which prevented the carrying out of William's will.[27] What was this trouble about?

It could have been (but certainly was not) about a marsh in Worlingham called 'le Park'. In his will William Garneys left this property to his brother Peter. It was all that he left to him; and it was not left to him directly. William Garneys' last will of 3 February 1421 was not proved until 6 April 1425. Peter Garneys was one of the three executors who were given administration.[28] So far as the will was concerned (rather than the brief and straightforward testament), they and William's feoffees had, over the succeeding years, complicated tasks to perform: they had to match William's careful instructions for every eventuality to those eventualities as they occurred. The park in Worlingham was among a group of properties in Wangford Hundred, Suffolk, of which the chief were the three manors of Redisham, Barsham, and Weston. This bundle of properties, some of which had once been Edmund Redisham's and William de Barsham's,[29] and others which William or his father Robert had bought, was left to William's widow, Elizabeth, for life. Out of the revenues of these estates she was to maintain their two sons, Ralph and Robert, and their daughter, Margaret, until they came of age. If she married, then on the boys' coming of age she lost the estates. Weston was to descend to Robert and his heirs, with remainder to Ralph and his heirs; Redisham, Barsham, and the rest, apart from the park in Worlingham, which Peter was to have, were to go to Ralph and his heirs, with remainder to Robert and his heirs. If both Robert and Ralph were to die without heirs, Margaret and her heirs were to inherit all these Wangford Hundred lands, including the three manors; if Margaret also died childless Peter Garneys and his heirs were to have them.

By 1432 or 1433, when Ralph was old enough to complain to the chancellor about his uncle's administration of the will and William's feoffees

[26] PRO, C1/71/80. Peter Garneys had also had problems with Roos Hall in Beccles, for help in solving which he turned to the chancellor; his petition (C/10/56) is badly faded; John Heydon, however, seems to be the culprit among a group of feoffees or executors.

[27] PRO, C1/12/138.

[28] Although the testament is dated 23 February the last will is dated 3 February. Sir William Phelip (the most important of William's feoffees) was supervisor of the testament: NRO, NCC Reg. Hyrnyng fs. 136–8.

[29] Copinger, *Manors*, VII, p. 219. Two account rolls of Weston for 1388–91 and 1404–8 survive: BL Add. Chs. 26061, 26062. It was a small estate, worth about £6 a year in the early fifteenth century (Add. Ch. 26062). There is an extent for Weston and Redisham of July 1495 in the Suffolk Record Office at Ipswich: HB29/384/19.

pointed out to Peter what they maintained was Ralph's sharp practice, Elizabeth was certainly, and Robert and Margaret were probably, dead, the two last without children, no doubt without having married. They were certainly dead by 30 November 1435 when Sir William Phelip, Lord Bardolf, Sir John Fastolf and the other feoffees of William Garneys granted Redisham, Barsham, Weston, Stockton, and Geldeston – everything, indeed, *except* the park in Worlingham – to Ralph and his heirs, with remainder to Peter Garneys and his heirs.[30] On 20 June 1436 Ralph appointed his own feoffees: Sir John Heveningham, William Paston, John Berney, the Wychinghams and company; on 22 July 1437 they duly made their grant to Ralph.[31] It was 'duly' because the agreement to abide by an award had intervened: 29 January 1437. That seems to have been a last, rather than the first, instalment of the complex process of sorting out the troubles of uncle and nephew over William Garneys' will of twelve or more years previously. Why nephew and uncle disagreed is probably no mystery. William's will was no more complicated than the circumstances warranted, while the quickly ensuing deaths of his widow, one of his two sons and his daughter (who did not, therefore, have to be married) simplified them. Yet the executorship of Peter Garneys must have been tiresome: as he waited for Ralph to come of age he cannot have known what was going to happen next. He is scarcely to be blamed for hanging on rather longer than he ought to have done.

William Garneys' two principal manors of Stockton and Geldeston lay a few miles from Beccles across the Waveney in Norfolk. These Bigot estates William left to Elizabeth for life; as they were hers he had no other option. Their son Robert and daughter Margaret were to have £100 each out of the revenues towards their marriages. The manors were then to descend to Ralph; if he died without heirs and Robert and Margaret died also, the feoffees were to raise 1,000 marks from the properties and spend them for the benefit of the souls of William and Elizabeth, of Matilda Bigot, sometime Countess of Norfolk,[32] of Sir Ralph Bigot, her descendant (and Elizabeth Garneys' father, from whom these estates came to William), and of Robert Garneys and Aveline, his wife. That done, the two estates were to go to William Garneys' right heirs. To the fate of Stockton and Geldeston after Ralph's death without heirs in 1446 we will have to return.

In 1446, as the two estates left the family, Peter Garneys' thoughts might have returned to the arrangements by which they had entered it. In 1403 Robert Garneys contracted with Sir Ralph Bigot for the marriages of William and Peter to Sir Ralph's daughters, Elizabeth and Cecily. Peter and Cecily

[30] BL Cotton Ch. V3. Charter V22 is a power of attorney of the same date.
[31] BL Harleian Chs. 50: F37, F39, cited by Copinger, *Manors*, VII, pp. 203–4.
[32] This is, I take it, Maud, daughter of William Marshal, who died in 1248.

came second best out of that marriage-making.[33] Whereas Stockton and Geldeston were to be held by Sir Ralph Bigot for life with reversion to William and Elizabeth;[34] whereas William and Elizabeth were to have two water-mills at Ellingham at once;[35] whereas Peter and Cecily were to enfeoff Robert Garneys and his wife Katherine with the manors of Redisham and Barsham for their lives with reversion to William and Elizabeth:[36] all Peter and Cecily were to have was the reversion of lands worth 40 marks in which William was to enfeoff his father and mother for their lives. Perhaps 'all' is not the correct word; yet, even if Peter was a second son, Cecily was a co-heiress: why were William and Elizabeth to get so much, Peter and Cecily so little? The bargaining had undoubtedly been hard and may have been bitter: it was agreed between the parties 'that when these things shall be performed, either party shall be quit of all actions for trespass, debt or account, saving to the said William his action, claim, and demand against Sir Ralph for the scullery vessels of silver and vessels of brass which Sir Ralph has by his livery'. Successfully marrying up, so to speak, the equal rights of co-heiresses and the less than equal ones of an heir and his brother cannot have been easy. What Peter's land worth 40 marks consisted of, it seems certain, was his father's Roos Hall in Beccles. When Robert Garneys died (perhaps in 1411[37]) it came to him. There, as we have seen, he lived after most of a life, characteristically for a second son, spent in service elsewhere; his career in the royal household probably erased any memory of any affront (if there had been one) in 1403.

There was a great difference in age between Peter and William; undoubtedly they were Robert's sons by two wives, Aveline and Katherine, the latter being Peter's mother. In 1403 Peter can only have been a boy, even perhaps a child, whereas William had already made his mark in de la Pole service. At the baptism of William de la Pole at Cotton in Suffolk on 16 October 1396 William Garneys 'capitalis pincerna et buttelarius' of the

[33] For what follows, see *CCR 1402–5*, pp. 274–6.

[34] Geldeston is not mentioned, but Stockton includes Geldeston here as often elsewhere, and Sir Ralph's will of 15 February 1416 (proved 16 September 1416) was made at Geldeston; he desired to be buried in the chancel of the church there. One of his executors was Sir Thomas Geney: NRO, NCC Reg. Hyrnyng, f. 4. Another was Elizabeth, Sir Ralph's widow. She was (according to Blomefield I, p. 329) a Mortimer. Her will was made at Great Ellingham near Attleborough, though she wished to be buried in the church of the Austin Friars at Norwich. She had remarried Thomas Manning, to whom she left her lands at Great Ellingham, Attleborough, and Rockland. That was forty-seven years later: her will (NRO, NCC Reg. Brosyard, f. 316) was dated 26 July and proved 17 August 1463.

[35] These were perhaps the reasons for (at any rate they set the scene for) the later troubles. It is (by this stage) almost a duty to record yet another deed box: 'an iron bound chest with two locks', Sir Ralph to have one key, Robert and William Garneys the other.

[36] I take it that this was a form of quitclaim, or possibly the couple's relinquishing of two estates settled on them by Robert, perhaps as jointure.

[37] So Copinger, *Manors*, VII, p. 159.

newborn baby's father, Michael de la Pole, Earl of Suffolk, performed his duties so perfectly that Sir William Elmham tipped him £2.[38] Whether he transferred to the service of Thomas, Lord Morley, or served two masters I do not know; he certainly became Lord Morley's right-hand man. He it was who travelled from Beccles to Calais in autumn 1416 to bring his lord's body back to Norwich for burial; he also who supervised the writing of the account which tells us so.[39] If he had been serving two masters, the previous autumn he might have undertaken the same task on behalf of the body of the other; for Michael de la Pole, Earl of Suffolk, died of dysentery at Harfleur on 18 September 1415; his body was buried at Wingfield in Suffolk.[40] Although there was at this time a marriage alliance between de la Pole and Morley – Thomas, Lord Morley's grandson, Thomas, was married to Isobel, Michael de la Pole's daughter[41] – it seems most likely that by then William Garneys was a Morley servant, no longer a de la Pole one. For example, he was one of those given administration of the goods of the intestate Lord Morley in March 1417; he is not mentioned in the Earl of Suffolk's will of July 1415.[42]

William was also a feoffee of Thomas, Lord Morley; so were Peter Garneys, Sir William Phelip, Henry Inglose, Sir John Rothenale, and Edmund Winter.[43] William Garneys also knew William Paston, for Paston audited Garneys' accounts of those Morley lands which were in the feoffees' hands in July 1421.[44] Neither can have foreseen the twists and turns which would bring William Paston to stay the night of 21 September 1443 at Geldeston with William Garneys' son, Ralph, and which brought William Paston's grandson to be born there in the following year.[45] Yet they would not have been surprised: casual death made life take such twists and turns. Both may have been more surprised if they had known what was to happen to Geldeston itself.

[38] H.A. Napier, *Historical Notices of Swyncombe and Ewelme* (Oxford, 1858), p. 65. William, Duke of Suffolk's birth and christening at Cotton was, it seems to me, the compelling reason for his reluctance to part with this property, even though he sold it to Sir John Fastolf in the 1430s. His widow, Alice, wrenched it back from the Pastons in the 1460s. For this instructive story of attachment to place and person, see a future volume.

[39] 'Thomas, Lord Morley', pp. 2–3 and note 26. If, as I say there, Geldeston was his home, it had only just become so: Sir Ralph Bigot's will was proved on 16 September 1416 (see note 34, above); Thomas, Lord Morley died on 24 September, William set off for Calais on 2 October.

[40] *CP* XII, part I, p. 442. The bones of his son, Michael, who was killed at Agincourt five weeks later may also have come back to Suffolk – to Butley Priory: *ibid* p. 443.

[41] See, for example, 'Thomas, Lord Morley', p. 11, note 46.

[42] *Chichele's Register* II, pp. 58–60, 112–13. William Garneys mentions neither Morley nor de la Pole in his own testament of 1421.

[43] *CPR 1416–22*, pp. 53–4; *CCR 1422–29*, pp. 288–9.

[44] 'Thomas, Lord Morley', p. 11, note 60, citing NRO, MAC/B4. William Garneys had made his will in February.

[45] Davis I, pp. 218, 219–20, 565–6.

As we have seen, William Garneys in 1421 allowed for every eventuality – the deaths of all three of his children, Ralph, Robert, and Margaret, without children. If that came to pass 1,000 marks was to be raised by his executors from Geldeston and Stockton and spent for the benefit of his and various other named souls. That done, the two manors were to go to his or Elizabeth's right heirs. They did not: they went, and they went almost immediately, to William de la Pole, Duke of Suffolk. Ralph Garneys died in 1446; they were the duke's by the following year.[46] Did William's executors (one of whom was Peter Garneys, William's heir) agree with the feoffees, or with Ralph's feoffees, who may have replaced them, to raise the 1,000 marks by selling the two manors? Peter Garneys, though heir to his mother, had no legal claim to these two estates for they had been Elizabeth Bigot's; it was to *her* right heirs that they ought to have descended. The Duke of Suffolk, and later his widow and son were careful to obtain quitclaims from those heirs (or some of them): Edmund Swathing esquire in 1446, Thomas Sharington esquire, and a William Garneys and Matilda, his wife, in 1461.[47] Even if the collection of 1,000 marks might have appeared to the executors so daunting (and long term) a proposition that an outright sale was their only sensible course, it is, none the less, suspicious that it was William de la Pole who obtained Geldeston and Stockton. Did the duke pay 1,000 marks for the two manors, or was (as one suspects) some other sort of deal struck?

So, the Garneys left Geldeston. The family had lived there for no more than thirty years. Time enough for William and Elizabeth to have given the inscribed font, which survives, and for Ralph to have commemorated himself in the glass of the east window, which does not.[48]

Two thoughts occur. What did John Paston make of the Duke of Suffolk's acquisition of his stepfather-in-law's house, of the house were his second son had been born? These last years of the 1440s in East Anglia were a time when bold, unscrupulous men set about getting what was not theirs: Sir Edward Hull at Titchwell, Robert Hungerford, Lord Moleyns at Gresham, the Duke of Suffolk at Dedham. When did the rot observably set in? When was the rubicon, which divided the acceptably normal behaviour of the great from their too outrageous manipulation of government and the law, crossed; crossed, that is, in the minds of men of property like John Paston, a

[46] Blomefield IV, pp. 234, 258–9. They were certainly in the duke's possession by February 1448: *CCR 1447–54*, pp. 38–9, cf. *Cal. Anc. Deeds* V, pp. 68–9, 71.

[47] Blomefield IV, pp. 258–9. Thomas Sharington was the son of Henry Sharington, who had married Elizabeth, daughter and heir of Edmund Swathing of Cranworth, Norfolk: see also Blomefield V, pp. 1177–8; *CIPM Henry VII*, I, p. 536.

[48] For the font, see Pevsner, *North West and South Norfolk*, p. 170; for the glass, see Blomefield IV, p. 234.

man as habitually anti-social as the next man of property? The attack on Titchwell began in October 1448,[49] Gresham was occupied in February 1448,[50] the Duke of Suffolk entered Dedham early in 1447.[51] If the duke was underhand at Geldeston, here at first hand and for the first time John witnessed that the corruption went right to the top, or as near to the top as mattered. What security for property was there under such a government? It was 1399 writ both smaller and larger: it was lesser men than Bolingbroke who were the victims, but there were more of them. The crisis of 1450 may have begun for John at Geldeston in 1446. At Gresham in 1448 he was touched more nearly, and from Sir John Fastolf he may have been hearing for some time of the particular iniquities of the Duke of Suffolk,[52] but true enlightenment may have come to him through his close observation of what happened to Stockton and Geldeston. The political position he held in 1450 and thereafter, his 'Yorkism', he may first have taken up, or (rather) was impelled to adopt, in response to the duke's aggressive acquisitiveness of four years previously. There is no evidence of any reaction on his part, then or later. There is a little of how the Duke of Norfolk reacted: he entered Stockton.[53]

[49] P.S. Lewis, 'Sir John Fastolf's Lawsuit over Titchwell 1448–55', collected (somewhat incongruously) in the writer's *Essays in Later Medieval French History* (London, 1985), p. 217. [50] See chapter 3, p. 53.

[51] Anthony Smith, 'Aspects of the Career of Sir John Fastolf, 1380–1459', unpublished Oxford DPhil thesis, 1982, pp. 126ff.

[52] For the soured relations of Fastolf and Suffolk after 1437, see Anthony Smith, *ibid.*, pp. 138–40.

[53] When is not made clear: but as he was being removed while the first protectorate of Richard, Duke of York was coming to an end, presumably it was some time in the autumn of 1453 after the king had collapsed that the duke and his thugs were taking advantage of the political vacuum, a vacuum which was not filled until the Duke of York was made protector in March 1454. It may be that it was the Duke of Norfolk who had engineered the verdict of an inquisition which took the estates into the crown's possession in 1450 as Alice, the dowager Duchess of Suffolk had a life interest in the two manors: *Cal. Anc. Deeds* V, no. A 10957. Nevertheless, it was Alice who was granted their keeping for a year on 12 November 1450 (*CFR 1445–53*, p. 181); the grant was renewed in July 1451 and June 1452 (*ibid.*, pp. 217, 263). Thus, the duke presumably entered after Alice's grant ran out at Midsummer 1453: in December 1453 he entered into a bond of £12,000 to do the duchess no injury (*CCR 1447–54*, p. 476). It was in the opening days of February 1455 that Alice was going about the expensive business of removing Norfolk from Stockton. Her retainer, Sir Philip Wentworth, rode there from London to take possession with her receiver-general, Andrew Griggs, after William Sevrale had learnt from William Buxton at Brantham, Suffolk, how many men the Duke of Norfolk had taken with him when he had ridden away to London. The escheator, William Brandon, received the vast sum of £10, clearly as a bribe for looking the other way in February when Alice re-entered and held a court at Stockton. Perhaps the sum had to be large, as traditionally Brandon is associated with the Duke of Norfolk: Wedgwood, *Biographies*, pp. 102–3. For all this see BL Egerton Charter 8779, the duchess's receiver-general's accounts of 1453–4 for Norfolk, Suffolk, and Essex, under various headings, including under receipts, 'Soca de Stockton'. There are also two badly damaged

Secondly, what a world of wills the Paston world was: William Winter's, Robert Mautby's, William Garneys', William Paston's, Sir John Fastolf's.

The Pastons' kinship with the Garneys (such as it was) ended soon after it had begun. John married Margaret Mautby in 1440; Ralph Garneys died in 1446. Thereafter, Garneys at Kenton and Beccles played no part in their lives. Calthorps did: Eleanor Mautby, sister of Robert Mautby, Margaret's grandfather, married Sir William Calthorp. He died in 1421. William Paston was one of his executors.[54] Ten years later Sir William Calthorp proved his age and inherited the lands of his grandfather.[55] This William (knighted in 1461[56]), became, on the death of Edward Mautby in 1479, next heir after John and Margaret's children to the Mautby lands.[57] He died in 1495. Although he once said he was John Paston's 'greete frende',[58] they do not appear to have been close: to whom, indeed, was John Paston I close? None the less, an agreeable and businesslike letter from Sir William to his cousin survives; it is a model of clarity and courtesy.[59] Also, for a time after John's death, his daughter Anne was in Sir William's household at Burnham Thorpe,[60] while John II and John III seem to have been closer to him than their father had been.[61]

John III and his wife Margery certainly trusted Sir William's second wife Elizabeth, daughter of William Paston's old enemy, Sir Miles Stapleton. When John wrote to his mother in July 1471 with the good news of his pardon for having fought against Edward IV at Barnet, he told her: 'I prey yow wyth-owght it be to my Lady Calthorp let ther be but fewe woordys of thys perdon.'[62] In 1481 Margery was reporting Elizabeth's attempts to get the dowager Duchess of Norfolk to bring together her husband and his uncle, William Paston. Between pilgrimages the ladies talked, but Margery doubted William – 'he intendes largely to have a peace wyth you, as he seth, but truste hym not to moche for he is not goode' – and suggested the duchess had her price – 'for fayne she wold be redde of it, wyth hyr onowre savyd, but yette money she wold have'.[63]

petitions of the duchess to the chancellor (PRO/25/77; C1/26/164), for which, see Lawrence James, 'The Career and Political Influence of William de la Pole, first Duke of Suffolk 1437–1450', unpublished BLitt thesis, Oxford University, 1979, pp. 264–5, but beware: check all references. As the first petition dates from 1455–6 and the second from 1456–60, perhaps the duke was not removed so easily.

[54] Blomefield III, p. 718; *CFR 1413–22*, p. 378.

[55] *CFR 1430–37*, p. 39; *CCR 1429–35*, p. 84. He was the son of Sir John Calthorp, who, like the second of Sir William's sons, John, died in the lifetime of his father.

[56] Davis II, p. 236. [57] See, for instance, John III's will: Davis I, pp. 507–8.

[58] Davis II, p. 299, but see *Hopton*, p. 182. [59] *Ibid.*, no. 695.

[60] Davis I, pp. lxii–lxiii and 348. [61] *Ibid.*, pp. 433, 540. [62] *Ibid.*, p. 568.

[63] *Ibid.*, pp. 664–5, 666.

At Easter 1487 Elizabeth, Margery (or possibly Anne Paston), and other handsome gentlewomen of Norfolk were to have paraded themselves at Norwich before Henry VII; that is what the Earl of Oxford wanted them to do:

it is my lordys mende that my syster [William Paston wrote from Sheen], wyth all other godely folkys ther-abowte, scholde acompeny wyth Dame Elsebethe Calthorp, be-cawse there is noo grete lady ther-a-bowte, ageyns the Kyngys comynge, for my lorde hathe made grete boste of the fayre and goode gentyl-women of the contré and so the Kynge seyd he wolde see them sure.[64]

Fair she may have been, for that is what Margery's husband had once called her: 'Dame Elyzabet Calthorp is a fayir lady and longyth for orangys, thow she be not wyth chyld'.[65] Nor was she only fair: 'And I remembere that water of mynte or water of millefole were good for my cosyn Bernay to drynke for to make hym to browke [rupture]; and yeve thei send to Dame Elesebeth Callethroppe ther ye shall not fayill of the tone or of bothe. Sche haith othere wateris to make folkis to browke.'[66] In this fashion, with one of them dying, we come to the Berneys.

John Berney was dying where Margaret Paston, *née* Mautby, had been born: at Reedham.[67] Her mother had returned to the family home, if she had ever left it, to have her first and, as it transpired, her only child. The Berneys of Reedham like the Berneys of Witchingham were descended from John Berney, who died in 1374, knight of the shire for Norfolk and a wealthy Norwich merchant, rather than the 'eminent lawyer' Blomefield wished him to have been.[68] One of his two sons was the influential Robert Berney, whose sister Matilda William Winter married. Robert founded the Great Witchingham branch of the family; John's other son Thomas founded the Reedham branch. Although Thomas died in 1383 and Robert in 1415, because Robert inherited from his father two manors in Great Witch-

[64] *Ibid.*, p. 654. William Paston is writing to John Paston III: 'my syster' is, therefore, ambiguous. If it was Anne, was she wearing the necklace her mother had left her, 'my bedes of silver enamelled' (*ibid.*, pp. 386–7)? Perhaps Margaret had got the necklace *after* she had similarly been presented to Margaret of Anjou at Norwich in 1453 – she wrote to John at Easter: 'I pray yow that ye woll do yowr cost on me ayens Witsontyd, that I may have somme thyng for my nekke. When the Quene was here I borowd my cosyn Elysabet Cleris devys [ornament], for I durst not for shame go wyth my bedys among so many fresch jantylwomman as here were at that tym' (*ibid.*, p. 250). Or, knowing John, perhaps she did not.

[65] *Ibid.*, p. 554.

[66] Margaret Paston probably to James Gloys in January 1473: *ibid.*, p. 371.

[67] As she says in her will: *ibid.*, p. 385.

[68] Norman P. Tanner, *The Church in Late Medieval Norwich 1370–1532* (Toronto, 1984), pp. 12–13; Blomefield V, p. 1483; cf. Trevor John, 'The Parliamentary Representation of Norfolk and Suffolk, 1377–1422', unpublished MA thesis, Nottingham University, 1959, p. 158.

ingham, Clay Hall and Street Hall, and Thomas just one, Turteviles in Little Witchingham (or Witchingham St Faith), Thomas, it seems, was the younger of the two. Yet, he made the better marriage, or ultimately the better marriage. His wife Margaret, daughter and heir of Sir William Reedham, brought him Reedham itself and Norton Subcourse;[69] moreover, this marriage (so it appears) brought John Berney, probably Thomas' son and unequivocably Margaret Paston's grandfather, the manors of Braydeston, Caston, Shipdam, and Rockland (or West) Tofts.[70] What appears to have happened is this.

Robert de Caston died in August 1369. He left two daughters as his heirs: Margery, aged seven, and Mary, aged four.[71] They were married, presumably by Sir William Kerdiston, who was granted their marriages in 1376,[72] Margery to Sir William Reedham, Mary to Sir Robert Carbonell.[73] The Caston lands were divided. The Carbonells' principal estate was at Badingham in Suffolk. Sir Robert died in 1397.[74] A minor at the death of his father, Sir John Carbonell (as he was to become) entered his inheritance in 1404.[75] He died between November 1423 and March 1425.[76] His enduring memorial is his splendid table tomb against the north wall of the chancel of Badingham church: Sir Richard, his son and heir, who took on the administration of his father's will, did not spare to fulfil Sir John's simply expressed wish to be buried in the chancel of St John the Baptist at Badingham.[77] This tomb indicates the quality of Sir Richard's aesthetic taste; the addition of St Ursula and the eleven thousand virgins to the Virgin Mary herself as saints to whom in his will Sir Richard commends his soul, also alerts us to a man of discrimination in religion, as does the fact that he

[69] For the latter, across the marshes to the south of Reedham, see Blomefield IV, p. 256.

[70] For Rockland Tofts Blomefield I, pp. 324–5 is utterly confusing (unless it was simply a particularly bad afternoon).

[71] *CIPM Edward III*, XIV, pp. 17–18.

[72] *CPR 1374–6*, p. 216. For sharp practice by him over the property involved, see *ibid*, pp. 328–9; cf. p. 315.

[73] Here I am attempting a rationalization of Blomefield, IV, pp. 7 and 8.

[74] *CFR 1391–99*, p. 268, writ of *dce* 23 September 1397.

[75] *CFR 1391–99*, p. 253; *CCR 1402–5*, pp. 342, 355.

[76] His will (NRO, NCC Reg. Hyrnyng, f. 134) is dated at London, 12 November 1423, and was proved 30 March 1425. The executors allowed Richard, Sir John's son and heir, sole administration.

[77] To Richard's wife Margaret Sir John left 'unam cathenam auream cum una tabula de Salutacione beate Marie virginis cum reliquiis in eadem inclusis'. To each 'mulieri servienti mee mecum existenti: tempore mortis mee' he bequeathed 6s 8d. He also desired a small sum to be paid out of his manor of Saxham in Badingham to Joan Crabdam 'quod si ipsa fuit inclusa vel anacorita apud Framyngham vel ubicumque sibi melius placuerit sicut provisi in presencia', Sir William Phelip (who lived at adjacent Dennington) and Thomas Berton parson of Badingham.

died in 1430 'going to Jerusalem on pilgrimage'.[78] He left a son, John, and a daughter Margaret; both were minors.

The next we know is that in 1440 the manors of Braydeston, Caston, Shipdam, and Rockland Tofts were being disposed of in his last will by John Berney of Reedham, Margaret Paston's grandfather. Sir Richard Carbonell had held these estates;[79] John, merely a baby when his father died, soon died also, as presumably did Sir Richard's daughter, Margaret.[80] Moreover, as Badingham and the other Carbonell Suffolk lands went to Sir Robert Wingfield of Letheringham, Suffolk,[81] apparently a descendant of the daughter of a distant Sir William Carbonell, all the daughters of the family since Sir Robert Carbonell's marriage to Mary Caston – Sir Richard's sister Elizabeth, whom he mentions in his will, for example – must have died without issue. Thus, John Berney as the right heir (through Margaret Reedham, daughter of Margery Caston) got these Norfolk properties[82]

[78] William Worcester, *Itineraries*, ed. John Harvey (London, 1969), p. 359: writ of *dce* 18 November: *CFR 1430–37*, p. 2. The inquisition jurors said he died in July 1430, the Suffolk ones reported the 2nd (PRO, C139/53/11), the Norfolk ones the 30th (C139/48/3). His will (NRO, NCC Reg. Surfleet, f. 66) is dated 24 November 1429, proved 30 December 1430. Sir Richard's will deserves close study. For example, to Margaret, his wife, he left two books: one 'de donacionibus', the other 'dives et pauper'; the church at Rockland Tofts was left three: 'unum Sendale [?] et unum Martilogium et unum Jurnale'; Penesthorp church got a missal; Margaret, his daughter, a primer and a psalter. His portable altar was to go to his wife and after her death to his son John. Caston church was to have a silver pyx, 'unum pyxidem de argento pro sacramento', Braydeston church 'totum apparatum altarum de Rubio Tarteryn betyn cum ymaginibus'. His executors were to maintain Philip Swan 'ad scolas' until he was ordained a priest. Sir Richard was presumably setting out on his pilgrimage, as he desired burial wherever God pleased and he had taken out letters of exchange from an Italian banker in London: *CCR 1429–35*, p. 378. Might not the bequest of his soul to St Ursula be connected with his setting out on a journey from Britain?

[79] PRO, C139/48/23. William Paston had been among Sir John Carbonell's feoffees for these manors: Blomefield IV, p. 8; cf. Gairdner II, no. 5 (BL Add. Ch. 17243, dated 1 May 1422). Sir John Carbonell had been a feoffee of Robert Mautby's: Davis I, p. 17.

[80] The Norfolk inquisition of 28 May 1431 (PRO, C139/48/23) stated John's age as two. The Suffolk inquisition (C139/53/11) of 4 October 1432 stated that John was dead and made no mention of Margaret.

[81] PRO, C139/53/11 (cf. Blomefield I, p. 567).

[82] He may not here have got them immediately. But this is a story I do not understand. The Norfolk inquisition jurors stated that Sir Richard had granted the manors to Sir Thomas Tuddenham for life on 24 November 1427 and that Sir Thomas was in possession of them (PRO C139/48/23. May he have been intending to travel at this time also, even if he did not? He had taken out letters of exchange in London in October: *CFR 1429–35*, p. 375). Sir Thomas Tuddenham was the supervisor of Sir Richard's will and Sir Richard bequeathed to him two gold brooches. Copinger (*Manors* IV, pp. 6–7) says Sir Richard's wife Margaret was Sir Thomas' daughter. This cannot be: Sir Thomas did not marry Alice Woodhouse, the daughter of his guardian, until 1418 (or thereabouts) and they only lived together until 1425 (or thereabouts) – Alice during that time had had a son but it was Richard Stapleton's, her father's chamberlain, not Thomas'. Alice became a nun; the marriage was annulled. See Roger Virgoe, 'The Divorce of Sir Thomas Tuddenham', *Norfolk Archaeology* 34, part IV (1969), pp. 406–18. It seems feasible, therefore, that Sir Richard's wife Margaret may have been Sir Thomas Tuddenham's sister Margaret, who died, the widow of Edmund Bedingfield, in 1465, leaving Alice Tuddenham (still a nun at Crabhous), 10 marks (Virgoe, p. 408), were it not for the fact that Sir Richard's widow Margaret died only a little over a

almost as unexpectedly and at about the same time as John Hopton got his Suffolk ones. In less than forty years four generations of Carbonells had come and gone – and gone for ever;[83] in under seventy years these Norfolk estates had been in the possession of four families: Caston, Reedham, Carbonell, Berney.

John Berney of Reedham was a feoffee with William Paston of both John Mautby, to whom his daughter Margery had been married, and of Ralph Garneys, whom she married after John Mautby's death.[84] He had three sons and three daughters, or rather, he mentions three sons and three daughters in his will of 1440.[85] Its supervisor was William Paston; they had just become or were very much in the process of becoming in-laws: John Paston had met Margaret Mautby at Reedham on 20 April;[86] John Berney made his will there on 16 June.[87] If the careful drafting of John's last will denotes the supervisor of his testament's influence, William did better by John than he did for himself four years later: John Berney's younger sons were adequately and unambiguously provided for.

William, Earl of Suffolk was, one presumes, his chief feoffee; John urged him to make estate of Caston to Philip Berney and his heirs and of Shipdam to John Berney and his.[88] John and his issue were also to have the manor of Turteviles in Little Witchingham; Philip was also to have for life the manor of Kirkhall in Rockland Tofts. Presumably provision for the eldest son, Thomas, to inherit Reedham (and Norton Subcourse) had already been made; Braydeston had certainly been settled on him five years before, in

year after her husband, late in 1431. As Margaret made her will at Kimberley, Norfolk, she surely was a Woodhouse, for that family owned and lived at Kimberley (Blomefield I, p. 751ff.). Thus, Sir Richard's wife Margaret was probably an older sister of Alice Woodhouse, Sir Thomas Tuddenham's 'wife'. She made the will at Kimberley on 25 October 1431; it was proved on 8 January 1432: NRO, NCC Reg. Surfleet, f. 82. Nicholas Bocking was one of her executors; the supervisor she named was Master William Bernham, Bachelor of Canon Law, rural Dean of Tofts, Norfolk, and much else (Emden, *Biog. Reg. Camb.*, pp. 57–8); as official of the bishop he was closely involved in Sir Thomas Tuddenham's divorce (Virgoe, p. 409ff).

83 Sir Richard Carbonell duly appears in NRO, Norwich Public Library MS 7917 on f. 305v. Nicholas Bocking, on whose information William Worcester made up his list in 1463, had been a close witness of the sudden and complete end of this family in 1430–2: see note 82. But which 'John Bernay' (f. 306) did William Worcester mean?

84 Davis I, p. 16; *CCR 1435–41*, p. 109.

85 Two sons, Robert and Bartholomew, died young: see below, note 114.

86 Davis I, p. 26.

87 NRO, NCC Reg. Doke, fs. 126–8: brief Latin testament of 9 June followed by last will in English of a week later. Only proved 5 September 1445 (not 1440, it looks to me).

88 Or, is there a less straightforward reason for 'besechith my lord of Suffolk in as lowly wyse as he can that he wole of his gracyows lordschep make a stat' (NRO, NCC Reg. Doke, f. 127)? There was a doubt that Suffolk would make the required estate of Shipdam to John, as alternative provision was made for John if he did not. Given Sir Thomas Tuddenham's life interest of ten years earlier (see note 82), the delayed proof of the will (see note 87) in conjunction with the non-proof of his son and heir Thomas' will of 1441 (see below, note 92), and Thomas Daniel's attack on Braydeston in 1450 (though see note 89, below), one begins to ponder the sinister once again.

April 1435.[89] Thomas was to have 400 sheep on Fouleholm marsh in order to pay Sir John Fastolf 40 marks, which John Berney owed him. Another 160 sheep and 80 lambs at Reedham were to be sold to pay other debts and to perform works of charity. Thomas got all his father's 'utensilies' and household goods 'longyng to myn halle chaumbir pantery botery kechon [and] bakhows', except two beds of red worsted, which were to go, one apiece, to Margery and to Philip. The set of 'vi spones of myn Alle gylt' was to be broken up: one to Thomas, one to John, one to Philip, one to Margery, one to Margaret, and one to 'my lady hevenyngham'. Thomas was to have his father's 'ambelyng hors and j of my Foles wheche he wole chese'; John Lesse[90] was to have another, and John and Janyn were to have 'alle the clothes that lyn a bowte me at my passyng to be departyd be twene hem tweyne.' However, John Berney wished 'non entirement be made for me'. Braydeston 'ton' (town) was to have 40 shillings for the making of their church steeple; the church at Reedham was to be given 10 marks to buy 'a legend comown and sanctorum'. To Elizabeth, his daughter-in-law, John bequeathed 'a cors of gold and 1 agnus dei of silver and amet [amulet?] of the sepultur of our lady with othir'; she was to have these valuable objects for life only; after her death they were to remain at Reedham 'fro heir to heyr'.[91]

Thomas died the year after his father. On 27 April 1441 he made his will.[92] The 'utensilia et necessaria' of hall, chambers, pantry, buttery, kitchen and bakehouse, which he had enjoyed for so short a time, he left to Elizabeth, his wife. She was to have sufficient means to maintain herself, their young son John and their daughters, and to provide for the marriage of the girls. Apart from livestock and the equipment of husbandry, her dower was thirds of Reedham and Braydeston, the manor of Norton Subcourse,[93] and the marsh of Fouleholm. Elizabeth was still living thirty-two years later; she remarried Osbert Mountford; her son John Berney made her one of his executors in 1473: Elizabeth Mountford, 'my mother'.[94]

[89] In his last will of 1441 Thomas recites his father's enfeoffment to him of Braydeston of 2 April 1435 (NRO, NCC Reg. Doke, f. 157).

[90] John Lesse, apparently a servant, was also a feoffee of John's: see Thomas Berney's last will.

[91] He calls Elizabeth his daughter, but it is clear from the bequest itself, and her non-appearance among the remaindermen of the manor of Braydeston that she was his daughter-in-law, the wife of his son and heir Thomas. Her son, John Berney, in his will of 1473, calls her Elizabeth Mountford, my mother (Bodleian Library, Oxford, Norfolk Charter 418). Thus, confusion is cleared away: Elizabeth, daughter of John Berney (d. 1440) did not marry Osbert Mountford (see Davis II, p. 266 and everywhere else); Osbert Mountford married Elizabeth, widow of Thomas Berney (d. 1441). Davis II, p. 78, lines 9–12 now make sense, as does why Osbert Mountford was in possession of Braydeston: it was Elizabeth's dower (see below, p. 155).

[92] NRO, NCC Reg. Doke, fs. 157–8. No proof is recorded.

[93] Norton Subcourse on her death was to go to Thomas' brother Philip for life, Philip relinquishing (I think the meaning is) Rockland Tofts, left him by his father for life, to John their remaining brother, also for life. For Rockland Tofts see also below, p. 165, note 150.

[94] His will is Bodleian Library, Norfolk Charter 418. And see note 91, above. According to Blomefield (IV, p. 8) Elizabeth was the daughter of John Clippesby esquire.

Elizabeth and her second husband had been forced to fight hard for Braydeston in the early 1450s. Thomas Daniel, who made such a nuisance of himself on the other side of the county at Roydon near King's Lynn,[95] also descended on Braydeston in the spring of 1450;[96] Osbert Mountford re-entered on 7 September, but on 7 February 1452 Daniel again took possession while Mountford and John Berney were in the king's service at Calais.[97] His occupation, or rather that of Roger Church and Charles Nowell's gang was probably not as brief as previously, but Daniel was gone by November 1453, when Mountford's servants at Braydeston were besieged (and two others, on coming back from Acle market, were chased on horseback) by another of the gangs which were committing outrages in the county at that disorderly time.[98] John Paston was involved on Osbert's side throughout: we would know little of these events if he had not been.

There was, however, another angle of vision: in December 1458 the government ordered the arrest of Osbert, his brother-in-law John Berney, and John and William Paston as leaders of a gang just like those which earlier in the decade John Paston had considered the bane of East Anglia. Among those required to do the apprehending were (according to John Paston) the mobsters of yesteryear: Sir Thomas Tuddenham, John Heydon, Sir Miles Stapleton, and Thomas, Lord Scales.[99] Times were getting thoroughly bad; knowing who to trust or even who to believe was impossible. John survived; Osbert did not: he was beheaded at Risbank in the Calais pale in June 1460.

In November 1460, after her second husband's execution, Elizabeth was left with Osbert's heir, a daughter Mary, not yet of age. John busied himself in London on Elizabeth's behalf about Mary's wardship. Margaret reported to John,[100]

> And she thankyth you hertely for the greet labour and besynesse that ye have had in that matre, and in all others touchyng her and hers, wherfore she seithe she is ever bounden to be your bedwoman [bedewoman] and ever wolbe whyle she levethe. My cosyn, her sone, and hise wife recomaundethe them unto you, besechyng you that ye woll weche-safe to be her goode mastre, as ye have ben a-fore tyme. For they be enformed that Danyell is comen to Rysyng Castell and hes men make her bost that her mastre shal be a-yene at Brayston wythinne shorte tyme.

Daniel's men did not get beyond boasting: the Berneys did not lose Braydeston. But a widow's cares, particularly a 'political' widow's in

[95] See a future volume. [96] Davis II, pp. 34–5; Gairdner II, p. 145.

[97] Gairdner II, p. 145; Davis I, pp. 72–3; Davis II, pp. 77–9 (nos. 483–5).

[98] Davis I, p. 79.

[99] *CPR 1452–61*, p. 491. Concerning this (or another matter) Osbert wrote to John, or rather had written for him, an elegant letter in French: Davis II, no. 607. Was the 'petit homme d'armes' among John's children John Paston II or III?

[100] Davis I, p. 262. Mary carried Hockwold, the Mountfords' principal estate, to Sir William Tindale: Blomefield I, p. 493; *CIPM Henry VII*, II, pp. 22–3.

troubled times, were many. The over-mighty man who had killed her husband, Richard Neville, Earl of Warwick, at his most overbearing in the early 1460s, had become involved with those who had dispossessed Elizabeth of her jointure, the manor of East Lexham.[101] She informed John Paston: 'And if I hadde very undyrstandyng that my lord [Warwick] would take no parte in the mater a-bowe seyd I would trust to Goddys mersy and to you and other of my good fryndes to have possession a-geyne in right hasty tyme.' In the short term, it was wishful thinking; in the long term, she outlived the amoral earl, and East Lexham was recovered.[102]

Elizabeth had addressed John as her 'right good neveu'. Margaret called her 'myn aunte Mondeforthe'.[103] Their kinship we would think distant, in John and Elizabeth's case, one would barely consider them related at all. None the less, they considered themselves and thus were 'family'. As very much for Margaret were her Berney uncles. Thomas died (in 1441) before we can know what sort of relationship they may have had. William and (at sixteen years of age) Edmund Paston were among his feoffees. Philip Berney was one of William Paston's.[104] William he named supervisor of his will – as his father had done less than a year before. When Margaret was at Oxnead a year or two later, she told John her stepfather intended to come up from Geldeston the following week, 'and myn emme [uncle] also, and pleyn hem here wyth herre hawkys; and thei xhuld have me hom wyth hem'.[105] Which uncle was it? I fancy it may have been Philip Berney. He lived at Reedham, no distance from Geldeston. He and Ralph Garneys would have had good hunting in the marshes of the Waveney or the Yare; perhaps they wanted a change: the lush water meadows of the Bure at Oxnead.

Sadness is the keynote. Not of the relationship between Margaret and her uncle Philip, but of Philip himself, or of the information we have of him. Not at first: we have just observed him anticipating going hawking at Oxnead. And the picture of him in his lodgings at King's Lynn in March 1451 learning by chance of an intended visit of Lord Moleyns to North Norfolk is a felicitous one.[106] Thereafter, however, the gloom begins to break in. In July 1451 Margaret sent him the pot of treacle John had bought for him in London.[107] By the following Easter events had taken a sorry turn for him:

Item on the Monday next before Estern Day x of the seid persones [the Nowell gang] lay in wayte in the hey weye undyre Thorp woode up-on Phelep Berney, esquiere, and hese man, and shet at hem and smet her horse wyth arwes, and then over-rede hym and brake a bowe un the seid Phelippis hed and toke hym presoner, callyng hym traytour.[108]

[101] Davis II, pp. 266–7.

[102] *CIPM Henry VII*, v. II, p. 23. Osbert Mountford appears among the sonless esquires of Norfolk in William Worcester's list: NRO, Norwich Public Library MS 7917, fs. 306–306v.

[103] Davis II, p. 266; Davis I, p. 262.

[104] For East Beckham no less: Davis I, pp. 18–19 and chapter 3.

[105] *Ibid.*, p. 218. [106] *Ibid.*, p. 240. [107] *Ibid.*, p. 243, lines 30–31. [108] *Ibid.*, p. 59.

It was the same day, 6 April 1452, as John Paston was set upon by six other members of the Nowell gang at the door of Norwich Cathedral; though he was manhandled, he was not beaten up: he duly recovered. Philip did not. He was very ill in November 1452: 'he hath been so seke [wrote Margaret] sith that I come to Redham that I wend he shuld never an askapid it, nor not is leke to do but if he have redy help; and therefore he shal into Suffolk this next weke to myn aunt, for there is a good fesician and he shal loke to hym'.[109] Yet he survived the winter. He made his will at Reedham on 23 May 1453 and lingered on: painfully. He died on 2 July 1453, as Agnes informed her son: 'And as for tydyngys, Phylyppe Berney is passyd to God on Munday last past, wyt the grettes peyn that evyr I sey man'.[110] John Paston knew where to put the blame – 'Which affray shorttd the lyffdayes of the sayd Phillippe, whiche dyed withynne shorte tyme after the said affray' – even if fifteen months is not a short time.[111]

Philip died a bachelor. Neither wife nor children feature in his will.[112] There was a trusty servant, William Bedford, who was to have 20 shillings, a couple of stotts, a plough, and a cart. There was Davy, another servant, who also got 20 shillings. There was Philip's sister, Margaret Naunton, who was to have a silver cup, William Naunton who was to have 40 shillings to pray for him,[113] and his godson Philip Holler, who was to have 6s 8d. And there was his brother John. That is all: neither Margaret nor John Paston did he remember. Perhaps the 40 shillings he left to the brothers of the gild of St John at Reedham reveals him: was the convivial company of men his natural habitat? Like his father before him Philip wanted no funeral: 'nullam enteramentum pro eo teneatur'. He did want a priest to pray for his soul at Reedham for a year, and each priest at his burial was to have fourpence, each clerk twopence. One's impression is that Philip's soul would not have had a harsh journey through purgatory: penance enough he may already have done.

John Berney was his only executor. John, for a reasonable price, was to have his moveable goods. He and his heirs were also to have Philip's manors of Caston and Shipdam. According to their father's will John should already

[109] *Ibid.*, p. 246. Who was her aunt in Suffolk?

[110] *Ibid.*, p. 39. Margaret's report (*ibid.*, p. 250) was more restrained: 'And as for the chamer that ye assygnyd to myn unkyl, God hath purveyd for hym as hys will is: he passyd to God on Monday last past at xj of the clok before none.' The following morning Sir John Heveningham died suddenly and (it seems) painlessly. Both women clearly regarded the suddenness as unusual; as well they might.

[111] *Ibid.*, p. 76.

[112] NRO, NCC Reg. Aleyn, fs. 157–8, dated 23 May, proved 6 August 1453.

[113] Was this Margaret's husband and thus John Paston's cousin, who once acted as a go-between on Walsingham business for Paston and William Yelverton (Davis II, no. 599)? This letter throws an unexpected gleam onto the religious outlook of the judge, especially his 'for trewly if I be drawe to any worchep or wellfare, and discharge of myn enmyes daunger, I ascryve it unto Our Lady', and his dating of it 'on Sent Fraunces Day'.

have had Shipdam. Presumably other arrangements had been made between the brothers, perhaps after Thomas' death in 1441. So we come to the last of this trio of Berney brothers.[114]

John Berney and John Paston knew one another well. They were both 'highly regarded' by Sir John Fastolf, whose legal (and other) counsellors they were.[115] Not long after their master's death William Worcester wrote to John Berney at Caister a revealing letter;[116] characteristically it reveals William himself, but it also discloses the tensions among Fastolf's servants just two months after he had died:

Ryght worchypfull ser, I recommaund me to yow. And the cause of my commyng and tareyng yn London ys forasmuch as I obliged me by my lettre to be here now and to reken wyth all the credytours that I caused my maister frendes, God blesse hys soule, to be suertee for me for the cloth I made be bought for my maister entierment. I dyd but hald the candell amonges you yn Norffolk, for I was not put yn favour ne trust to commaund and yeve yn my maister name and for hys sake a goune cloth to none of hys frendes, servauntes, or almesfolk, but most beg and pray as I were a straunger. Yff I caused Maister Paston and myne oncle the parson [Thomas Howes] that they hafe such autorité as they hafe, they ought to be the fayner and desyrouse of the contynaunce of myne autorité, that ys as grete as theyrs or gretter, whate so evyr Frere Braklé or they sey, and so it ys to op-ynly knowen of record . . . Ser, at reverence of God, and for the verray and faythfull lofe ye hafe to my maister yn the yeeres and dayes that ye dyd hym servyce yn the werres, suffred prysonment[117] and manye a sherp day for hys sake not rewarded, yhyt meove ye myn oncle the parson, and othyrs havyng autorité wyth hym, to peyn hem to do that at ys moste nede for the helthe of my maister soule and for the relieve of all Cristen soules, and namely for the sustenaunce and encresyng of a comyn weelle. Hyt ys not a comyn proffyt to gefe manye blak gonnys to such as nede none of yeft, and namely yff they be yoven, to my maister ennemyes as som seyn there been.

With John Paston and Thomas Howes, his uncle, William Worcester had become (it is clear) speedily disillusioned. Eventually he would break with them. Had he lived, who would John Berney have supported? The freedom with which William Worcester wrote to him indicates that Worcester, freely though he always wrote, saw John Berney as sympathetic to his complaints, possibly even sharing his unease. Had John Berney lived, his former colleague John Paston's single-minded pursuit of his own interest may have

[114] In this John Berney's will of 1460 among the souls he wishes prayers to be said for are those of Robert and Bartholomew his brothers (PRO, Probate 11/4, fs. 181–2). They must have died in infancy.

[115] Anthony Smith, 'Sir John Fastolf', p. 111; Davis II, p. 44, p. 93 (lines 28–9), p. 94; Gairdner II, p. 212. The reference to Rockland Tofts should be compared with Davis I, p. 60 and with note 93 above. The John Berney outlawed in July 1453 was of Great Witchingham, that is of the other, senior branch of the family; he was the writer of Davis II, nos. 481, 637–9. For the connecting evidence, see *CFR 1452–61*, p. 36; *CPR 1452–61*, p. 274; Davis II, no. 481, headnote and lines 6–8.

[116] Davis II, no. 888, pp. 539–40.

[117] This appears to prove that it was this John Berney who was the prisoner of war Fastolf ransomed before 1420 (Gairdner II, p. 50; for further comment see chapter 7). He bequeathed his armour to his only son Osbert, who evidently, being a minor in 1460, was a child of John's maturity, if not old age.

been too much for him to swallow too. And if we are tempted to feel that it may have been as well that John Berney did not live to see what John Paston did as Fastolf's executor, how much more strongly are we likely to feel that it was a blessing he was not able to observe what John Paston did as his.

He made his will at Caister on 2 June 1460.[118] John informed Margaret of his death in a letter as characteristic of him as the last was of William Worcester (how could John Berney *not* have sided with William?):

I recommaunde me unto you, letyng you witte that your unkyll John Berney is deed, whoos soule God have mercy; desyryng you to sende for Thomas Holler and enquere of hym wher his goode is and what he is wurthe, and that he take goode eede to all suche goodes as he had, bothe meveable and on-mevable, for I undre-stande that he is wurthe in money v c marke and in plate to the valwe of other v c marke, beside other goodes. Wherfor I wolde ye schulde not lete hym wete of his dissese unto the tyme that ye had enquered of the seide Thomas Holler of all suche maters as be a-bovyn wreten. And whan he hathe enformed you therof, than lete hym wete verely that he is deede; desiryng hym that no man come on-to his place at Redham but hymselfe unto the tyme that I come.

Item, I lete you witte that gret parte of his goode is at William Taverners, as I undrestande. Thomas Holler wolle telle you justely the trouthe, as I suppose; and desyre hym on my behalfe that he doo soo. And ther is writyng therof, and telle Thomas Holler that I and he be executours named. And therefore lete hym take heede that the goodes be kept saffe, and that no body knowe wher it shall lie but ye and Thomas Holler. And Thomas Holler, as your unkyll tolde me, is prevy wher all his goode lithe, and all his writyng; and so I wol that ye be prevy to the same for casualté of deethe, and ye too schalbe his executours for me as longe as ye doo trewly, as I trowe verely ye woll.

Richard Calle wrote the letter for him; John added the postscript. Is he expressing sympathy: 'I requer yhow be of god cumffoort and be not hevy if ye wil do owth for me'?[119] As John Berney's son Osbert was under age, had been left all his father's household goods, and was put under the governance of the executors, their role was an important one. But Margaret was not quick enough. William Taverner or Perse had been quicker. Margaret wrote to John:[120]

Perys is stylle in presone, but he wolle not confese mor thane he ded when ye wer at home. Edmond Brome was wyth me and tolde me that Perse sent for hym for to come spek wyth hym, and he tolde me that he was wyth hym and examynyd hym, but he wold not be a-knowe to hym that he had no knowlage wher no goode was of hys masterys more thane he hade knowlageyd to yow. He tolde me that he sent for hym to desyir hym to labore to yow and to me for hym if ye had be at home, and he tolde me that he seyd to hym a-yen that he wold never labor for hym but he myth know that he wer trwe to hys mastyr, thow it lay in hys power to do ryth myche for hym. I suppose it schulde do none harme thow the seyd Perse wer remevyd ferther. I pray to Gode yeve grace that the trowthe may be knowe, and that the dede may have part of hys owne goode.

[118] PRO, Probate, 11/4, f. 181.

[119] Davis I, pp. 92–3. Thomas Holler was of Moulton, a few miles north of Reedham. Philip Holler, Philip Berney's godson (see above, p. 157), was no doubt Thomas' son.

[120] *Ibid.*, p. 260.

It was a pious hope, devoutly wished. Margaret could have wished, and probably did wish, the same on Sir John Fastolf's behalf. Or, for that matter, her father-in-law's.[121] Whenever the lively John Paston was an executor there was small chance of the dead having 'part of hys owne goode'.

He was not the only one. The prior of Bromholm was sniffing about to see what he could get (as he put it) 'to releve our poure place'. He had spoken to Thomas Howes, Fastolf's other executor, and wrote to John Paston:[122]

He answered a-geyn in these wordes: 'Nere is my kyrtyl, but nerre is my smok'. And this was his menyng, that ye shulde be more nere us and tendere to us than he, and that ye shulde rather owe us good wyl than he, and that we shulde labour rather to yowr maystirship than to hym. And also that good that he had to dispose he had besette it, and of passel he tolde me he had delyvered the Abbot of Langelé fourescore li., where-of, as he seyd to me, ye grutched and were in maner displesed, not withstandyng ye seyd a-geyn to hym ye shulde geve as moche. And he seyd to me ye named the places where, and therfor he avysed me to labour effectualy to yowr good maystirship for ye myth helpe us wele; for he seyd ye had moche good of the dede to dispose, what of yowr fader, God blisse that sowle, what of Barney, and what now of his good maystir Fastolfe. And as for Sire John Fastolfe, on hoose soule Jesu have mercy, he seyd to me ye had of his good foure, foure, and foure more than he, in these same termes with-owte ony summe.

His obsequiousness – 'Over-more, that hy and myghty Celestial Prince preserve yow body and soule, and sende yow counforte of the Holy Goost wele to performe all yowr hertis desire in all yowr materes, to his plesaunce and yowr wirship and solace to alle yowr wele-wylleres' – was, there can be little doubt, entirely in vain.

But what of Perse? A year after John Berney's death he was still in prison. Using (of all people) Richard Calle as his secretary, he wrote with dignity and some spirit to Robert Rokesby:[123]

Godwot, it stonde right straunge with me; for the false chayler that kepeth me entretethe me worse thanne it weere a dogge, for I am feterid worse thanne ever I whas, and manacled in the hands by the daye and nyght, for he is feerde of me for brekyng a weye. He makethe false tales of me, throw the means of a false qwene that was tendyng to a Frensheman that is presoner to my Lord Roose, and for be cause of that he bronde me every day be John of Berney, that is goone to the tother Lords; but I truste to God oonys to qwite hys meede. And, Sir, I thanke you mekel of that ye have doone for me or seide; and, Sir, I shal deserve it a yenst yow, be the grace of God, for i' feythe I am holden to you more thane to all men that ever I fonnde syn I cam in preson.

[121] As a reminder, Agnes (Davis I, p. 46): 'And after that swyche tresowre of my husbons as wasse leyd in the abbey of Norwyche by the seyd John Paston, John Bakton, John Dam, and me, to delyvere agen to us all excectorys the seyde John Paston owte of the seyde abbey, unknowyn to the Priour ore ony oder person of the seyde abbey, and wyth-owte my wetyn and assente ore ony of owre felawys, toke and barre awey all.'

[122] Davis II, pp. 228–9.

[123] The letter is BL Add. MS 34888, f. 156 (Gairdner III, no. 425); see Davis' comment, II, p. 342.

To Margaret in his own hand he wrote imploringly:[124]

Right reverent and wurchipphull maisteres, I recomaunde me un-to youre god maistereschipp, bescheching yow to be myn good maisteres to remembre and to thynk up-on me, youre pore presoner queche is lyeng in grevous jeryns, queche jernys [hole in paper; room for about six letters] most lost myn leggis; bescheching yow of your god maistereschipp to speke un-to myn maister your husbond to be myn good maister and that he of his good maisterschipp will take me un-to his grace; for be myn trewthe I never deserved othir ne nevir will in non maner wyse. And as for good I have non. As for myn body he may don ther-wit as it please hym. And therfore I bescheche yow to informe his good masterschipp that he will have compassion up-on me, for I nevir knew of the goodis queche he put it a-yens me, and thus to be kepte in preson for sqech goodis that I nevir had knowyng of. I may rewe the tyme that I ever ded hym service, thus myschevously to be presoned for his goodis. And therfore I bescheche you, for the love of Good [*sic*] and for the love of myn maister that ded is (up-on his sowle Jesu have mercy) and in the wey of charité, that ye se that I be nout lost in prison as ittis non othir lyche, for it was nevir myn Maister Berneys will, &c.

Be your pore servaunt PIERS, late the servaunt of John Berney

The note of desperation appears to have touched Margaret. She wrote to John telling him of the condition of Perse's legs and hoping that he would accept Perse's security for his release.[125] John was unmoveable.

When Perse did get out of gaol six months later it was as a consequence of a general pardon. Margaret wrote to John on 27 January 1462:[126]

Plesyt yow to wet that Perse was delyveryd owt of preson by the generall pardon that the Kynge hathe grantyd, whyche was opynly proclamyd in the gyld-hall. A-none as he was delyveryd he cam hedyr to me, God wote in an evyll plyte, and he desyiryd me wepyng that I wold be hys good mastres and to be mene to yow to he hys good mastyr, and swore for that he was nevyr defawty in that ye have thowte hym defawty in. He seyd that if ther wer ony coyne in the cofys that was at Wylliam Tavernerys it was ther wyth-owt hys knowlage, for hys mastyr wold nevyr lat hym se what was in that cofyr; and he tolde me that the keyis wer sent to Thomas Holler by Mastyr John Smyth. What Holler leyd in or took owte he wot not, as he sweryth. He offyrd me to be rewlyd as ye and I wold have hym, and if I wold comand hym to go

[124] Davis II, no. 715; no. 714, also to Margaret and altogether more sprightly, seems, as Davis suggests, to be earlier, probably some months earlier to judge by its tone.

[125] Davis I, p. 266.

[126] *Ibid.*, pp. 280–1. For the moment and reluctantly I reject Gairdner's identification of Perys of Legh (Davis II, p. 269) with the Perse imprisoned by John Paston. John Berney's Perse had been shackled either in Norwich Castle or Norwich Guildhall (Davis I, p. 280, line 13). Was he the Edmund Piers who had been a feoffee of Thomas Berney (NRO, NCC Reg. Doke, f. 157)? That seems more likely than that he was Perse (Moody), the servant of John Paston II and III: Davis I, p. 366, lines 23–4; p. 501, line 2; p. 502, line 6; Davis II, p. 421, lines 10–13, p. 437, lines 13–14, p. 456, lines 7–8. As to Perys of Legh, if Gairdner's identification is not accepted, John Douebiggyng's letter (Davis II, no. 659) does not have to be dated 1460–2; from its peculiar address. 'To the ryght reverent and worshipful ser, John Paston, sum tyme lorde of Gresham and now fermour thereof, as hit is seide', a date of 1450–2 might be more suitable. That is about the time of the only other reference to John Douebiggyng, servant of Thomas, Lord Scales, in the Paston letters: Gairdner II, p. 82, an abstract of Magdalen College, Hickling Deed 104. Still, even *c.* 1450, what is the context of Douebiggyng's 'I and other *youre* presoneres' (Davis II, p. 269, line 3)?

a-geyn to preson, whedyr I wold to the castyll or to the gyld-hall, he wold obey my comandment; and seth that he cam of hys owne fre wyll wyth-owt ony comandment of ony man or desyir. I seyd I wold not send hym ageyn to preson so that he wold a-byde yowyr rewyll when ye came home, and so he is her wyth me and schall be tyll ye send me word how ye wole that I do wyth hym; wher-for I pray yow that ye wole let me have knowlage in hast how ye wole that I do wyth hym . . . Dawbeney and Playter avise me to lete Peers go at large, and to take a promys of hym to com to me a-mong un-to your comyng hom; and in the mene while his demenyng may be knowyn and espyed in mo thyngs.

We shall never get to the bottom of this. Did John Paston? It had not been until 1 December 1461 that John Berney's will was proved; Thomas Holler was given administration for the time being; he was to submit accounts before 26 January; if John Paston appeared to claim administration before that date he was to have it. John Paston did not appear: on 26 January 1462 he was duly and formally excluded from administrating John Berney's will.[127] Holler, Taverner, Perse, Paston: who was to blame that John Berney's soul[128] did not have the full benefit 'of hys own goode', of that more than 1,000 marks in money and plate?[129]

Did the others named in John's will get what he wanted them to have? The folk of Reedham, for example, the 66s 8d for the 'emendacionem et exultatacionem campanilis' of their church? Or the blind Nicholas Mynstrall the 3s 4d John left him to pray for his soul? Or the lepers at the Gates of Yarmouth their 20d? Or his godson John Bedford his 6s 8d? Was the cypress chest bound with iron for the ornaments to be kept in ever given to Reedham church? One hopes (at least) Osbert his son got his father's armour: he was going to have need of it when he helped John Paston III defend Caister in 1469.

Osbert was John Berney's only child. He was a bastard: John, like Philip, had never married.[130] Had the two younger brothers deliberately refrained from marrying, staying bachelor uncles to their elder brother Thomas' son, John? Osbert's illegitimacy is shown not only, not at all perhaps, by his serving the Pastons, but by the manner in which John Berney disposed of his

[127] PRO, Probate 11/4, f. 182; cf. Gairdner III, p. 223, note 2.

[128] Not only his: he required his executors, once his bequests had been fulfilled, to dispose of the remainder of his goods for the souls of John Berney his father, of Isobel his mother, of his brothers Philip, Robert, and Bartholomew, of his sisters Margaret and Isobel, and of Sir John Fastolf and John Wakering, Bishop of Norwich. The latter had died as long before as 1425: the clerk did not know his christian name and left it blank.

[129] But see one of Richard Calle's jottings on the dorse of Margaret's letter to John of early 1463 (Davis I, no. 173; Gairdner IV, p. 71): 'Rec. de Willelmo Norwich et M. Johanne Smythe renditio Jocalium Johannis Berney de Redham pro tant' denar' pro me pro debito ipsius Berney apud Redham solut', xxli. xvjs.'

[130] No wife features in his will, particularly not among those whose souls were to be prayed for: see note 128. Osbert was the consequence of an old soldier's liaison: with whom?

lands. Osbert was to have for life the manors of Shipdam and Turtevilles in Little Witchingham; they were then to revert to John Berney, the son of Thomas Berney. John Berney, the representative of the main branch of a family whose subsidiary branches had ceased to grow, was to have the manor of Caston immediately; over the first three years, however, he was to pay £20 for masses for John Berney's soul and £20 towards Osbert's maintenance – Osbert being under age and under the governance of Thomas Holler and John Paston, John Berney's executors.[131] The only property Osbert was to have for himself and his heirs was a messuage in Reedham.[132]

None the less, it is of Osbert that we hear most after 1460; there is little to learn of John Berney of Reedham. Called in 1458 'of Hockwold',[133] where no doubt he was living or had lived with his mother and her second husband, Osbert Mountford, in 1460 he was termed 'of Reedham'.[134] He was an accommodating juror at the *inquisition post mortem* on Sir John Fastolf held at Acle on 21 October that year.[135] After that, to the Pastons he was a cousin who meant next to nothing. It was with their far more distant relative, John Berney of Witchingham, that John Paston was elected to the Commons as knight of the shire in June (and August) 1461.[136] That John got into other sorts of trouble in 1469[137] and died in November 1471.[138] John Berney of Reedham died in January 1473.

We have observed him dying: Margaret Paston urged James Gloys to send to Elizabeth Calthorpe for medicines.

> And I am soré [Margaret wrote] that my cosyn Bernay is seke, and I pray you yeff my white wine, or ony of my wateris, or ony othere thyng that I have that is in youre awarde may doo hym ony comforth, lette hym have it; for I wold be right sory yf ony thyng schuld comme to hym botte good. And for Godsake advise hym to doo make hys will, yeve it be not doo, and to doo well to my cosyn his wiff, and els it were peté.[139]

She wrote on Monday 18 January; on Wednesday 20 January, the feast of Saints Fabian and Sebastian, John died.[140] On the day he died he made his

[131] Possibly, Osbert was the 'praty boy' baby fetched 'hom' from Rockland Tofts in January 1454 or earlier (Davis I, p. 253, lines 18–19); indeed, probably earlier, as aged fifteen he would have been a particularly young fighter at Caister in the summer of 1469.

[132] Which, perhaps, John had bought from Ralph Lampet and not fully paid for: Davis II, p. 552. [133] *CPR 1452–61*, p. 491. [134] Davis II, p. 542.

[135] Davis I, p. 259; II, p. 220.

[136] As the connection of *CFR 1452–61*, p. 36, *CPR 1452–61*, p. 274, and Davis II, no. 481, headnote and lines 6–8, demonstrates. For this disputed election see K.B. McFarlane, *England in the Fifteenth Century* (London, 1981), pp. 6–9.

[137] He was assaulted in the cathedral at Norwich by servants of the Duke of Norfolk: NRO, Norwich Chamberlains' Accounts, 1469–70, f. 7v. His arrest was ordered in September: *CPR 1467–77*, p. 197. [138] Davis I, pp. 351, 354, 355. [139] *Ibid.*, p. 370.

[140] *Ibid.*, p. 369 citing the *inquisition post mortem*: PRO, C140/43/17.

will.[141] His wife Elizabeth was to have her jointure in the manors of Caston, Shipdam, and Turtevilles in Little Witchingham,[142] and half her husband's moveable goods. She was to be one of his executors; the others were Elizabeth Mountford, his mother, William Yelverton, his brother (which means John's wife was Elizabeth Yelverton), James Gloys, and none other than Thomas Holler. They had considerable responsibility. Both John's children, John and Elizabeth, were minors. The executors were to have the profits of the manors of Reedham, Braydeston, and Stokesby[143] and of his sheep flock for the children's maintenance; out of these profits they were also to find 200 marks for Elizabeth's marriage and the hire of a priest for two years to pray at Reedham for the souls of John and his friends. No Paston features in this will (though the Pastons' Norwich church does: to St Peter Hungate John Berney left £1[144]). John Berney's other relatives do: for example, his 'brother Tindale'[145] was to have his great horse and John Blanerhasset[146] was among the witnesses to the will. Do these two facts, that Thomas Holler was an executor and that no Paston is mentioned, tell us something about what happened after John Berney died in 1460? Did this John Berney, who seems to have had little or nothing to do with the Pastons during his life, recall only too well as he was dying, because he had never forgotten it, what John Paston had done or not done after his uncle's death a dozen years before? Thomas Holler, at any rate, he trusted.

Should he have done? The young John Berney's wardship was claimed by the crown (because it had held the temporalities of the bishopric of Norwich during the vacancy after Bishop Walter Lyhert's death, which was when John Berney died[147]) and promptly granted away.[148] There was also, a few

[141] Bodleian Library, Norfolk Charters 418. According to a note on the dorse it was proved at Norwich on 31 May 1473.

[142] Osbert (according to his father's will) ought to have been in possession of Shipdam and Turtevilles. I suspect he may have given them up for an annuity; John Paston II wrote to John Paston III in November 1473 (Davis I, p. 472): 'Item, I praye yow doo for Berneye as ye kan so that he maye be in sewerté for hys annywté, and that it be nott costius fro hense forthe to hym any more to come ore sende for it. I pray yowe wynne yowre sporys in thys mater.'

[143] James Gloys had very recently been appointed rector of Stokesby by John Berney, who held advowson and manor: Davis I, p. 582; Blomefield V, pp. 1584–5. Gloys himself died later in 1473: *ibid.*, p. 470.

[144] Fittingly (or oddly) enough, in the museum that St Peter Hungate now is, there is the head of this John Berney from his brass at Reedham.

[145] Sir William Tindale, who had married Mary Mountford, John Berney's half-sister: see above, note 100.

[146] For him, whom John Paston called cousin, see Davis I, p. 589; Gairdner V, p. 178, note; *CIPM Henry VII*, II, p. 290. He came from Frenze near Diss and died in 1510. For the brasses of himself, Jane his wife, Joan his mother, and Ralph his father, see Blomefield I, pp. 93–5 and Pevsner, *North West and South Norfolk*, p. 165. John Paston II did not think much of Ralph, or so I interpret this difficult passage: Davis I, p. 456.

[147] Some sniffing out was done here, I suspect: Walter Lyhert's successor James Goldwell, consecrated in October 1472, had been granted the temporalities on 25 February 1473;

years later, a renewed challenge by Thomas Daniel to John Berney's ownership of Braydeston; John and his guardian, Richard Southwell, had to fight it off by arbitration.[149] John survived all the rigours of a minority, married his guardian's daughter Alice, fathered another John Berney, and died in January 1506.[150] He held all the Berney estates his great-grandfather John Berney had held but had dispersed among his three sons at his death in 1440. Male infertility, as McFarlane would have commented, and a sensible remaindering policy, as John Paston II would have considered it, in less than three generations ensured the return of those estates to the head of the senior line of the Berneys of Reedham. But had the male infertility been deliberate? Only Osbert Berney might have known that. He is the last of the Berneys with whom we have to deal.

Unlike his half-nephew John Berney, Osbert was close to the Pastons.[151] He was in John Paston's service by 1465.[152] And although John Pason III told his brother that Osbert had become a sworn man of the youthful Richard, Duke of Gloucester in June 1469,[153] he was with John Paston III defending Caister against the Duke of Norfolk later that summer – and wrongly reported dead to Margaret.[154] He was with John Paston II in February 1470 at London[155] – Sir John having acted (one hopes and presumes) on his brother's advice of the previous October.[156] In 1472 he

the *inquisition post mortem* was held at Acle as late as 5 November 1473; the always amenable Robert Curzon was the escheator (PRO, C140/43/17). The inquisition was held some months after the wardship had been granted, which had been the previous May and July: *CFR 1471–85*, pp. 66–7, 72. As Henry Heydon was a mainpernor in the grant of wardship and wanted John Berney as a husband for his daughter (Davis I, p. 590) suspicions have somewhere to lodge.

[148] PRO, C140/43/17; *CFR 1471–85*, pp. 66–7, 72. The inquisition jurors correctly reported that the young John Berney was twelve years old: Friar Brackley had informed John Paston on 24 October 1460 that the wife of John Berney had given birth to a son within the last three days: Davis I, p. 222. [149] *CCR 1476–85*, p. 81.

[150] Blomefield V, p. 1484; *CIPM Henry VII*, III, pp. 150–1. (This is where Rockland Tofts reappears: I may have conflated it throughout with their manor of Castonhall in West Tofts, for which see Blomefield, I, p. 545.)

[151] Among John Berney's many feoffees there are no Pastons: *CIPM Henry VII*, III, pp. 150–1.

[152] Davis I, pp. 127, 131, 319–20. [153] *Ibid.*, p. 545. [154] *Ibid.*, pp. 344 and 346.

[155] *Ibid.*, p. 413.

[156] After the failure to hold Caister John III wrote to his brother in London about the servants who had helped in those darkest of days (Davis I, p. 547): 'Ryght worchepfull syr, I recomand me on-to you, praying yow that ye wyll in all hast send me word how that ye wyll that Syr John Styll, John Pampyng, W. Mylsent, Nycolas Mondonet, T. Tomson shall be rwlyd, and whedyr that they shall sek hem newe servysys or not . . . Notwythstandyng, if ye kowd get Barney, or eny of thes seyd folkys whyche that ye wyll not kepe, eny servyse in the mene seson it wer more worchep for yow then to put them from yow lyek masterles hondys, for by my trowthe they ar as good menys bodys as eny leve, and spescyally Syr John Stylle and John Pampyng. And I wer of power to kepe them, and all thes befor rehersyd, by trowthe they shold never depert fro me whyll I leveyd . . . so God help me I have neythyr mony to com up wyth nor for to tery wyth yow when I am ther but if ye send me some; for by my trowthe thes werkys have causyd me to ley owt for yow bettyr then x or xij

was also in London with Sir John,[157] but in 1473 he was in Norfolk with John Paston III, and probably unsettled: 'I wold not that he pleyed the fooll nere wastyd hys tyme nere hys sylver', wrote Sir John.[158] A year later he was found a place in the retinue of the lieutenant of Calais by the lieutenant himself, William, Lord Hastings. Sir John expressed his relief to his brother:

> Item, I had answere from my lorde that he is my speciall goode lorde, and that by wryghtyng; and as for Bernaye, he sette hym in hys owne wagys for my sake, and that whan so ever I come to Caleys I shall fynde all thyng there as I woll have it, and rather better than it was heere-tofor.[159]

But it was not for ever. In May 1478 Osbert was once more in Norfolk serving John Paston and the family.[160] He was evidently valued: the last to be learned of him is the 10 marks annuity Margaret left him in her will of February 1482.[161]

For Margaret, had her cousin's bravery at Caister in 1469 cancelled out her uncle's cowardice at Gresham in 1448? It is a story told before.[162] But who was this less than lion-like uncle of 1448? As he had been riding to Gresham via Cawston, he is likely to have been coming from Great Witchingham. None the less, it is the loose-tongued Davy who gives the game away (as he did in 1448), for in his will of 1453 Philip Berney left 20 shillings to his servant Davy.[163] Alas, that so timid a man should have had so painful a death.

li. besyd that mony that I had of my modyr, whyche is abowt an viij li. God amend defawtys, but this I warant yow, wyth-owt that it be Mathew whyche ye sent woord by John Thressher that ye wold have to awayt on yow, ther is no man that was hyryd for the tyme of thys sege that wyll axe yow a peny.' [157] *Ibid.*, p. 577.

[158] *Ibid.*, pp. 471 (cf. p. 454?), 472. [159] *Ibid.*, p. 479. [160] *Ibid.*, p. 508.

[161] *Ibid.*, p. 387. He was buried at Braydeston: Blomefield IV, p. 8. Why Braydeston?

[162] Davis II, p. 28, quoted in full in chapter 2, p. 54.

[163] NRO, NCC Reg. Aleyn, f. 157.

Chapter 6

THE DEATHBED OF WILLIAM PASTON AND ITS CONSEQUENCES

If, as the Russians say, the end crowns the matter, that is, the manner of a man's dying strips his personality bare, we may observe from the accounts of the deathbed of William Paston that he was indecisive, inefficient, and indifferent to the interests of his family. Also, he was negligent, lacked vision, could not discern character, had neither shrewdness nor insight, perspicacity nor sensitivity. Precisely the qualifications, the cynic would maintain, of a judge, particularly of a good judge. On his deathbed William Paston was a poor judge: of everything. To the pig's ear he made of ending his successful life we will return, but one conclusion is both inescapable and irresistible: what a simple matter it is to make money, especially from the weaknesses of men and women, how difficult to discover their strengths and to ensure that they are sustained and developed.[1]

The no more than thirty documents among the Paston letters which survive from William Paston's life before its last moments reveal little. They show us what a busy man he was: yet another of those capable lawyers who appear to dominate fifteenth-century English life; 'appear to' because of the quantity of paper their business generated. It would be tedious to list all those (all those we know of) whose feoffee or executor he was – uninstructive as well as tedious. Attorney of Sir Robert Swillington, feoffee of Sir Thomas Erpingham, of Sir Simon Felbrigg, of Sir John Fastolf, of Robert, Lord Willougby, of Ralph, Lord Cromwell, executor of Alexander Tottington, Bishop of Norwich, steward of the East Anglian properties of the Duke of Norfolk, retained by the Prior of Norwich and the towns of Great Yarmouth and King's Lynn, etc., etc.: we know him no better.[2] That he was

[1] I also have in mind here Francesco di Marco Datini.

[2] *Deputy Keeper of the Public Records, 41st Report* (London 1880), pp. 690, 793. *CPR 1416–22*, pp. 16, 92, 99, 248; *CPR 1422–9*, pp. 212, 270; *CPR 1429–36*, pp. 368–9; *CPR 1436–41*, p. 292; Davis I, p. 11; Davis II, pp. 4, 76, 508–9; Gairdner I, pp. 30–1; *Cal. Papal Letters, 1431–47*, pp. 159 ff. He was also a feoffee of Sir Thomas Kerdiston; almost all of Kerdiston's feoffees are familiar names to us: Thomas, Lord Morley, Sir Thomas Erpingham, Sir Simon Felbrigg, Sir John Carbonel, Sir Henry Inglose, Sir Edmund Barry, John Berney of Witchingham, John Berney of Reedham, William Garneys: *Cal. Anc. Deeds*, III, nos. 426, 1020.

not associated with William, Earl of Suffolk, may tell us something, but what is it? Only if we had the answer to another question – 'why wasn't he?' – could we know; but we do not have the answer. All we have is Judge William's advice to William Burgeys:[3]

> and than he rod up to Lundun and wente to Pastun the justyse and preyd hym of consel and tolde hym al the mater, and he bad hym not plete wyth hym [Reynald Rous] be non wey, 'for gyf thu do', he seyd, 'thu xalte halfe the werse, be thi cawse never so trewe, for he is feid wyth myn lord of Sowthfolke and mech he is of hese consel, and also thu canste no man of lawe in Northfolke ne in Sowthfolke to be wyth the a-gens hym, and for sothe nomore myth I qwan I had a ple agens hym; and therfore myn consel is that thu make an end qwhat so ever thu pay, for he xal elles on-do the and brynge the to nowte'.

It is enough, more than enough, to tell us Paston, an old judge, was not of the young earl's clique. Thereafter, that is for the rest of the century, Pastons and de la Poles never got on. A continuity had been created, a stance adopted. However the non-association had come about, it stuck. That is its significance.

There were other continuities begun, possibly determined, in William Paston's lifetime: the Mowbray connection, for instance. Perhaps this was the reverse of the coin whose obverse was the antagonistic relationship with the de la Poles, for the Pastons, even when the Duke of Norfolk in the 1460s and early 1470s did not want to know them, persisted: as if the connection was (for them) a 'natural' one, despite the duke's 'unnatural' conduct towards them. There was also William Paston's association with Sir John Fastolf, strengthened by the marriage of John Paston to Margaret Mautby in 1440. John developed, some might say exploited, this connection; he did not begin it.[4] Where he did take an initiative, if that is the right

[3] Davis II, p. 518.

[4] Elizabeth, widow of Sir John Rothenhale, wrote to William Paston, one of her late husband's 'best trosted frendes', asking his help; as her former husband's executor, she was being sued by William Steyard of Yarmouth, deputy of Thomas Chaucer, chief Butler of the crown, for money he claimed was owing on wine which had been imported by Sir John; Elizabeth believed 'his askyng is on-trewe'. William took up her cause and satisfactorily concluded it (Davis II, pp. 2–3, and p. 509, note; Gairdner II, no. 13). That was in 1426; Sir John had died in 1420. Elizabeth wrote her letter from Caister. She had remarried John Clere of Ormesby, who also had the manor of Horninghall in Caister (a manor later sold to William Paston II). Elizabeth's two sons by John, Robert and Edmund Clere, were involved with William Paston in his exchange of lands with the Duchy of Lancaster (see, for example, Gairdner II, nos. 42 and 48) and were his feoffees (Davis I, p. 22). Friendship with the Cleres was to become important to the Pastons (NRO, Rye MS; Farrer, 'A Norfolk Armory of the Fifteenth Century', *Norfolk Antiquarian Miscellany*, 8 (1887), pp. 61–2; and a future volume), but Elizabeth Rothenhale was also Sir John Fastolf's niece: she was the daughter of his half-sister Margaret and her husband Sir Philip Braunch, who, like Sir John Rothenhale and Sir John Fastolf, had fought in Normandy for Henry V. Margaret Braunch, after her husband's death, lived at Caister, probably as the 'gentlewoman' of Milicent, Fastolf's wife: a household account of 1430–1, noticed in HMC *8th Report*, p. 268a (Magdalen College, Oxford, muniments). Margaret's grandmother, Katherine Braunch, had made her will at Caister in

way of putting it, was with John de Vere, Earl of Oxford. In what eventually, and after a breath-holding hiatus between 1471 and 1485, was to be the most fruitful of the family's associations (that with Fastolf included), William Paston did not play the role of creator.

Yet creating connections, like creating wealth, was what he was good at, was his contribution to the future of the Pastons, his positive contribution we should add, having in mind the negative one he contrived on his deathbed. Can we say that he was good at anything else? At making enemies certainly. It is almost the only time emotion breaks through the crust of his businesslike manner:[5] 'I prey the Holy Trinité, lord of yowr cherche and of alle the werld, delyvere me of my iij adversaries, of this cursed bysshop for Bromholm, Aslak for Sprouston, and Julian Herberd for Thornham.' We have seen how, according to her, he treated Julian Herberd – ruthlessly, viciously, a strong man preying upon a weak woman.[6] He was probably also expecting to cheat Joan Marriot. There were, no doubt, numerous, perhaps countless (because unkown) others, victims of his 'know-how'. Still, and typically of such folk, it is he who feels persecuted:[7] 'I have nought trespassed a-geyn noon of these iij, God knowith, and yet I am foule and noysyngly vexed wyth hem to my gret unease.' One of the three, the 'cursed bysshop', got him excommunicated.[8] For his many sins he deserved it. But, like his sense of justice, whatever religion he had was only skin-deep:[9] excommunication can have been no more than an irritation.

1420; she named William Paston as its supervisor; he was to have 40 shillings. One of her executors, William (Sheringham), rector of Holt, 'habeat bibliam', while another priest, John Gumete, 'habeat Kalendarium quod scripsit'. She made a request to John Rothenhale, son of Sir John Rothenhale, but did not mention Elizabeth. She wished to be buried in the chantry of St Thomas in the church of St Germans, Wiggenhall: NRO, NCC, Reg. Hyrnyng, f. 64, dated 4 August, proved 5 September 1420. William Sheringham also desired prayers for his soul at the same chantry, and he left 15 marks towards the building ('fabricacionem') of the church. One of his executors was Katherine's son, John Braunch of Stody (a manor she left to him): NRO, NCC, Reg. Hyrnyng, f. 94, dated 10 February, proved 27 March 1422. When Elizabeth Rothenale leased the Clere manor of Keswick in February 1436 it was to Harry Collis of Eton, yeoman, and his son John Collis, yeoman (NRO, NRS 10858). Can this be Harry Collis, servant of the timorous Philip Berney (Davis II, p. 28)? If Elizabeth Rothenhale was part of the 'Fastolf connection' it would not be surprising; that connection might be said 'to have run and run', mainly through the numerous marriages of Sir John's three half-sisters, Cecily, Margaret (both of whom and many of whose progeny he remembered in his will: Gairdner III, pp. 155, 157), and Elizabeth. The latter's first husband was Sir Ralph Bigot; their daughters we have encountered marrying the Garneys brothers (see chapter 5, above). Through Fastolf himself, through Katherine Braunch and Elizabeth Rothenhale, William Paston, well before 1440, was part of this nexus.

[5] Davis I, p. 7.

[6] See above, pp. 35–7; Davies II, pp. 514–15.

[7] Davis I, p. 7.

[8] Davis II, pp. 507–8 and Davis I, pp. 2–6; II, pp. 1–2; Gairdner II, p. 29; *Cal. Papal Letters 1417–31*, pp. 180, 405. The affair is summarized, in so far as it can be, by Gairdner, I, pp. 33–4.

[9] Is there anything to suggest otherwise? Not Davis, I, no. 6; Gairdner II, no. 53, *Cal. Papal Letters 1427–47*, p. 435; Gairdner I, p. 38 note 2; but just possibly the provisions of his will, described below, p. 172.

One other thing he was good at: pleading in court. E.A. Robbins in his *William Paston, Justice,*[10] citing the year books, remarks on William's 'delightful sarcasm' and notices that 'his witticisms were few and somewhat caustic'. In the published *Year Book* for 1422,[11] William's interventions, to my unpractised ear, appear banal. A single year book, however, may be thoroughly unrepresentative. Moreover, the sarcasm and caustic wit ring true: in court, 'at home' so to speak, he could perform with the assurance that his fellow professionals would appreciate his displays of esoteric and arcane learning – the sarcasm and caustic wit were not directed at them but were at the expense of non-members of 'the club'.[12]

Have I painted too black a character? Of course, it is not easy to keep indignation in check; or imagination. Yet, James Gairdner's judgement is the opposite of the truth. He wrote of William:[13] 'Of his personal character we are entitled to form a favourable estimate, not only from the honourable name conferred on him as a judge, but also from the evidences already alluded to[14] of the general confidence felt in his integrity.'

The undeniable charge against William at his deathbed would be one of incompetence; of that he would be indicted by any and everyone. There are two counts to the charge: not all his lands were included in his will; that will was out of date. To the charge William pleaded guilty: 'Swynne of slowthe', he said on his deathbed, 'hijs wyll wasse not made up'. This is not the place, and it is besides unnecessary, to discuss the medieval concept of the sin of sloth; what William meant in his use of the word was, I think, no more than laziness, lassitude, 'not getting around to it'.[15] The fact that his written will (ostensibly of January 1444, actually of some time before April 1442)[16] did not embody his intentions of August 1444 not only led to distressing scenes

[10] Published at Norwich, 1932. I quote from p. 31.

[11] Edited by C.H. Williams for the Selden Society, vol. L (London, 1933). I owe this reference to the kindness of Diana Spelman.

[12] The scene has been described by E.W. Ives, *The Common Lawyers of Pre-Reformation England* (London, 1983), chapter 8; cf. my review of this book in *History*, 69 (1984) p. 310. Looked at from the non-members' angle Paston and his fellows were 'ransacking lives'.

[13] Volume I, pp. 31–2.

[14] Following a list of some of those for whom William was a feoffee or executor, Gairdner comments 'the confidence reposed in him by so many different persons is a remarkable testimony to the esteem in which he was held'. Esteem is the wrong word.

[15] Davis I, p. 46. There is no reason to doubt Agnes' twenty-two-year-old recollections (recorded in 1466) of her husband's last days: *ibid.*, pp. 44–8. Being a non-writer she would have had a good memory; moreover, those days were dramatic, even traumatic. Still, Edmund Paston considered his mother unreliable (*ibid.*, p. 147): 'Ryth worschipfull brothir, I recomaund me to yow &c. I preye write to myn modre of your owne hed as for to consell her howh that sche kepe her preuye and tell no body ryth nowth of her counsell, for sche woll tell persones many of her counsell this day and to-morwe sche woll sey be Goddis faste that the same men ben false.'

[16] After John and Margaret's marriage, but before they had any children, that is before 15 April 1442 (Gairdner II, no. 43). This the wording of the will discloses (Davis I, p. 24, lines

at his deathbed, both before and after his death, but also and far more unfortunately to discord within the family over the succeeding forty years. On the other hand, if William's final intentions had been embodied in the written will that discord is likely to have been far more damaging, for John Paston, instead of being momentarily disconcerted would have been permanently and understandably outraged. As it was, John was able to stop the great fire by lighting a smaller. Agnes describes what happened:

Swynne of slowthe that hijs wyll wasse not made up, 'but wat swm ever cwm of me, dame, I wyll ye know my wyll'; and seyed that swyche lond as he hadde not wrytyn in hijs wyll, wat xwlde be do wyth-all he wolde hijs ij yongest sonnys Wyllam and Clement xwlde have, and owte of Sweynthorpe to have hijs perpetuell masse. And of thys prayd me to reporte, record, and berre wyttnesse; in qwyche disposicion and intent he continuyd on-to the day off hijs dethe. And I darre rygh largely deposse that that sam wasse hijs last wyll the tym of hijs dethe, qwyche wyll inmediatly after my husbondys decesse I hopynd and declaryd to John Paston and al the other excectorys of my husbond, desyeryng hem to have performyd it. And the seyd John Paston wold in no wysse agree there-to, seyyng that by the lawe the seyd manerys xulde be hijs, in as moche as my husbonde made no wyll of hem in wrytyn; and gatte the dedys owte of my possession and estat of the feffeez in the seyde manerys myn unknowyng.[17]

We must now explain. The place to begin is William's written will.[18]

To Agnes William left property for life worth £100 per annum. This

127–41) despite its dating clause of 21 January 1444 (*ibid.*, p. 25). If we accept the dating clause at its face value, either William had not brought up to date an earlier will – in which case we catch him nodding – or John II had not been born. The John of April 1442 will then have to have been another John who had died before January 1444. This leads to the twins hypothesis, for which see above (p. 121). As John and Margaret had 'chyldyrryn' by July 1444 (Davis I, p. 220) and the twins hypothesis is far-fetched, it looks as if William had been lax when reviewing his will in January 1444. Perhaps because it was not absolutely necessary to alter these clauses (cf. Davis I, p. 22, lines 46–52) I am being unnecessarily, even gratuitously censorious. On the other hand, if William did thoroughly overhaul his will in January 1444 (rather than merely give an earlier version his cursory approval) his changes of mind six months later display him as an even greater ditherer.

A John who died in infancy is somewhat less far-fetched; John I, after all, had had a brother Henry who had died young; Henry was remembered: our putative John would surely also have been, but was not. Margaret it was who remembered Henry, probably when she was pregnant (Davis I, p. 255): 'I pray yow [she wrote to John] if ye have an othere sone that ye woll lete it be named Herry in remembrans of your brother Herry. Also I pray yow that ye woll send me datys and synamun as hastyly as ye may.' Thinking of children, it is in her letter of July 1444 (Davis I, p. 220) that Margaret related John Heydon's reaction to the birth of a child to his wife which was not his. John Heydon's wife was Eleanor Winter. It is a strange coincidence that both of the greatest enemies of the Pastons at this time, John Heydon and Sir Thomas Tuddenham were cuckolds; obviously, they were as unpleasant to their wives as they were to others. For Heydon, see also Davis II, p. 51, and Vanessa Donoghue, 'The Heydons of Baconsthorpe', unpublished BA dissertation, Keele University, 1985, pp. 27–8. For Tuddenham, see Roger Virgoe, 'The Divorce of Sir Thomas Tuddenham', *Norfolk Archaeology* 35 (1969), pp. 406–18.

[17] Davis I, p. 46.

[18] For the will, see Davis I, pp. 22–5 and Gairdner VI, pp. 190–8. For the lands in greater detail see chapter 3, above.

included her jointure, Oxnead, and her inheritance, Marlingford, Stansted, and Horwellbury, but there was also Cromer, Paston itself, and much else. None the less, William thought it not enough, or so Agnes in 1466 remembered him saying:[19]

> my seyd husbond, lyyng sek on hijs bede, sent fore me, John Paston, Bakton, and John a Dame to here hijs wyll rede. And in owre presens all he began to reede hijs wyll, and spak fyrst of me and assynyd to me the maneris of Paston, Latymer, and Schypden and Ropers in Crowmer fore term of my lyffe, and the manerys of Merlyngforthe, Stonsted, and Horwelbury, wyche wasse myn own enheritans, and Oxned, wyche wasse my jontore; and seyde and he hadde do to lityll to ony it wasse to me, for for me he faryd the better and so dede he for noon of hem all.

That was no more than the truth, but it did not mollify John Paston. He grasped at once that his father's generosity to Agnes was likely to entail parsimony towards himself. It did: 'And then he red John parte and assynyd to hym and to hys wyffe the maner of Gressam and after my decesse the maner of Oxned . . . thynkyng by John Pastons demenyng that he wasse not plesyd.'[20] Crucial to John was what his father had left to his younger brothers and what provision had been made for Elizabeth, his sister. To the eighteen-year-old Edmund,[21] when he reached twenty-one, William left the Cambridgeshire manor of Snailwell. Meanwhile, half its annual revenue of 40 marks was to be spent in masses and alms deeds for William's soul, half in completing Edmund's education in the law. To William, who was only seven, were to go the manor of Holwellhall and other property in East Tuddenham and elsewhere in central Norfolk, when he became eighteen. These estates were worth 25 marks per annum; for eight years an annual 5 marks was to be spent on masses and pious works, the rest was to go towards William's maintenance and education, an education which was to be the same as Edmund was undergoing. To Clement,[22] when he became eighteen, William left the lands in Somerton, Winterton, and elsewhere which had been Geoffrey Somerton's. They were also worth 25 marks a year. Clement (and his sister Elizabeth) were to be maintained by Agnes out of that sum and Clement educated at grammar school and in the law like his two elder brothers; 5 marks annually, however, she was to give to the poor and aged, 'manu propria', in honour of the five wounds of Christ and the five joys of the Blessed Virgin Mary. Finally,

[19] Davis I, pp. 45–6. As John, according to the recollection of Elizabeth his sister (Davis I, p. 627), was not at their father's deathbed in London, William's sickness was not quite his last. The confrontation with his eldest son was.

[20] Davis I, p. 46. Gresham, clearly, was Margaret's jointure: Davis I, p. 24, lines 131–8 (cf. *ibid.*, p. 385, lines 70–2).

[21] These ages too seem more appropriate to 1442 than 1444 – as John was said (*ibid.*, p. 24, line 132) to be twenty, and we know he was born in October 1421.

[22] Whose age is wanting because of damage to the will at this point: *ibid.*, p. 23, line 108.

Elizabeth was to have 200 marks towards her marriage according to certain conditions – which we shall discuss in the proper place.

At this point, with the reading of the will completed, John's sigh of relief might have been audible. Although he had been left only Gresham and reversions, there were a good many estates William had not included in his will: these would fall to John.[23] His relief was short-lived, was transformed into consternation, apprehension. As we have seen, William began to talk of giving William and Clement some of these estates. He also raised the matter of a perpetual chantry. Agnes gives another version of her husband's thinking on these issues:[24]

> myn husbond, whos soule God assoile, dyverse tymes . . . rehersed to me that the lyvelod which he had assigned to his ij yongest, William and Clement, by his will in writting was so littill that they might not leve theron wythought they shuld hold the plowe be the tayle, and ferthermore seying that he had dyvers oder maners, that is to say the maner of Sporle, Sweynsthorp, and Bekham, which maner of Bekham he was purposed to chaunge wyth the maner of Pagrave, and if he myght bring it abought then xuld on of his ij yongest sones have the seid maners of Sporle and Bekham and no more, and the other yongest sone xuld have al the remenaunt, and he that had the maner of Sweynsthorp xuld be bound in a gret some to the Prior of the abbey of Norwiche to paie for ever to the monke that for the day singeth the masse of the Holy Goste in Our Lady chapell in Norwiche, where he purposed to leye his body, every day iiij d. to sing and pray for his sowle and myn and al the sowles that he and I have hade any goode of or be beholdyn to pray for.

Hearing such talk, John's heart sank; his ire rose.

This his father detected, 'asking hym the question wheder he held hym not content, so seying to him in these termes: "Sir, and thow do not I doo, for I will not geve so mekyll to on that the remenaunt xal have to littil to leve on."'[25] To get the balance right between the heir and his younger brothers, especially when there were three of them, was no easy matter – we should not be over-critical of William on that score – but the written will was better balanced than the last-minute amendments William proposed. Agnes was a young woman; John's expectations there might be long delayed. Besides, he needed revenue now not later. For one thing his brothers and sisters were young too; they were as much in his charge as in Agnes'. For another he, with a wife and child (soon to be children), was to be head of the family in times which were becoming unpropitious, as the East Beckham and Oxnead affairs in his own experience all too clearly were showing; with the grand old man dead, he knew they would get sharply worse. He needed more landed security than Gresham. Palgrave, and Cressingham would give him. Thoughts akin to those expressed by Gervase Markham in 1598 undoubtedly were in John's mind: 'If I shall leave my land and living equally divided

[23] He also had, or had the prospect of, the Mautby property of his wife: see chapter 4, above.
[24] Davis I, pp. 44–5. [25] *Ibid.*, p. 45

amongst my children . . . then shall the dignity of my degree, the hope of my house . . . be quite buried in the bottomless pit of oblivion.'[26] We do not have to believe John was other than a hard and covetous man – or, at any rate was to become one – in order to understand the ill-feeling he displayed at his father's deathbed. Indeed, may not his father's lack of understanding of the needs of his eldest son have developed in John that hardness, that covetousness? John cared much, much more for his birthright than did Esau; he set about securing it with all the dispatch (he did not need to use the craft) of Jacob.

What John did was to ignore the last wishes of his father: '. . . and the seyd John Paston wold in no wysse agree there-to, seying that by the lawe the seyd maners xhuld be hijs, in as moche as my husbonde made no wyll of hem in wrytyn.'[27] Fifteen years later at another old man's deathbed, John was desperate to catch Sir John Fastolf's final thoughts on the disposal of his landed estate, and would commit himself and his family to the carrying out of what he thought he had heard or thought he ought to have heard. At his father's deathbed it was the other way about: he had heard only too clearly the dying man's decisions. Having heard the worst, he set about preventing it: '. . . and gatte the dedys owte of my possession and estat of the feffeez in the seyde manerys myn unknowyng'. Not only that: seeking greater security, John endeavoured to get his mother to alter William's will to put in the manors of Sporle and Swainsthorp as left to him. John Damme, the executor sympathetic to John Paston, seems to have suggested to Agnes that this was a pardonable sin.[28] Agnes told the other executor, William Bacton, 'how they had sayde to me, and [I] told hym I coude not fynde in my herte to sette in the wyll that I knewe wel was the contrary. And he sayde he wolde not councell me thereto.' Thus Sir John Fastolf's will was not the first John Paston considered tampering with. November 1459 saw Thomas Howes in the role of John Damme, the collusive executor, but at Caister there was no strong-minded widow; there were, however, plenty of other tough-minded executors who did not let John get away with what he got away with in 1444.

One of the things John wanted and got away with was his father's cash:[29]

[26] Cited in Mervyn James, *Family, Lineage, and Civil Society* (London, 1974), p. 26.

[27] For this and the other quotations in this paragraph, see Davis I, pp. 46 and 48.

[28] The passage (*ibid.*, p. 48) is obscure because the document is severely damaged: 'And I sayd it was never my husbondys [GAP] the advys of my lord of Lyncoln. And John Dam lenyng up-on a stole, I syttyng by hym, sayd [GAP] to a prest to aske hym counsell of suche a thyng he wolde nat byde hym dowte, but if he do it and go to the prest he wyll asoyle hym.' William Paston had named William Alnwick, the Bishop of Lincoln, as supervisor of his testament: *ibid.*, p. 22.

[29] *Ibid.*, p. 46.

And after that swyche tresowre of my husbons as wasse leyd in the abbey of Norwyche by the seyd John Paston, John Bakton, John Dam, and me, to delyvere agen to us all excectorys the seyde John Paston owte of the seyde abbey, unknown to the Priour ore ony oder person of the seyde abbey, and wyth-owte my wetyn and assente ore ony of owre felawys, toke and barre awey all, and kepying it styll a-gens my wyll and all the tothere excectorys wyllys, nothere restoryng the seyd Wyllam and Clement to the forseyd lond nore of my husbondys tresore recompensyng theim and ordeynyng fore my husbondys sowle in havyng of hijs perpetuell masse acordyn to hys wyll.

The money had been deposited at the cathedral by the executors as a form of assurance that William's perpetual chantry would be founded there and permanently funded out of the manor of Swainsthorp, as Agnes stoutly maintained William had wished. John maintained otherwise: he said the chantry should be financed out of the manor of Streethall in Great Cressingham. There was also dispute as to whether the chantry should be for eighty years rather than in perpetuity.[30] This wrangling may have gone on for years rather than weeks,[31] John no doubt being the stumbling block, before he pre-empted a decision by carrying off the money:

and after that dede don [the prior wrote] ther was no more money yoven us nowther to kepe the seide obit ner to pray for the soull of the seide William as be the seide executours, savyng that the seide Annes duryng here lyve yaff us of hir owne cost yerly to remember the soule; and that that hath be done sythen hath be don of oure owne devocion, and this many yerys ther hath no thing be yoven us. Not withstondyng of oure own devocion we have rehersid his name in oure bederolle every Sonday.[32]

Once again, there are premonitions of 1459. It was neither a simple nor a cheap undertaking to get a licence in mortmain: neither Sir John Fastolf nor William Paston had either the determination or the willingness to part with their money to ensure that their chantries were established in their lifetimes. At what cost to their souls – for their bickering executors did not repair their omission? In both cases John Paston was the principal beneficiary; of the non-foundation of Sir John Fastolf's college of priests and poormen at Caister and of William Paston's chantry in Norwich Cathedral. It is difficult not to despise this man (the very opposite of the literary model, 'The Childe of Bristow'[33]), who cared so little for the dead, his own dead: his father and his patron. If it had not been for Agnes and William Worcester, these two sinful souls would have been entirely bereft of aid from the living.

[30] Davis II, pp. 609–10. [31] *Ibid.*, lines 60–5. [32] *Ibid.*, lines 67–74.

[33] Ed. Clarence Hopper, *Camden Miscellany* IV, Camden Society, original series, LXXIII (London, 1859).

There was less excuse for John Paston in 1444 than in 1459.[34] Controversy inhibited action in both instances; it did not absolutely prevent it. Moreover, John genuinely seems to have started the college at Caister;[35] he did nothing at all about his father's chantry. Agnes' insistence that it had to be perpetual and the money had to come from Swainsthorp may have been an obstacle to any other scheme he had, but powerful filial piety would have got round that. I think we have to assume the rift between him and his father during William's last days was as deep as the one which opened up between him and his mother – 'After that', Agnes wrote in 1466, 'my sonne John Paston had never ryght kynde wordys to me.'[36] For John was not Jacob: he did not get his father's blessing.[37] He was not present when William died in London, and it was almost a week before he set out from Norfolk to see his father's body.[38] In the end, are we ready to say that John did not want to do anything for his father's soul, or, at any rate, that he did not care whether anything was done or not?[39]

If John would release no land to save the dead, he was certainly not prepared to let go of any to benefit the living. It was not simply that he kept Sporle, Swainsthorp, Streethall in Great Cressingham, and Woodhall in Great Palgrave, some or perhaps all of which manors in August 1444 William had stated should go to augment what he had left William and Clement in his written will of January 1444 (or earlier).[40] Within five years,

[34] Such excuse as might be offered in 1444 would have to be based upon confusion as to what William actually wanted. In his testament (Davis I, p. 21) he had desired masses at Norwich for no more than seven years. Thus, in 1444 as in 1459 John's reaction may have included exasperation: interpreting what these indecisive old men really intended must have been a difficult task.

[35] See a future volume. Sir John Paston in his draft will of 1477 still had good intentions with regard to a college of priests at 'my seid maner and fortresse' of Caister: *ibid.*, p. 507.

[36] *Ibid.*, p. 48. He was unmoveable: John, Agnes said in 1466 (*ibid.*, p. 47), 'at thys day will in no wysse by any fayere menez ore spekyng tendere my seyd husbondys sowle and myn, were perform the wyll of my seyd husbon'.

[37] Or so I construe the admittedly ambiguous letter of Agnes' of perhaps 1465 (*ibid.*, p. [illegible]3): 'Sonne, I grete yow wele and lete yow wete that, for as myche as youre brodir Clement letyth me wete that ye desyre feythfully my blyssyng, that blyssyng that I prayed youre fadir to gyffe yow the laste day that ever he spakke, and the blyssyng of all seyntes undir heven, and myn, mote come to yow all dayes and tymes. And thynke veryly non other but that ye have it, and shal have it wyth that that I fynde yow kynde and wyllyng to the wele of youre fadres soule and to the welfare of youre bretheren.' Agnes' blessing, it should be noted, continued conditional.

[38] *Ibid.*, p. 47, lines 1–5; p. 627.

[39] To be entirely just, it should be pointed out that Agnes survived him and did not do anything either; she had the independent means to do something long before 1466.

[40] *Ibid.*, pp. 44, 46. As regards to some or all, the following is unclear: 'seying that he had dyvers oder maners, that is to say the maner of Sporle, Sweynsthorp, and Bekham, which maner of Bekham he was purposed to chaunge wyth the maner of Pagrave, and if he myght bring it abought then xuld on of his ij yongest sones have the seid maners of Sporle and Bekham and no more, and the other yongest sone xuld have al the remenaunt'. What is

on Edmund's death in 1449, Snailwell fell to him – as, in such an event, William in his will had stated that it should.[41] By then he had most of the Mautby property, and a year or so later when Gresham had been recovered from Lord Moleyns, John had enough resources to have established his father's perpetual chantry and to have augmented his father's settlement on William and Clement. He did neither. In 1455 William became eighteen and should have entered into the manor of Holwellhall and the other lands his father had bequeathed to him. John clung on even to this small property:[42] far from adding, he took away. It may be that some other arrangement – the purchase of lands for William[43] – was being negotiated by John and the other executors; nothing, however, came of this.[44] William did not get Holwellhall until John was dead.[45] Clement became eigtheen in 1460.[46] He did get Geoffrey Somerton's lands, which his father had intended he should have: Clement was the brother whom John favoured.[47]

If Clement was the lucky one, Elizabeth his sister most certainly was not. We have come even closer to condemning John for meanness, meanness of spirit as well as miserliness: in 1454 he was rumoured to be saving £100 a year. William, signing himself (and meaning it) 'yowre pore brodyer', reported with much relish to John, the opinion of his much older friend, Thomas Billing, Recorder of London: 'As for Paston, he ys a swyre of wurchyp, and of gret lyvelode, and I wothe he wyll not spend alle hys good at onys, but he sparyt yerely c mark or jc li.' From trying to sympathize with

unclear is 'al the remenaunt', as well as the proposed exchange: was Streethall included in 'al the remenaunt'? East Beckham, which according to Agnes featured in William's thoughts as a manor one or other of the younger sons should have, is a special problem: see above, chapter 3. [41] Gairdner VI, p. 194; for Snailwell as John's see Davis II, p. 328.

[42] Davis I, pp. 622–3. [43] *Ibid.*, p. 623, lines 29–32.

[44] Probably in 1452 Agnes wrote to John (*ibid.*, p. 38), 'Item, John Dam told me that the Lady Boys will selle a place called Halys, but he seith sche speketh it prevyly and seith it is not cryed; as John Dam knoweth will, she hath seide as largely of other thyng that hath not be so. Item, he tolde me as he herd seyn Sere John Fastolf hath sold Heylysdon to Boleyn of London, and if it be so it semeth he will selle more; wherfore I preye you, as ye will have my love and my blissyng, that ye will helpe and do youre dever that sumthyng were purchased for youre ij bretheren.' The connection of land purchase with the will is made by her blessing, for which see above, p. 176, note 17. For what lands William did have see below, p. 183, note 82.

[45] Ironically, John Paston III in 1484 complained (Davis I, p. 623): 'The ryght off the whyche maner, londis, tenementes, and othire the premysses afftyr the desses of the seyd John the fadyr owith to come to the seyd John now compleynaunt as sone and heyre off the seyd John Paston for as myche as the seyd John and fadyre made no wylle nor mencyon of the aforseyd maner, londis, tenementes, nore off other the premysses, whyche maner, londis, tenementes and othire the premysses the seyd William Paston hath agenst the cours of the lawe ocupyeth.'

[46] If he was aged two in 1444 as Davis says he was: I, p. 43 headnote to no. 30, where he cites William Paston's will (*ibid.*, p. lviii), though I cannot discover Clement's age there.

[47] See below, p. 182.

John in 1444, when he was faced with having only Gresham as his livelihood, we have followed his deterioration into hardness of heart against father, mother, and brother. He was no gentler towards his sister. How unlike a gentleman ('a swyre of wurchyp') John Paston was; odd that for so long he has been taken as typical of his class, unless one faces the paradox of English gentlemen rarely being gentlemen at all – a semantic contradiction Thomas More took such delight in making use of in *Utopia*.[48] John Paston as anti-gentleman? Far from it: being small-minded, hard-headed, and cold-hearted, John Paston was every inch an English gentleman, 'ein Gentleman durch und durch', as the Germans (who had gentry but no gentlemen) were wont to say. We have been sympathetic long enough; in the 1450s there are no excuses for him. It will be a relief to get to his eldest son, to arrive at gentility proper. Meanwhile, John Paston has to be observed briefly but at his worst, in the way he mistreated his sister.

In his will William Paston directed that Elizabeth was to have £200 towards her marriage, if she married according to the advice of Agnes and his other executors, 'proviso semper quod eadem Elizabeth pari sexu et etate in bona et competenti consanguinitatis linea meritata sit', and so long as her jointure was of lands worth not less than £40 per annum.[49] William's *nouveau riche* snobbery is apparent: 'of equal class', 'of sound lineage' is what one might have expected from him, yet is surprised to discover articulated. In 1444, as Elizabeth recalled forty years later, she 'was xiiij, xv yer, or xvj yer old'.[50] She was not married until she was 28, 29, or 30.[51] Why did it take so long? There were suitors enough. Edmund, Lord Grey of Ruthin's ward, 'a grete gentylman born and of gode blode', would have satisfied one of William's conditions almost to the letter; he had 'iijc marc of lyvelod', so would have been satisfactory on the score of wealth also.[52] William Clopton was willing to offer a jointure of £40 with his son John, the bargaining over Elizabeth's 'chambyr' and 'here bourd aftyr the day of the mariage' seems to have been amicable enough – at any rate on John Clopton's part. As the negotiations got as far as a draft settlement it is not likely that the Pastons considered the Cloptons beneath them. Perhaps in the end John baulked at the 400 marks marriage portion, or Agnes and he fell out over it, or Agnes had second thoughts about paying for Elizabeth's 'chambyr' and 'the costages theof the day of the wedding'.[53]

[48] J.H. Hexter, *The Vision of Politics on the Eve of the Reformation* (London, 1973), pp. 194–8.
[49] Davis I, p. 24. [50] *Ibid.*, p. 627.
[51] For what follows see 'The Pastons Revisited: Marriage and the Family in Fifteenth-century England', *BIHR*. 58 [1985], pp. 35–6. [52] Davis I, p. 155; II, p. 96.
[53] Davis I, pp. 40–1; Davis II, p. 89. John Clopton was certainly nervous on the issue of Elizabeth's 'chambyr': 'and syr I besheche you, sethyn that I do myn part to fullefelle youre wyll, that ye wolle shew me youre good maystyrhod in here chambyr, as myn full trust js, jn

John, on the other hand, sometimes freely interpreted his father's condition of 'equality of age' when seeking a husband for his sister: Sir William Oldhall, for example, was nearly fifty when Elizabeth was but twenty.[54] She was only nineteen and Stephen Scrope fifty when their marriage was under discussion in 1449. Elizabeth was unhappy then, being kept in *purdah* by her mother and getting regular beatings, and desperate enough, Elizabeth Clere thought, to marry if not anyone, certainly not as William had directed she should.[55] Yet, five years later Scrope was still a candidate. An unlikely one it was thought, not only (one supposes) because, as Elizabeth Clere wrote, 'his persone is symple', or he was a widower with a daughter, but rather because his stepfather, Sir John Fastolf, had contrived to keep him out of his inheritance: thus, Stephen had nothing to offer.[56] By 1454, even the eighteen-year-old William Paston was voicing his concern at what was becoming a scandal: his twenty-five year-old sister was still a spinster. He wrote with some heat to his elder brother and head of the family: 'At the reverens of Good, drawe to summe conclusyon, it is time.'[57] Moreover, William's 'Ye knowe ho is most wurchipfull better than I' perhaps reveals who it was who was keeping Elizabeth a spinster and possibly indicates why. Did Elizabeth continue to wait for another four years because John could not find someone 'wurchipfull' enough for him, not for her?[58]

There are other hints that John, for whatever cause, dragged his heels. It was not Elizabeth: she had been ready to marry even Stephen Scrope.[59] In 1453 or thereabouts, she urged her brother to do more than he was doing about another suitor; Margaret reported to John:[60]

so moche that jt xall nowth hurthe you nor non of youris, and the profite there-of xal be on-to the avayle of myn maystress youre suster and to me, and to non odyr creature.' He offered to pay for Elizabeth's 'bourd aftyr the day of the mariage . . . to ease me that hat here chambyr may be non contradiction': Davis II, p. 89. The draft settlement was in the names of Agnes, John Paston, and John Damme; this, as well as the fact that Elizabeth was to remain with Agnes after the wedding, suggests she was younger than twenty-five, which she would have been if 1454 was the date of these abortive negotiations. Some time in the 1440s might be more appropriate for them.

[54] Davis I, pp. 31–2; 'Pastons Revisited', p. 35. [55] Davis I, p. 30; Davis II, pp. 31–2.

[56] For this, yet another story of injustice, see G. Poulett Scrope, *History of the Manor and Ancient Barony of Castle Combe* (London, 1852), pp. 264 ff. In 1450 Stephen Scrope was translating from the French – a fairly accurate translation – *The Dicts and Sayings of the Philosophers* for the 'solace' of his stepfather: edited Curt F. Buhler, EETS original series, no. 211 (London, 1941 for 1939), pp. lxii and 2. Scrope, unprepossessing though some may have thought him, was a man whose anger against a servant did not prevent that servant giving him 'a mervelows good name . . . and he hath seyd the best of yow lyke a nonest man shold sey of hys master': see the letter from Thomas Bamfield to Scrope in BM Add. MS 28212, f. 32.

[57] Davis II, p. 155.

[58] His reply to Edmund, Lord Grey, who had written concerning 'a gentylman of iij C. marc. of lyvelod' (*ibid.*, p. 96), was, however, rightly cautious as well as tendentious: Davis I, p. 82.

[59] Davis II, p. 32. [60] Davis I, p. 247.

And she desyrith, if itt pleased yow, that ye shuld yeve the jantylman that ye know of seche langage as he myght fele by yow that ye wull be wele willying to the mater that ye know of; for she told me that he hath seyd before this tym that he conseyvid that ye have sett but lytil ther-by.

The suitor's belief that John 'sett but lytil ther-by' is illuminating. Elizabeth and her mother were getting on no better in the mid-1450s than they had been in the late 1440s, Agnes, on one occasion at least, descending to crude sarcasm; the hurtfulness of her 'ther is gode crafte in daubyng' echoes resoundingly over five hundred years to demonstrate Elizabeth's humiliating plight.[61]

The years, many years, passed. Eventually, by January 1458 Elizabeth had escaped from 'home'; she was boarded out with 'Lady Pole' in London. She had not escaped her mother: 'And sey Elyzabet Paston that che must use hyr-selfe to werke redyly as other jentylwomen don, and sumwhat to helpe hyr-selfe ther-wyth', Agnes noted as one of her 'Erandys to London', 'Item, to pay the Lady Pole – xxvjs viiiid. for hyr bord.'[62] It looks as if Elizabeth had become resigned, quietist even. Her spirit, none the less, was not broken. By August William Paston was writing hopefully to Margaret,

Myn suster and myn broder recomand hem to yow bothe, and I may say to yow jn counsayll sche is op-on poyn of mariage so that moder and myn broder sett frendely and stedfastely there-on, leke as I wothe well ye wolld and it lay in yow as it dothe jn hem, &c. I pray yow to yowre parthe to kall there-on. It were to long to wrythe on-to yow all the maner of demenyng of this mater, and there-for I have spoke to Wyllyam Worsetere and to Wethewell to tell it yow holly as it is. I wothe ryth well yowr good labore may do moche; and send me word how ye here as hastely as ye may.[63]

We can catch the held breath: 'so that moder and myn broder sett frendely and stedfastely there-on' reveals the truth. Why this time John and Agnes went through with it, for we assume that the marriage Elizabeth was on the brink of was the one that came off later in 1458 to Robert Poynings, we do not know. The 'jointure', as Robin Jeffs wrote, 'was not ungenerous even if Poynings had a dubious title to some of the lands which formed part of it';[64] John and Agnes put Robert under a bond of £1,000 to make it – 'the which neded no such bond', Elizabeth wrote pointedly to her mother after the wedding.[65] John and Agnes, on the other hand, were in no hurry to hand over the marriage portion,

I beseke you, gode mother [wrote Elizabeth] as oure most syngler trost is yn youre gode moderhode, that my maystre, my best beloved, fayle not of the c marc at the begynnyng of this terme the which ye promysed hym to his mariage, wyth the remanent of the money of my faders wille.

[61] *Ibid.*, p. 248. [62] *Ibid.*, p. 42. [63] *Ibid.*, pp. 156–7.
[64] 'The Poynings–Percy Dispute: an Example of the Interplay of Open Strife and Legal Action in the Fifteenth Century', *BIHR*, 34 (1961), p. 157. [65] Davis I, p. 206.

They still owed 'Lady Pool' too; Elizabeth had to remind Agnes to pay her 'wyth hom I soiourned . . . all the costes doon to me before my maryage'.[66]

Married at last, Elizabeth wrote to her mother on 3 January 1459.[67] Her tone of delicate irony may have been familiar to Agnes. One senses those two women had got to know most of what there was to know about each other. Elizabeth Paston was a businesslike and capable woman, as her one other surviving letter, to John Paston II, shows.[68] Her letter of January 1459 to Agnes displays relief, perhaps tinged with apprehension, certainly (I detect) coloured by humour.[69] She must not be made into what she was not; she was, for example, always (or apparently always) submissive to her brother.[70] She was no rebel before her time: though she had cause. From the age of fifteen to the age of thirty she lived at home with her mother. In all that time no husband was found for her. It was not for want of a 'jantlymanly man':[71] such sought Elizabeth out. It was not because John and Agnes could not afford the marriage portion of £200. Thomas Billing knew there could be no plea on that score, as we have already observed William Paston reporting him as saying in July 1454:[72]

> As for Paston, he ys a swyre of wurchyp, and of gret lyvelode, and I wothe he wyll not spend alle hys good at onys, but he sparyt yerely c mark or jc li. He may do hys ennemy a scherewd turne and never fare the warse jn hys howsholde, ner the lesse men a-bowthe hym.

Undoubtedly John was negligent (like his father) – what can taking fifteen years to get your sister a husband be but negligence?[73] It was also, of course, inconsiderate, discourteous, unchivalrous. Ungenerous: is that not the final word? If John (and Agnes) had wanted it, Elizabeth might have been married before she was twenty. Their miserliness of spirit, not of means, was what kept Elizabeth miserable for so long.

How did John treat his brothers? Edmund, eighteen in 1444, had little time to enjoy Snailwell, which his father left to him; he was to have it when he became 21; he died in 1449. John duly inherited Snailwell.[74] William, who was seven in 1444, was to have what his father intended for him when he became eighteen. Because he did not get some of it until the death of John

[66] *Ibid.*, p. 207. [67] *Ibid.*, no. 121, the letter from which we have just been quoting.
[68] *Ibid.*, no. 122.
[69] I wish I understood more fully the meaning of Agnes' 'she hath no fantesy ther-inne, but that it shall com to a jape', her comment on Elizabeth's attitude towards a proposed match in 1453: *ibid.*, p. 248. [70] For example, *ibid.*, pp. 31–2, 248; Davis II, p. 32.
[71] Davis I, p. 155. [72] *Ibid.*, p. 154.
[73] As William Paston wrote to Margaret in 1458 after reporting the offer of a marriage for Margery, her daughter, his niece (*ibid.*, p. 157), 'It were well do suche materes were nawthe sclawfully laboryd; it is wurchypffull &c.' He may have had Elizabeth's case in mind, for in the preceding paragraph (that is, the paragraph quoted above) he had told Margaret 'sche is op-on poyn of mariage'. [74] *Ibid.*, pp. 22–3, 148; Davis II, p. 327.

I allowed him to in 1466, because most he never did get, and because he lived until 1496 he became (not all at once in 1455, but by uneven leaps and bounds thereafter) first a disgruntled and then an alienated member of the family, ending as a fairly implacable opponent of his nephew John Paston III, the head of the family after 1479. The story of the family at odds with itself as a consequence of Judge William's bungled deathbed is William II's story: he, as the survivor, kept the cause of the badly done by younger sons going into the next generation. William is the main attraction, once we have dealt with what little there is to deal with on the last and youngest of the brothers, Clement.

If Clement was two years old in 1444,[75] he was the same age as his nephew, John Paston II. Perhaps the almost generational gap between them was the reason why John Paston I treated Clement better than he did William: more like a son than a brother. In May 1460 he was in possession of the lands in East Somerton his father in 1444 had wished him to have when he became eighteen.[76] A year later he wrote to John,[77]

> Brodere, I pray yow delyver the mony that I xld have in-to swm priore of swm abbey, to swm mayster of swm colage, to be delyveryd qwan I can espy ony londe to be purchasyd. I pray yow send me word wyder ye will doo thus ore no.

What was the money that he should have had? Is there a lack of trust in the last sentence? That he did not fall out with his brother the handful of his surviving letters to John show. After John's death in 1466, and apart from Agnes' concern that he should get what Judge William really intended he should have had (expressed in the drafts of her will of later that year, one of which drafts Clement wrote[78]), he almost completely disappears from view. The single and oblique glimpse of him is in February 1470, when John II asked John III to discover what their uncle William's current attitude was on the matter of the lands he reckoned he ought to have had,

> whethere he be off the same dysposicion in my grantdamez londe as he was at hys last beyng here, at whyche tyme he tolde me that he scholde and wolde have suche londe as I loked afftre, rehersyng moreovyre that myn oncle Clement had laboryd the same.[79]

He was dead when Agnes composed another and probably final will.[80] He had died unmarried; his lands went, as Judge William said they should, to his brother William.[81] Clement's death left William alone, save for Agnes' somewhat unreliable support, to fight for a reversal of 1444 and for his rights.

[75] See above; p. 177, note 46. [76] Davis I, p. 163, lines 13–15; cf. Davis II, p. 258, lines 40–9. [77] Davis I, p. 199. [78] *Ibid.*, p. 45. [79] *Ibid.*, p. 415. [80] *Ibid.*, p. 49.

[81] *Ibid.*, p. 623; Gairdner VI, p. 195; Davis I, p. 176, line 30, which shows, I think, that Clement was dead by August 1477.

William, aged seven in 1444, according to Judge William's will, should have entered on what his father left him in 1455. John denied these estates to his brother; nor is there the slightest indication that anything resulted from the proposed alternative of purchasing lands for him.[82] No more than Clement, though he had every reason, did William fall out with John. Not, at any rate, for some years: he was John's loyal ally in the cause of Fastolf's will in 1460.[83] But he had not forgotten his just grievance; in 1462 he reminded his brother (not for the first time) of this matter which divided them; he wrote with feeling, dignity, and wisdom:[84]

Ryththe wurchipfull broder, I recomand me to yow. Lekit it yow to wethe Jon off Dam is come to towne and purposit hym to tary here a day are ij, are lengar, I can thynk, and he be desyryd; were-fore I pray yow, and as I have a-fore this tyme desiryed yow the same, that suche materis as hathe be comunyd now lathe be-twyx myn moder, yow, and hym may take some good conclucyon be-twyx owre-selff here at hom. And yn myn consayt, savyng yowr better avyse, it were so most covenyent and wurchipfull for us all and comforthe to all owre fryndis. And for this ententhe I wold tary here the lengare, for I wold be as glad as any man a-lyve that su̇che an ende mythe be take be-twix us that jche off us all schuld jnyoy the wylleffare off odyr, qweche I trust wyth yowre good help schall be rythe wyll.

There was the heart of the matter: 'that jche off us all schuld jnyoy the wylleffare off odyr'.[85] The appeal to solidarity, to community fell on the deaf ears of such a committed individualist as John Paston.[86] That was the last time William wrote to John; at least John kept no more of William's letters, if there were any. There are no letters at all from John to William, or indeed from Margaret, John II, or John III to him (which survive). It seems likely that after 1462 William, as he said in the postscript to this letter, was not, or was no longer 'in a folis paradyce'.[87] His last words had been more in

[82] See above, p. 177. Unless the manor of Horninghall or Caister Clere (Davis I, pp. 176, 196; II, p. 608) in Caister was brought for him. Edmund Clere (according to Blomefield V, p. 1553) owned it in 1457. In 1458 William thanked Margaret Paston for 'gaderyng of myn mony' (Davis I, p. 156). Nevertheless, the purchase seems not to have been made until 1464, when in May seisin was made to Agnes, William, and his feoffees: Bodleian Library, Oxford, Norfolk Charter a.8, 734.

[83] Davis I, pp. 157–64, for instance.

[84] *Ibid.*, pp. 166–7.

[85] Cf. Margaret's postscript to her letter to John of 16 November 1461 (*ibid.*, p. 273): 'My modyr wold ryth fayne know how that ye and my brodyr Wylliam wer a-cordyd; sche wold ryth fayne that all wer well be-twen yow.'

[86] No more successful was the involvement in 1462–3 of Chief Justice Markham as an arbiter between the brothers: *ibid.*, p. 167, line 12; Davis II, p. 291, lines 36–7. Probably his involvement did not get beyond a preliminary stage.

[87] The postscript is about a possible marriage for John II (rather than any longer William himself) with a daughter, or some other relation (or possibly ward) of Lord Scrope, 'the mater towchyng the Lord Scrop' of the last paragraph in the main text. John, Lord Scrope of Bolton, was a feoffee of William's in 1464 (Bodleian Library, Norfolk Charter a.8, 734). William concludes: 'For as for me, I know so moche that sche will non have but iff he have, ar be leke to have, meche more lond than I have; and iff I knewe the contrary it schuld nat be left for the labore, but I wold nat be in a folis paradyce.'

desperation than expectation: 'And ye by myn good brodir I trust thow to do rythe will etc.'

Having got nothing from John I, he got nothing from John II after John I's death in 1466.[88] John I seems to have made no written will at all; even if he was overtaken by a sudden death, even though he died before he was forty-five, his failure to have done so is remarkable for a man trained in the law, and as shortsighted, given the far from unfinished business of Fastolf's will, as was his father's omission to incorporate his final intentions in writing. The will, which was only proved several years later in 1473,[89] must have been (like Fastolf's) nuncupative.[90] Even at that late stage there was doubt as to whether William was his brother's executor or not: John II wrote to John III[91]

> for as God helpe me I cannot say verrely iff my fadre, God have hys sowle, agreyd that he [William] shold be on, but in my sowle he never thowt that he sholde, for he never namyd no moore butt my modre and me, and afftre yow whan I rehersyd myn oncle Clement, yow, and Arblaster, and than he chase yow, seyng he thoght that ye were good and trewe. Kepe thys secrett. Iff myn oncle be noon executur it maye happely brynge ageyn a trussyng coffre wyth cc old peyse noblis whyche he toke from me as executur.

In 1466 and immediately thereafter William had certainly behaved as if he were John's executor – along with Margaret, James Arblaster, and John II.[92] Margaret was worried what William might attempt 'twochyng hys lyflode',[93] while William reminded Margaret of what John had failed to do: 'Hit nedis nat to put you in remembraunce of my mater touchyng my fadirs soule, my modir, and me.'[94] For, we might remind ourselves, if the living had not received their due from John Paston nor had the dead: his father's soul had been struggling unaided through purgatory for over twenty years.

Neither the dead nor the living, however, got any more out of the son than they had out of the father. If Judge William could do nothing to alter his fate, William could try to do something about his. He nagged at John II and threatened him through Agnes,

[88] Except that he got after John I's death Holwellhall and the other properties he should have had in 1455 by virtue of his father's written will: Davis I, pp. 176–7, 622–3.

[89] *Ibid.*, p. 467.

[90] William Paston III sent a copy of it to his brother Edmund *c.* 1480 (*ibid.*, p. 651): 'here is closid in thys same byll the wyll of my fadyr, suche as my brodyr hathe, and he seyth that it is the very wyll of my fadyr and that he had it owt of the regestyr'. Why is it no longer in the register Wattys?

[91] *Ibid.*, p. 468.

[92] So the missing 'trussyng coffre', the other business with coffers of Davis I, p. 170, lines 9–19, and *ibid.*, p. 168, lines 1–4, and the authoritative mode of these memoranda to his nephew of 1466 or 1467 suggest Margaret thought him an executor: *ibid.*, p. 341, lines 4–5. Cf. *ibid.*, p. 356 lines 17–18. William seems to have been at John's deathbed in London; Margaret and John II, apparently, were not: *ibid.*, p. 333, lines 12–20.

[93] *Ibid.*, p. 334, lines 29–33.

Item [John wrote to his mother in October 1469[95]], myn oncle William scholde have comen home every daye thys vij nyght, and thys daye or to-morow he comyth homwardys. He and I be as goode as fallyn owt, for he hathe laten me pleynly wete that he schalle have all my grauntdames lyfflod off here enherytance and of hyr joyntore also, wherin I trust to God that he schall helpe. I woll not yit speke of it, ner I praye yow doo not.

For what Agnes had threatened to do[96] in order to recompense William (and Clement) for the additional lands which, she maintained, William had wanted to leave them but had not included in his written will, and which John had refused to release to them, was to bequeath to them for as long as they were denied those properties, lands of the equivalent value from her own inheritance, the manors of Stansted, Marlingford, and Horwellbury. Between them, Agnes and William got as far as initiating legal action in London to make William 'swyr of hyr lond', or so John III reported to his brother in 1470.[97] Yet they never got far enough[98] and on Agnes' death in 1479, whatever claims to these three estates William pursued, and he pursued them vigorously, as we shall see shortly, they were not sufficiently sure to bring him unconditional victory. In the end Agnes probably promised more than she really wished to deliver.

Before arriving at the critical year of 1479 two points need to be made. First, if the excuse for John Paston's uncompromising attitude towards his younger brothers in and after 1444 was that he, as head of the family, had not been as generously treated by his father as was his due, then the excuse for John II's opposition to his uncle William's claims after 1466 was weightier, for he was in direr straits after his father's death than was his father after *his* father's. In 1466 Agnes had another thirteen years in which to enjoy her inheritance, her jointure, and her dower, but now there was a second dowager, Margaret, who carried away with her to Mautby her

[95] *Ibid.*, p. 409. [96] In the draft will of 1466: *ibid.*, pp. 46–7.

[97] *Ibid.*, p. 561, lines 10–13. In the same year William was also boasting, as John III said, to 'stryp me fro the maner of Sweynsthorp': *ibid.*, p. 559, lines 37–8. Swainsthorp was to have gone to William or Clement and out of it ought to have come the annuity for Judge William's perpetual chantry (*ibid.*, pp. 44–5, 46). It was settled on John III and Margery Brews in 1477 (see, for example, *ibid.*, pp. 607–8). It certainly looks as if it had been left to John Paston III by his father. John I also left 10 marks annually to another of his younger sons – William, as it turned out: see below p. 186, note 105. Moreover, he also seems to have bequeathed Cressingham and Palgrave to his younger sons: Walter got Cressingham (Davis I, pp. 647–8) and Edmund Palgrave (see note 103). All of which, considering the events of 1444, is most interesting. John even had one more son than his father to consider: five to four. The same number were under age, three, but as Edmund in each case was on the threshold of legal maturity there were the same number of boys in 1444 and 1466 whose more distant future had to be catered for: William and Clement in the first case, Walter and William in the second.

[98] Despite the rumours related by Margaret to John III, 28 January 1475: Davis I, p. 374, lines 22–5.

Mautby inheritance and Gresham, her jointure.[99] She seems not to have been dowered. Moreover, William in 1466[100] had at last got possession of what according to Judge William's written will he should have had in 1455, the manor of Holwellhall in East Tuddenham and other property there and elsewhere. Clement already had the Somerton and Winterton lands. Furthermore, in 1466 John III was given Swainsthorp,[101] Walter, Cressingham,[102] and Edmund, Palgrave by their father.[103] What was there left to John II? Very little, as he complained and enumerated in 1477 when telling John III he could or would not give him a manor in order to marry Margery Brews: 'I wolde be as gladde that one gaffe yow a maner off xxli. by yeere as if he gave it to my selffe, by my trowthe', but that one is not going to be me, he went on to gloss at length.[104] In fact, of Paston lands for John II all there was were Sporle (which was mortgaged)[105] and Snailwell.[106] Not much for the head of the Paston family: 'my fadre, God have hys sowle, leffte me scant xlli. londe in rest'.[107] All the chief estates were in the tight and long-lasting clutch of heiress dowagers: Agnes had Paston and Oxnead, Margaret had Gresham and Mautby.

By 1477, of course, John II had (and he listed them) Caister and a handful of other much smaller, former Fastolf manors. But he did not securely have them in 1466, however much the Fastolf estate may have entered into his father's calculations when he was apportioning property among his five sons. John II was shown less understanding and given less consideration by John I in 1466 than John I had been in 1444 by William. So much for fathers' predilection for their eldest sons in England in the later Middle Ages.[108] And mark how daunting the power of women. For John II in 1466

[99] For which see above, p. 172. In her will she left 6d to 'ich pore houshold that be my tenauntes there': Davis I, p. 385.

[100] For so I interpret Davis I, pp. 622–3. He had these properties in 1477: *ibid.*, pp. 176–7.

[101] See page 185, note 97 above.

[102] When he died in 1479 Walter left it to John III, unless he became head of the family, in which case it was to go to Edmund, to whom, as John did become head of the family, it presumably went: Davis I, pp. 647–8.

[103] I infer this because Palgrave, like Cressingham, is not mentioned by John Paston II in his list of landed assets in 1477: *ibid.*, p. 503. The 'disappearance' of Woodhall in Great Palgrave into Sporle after 1466 (Blomefield III, p. 447) might be explained by its temporary absence in Edmund's hands between then and the early sixteenth century.

[104] Davis I, p. 503.

[105] Moreover, 10 marks out of the 30 it was worth per annum, were earmarked for William Paston, the youngest of John Paston's five sons, by John in 1466; as maintenance in the first instance (*ibid.*, p. 451, lines 1–3), as an annuity when he came of age; because the manor was mortgaged, John II in 1479 had to leave William the former Fastolf manor of Runham as he predicted in 1477 he might have to: *ibid.*, p. 503, lines 18–23; p. 652, lines 9–12.

[106] He did not mention East Beckham, but then he did not have it.

[107] Davis I, p. 466.

[108] An example of another Norfolk landowner dividing his estate is Oliver Gros esquire (his will is NRO, NCC Reg. Aleyn, f. 186, dated 1 July 1439 with a codicil of 16 June 1440, proved 16 March 1453). Oliver (evidently a reader of chivalrous texts) stated that if his son

we are compelled to have sympathy. For him a speedy settlement of the Fastolf affair on almost whatever terms was essential; he could not afford to wait. It is, therefore, hard to understand his mother's particular reluctance to lend him money in 1472 and her general lack of sympathy for him: in her situation and in his.[109] It is far easier to grasp why so much hung on the recovery of Caister from the Duke of Norfolk in the early 1470s: Caister was not simply a jewel in the Paston crown, it was the only jewel in what had become a coronet. Having (somewhat luckily) got back the vital Caister in 1476, here Sir John's good fortune ceased: he died barely three months after his grandmother and five years before his mother. He above all might have said: a plague on the power of women. He never did: if anyone was a gentleman among the Paston menfolk it was Sir John. His collected, cool but

Rowland inherited the manor of Sloley, then his son John was to have the manor of Irstead, the property called Malousells in Swannington, purchased from Margery Geney, and other lands in Worstead and Westwick, once Sir John Colville's, bought from the executors of Sir Thomas Geney. Oliver was also generous to his daughter Cecilia: a £5 annuity out of Sloley, and for life the ornaments and vestments in the chapel of St James at Sloley church – in that chapel Oliver was to be buried. The manor of Crostwick, Rowland already had (Blomefield V, p. 1396). Oliver's will disguises more than it discloses. The phrasing 'if Rowland should inherit Sloley' and the long-delayed proof are the faintest of clues to the grinding contest over that manor which was to take place in the 1450s and 1460s. Oliver does not mention his dead eldest son Simon nor Simon's daughter Amy. Simon had married Margaret, daughter of Sir Henry Inglose; Sloley was their jointure. After Simon's early death Sloley was held first by Oliver Gros then on Oliver's death by Rowland, and when Rowland died by his brother John, each of these 'leasees' paying Margaret (and her second husband Thomas Beaupre) an annuity of £20 handed over in four yearly instalments in the Lady Chapel of Norwich Cathedral – out of an estate valued variously at £20, £30, and £40. Rowland had a son, John. The struggle in Chancery was a straightforward contest between him, the heir male, and the heir general, Robert Ashfield, Amy's son by her husband John Ashfield (PRO, C1/31/216, 217, 218, 219). The issue turned, of course, on a deed in a deed box. John Gros claimed Sloley by a male entail of 1372; Robert Ashfield by a settlement on heirs general of 1368. There was doubt about the existence of the deed of 1368, and if it existed who had it, but William Wayte told a circumstantial story (*CCR 1461–8*, pp. 86–7) of copying it out for William Yelverton, his master. Yelverton visited by John Gros, Oliver's youngest son, saw the deed in the deed box John had brought with him. As Yelverton's wife Jane was a daughter of Oliver's, he thought a copy of the deed was worth having for himself; he, therefore, got John Gros to take the box with him and had William Wayte make the copy. It must have been the deed itself, however, which Yelverton produced in Chancery (PRO, C1/31/217), presumably to settle the case: in 1478 Robert Ashfield sold Sloley to Edmund Jenny (Blomefield V, p. 1434).

John Gros, Oliver's son, was married to Margaret, daughter of Sir John Heveningham. Margaret Paston's word for him, 'gentyll', when he was endeavouring to persuade his widowed mother-in-law to marry John Windham (Davis I, p. 256, line 39), must be ironic.

Oliver's naming of his second son Rowland is interesting, as interesting as the fact that in the Fastolf family Alexander was a common name in the fourteenth century. There was, for example, 'Blak Alysaunder de Gapton', who died in 1405, leaving his armour to his son Thomas. There was also (among others) an Alexander Fastolf who was a monk at St Benets at Holm: see the fifteenth-century Fastolf genealogical notes of Bodleian Library, Norfolk Charter a.8. 722.

[109] Margaret's almost anti-Paston stance after 1466 will have to be examined on a later occasion.

uncalculating demeanour throughout all his vexations comes as a relief, at least to this explorer of the family's past.[110]

Secondly, to what extent did William's less than complete solidarity with his brother's widow and nephews after 1466 hinder, if it hindered at all, the final settlement of the Fastolf affair? A brief answer might be a couple of years. A full answer must be delayed until the story of the Fastolf will is related at its proper length and in its proper place. What needs to be said here is that William's involvement from the beginning in 1459 (as a feoffee of Fastolf if nothing else[111]) ensured his involvement to the bitter end, and that his entirely legitimate concern for his own property in Caister, that is the manor of Horninghall or Caister Clere[112] and his tenement of Methis or Holkhams (the latter sold to him by Thomas Howes and William Worcester[113]), ensured that 1473 and not 1471 was when William Wainfleet and Sir John Paston at last tied up all loose ends – the Duke of Norfolk actually occupying Caister always excepted.[114]

What was it William Paston had written to his elder brother in 1462: 'that jche off us all schuld jnyoy the wylleffare off odyr'? John Paston's self-regarding treatment of William was ill-considered; it damaged the interests, even as he, John, would have seen them, of the family. William gave no help to John III besieged at Caister in 1469, he did not speed but impeded agreement with Wainfleet, and after 1479 (as we shall see) he was in outright and successful opposition to a family which continued to deny him his rights. Before 1479 he was not so thoroughly alienated. Although Margaret and her two eldest sons were suspicious of him,[115] yet they valued his advice in the years after John I's death,[116] and they borrowed his money, though not willingly.[117] He, on the other hand, offered them advice[118] and

[110] To his brother, John III, he did, however, let his feelings show towards the uncle who had lent him £400 (Davis I, p. 476): 'as for chevysshaunce [borrowing at interest] that myn oncle W. spake off, as God helpe me itt canne nott be . . . by God I had lever than c noblys that I weer qwyte off hym . . . I am in an agonye wyth hym that vexithe all my spyrytys' (*ibid.*, p. 481). Even here the tone is more of sadness than of wrath. This financial business between uncle and nephews must also be deferred until later.

[111] Davis I, p. lvii; *CPR 1452–61*, p. 386.

[112] See above, p. 183 note 82.

[113] Davis II, pp. 607–8: in recompense for all he had done on Fastolf's behalf, both while Sir John was alive as well as after his death, declared William Barker and Margaret Worcester *c.* 1485. Cf. Davis I, p. 17, line 24.

[114] See, for the moment, Davis I, pp. 421, 423, 437, 576 (line 32); Gairdner V, nos. 807, 835; Magdalen College, Oxford, Fastolf Papers 103/21, 24; PRO, C1/40/18, 19; C1/20/80; C1/12/28.

[115] Davis I, pp. 368, 596. There was necessarily a mutual lack of confidence here which went back to John Paston's time: Davis I, p. 271–2, Davis II, p. 288.

[116] For example, Davis I, pp. 336–7.

[117] For instance, *ibid.*, p. 476, the revealing encounter of lines 10–28 and John's conclusion: 'But iff I maye doo other wyse I purpose nott to chevyshe any mony by hys meane.'

[118] *Ibid.*, pp. 167–70.

lent them money, albeit on security.[119] That he was not their enemy is beside the point; the point is that he was not their committed ally: which he might have been. Their loss was considerable.[120] William's wholehearted support would have been a formidable augmentation of their limited resources. For by then William Paston was a man of substance; in 1466 he was well on the way to becoming one.

He was William Paston of London, gentleman.[121] He is the very epitome of David Morgan's gentleman:[122] a younger son who makes himself someone to be reckoned with by service to the great at the centre of things, London. He was a Norfolk JP (and of the quorum), but the towns for which he sat in the Commons – and he sat in many parliaments – show he was not a man of Norfolk. One of them was Newcastle-under-Lyme, which he represented with John Wood of Keele in the parliament of 1472–5. Another was Bedwin.[123] Who put him forward for these 'rotten' boroughs? There is little evidence of a close connection with the Staffords, though we should note his accompanying Henry, the young Duke of Buckingham, on pilgrimage to Walsingham, or, at any rate, coming with him into Norfolk, in summer 1478,[124] and in the autumn of the following year his successful handling of a matter which lay between Duke Henry and Elizabeth, dowager Duchess of Norfolk.[125] It would be a long way wide of the mark to

[119] *Ibid.*, pp. 371, 373; no. 97 (pp. 174–5); cf. p. 478, lines 35–6. The estate mortgaged to him in 1474 was probably Sporle.

[120] While there was not a splintered family, Agnes and William against the rest, these two were regarded with mistrust and, considering what Agnes might do with Marlingford, Stansted, and Horwellbury, or indeed Oxnead, apprehension by the others, for example, Margaret to John III, 28 January 1475 (*ibid.*, p. 374, lines 20–2): 'Recomaund me to yowyr grauntdam. I wold she war her in Norfolk as well at es as evyr I sy hyr, and as lytyll rewlyd by hyr son as evyr she was; and than I wold hope that we alle shuld far the bettyr for hyr.' By this time Agnes lived in William's London house, Warwick Inn, near Newgate (*ibid.*, p. 476). The measure of William's influence upon his very elderly mother in the last years of her life is shown in Davis I, nos. 98–103: he was her Norfolk agent, so to speak.

[121] *Cal. Anc. Deeds* I, p. 498, C1130. Only much later, two years before his death in 1496, when we might think of him as 'retired', does he become William Paston of Caister, gentleman: (*CCR 1485–1500*, p. 219); by then it is his nephew who has become William Paston of London, gentleman (*ibid.*).

[122] D.A.L. Morgan, 'The Individual Style of the English Gentleman', in Michael Jones (ed.), *Gentry and Lesser Nobility in Late Medieval Europe* (Gloucester, 1986), esp. p. 8 ff.

[123] For this see Wedgwood, *Biographies*, pp. 667, 967. Colonel Wedgwood's entry on this predecessor of his in the Newcastle seat is a particularly idiosyncratic one, even for him.

[124] Davis I, p. 511: 'Syr, it is too that the Duke of Bokyngham shall come on pilgrymage to Walsyngham, and so to Bokenham Castell to my lady hys sustre [his aunt?], and then it is supposyd that he shalle to my lady off Norffolk; and myn oncle William comythe wyth hym.' He was also a feoffee of the duke's in 1481: *CPR 1476–85*, p. 257.

[125] From his manor of Wood Norton William wrote to his friend Richard Roos at Reepham (Davis I, p. 189): 'ser, I remember that ye tolde me the last tyme that I was with you at Refham that ye wolde dispose your-silf affore this Cristenmas to take a journey to se my lady of Norffolk; which if ye will parfourme nowe I wolde be verrey glade to awaite upon you and to accompany with you thider. And ye coude not take your journey thider in a better

connect William Paston with a single great man, even to conclude that he served one more than he served others. That was not the way to modest fortune for the sort of gentleman William Paston was. The way was: to put yourself about, to be useful to many.[126] William was educated in the contemporary fashion;[127] his letters show he had a lively intelligence, was urbane (as who would not be who lived in London society), and affable; he was a man who could do the work when necessary and keep his counsel when required to. He was, for example, consulted on how to write a stiff letter to Alice, dowager Duchess of Suffolk; the chancellor, George Nevill, Archbishop of York, thought the letter too long 'and mad on after is owune entent'; as Alice ignored it, perhaps George should have sent William's longer version.[128] It was William, said John III, who got John II to lend George Nevill 1,000 marks, which, as almost all of that sum was never repaid,[129] shows William was far from infallible, even if it was unpredictable politics that were chiefly to be blamed. Probably it was William who had John II take Nevill's 'lytell clokke' to the clock repairer's;[130] one hopes he knew better what he was doing on this occasion.

season, for ther is commyn hider to me a servaunte of my lord of Bukynghams, which hath abiden her this iij or iiij dais and wil not departe hens till he have me forth with hym to my lady of Norffolk for a serten mater touching my said lord of Bukyngham, which mater I trust if ye com I shal handill it so that ye shal do both my lorde and hir a plesure.' Richard was not persuaded. A little later William wrote to him again (*ibid.*, p. 190): 'Master Roos, I recomaund me to yew in myn most humbill maner. Syr, myn lady of Norffolk faryth welle and recomaund her to yew, and gladly wold se yew: We sped all myn Lord Bokyngham intent with hyr grace.' The dowager duchess was presumably living at Kenninghall in the south of the county. In 1491–2 the hall and barn at Kenninghall were repaired at a cost of 53s 9d: see the slip of paper stuck in at f. 48 in the accounts of the duchess' lands of that year, the fourth item in the volume formerly Phillipps MS 3840 and now in the possession of Mr Brian Spencer. In the later 1490s, however, she was (or was also) living at Earl Soham in Suffolk: Davis II, pp. 475, 476. At some point, perhaps around 1480, she was at Smallbridge Hall in Bures, on the Suffolk–Essex border: Davis I, p. 193, lines 5–6. For Smallbridge Hall, see Pevsner, *Suffolk*, (revised edition) p. 126.

[126] From, for example, Robert, Lord Willoughby, in the 1450s to Thomas, Earl of Ormond, in the 1940s *via* Sir Thomas Burgh in the 1470s; *CCR 1461–8*, p. 143, *Cal. Anc. Deeds* II, C2550; IV, A7701, A7720; *CPR 1467–77*, p. 523. The list of his feoffees for Horninghall in May 1464 (Bodleian Library, Norfolk Charters a.8, 734) is revealing: Elizabeth, Countess of Oxford, John, Earl of Oxford, John, Lord Scrope [of Bolton]; William Yelverton, Elizabeth Clere, William Jenny, John Greenfield (sergeant-at-law), John Catesby, sergeant at law, John Hastings, John Clopton, John Calthorpe, Hugh Fenn, Thomas Cornwallis, Thomas Howes, clerk, Roger Marshall of London, Henry Spelman, William Lomnor, Bartholemew White, William White, John Appleyard, James Arblaster, William Worcester, Richard Mariot.

[127] Cambridge and (almost certainly) the Inns of Court: Davis I, nos. 83, 84, and his friendships with other sergeants at law besides Thomas Billing suggest this; it is likely he was at Gray's Inn, where Thomas Billing was Reader in the early 1450s (Wedgwood, *Biographies*, p. 76).

[128] Davis II, p. 383. Once Alice had got Drayton and Helsdon back into de la Pole possession there was no chance of anyone getting her out of them. Or Dedham, or Cotton for that matter.

[129] Davis I, p. 626; cf. Davis II, p. 394, and future volumes.

[130] Davis I, p. 413.

Being a familiar of such elevated folk William was well aware politicians' promises signified nothing (the loan to George Nevill was a risk which had to be taken):

And as for the Lord Revers, he seyd to myn oncyll William, Fayirfax, and me that he shold meve the Kyng to spek to the two dwkys of Norffolk and Suffolk that they shold leve of ther tytyls of syche lond as wer Syr John Fastolffys . . . whedyr he mevyd the Kyng wyth it or nowt I can not seye. Myn oncyll Wylliam thynkys naye.

On the other hand, and on the same famous occasion of Edward IV's visit to Norfolk in June 1469, the king spoke the truth to him after making a joke:[131]

myn oncyll William seythe that the Kyng told hym hys owne mowthe when he had redyn forby the loge in Heylysdon Waren that he supposyd as well that it myght falle downe by the self as be plukyd downe . . . And then myn oncyll seythe how that he answered the Kyng that ye trustyd to hys good grace that he shold set yow thorow wyth bothe the dwkys by mene of treté, and he seyth that the Kyng answerd hym that he wold neythyr tret nor spek for yow but for to let the lawe proced; and so he seyth that they depertyd.

If it was a joke; it says little for Edward IV if it was not.

By this time William had married Anne, daughter of Edmund, Duke of Somerset.[132] Her father and eldest brother, Henry, had given their lives for the Lancastrian cause; two other brothers, Edmund and John, presently in exile for that cause, would do so at Tewkesbury in 1471. In 1464 William had been a feoffee of George, Duke of Clarence.[133] We have noticed his association with George Nevill. William was pardoned in December 1471, the same month as John II, two months before John III:[134] they had fought against Edward IV; it is difficult to believe William had. It is not that his nephews were 'political' (whatever that term means) and he was not. They fought at Barnet with the Earl of Oxford because the earl had shown himself their effective patron during the Readeption; the return of Edward IV would mean their enemies, the Dukes of Norfolk and Suffolk, would recover their power to strip the Pastons of what was left to them of the Fastolf estates.

[131] *Ibid.*, pp. 543, 544–5. [132] *Ibid.*, p. lvii, esp. note 13. [133] *CPR 1461–67*, p. 323.

[134] Davis I, pp. lvii, lvix, 566 (headnote). He had obtained a general pardon on 16 July 1468 (BL Add. Ch. 17248; Gairdner, IV, p. 299). This was during an unnerving summer, after the Thomas Cook affair but before the arrest of the Pastons' patron, the Earl of Oxford, in the autumn. (Had William gone with the Duchess of Norfolk, 'the noblest of the ladies' who accompanied Margaret of York to Bruges for her marriage to Charles the Bold in June? See, C.L. Scofield, *The Life and Reign of Edward the Fourth* (London, 1923), I, pp. 455–6; Richard Vaughan, *Charles the Bold* (London, 1973), p. 52. His nephews were there: Davis I, p. 538.) Did Sir John Paston have to purchase William's pardons for him? In 1484 in his draft bill of complaints against his uncle (Davis I, p. 626) John III noted the following: 'Item, the seid John axith restitucion of suche jnportable charges as the seid William hathe put the forsaid Sir John on-to by the space of many yeres as in plesures doyng and rewardis which apperith by writyng of the hande of the seid Sire John, which pleasures and charges the seid Sir John was constreyned to doo in defence of the seid William; where-of the seid John axeth to have amendys of cc mark.'

Their family interests dictated a commitment which did not fall short of putting their armour on. But William's interests – as we have seen – were not those of his nephews. His life was a London life of service to many, as many, one presumes, as possible. If his sympathies in 1469–71 were 'Lancastrian', and one suspects they were and not held lightly either, he wore them lightly: that had to be, it was one of the constraints imposed on the type of gentleman William was.

After 1471 he buried his feelings, but not so deep that they did not show. Thus, when in 1473–4 Elizabeth, Countess of Oxford was forced to make over many of her East Anglian estates to the king's brother, Richard, Duke of Gloucester, William was the last of her feoffees to bend to the will of the over-mighty duke; he was also the most outspoken: 'I never knewe that hit was the fre wil of the seid countes that I shulde release', he told the duke when finally *subpoenaed* into Chancery. The courageous integrity William displayed throughout this nasty episode seems characteristic of this attractive man; no wonder he got on better with his nephew, John II, than his brother, John I.[135] One of the Norfolk manors Duke Richard plundered from the countess was Knapton in North Erpingham hundred, neighbour to Paston. If Elizabeth had fee'd William out of the revenues of that property his fee was continued by the duke:[136] perhaps so loyal a gentleman was to be wooed, not further alienated.

More to William's taste in the 1470s would have been to observe (from the vantage point of being his feoffee) his old friend and now Chief Justice Thomas Billing's no doubt advantageous business dealings with Isobel, dowager Marquess Montague. This rich Cambridgeshire heiress had run up a bill of £1,000 with her London dressmaker, William Parker, and her lands and those of her widowed mother Jane Ingoldesthorp had to be settled in such a way as to clear her and her second husband, Sir William Norris, Knight of the Body, of it. Unless William had mixed feelings, which one of his fellow feoffees, John Morton could have shared, at what may have been another instance of Yorkist sharp practice.[137] Thomas Billing was an old

[135] Gairdner V, no. 845; *CCR 1468–76*, pp. 334–5; M.A. Hicks, 'The Last Days of Elizabeth Countess of Oxford', *EHR*, 103 (1988), pp. 76–95, esp. pp. 92–4.

[136] Davis I, p. 176, line 10; pp. 186, 188.

[137] *CCR 1468–76*, pp. 329–30. This transaction requires more attention than I can give it here. Jane Ingoldesthorp was a sister of John Tiptoft, Earl of Worcester; it was he who had got her daughter Isobel the marriage with John Neville in 1457 (Davis II, p. 172). Isobel seems to have remembered her uncle in the windows she gave for the north aisle of the elegant church of Wiggenhall, St Mary Magdalen, Norfolk; the exotic range of Italian and British saints they portrayed reflected his (and possibly her) 'uncommon and specialized taste': R.J. Mitchell, *John Tiptoft* (London, 1938), pp. 144–5; C. Woodforde, *The Norwich School of Glass Painting in the Fifteenth Century* (London, 1950), pp. 165–6. Thomas Billing, according to Wedgwood (*Biographies*, p. 76) of 'plebian parentage', I presume bought and built Astwell Castle, Northants.

acquaintance. John Morton, Richard Roos, and Henry Colet were new friends; they had been either actively Lancastrian or Lancastrian sympathizers during the Readeption. The 'circle' they composed, which in Norfolk had at its centre Elizabeth Talbot, dowager Duchess of Norfolk, is an intriguing one – especially if we add to it, albeit probably on its circumference, Henry, Duke of Buckingham.[138] If they were hardly Lancastrian any longer – though we should remember, as they undoubtedly remembered, the Earl of Oxford, who landed in East Anglia in May 1473, and remained after 1474 their lost leader across the water, imprisoned in Calais – they certainly were reluctant, unconvinced Yorkists. The dowager Duchess of Norfolk, who had been obliged to make an agreement over her dower (even if it was not financially an unsatisfactory one[139]) with the king, his second son Richard marrying her heiress daughter, Anne, in 1478, may be thought to have had a particular antipathy towards Edward IV until it is recalled that her late husband's method of separating the Pastons from their property was far more brutal, his attitude towards them far less generous. Of course: she could have been antipathetic to him too.[140]

If the political tendencies of the members of this circle were such as to make them, in the later 1470s, less than enthralled observers of the *status quo*, they were by no means gloomy. Witness the prank they played on William Paston at Christmastide 1479. William is writing to Richard Roos:[141]

Syr, myn lord of Ely, be the menys of myn Lady Norffolk and myn lady Anne, and myn cosyn Southwell that was masengere, sent me a suppena to a-pere a-forn the Kyng in the peyn of a m[1]li. be-fore Crystmes; and I wold nat be in the case that I was in to dayes, tyl I knw the mater, nat for xxli. And myn lady of Norffolk wold nat dyscover the mater tyll I had wretyn and sent myn servauntes to London; and qwan thei were gon, than myn Lady Norffolk told me the mater and tornyd to a jape that was ernest with me a-fore, &c.

Light-hearted this 'jape' may have been, but given the political proclivities of the perpetrators and their victim *and* his and their knowledge of that *subpoena* of 1474, it carried a heavy ironic weight. In the circumstances a *subpoena* to the effect that the king wants to see you at once seems an

[138] See above, p. 189.

[139] In the settlement made in 1476 and embodied in an act of Parliament in 1478 (*Rot. Parl.* VI, p. 169) her allotment of Mowbray lands gave her a net cash income of over £1,400: calculated by Mr Brian Spencer from the accounts of her lands for 1491–2, part of a miscellaneous volume, formerly Phillipps MS 3840, and now in his possession.

[140] They were married as children before 1448. She was, or gave the appearance of being, sympathetic to the Pastons in their attempts to get her husband to give up Caister; see a future volume and, meanwhile, Davis I, pp. 585–6. Moreover, she wanted Margaret Paston to be with her at her confinement in March 1476, that is, after her husband's death in January but before John II recovered Caister in June (Davis I, p. 602).

[141] Davis I, p. 191.

especially sure device to unnerve William: or did they take the politics of the 1470s more lightly than its historians do? That the counterfeit summons came from the royal councillor, John Morton, enhances our pleasure at their sense of comedy and at the fact of that clever man's involvement in such an amusement. It should be noted, however, that he did not invent it; that was the doing of the Duchess of Norfolk and William's wife, Anne.

William lent 500 marks to Morton.[142] Henry Colet lent that sum to John Paston III.[143] William was a feoffee of this wealthy London merchant, who had been active on Henry VI's behalf in 1470 (and was pardoned in December 1471), and who had married the remarkable Christian Knevett, sister of Sir William Knevett of Buckenham Castle, counsellor of both Elizabeth, dowager Duchess of Norfolk and Henry, Duke of Buckenham.[144] Sir William was another of this 'old Lancastrian' Norfolk group; he was certainly an old Lancastrian, having been one before 1461 as well as between 1469 and 1471. Henry Colet, who was to be twice mayor of London after 1485, was a younger man; he also had estates in Norfolk.[145] It was in Colet's house, but undoubtedly his London one, that a strange scene was played out by the disputing Pastons:

Item, where on Lomnore had a cofure in kepyng and v ml mark in the same be extymasion to the use of John Paston, fadire of the forsayed Sir John and John, the seid William Paston fraudelently atteyned the seid cofure wyth the seyd sume off money after the dissece of the seid John the fadire, and had it in his kepying serteyn dayes and did with it his pleasure unknowyn to the seid Sir John Paston and John Paston his brothere, and after at Herry Colettes house the seid William brought the seid cofure to the seid John Paston, knyght, and there openyd the seid cofure, where was then lefte but cc old noblis which were by extimacion in value c li., and the seid William toke there the seid gold awey with hym ageyn the will of seid Sire John, and withholdith the same wereof the seyd John preyeth to be restored.

So complained John Paston III in 1484.[146] The coffer was that mentioned by John Paston II in 1473.[147] Into it John Paston I had put his father's cash and plate, which he had carried off from Norwich Priory some time after

[142] *CCR 1476–85*, p. 173.

[143] College of Arms, MS 326/91; BL Stowe Charter 194; and see a future volume.

[144] *CPR 1476–85*, p. 53; Wedgwood, *Biographies*, pp. 205, 520; Davis II, p. 474. Christian was remarkable because having had twenty-two children, of whom only one, the equally remarkable John Colet, survived, she looked sufficiently youthful in her seventies to impress Erasmus. She outlived her distinguished son and died in 1523: Mary L. MacKenzie, *Dame Christian Colet* (Cambridge, 1923). I suppose the irony is that John Paston had borrowed from Henry Colet partly to pay off the costs of combating William's assault on the Paston estates in 1479.

[145] *CChR 1427–1516*, p. 267 (cf. Blomefield IV, p. 504); among his Norfolk lands was property in Clippesby and elsewhere in the hundreds of East and West Flegg: Samuel Knight, *The Life of John Colet* (new edition, London, 1823), pp. 279, 404.

[146] Davis I, p. 625.

[147] *Ibid.*, p. 468: 'Iff myn oncle be noon executur it maye happely brynge ageyn a trussyng coffre wyth cc old peyse noblis whyche he toke from me as executur.'

1444:[148] what he had done, had been done to him. But can there really have been as much as 5,000 marks still in the coffer in 1466?

The man in this circle to whom William was, or seems to have been, closest was Richard Roos esquire.[149] Richard was William's brother-in-law.[150] These two, together with the Knevetts, Thomas Billing, John Paston II, John Paston III, John Heydon, John Jenny, John Fincham, and others, were on Norfolk commissions during the Readeption.[151] Richard, after a hectic earlier life, had settled with his Norfolk wife at Reepham near Roos, estates restored to him in 1463.[152] William addressed two letters to him there;[153] they reveal their friendship, and (in the following passage) the quality of that friendship:[154]

> Master Ros, I recommand me to you as humbly as I can, thankyng you nat allonly . . . for your brawne and your crane, but also for the labour that ye toke for me in commyng hider to Wodnorton to your gret disese. For I undirstonde be Master [gap in MS] that was her with me agein yisterday that ye cam home both colde and late and causid hym and his broder both to abide with you al nyght and made them ful goode chier, as he saith.

When Elizabeth, dowager Duchess of Norfolk wrote to Richard she did so equally warmly:[155] he was manifestly someone who could be warmed to. Perhaps having been a youthful prisoner in France for ten years in the custody of that other devoted Lancastrian, Pierre de Brezé, [156] had made him into a real gentleman.

In his two letters to Richard Roos, William Paston signs himself 'yowre servaunt'. This was courtesy; it was also recognition of, and it brings us back to, what William Paston was. He was a servant long before modern concepts of servility became attached to service. Service brought him money. The money brought him land.[157] His manor of Horninghall at Caister (acquired

[148] *Ibid.*, p. 46; Davis II, p. 610.

[149] Richard Roos, Sir William Knevett, and Henry Colet are caught together in HMC, *Rutland Mss.*, I, p. 7: Knevett acknowledges receipt on 18 Nov 1481 of £20 from Roos for Colet.

[150] Ethel Seaton, *Sir Richard Roos* (London, 1961), p. 40, and for Richard Roos esquire, pp. 35–42.

[151] *CPR 1467–77*, pp. 245, 247, 249; see also Davis I, p. 432, lines 1–8. For John Fincham see below, p. 196, note 160. Richard Roos was the most intransigent of these Lancastrians, being named as a rebel (with William Knevett) in April 1470 and not being pardoned until March 1474: *CPR 1467–77*, pp. 218.

[152] *CPR 1461–7*, pp. 285–6; Seaton, *Sir Richard Roos*, pp. 39–40.

[153] Davis I, nos. 108, 109.

[154] *Ibid.*, p. 189. Can the Simon Gunnor, Roos' servant of the next line, be *the* Simon Gunnor of East Beckham?

[155] HMC, *Rutland Mss.*, IV, p. 188.

[156] Seaton, *Sir Richard Roos*, pp. 35–8.

[157] The money (presumably) made him more money when he lent it, as we have seen him lending it to John Paston II and John Morton; see also, *CCR 1476–85*, p. 289. Was he wealthier than his nephews? I fancy that by the 1480s he may have been. Perhaps because he was not primarily a landed gentleman, he seems to have been less disputatious than his elder brother; he did, however, quarrel in 1486 with his illegitimate Beaufort relatives as well as with John Mills, yeoman, or they with him: *CCR 1485–1500*, pp. 18–19, 21.

in 1464) and his house in London have already been noticed.[158] He purchased two other estates in Norfolk: Wood Norton, from where he wrote to Richard Roos and Henry Waryns in 1479 and whose church of St Peter was the only one to which he made a bequest,[159] and the manor of Talbots in Fincham, in West Norfolk, which he acquired from Christopher Talbot soon after the death of Christopher's father, Thomas, in 1478.[160] He also had a house in Norwich.[161]

London apart, Wood Norton was clearly William's favourite place. His manor there was called 'Gerbridges and Genyes': it had belonged to his mother's Gerbridge ancestors.[162] William probably bought it from a member of the Crane family, possibly from Adam Crane; Cranes corresponded with Pastons in the 1450s[163] and it was Adam Crane's daughter, Elizabeth, who quitclaimed it to William in 1494.[164] She had probably just come of age: in his will of two years[165] later William wanted her to 'be wele maried at my costis, or ellis by the menes of my doughters, un-to suche a persoune as may dispende by yere xx merc, or ellis to a gode marchaunt or other craftisman'. It was from such folk as Christopher Talbot and Adam Crane, on the gentry–yeomanry border and when they were in difficulties, that younger sons, who had very certainly succeeded and very definitely were gentlemen, bought the rural properties, which, while not turning them into country gentlemen, for (we have been assured) there was no such creature in fifteenth-century England, did give them security and influence: a gentleman had to have his own place from which to hunt and hawk and where he might 'lord it' over *his* tenants. For such as William Paston, Wood Norton demonstrated he had arrived.

[158] See above, pp. 183 and 189. [159] Davis I, pp. 186–7, 189, 195.

[160] *CCR 1476–85*, p. 246; Blomefield IV, p. 98. Part of the deal that was (one suspects) the buying of Christopher Talbot out of his patrimony was a grant to him of a life annuity of 5 marks: Davis I, p. 195. Thomas left another son, John, and a daughter, Florence; they were given money and were Thomas' executors; Christopher was not. They were to have Thomas' Norwich property if Christopher prevented them having their money. The will of Thomas Talbot, gentleman, is NRO, NCC Reg. Gebur, f. 211v, dated 18 March 1478, proved 13 January 1479. John Fincham esquire was a supervisor of Thomas Talbot's will. John owned the main manor in Fincham, was a benefactor of the grand church of St Martin there, had perhaps 'Lancastrian' leanings in the Readeption, and died in 1495. He was another lawyer: Davis I, p. 190; II, pp. 139, 140, 157. In his will John desired his brother Nicholas Fincham to be his chantry priest either in St Martin's church 'or els in tyme of Necessite in the Chapell of oure Lady being edefied in my Maner of Fincham . . . that is to say in tyme of necessite Whanne any woman or women being in the said Maner be grete with child and may not labour to goo to the parissh Church or in tyme of Sikenes or trowbelous or fowle wedir or at any other convenient tyme Whenne it shall like any of my said heires to have Masse in the said Chapell.' Later priests were to be appointed by John's heirs, whom he also empowered to dismiss any priest they considered to be 'not of good conversacion and disposicion'. The will is PRO, Probate 11/11, f. 61v, dated 10 March 1494, proved 7 February 1496.

[161] Davis I, p. 196. [162] Blomefield IV, pp. 451–2. [163] Davis II, pp. 36, 115, 339.

[164] *CCR 1485–1500*, p. 219. [165] Davis I, p. 195.

William had clearly done that by 1479 when, at last, Agnes died. Being a year of plague, it was an extraordinary year for deaths. Three Pastons died: as well as Agnes, there were her two grandsons, Walter, newly graduated from Oxford, who died in August, in the same month as his grandmother, and John II, who died in November.[166] It was Agnes' death which took the family by surprise. They were at Walter's funeral in Norwich on Saturday 21 August when the news was brought.[167] Agnes died alone in London. John Paston II was not with her,[168] nor (almost certainly) was John III.[169] William, her son, was certainly not. He was riding (perhaps from London, perhaps from Wood Norton) to Norwich for Walter's funeral when he was told of his mother's death. At once he turned his horse and rode off to Marlingford, where between three and four o'clock that afternoon he urged the tenants 'to attorne to hym withoute wrytyng or ony evydence shewed to hem'.[170] William was in such a rush to gain this advantage over his nephew that he appears not to have wasted time riding *via* the Duchess of Norfolk to collect the sixty followers Thomas Docking told Edmund Paston he would.[171] No more than he wasted time at Walter's funeral: so much for family feeling. In this irreligious fashion the contest between uncle and nephews commenced.

John II and his brothers quickly counter-attacked – at Marlingford within less than a week. On their side they enlisted friends like William Lomnour and William Yelverton, and the friendly great like Sir John Radcliff and the Bishop of Ely.[172] The bishop, John Morton, might have been expected to favour his friend, William Paston; perhaps he did, when in October he counselled both parties to delay Agnes' *inquisition post mortem* until some accommodation had been reached between them. It was the escheator or under-escheator who would not delay; whether he was awkward, of an independent cast of mind, or simply favoured John Paston II, he went ahead early in November and found as John wished. This worried John III: how

[166] Three Pastons and a Yelverton died. Edmund Paston wrote in his letter which told of his brother's funeral and his grandmother's death, 'My syster ys delyuerd, and the chyld passyd to God, who send uus hys grace': *ibid.*, p. 639. This was almost certainly Anne, married to William Yelverton, rather than Margery, married to Richard Calle. The child was perhaps the only one she ever had: *ibid.*, pp. lxii–lxviii.

[167] For what follows, see Edmund's letter of that day, *ibid.*, pp. 638–9. I infer that the funeral was at Norwich from the first line of the letter.

[168] As his memoranda of this month show: *ibid.*, p. 514.

[169] Edmund's letter was endorsed by John III 'dies mortis A.P.' There is no address (*ibid.*, p. 638); it does not read like a letter to a brother. If John III was not at Walter's funeral, where was he?

[170] Davis II, p. 599.

[171] Davis I, p. 639. Or did he? Later, he reminded the duchess of John Barell (*ibid.*, p. 193, lines 9–10): 'This same John Barell cam with me whan I com to youre grace incontinent afttur my modirs decesse.' Was this Docking the Thomas Dokking to whom William Paston left an annuity of 40 shillings in 1496 (*ibid.*, p. 195, lines 67–8)?

[172] *Ibid.*, p. 515; Davis II, p. 599.

would uncle William and the bishop take what to them had to appear as the reneging on an agreement, merely verbal though that had been. For some fumblings towards an agreement had occurred, an 'apoyntment befor th'arbytrors' (one of them Sir John Radcliff) having been taken.[173] This did not prevent competitive rent collecting at Paston, where Harry Waryns was a stout supporter of William Paston;[174] there, indeed, William had been put into possession by Agnes three months before she died. On 21 May 1479 the tenants of the manor of Huntingfield, none other than Warin King at their head, had been summoned by Harry Waryns to witness to Simon Gunnor (none other) transferring possession from Agnes to William. This was an illegal procedure: Paston was Agnes' for life only. Possibly Agnes was beyond caring about such things; it is evident from the deposition of the tenants William took care to have drawn up that he was not.[175] As the family apparently began to disintegrate, it suffered a further and heavy blow: John Paston II died in November.[176]

This gave William one opponent fewer. John III, who went at once to London to bring home his brother's body for burial but found (to his surprise, but not to David Morgan's) that his London-based brother had chosen to be buried there,[177] was, none the less, not an isolated opponent. In Norfolk, he counted, and counted on, his friends:[178]

If myn unkynd oncle make eny mastryes to gadre money, areragys or other, my Mastyr Fytzwater, Syr Robart Wyngfeld, Syr Thomas Brews, my brodyr Yelverton, my brodyr Harecort, and other of my frendys I trust wyll sey hym naye, if they have knowlage.

In London he sought friends – in the highest places:[179]

But thys I thynk to do when I com to London, to spek wyth my lord Chamberleyn and to wynne by hys meanys my lord of Ely if I can. And if I may be eny of ther meanys cause the Kyng to take my servyse and my quarell to-gedyrs, I wyll; and I thynk that Syr George Brown, Syr James Radclyff, and other of myn acqueyntance whyche wayte most upon the Kyng and lye nyghtly in hys chamber wyll put to ther good wyllys. Thys is my wey as yet.

By December[180] he had found some and wrote with relief and self-satisfaction to his mother,

[173] Davis I, pp. 515–16, 614–15. John Paston III writes straightforwardly of 'th'exchetore Palmer' (Davis I, p. 614, lines 3–4), but the escheator of Norfolk and Suffolk at this time was Humphrey Grey: *CFR 1471–85*, p. 154. William Paston had got the writ of 'diem clawsyth extremum' (Davis I, p. 515, lines 20–1) on 5 September: *CFR 1471–85*, p. 174.

[174] Davis I, p. 615; II, pp. 367, 412, 428–9. For William Paston and Harry Waryns, see Davis I, no. 106.

[175] Bodleian Library, Norfolk Charters 6.

[176] John II died between Monday 22 November and Thursday 25 November: Davis II, p. 437, lines 5–9.

[177] Davis I, p. 617.

[178] *Ibid.*, p. 618.

[179] *Ibid.*, p. 617.

[180] *Ibid.*, p. 619.

And sythe it is so that God hathe purveyd me to be the solysytore of thys mater, I thank hym of hys grace for the good lordys, mastyrs, and frendys that he hathe sent me, whyche have parfytely promysyd me to take my cause as ther owne; and those frendys be not a fewe.

Who exactly they were is not clear. John had seen the Bishop of Ely and learned that John II 'had promysed to a-byde the reule' of Morton himself and the chamberlain, William, Lord Hastings. He was hoping to see Lord Hastings the following day; meanwhile, the doubts William Lomnour was sowing in his mind – 'As for my lord of Ely, dele not with hym be owre avyse, for he woll move for treté and ell be displesid'[181] – remained:

I am put in serteynté by my most specyall good mastyr, my Mastyr of the Rollys, that my lord of Ely is and shalbe bettyr lord to me then he hathe shewyd as yet; and yet hathe he delt wyth me ryght well and honourably.

John Morton was playing the sort of game at which he was a master. It is strange to think of him, probably in this same month, playing with William Paston's friends another game, the hoaxing of William Paston with a fake *subpoena*;[182] strange, that is, until one realizes how confusing fiction with fact is eternally the way rulers and their agents rule: 'the great game', in Kipling's phrase.

Before John left for London at the end of November he had taken what measures he could to protect the Norfolk estates. He had himself ridden to Cressingham to hold the court: the family may have needed the cash he collected to pay the costs of Walter's final illness and of his burial.[183] John held the court on Thursday 25 November. On the following Sunday, after John had departed, Edmund rode to Marlingford (in the morning) and on to Oxnead (in the afternoon). At Marlingford the news was good: 'James, kepere there for Will Paston', was discovered not to have been at his post when John II died. At Oxnead 'Peris kepyd your brotheres possession at that tyme; and your uncle his man was not there, but he assyned anothere pore man to be ther': less good news. William Lomnour, who gave it, also reported John Wyndham's and John Heydon's lukewarmness:[184]

[181] Davis II, p. 437, lines 23–4. [182] Davis I, p. 191: see above, p. 193.

[183] Davis I, pp. 616–7. And compare John to his mother from London in December (*ibid.*, p. 619): 'Modyr, I beseche yow that Pekok may be sent to to [*sic*] purvey me as myche money as is possybyll for hym to make ayenst my comyng hom, for I have myche to pay her in London, what for the funerall costys, dettys, and legattys that must be content in gretter hast then shalbe myn ease.' Margaret, of course, worried about John in plague-ridden London, as William Lomnour wrote (Davis II, p. 438): 'my mastras your moder gretyth yow well and sendyth yow here blessyng, requiryng yow to come oute of that here alsone as ye may'. John reassured her (Davis I, p. 618): 'Pleasyt yow to undyrstand that, wer as ye wyllyd me by Poiness to hast me ought of the heyer that I am jn, it is so that I must put me in God, for her must I be for a season; and in good feyth I shall never, whyll God sendyth me lyff, dred mor dethe then shame. And thankyd be God, the sykness is well seasyd here; and also my besyness puttyth a-wey my fere.'

Your brothere Edmond sent to John Wymondham, and he sent word he wolle be a mene of treté but wold take noo parte, and as I sopose that was be Heydons avyse; for your uncle sent to be with hym, and also the same man rodd to Heydon and Wymondham &c.

One can appreciate their predicament. How much did they know of the story of Judge William's deathbed? What we do not know is how Agnes at the last disposed of her lands. Did she leave her inheritance, Marlingford, Stansted, and Horwellbury, as she had threatened in the 1460s,[185] not to the main stem of the family, but to William? Wyndham and Heydon, like us, may have felt William, ill-treated by a John Paston whom their fathers had known intimately enough,[186] deserved to have something after his mother's death, as he had got little or nothing after his father's. John III, while wanting possession to be taken of all the family estates,[187] understood the extent of the opposition; to be observed as one who wished to have all might lead to him losing much. At Oxnead and Marlingford, for example, Edmund was to take no money from the tenants:

I thynk if ther shold be eny money axid in my name, paraventure it wold make my lady of Norffolk ayenst me and cause hyr to thynk I dellt more contrary to hyr plesure than dyd my brodyr, whom God pardon of hys gret mercy.[188]

It is unlikely this diplomatic conciliation achieved what John required it to; no doubt it was seen for the window-dressing it was.

For one thing, William did not hold his hand; he 'occupied' for some time or from time to time over the next five or more years not only Oxnead and Marlingford, but also Stansted and Horwellbury; at Paston too (as we have noticed) he came; and also he went.[189] For another, John did not increase his support. Robert Browne wrote from Norfolk[190] of disarray and disillusion:

Ryght worshipfull ser, y recommaunde me to you as hertily as y can, desiring to undrrestond your welefare and also to knowe somwhat certainly hou your matier dothe with your uncle, and hou fer ye be; for in thies parties, y assertayne you, moche mater is shewed and proclamed in worshipful presence fer fro th'entent of your welewillers, of the discorage and reprofe in maner of you, and by such as men supposed you to have ben right wele favoured with; and the contrary shewed in the presence of right worshipful and right many, and as it is said iij scor in nombre, with such termes and under such forme, as it is reported, as is full hevy to diverse here.

[185] Davis I, p. 47. [186] For this was John Wyndham the son, and Henry Heydon.

[187] Davis I, p. 618, lines 20–3 and 30. [188] *Ibid.*, p. 618.

[189] See John's complaints, Davis I, pp. 620, 623–4; and also *ibid.*, p. 192; Davis II, p. 600 for Horwellbury – 'I nede no grete helpe there', William wrote to the Duchess of Norfolk: Davis I, p. 194; and *ibid.* p. 193 for Stansted, where William's farmer John Barell proved treacherous and paid his farm to John Paston; and *ibid.*, pp. 664, 665 for Marlingford – Margery's agitated and duplicated account of William's descent upon and dismantling of the mill there. [190] Davis II, p. 441.

Robert's letter was addressed 'to John Paston, squier, with my lord, Chamburlayn'. John, following his elder brother's example, had entered William, Lord Hastings' service; as Lord Hastings was captain of Calais, John served him there too, on one occasion so well that his 'tru frend Hastynges' thanked him heartily. The occasion was almost certainly in April 1483.[191] Within two months Hastings was dead, murdered by Richard, Duke of Gloucester, hell-bent on usurping the throne. John Paston lost his patron, the one man who, until the death of Edward IV at least, might have got for him what he wanted. Richard's murder of Hastings on 13 June was the end of the hopes and expectations of many clients like John Paston – they, John Paston among them, were unwilling to forgive the usurper so bloodily thorough an extinction of their prospects.

By the summer of 1483, therefore, John had no one to counter his uncle's Duchess of Norfolk. She had become tired of the affair, as had John's farmer at Oxnead. So Margery told John:[192]

> Item, ser, on Saturday last past I spacke wyth my cosyn Gornay, and he seyd if I wold goo to my lady of Norffolk and besech hyr good grace to be youre good and gracyous lady, she wold so be; for he seyd that on word of a woman shuld do more than the wordys of xx men, yiffe I coude rewyll my tonge and speke non harme of myn unkyll. And if ye comaund me so for to do, I trist I shuld sey nothyng to my ladys displeasure, but to youre profyt; for me thynkyth by the wordys of them, and of youre good fermore of Oxned, that they wyll sone drawe to an ende; for he cursyth the tyme that ever he come in the ferme of Oxned, for he seyth that he wotyth well that he shall have a grette losse, and yet he wyll not be aknowyn wheder he hathe payd or nought; but whan he seth his tyme he wyll sey trowth. I understood by my seyd cosyn Gornay that my lady is nere wery of hyr parte, and he seyth my lady shal come on pylgremage in-to this towne, but he knowyth not wheder afore Cristmes or aftyr; and if I wold thanne gete my Lady Calthorpe, my moder in lawe, and my moder and my-selfe, and come before my lady besychyng hyr to be youre good and gracyous lady, he thynkyth ye shull have an ende, for fayne she wold be redde of it, wyth hyr onowre savyd, but yette money she wold have.

Indeed, the weariness as well as the seeping away of revenue drove them, though it drove them gingerly, towards a settlement.

Margery's letter to John may have been of November 1481. It was not until 1486 or 1487 and after another unlikely political revolution that arbitrators were agreed on. Two, almost certainly William's two, were John Alcock, the chancellor and new Bishop of Ely, and Sir Reginald Bray; John's two we do not know.[193] It was a year or more later before a conclusion was

[191] *Ibid.*, p. 439. Cf. *ibid.*, p. 440, where William's brother, Sir Ralph Hastings, writing from Guisnes on 9 May was apprehensive, especially on his brother's behalf (lines 5–6).

[192] Davis I, pp. 665–6. For the altogether admirable William Gurney, see *Hopton*, pp. 253–4.

[193] Davis II, p. 610, lines 75–9. One feels it ought to have been John Morton rather than John Alcock, but Morton ceased to be Bishop of Ely in October 1486, and only became chancellor in March 1487. Davis II, no. 832 appears to be about a different dispute.

reached. The Duchess of Norfolk was still involved. Sir Henry Heydon, almost certainly from the manner of his writing, one of John's arbitrators, wrote to him,

As for your mater betwyx you and your wncle, I have shewid it soo to myn ladie of Norffolk and to hym that it is agreed yee to entre in to Marlyngfford and all other maners in debate in your name, and to kepe your courtes, sell your wodes, and to doo therwith as with your own. Wherupon I advise you as soone as yee may send som discrete man to kepe your courtes and to lette your fermys and selle your wodes to your most avayll . . .; and what is bee-heende in the fermourz or tenauntz handez sethyn the rekenyng last be-for myn ladiez servauntz and yourz, that thei bee warnyd kurtesly to paie it by a day, except in ony wise I avyse you nat to make ony thretes to ony fermour or tenaunt for ony dealyng affor this tyme, but to gett in fayernesse till I speke with you; and in ony wyse that yee nor ony your servauntz have noon wordes in this mater but that it is agreed bee myn ladie you to have your peasebill possession.

The reckoning for John had still to come. As Sir Henry put it: 'Your penauns off your wncles mater shall yee knowe whan I kom hoome.' He did not attempt to soften the impending blow: 'Ther is non other meane but to sell your wodes and tymber in all your maners.'[194] Thus, after ten years or so uncle and nephew arrived at a settlement, arrived at it, one suspects, through exhaustion and perhaps because since 1485 William's Lancastrian associations (even closer than his nephew's with the Earl of Oxford) made him an antagonist not to be denied.[195] Yet, William was old and had only

[194] Davis II, pp. 469–70. 'Huntyngfeldes' (of p. 470, line 16) is the manor of Paston itself: *CCR 1454–61*, p. 290 and chapter 2 p. 32.

[195] Three letters of William Paston in the Northamptonshire Record Office show his connection with the Butler interest, represented by his wife's sister, Eleanor Beaufort, widow of James Butler, Earl of Ormond and Earl of Wiltshire. All three letters are to Thomas Cary, of Moulsford, Berkshire, son of a Tewkesbury victim, Sir William Cary, and brother-in-law of Sir Robert Spencer, Eleanor's second husband. (See Wedgwood, *Biographies*, p. 156.) The five items of Fitzwilliam Roll 370 make up three letters. Item 4 is a letter written in London on 10 September – William writes of 'suche besynesse as the King hath commanded me'. Items I and 5 comprise a very long letter 'By your Frende William Paston', written at London on 9 November (1492?); it is full of interest, especially with regard to 'the boke of the Statutes of Werre with the portrature of the kynges armes and bagys', printed by Pynson – Pynson had delivered all the copies made for the king to Sir Thomas Lovell, who had distributed them to 'the capitaignes of his hooste . . . Nevertheless . . . I have be crafte gotten you one whiche I sende you by this berer.' Unfortunately, there had not been time to colour the arms and badges of the first page of the book; William describes at length what colours these should be. Once again, he writes of his involvement in royal matters: his servant, John King, is in Wales on the king's business. Items 3 and 2 comprise a letter, which is endorsed 'a letter that M Paston sent M Cary the vth day of January anno x h vij [1495]'; the letter ends: 'and our lorde preserve you. Wretten at London the vth day of January be your frend William Paston' – the last clause being in William's hand. He mentions the exchange of New Year gifts between the king and the bishops; characteristically, Henry was pleased with Thomas Langton, the Bishop of Winchester's, 100 marks in a purse. He also writes of the Book of the 'Justs', which would consist of six or seven sheets of paper when finished, and which the king wished to be kept secret until he had seen and approved it; Garter King of Arms had shown William as much

daughters. He needed the estates less than John Paston did. He settled for money.

How much money we do not know. What we do know is that this ten-year dispute cost John Paston dearly. In 1484 he estimated his losses at more than 1,000 marks;[196] a further five years of conflict could have doubled this sum, or, if it had been exaggerated in 1484, could have reached 1,000 marks by 1489. Then there were legal expenses and whatever he had to pay his uncle by way of settlement. We have seen that he had to borrow 500 marks from Henry Colet in 1485: he undertook to repay this in five years.[197] He had also borrowed from Sir Roger Townshend,[198] to whom East Beckham was mortgaged. His financial embarrassment was doubtless eased by the marriage of his son and heir, William, to Sir Henry Heydon's daughter Bridget, whose marriage portion was probably 500 marks.[199] No wonder Sir Henry wanted John Paston's punishing contest with his uncle concluded: he needed to see his son-in-law's lands unencumbered. One way and another John got out of debt. It may have taken more than the ten years it took him to get into it: it was not until 1503, for example that he was able to redeem East Beckham.[200]

There may have been more than a straightforward monetary price John had to pay for bringing to an end a dispute which had begun more than fifty years before and which had not been of his making: he may also have had to part with lands. I have said that William Paston had only daughters and settled for money. But those daughters, Agnes and Elizabeth, were his heirs. Soon after William's death in 1496 they were married; their husbands,

as had been done. This Butler circle's 'Lancastrianism' is well displayed by the prayers to Henry VI in the family's Book of Hours (BL Harleian MS 2887, fs. 10, 11v) and by the inclusion among the obits on f. 2 of Margaret of Anjou, Edward, Prince of Wales, and Henry himself 'qui obit inter xxj May et xxij May', an accuracy which is pathetic as well as illuminating.

[196] Davis I, pp. 623–6. They may be set out thus: (1) 'decayed howsyng' (including two watermills at Oxnead and Marlingford) at Oxnead, Marlingford, Stansted, and Horwellbury: 500 marks; (2) damage at Paston: £40; (3) stock, grain and 'hotilementis' taken from Paston, Oxnead, Marlingford, Stansted, and Horwellbury: £40; (4) timber felled at Oxnead and Marlingford: £20; (5) costs of John's men defending the manors, and money collected by William's men there for the same purpose: £40; (6) lost revenues of four and three-quarter years: £200.

[197] BL Stowe Charter 194: John enfeoffed Colet in certain manors (including Mautby and Fritton), which Colet then released to him for an annual rent of 100 marks.

[198] See for example, Davis I, p. 642.

[199] *Ibid.* The wedding was already in sight when Sir Henry informed John Paston of the conclusion of the dispute with William Paston (Davis II, p. 470): 'How yee and myn ladie, and in what sylk or clooth yee will have these tweyn yong innocentes maried jnne, iff it shuld be purveyed at London to send me word, or ellys at Norwich, as it shall please you and myn ladie ther-affter I shall applie me; for it must bee ordyrd be you in the yong husbondes name.' 1489 seems the year in which to place the end of the controversy and the marriage, as on 10 February 1489 Margery, in writing to John, refers to 'my brodyre Heydon': *ibid.*, p. 669, line 48.

[200] Davis II, p. 612.

respectively Gilbert Talbot esquire and Sir John Saville,[201] desired to have all that their heiress wives should have. They and John Paston are to be discovered disputing what that was. Sir Henry Heydon was once again among the three umpires called to adjudicate; even after they had, John, according to Agnes and Elizabeth's great aunt, Lady Margaret Beaufort, was refusing to disgorge the property Talbot and Saville had been awarded,

> divers lands which they ought to have in right of their wives . . . which lands ye by mighty power kepe and withholde from them without any just title, as they afferme; and albeit the said agrement was made by your minde and consent, yet ye ne doe performe the same to our merveile if it be so.[202]

What were these lands? It seems unlikely they were William's own manors of Holwellhall in East Tuddenham, Gerbridges in Wood Norton, Talbots in Fincham, Horninghall at Caister, and his other Norfolk estates.[203] Could they have been Agnes' Stansted in Suffolk and Horwellbury in Hertfordshire? It seems not. These do not appear, as does Marlingford, in the Paston estate accounts of 1552–3,[204] but in the case of Horwellbury that is because John's son William had sold it in 1507.[205] Perhaps it was only Stansted which John lost in 1489 – if he did.[206] There were also the manors 'mortgaged' to Henry Colet in 1485. One of them, Margaret's Fritton, does not feature in the 1552–3 estate account. Neither does it, however, in the *inquisition post mortem* of Henry Colet, nor in his estate documents or those of this son, Dean John Colet.[207] Perhaps William Paston sold that too. It may be that in the end John Paston III gave up no land to his uncle, or to anyone else; on the other hand, it may be that his son had to sell at least one estate his father did not relinquish to clear debts John had accumulated possibly in order not to get into debt himself.

201 So Elizabeth Paston became a Yorkshirewoman. When she died in 1542 her bequests were all to northern folk and she chose to be buried in Thornhill church beside her husband, who had died nearly forty years previously in 1504: *Test. Ebor.* VI pp. 139–40.

202 Davis II, p. 484. It is difficult to believe Margaret Beaufort could be resisted, particularly as William's daughters were her great-nieces, and considering (Dr Michael Jones has informed me in a letter) the importance to Margaret of the extended family, 'especially through the female line'. Moreover, William had managed some of the Lady Margaret's estates: 'it is clear', Michael Jones writes (citing Westminster Abbey Muniments, MS 32355), 'that he was one of her officials'. Also, Margaret had acted as umpire in a dispute between William and Sir Charles Somerset, the illegitimate son of Henry Beaufort, Duke of Somerset: *CCR 1485–1500*, pp. 18–19. William's involvement in Beaufort affairs is evidenced in PRO SCI/60/67. Is this memorandum in Thomas Danvers' hand? It ends 'Item, to speke unto Ivers to labour for me to be Receyvour to my lord Lovell of all his londes in Wilts, Oxon, Berks or ells Surveyour . . .', so must be dated before 1483.

203 Sir John Saville certainly got Wood Norton: Blomefield IV, p. 452.

204 The Brian Spencer MS, for which see previously, p. 193.

205 *VCH Herts.* II, p. 243; BL Add. Ch. 27442.

206 Copinger, *Manors* I, p. 208, says that it remained a Paston estate.

207 *CIPM Henry VII*, III, no. 52 is Norfolk – there was no inquisition for Suffolk; Samuel Knight, *The Life of Dr John Colet* (Oxford, 1823), pp. 278–82, 398–400.

What is not in doubt is the damage done to the family by the split between the main stem and the cadet branch. After Clement's death, and particularly after Agnes' death, William was a sturdy representative of that branch. He was a vigorous opponent, who gave as good or better than he got, and had no intention of knuckling under, especially under his nephews after 1466. Family fragmentation was harmful in numerous ways: loss of revenue, the disruption of estate management, the alienation of tenants and farmers were bad enough at a time when landowners had to labour for every penny they could get from rents and leases. There was also incalculable loss from the failure to present a common front in the campaign for Fastolf's will. What was the result? Might John II have got more than Caister? That is doubtful. Less so is that the family could have sailed into calmer waters in the later 1470s, and ought to have done in 1485, but did not do so (as we have seen) until after 1489, almost certainly as long after as the early sixteenth century.

The delay in the Pastons reaching a secure social harbour, their 'right' place in Norfolk society, was due to two things: Judge William's uncharacteristic, or at any rate unexpected, indecisiveness, and his eldest son's greed. Allowances may be made, and have been already: John Paston in 1444 was in an unenviable position. Yet, as time went on and his position became easier he showed no inclination to be just, let alone generous to his younger brothers and sister; in addition, he was uncompromisingly covetous so far as the Fastolf inheritance was concerned. Judge William's failure to know his own mind did not present an insurmountable obstacle to family harmony. With good will and in good faith it could have been got over and forgotten by the mid 1450s. John Paston is, therefore, the culprit. If he had been other than he was, the family would have been a happier one, an accepted, and an achieved one forty or fifty years earlier than in the event it became so. Character determines all.

Chapter 7

SIR JOHN FASTOLF AND JOHN PASTON

In the film *Chimes at Midnight* it is the scenes of those old men, Falstaff and Shallow, remembering their younger days which, even among so many vivid images, remain in the mind. Shakespeare and Orson Welles together are twice as large as life. We are left in no doubt: Shallow's earlier years were as boring as his later ones are tedious. Falstaff, given the occasion to reminisce, undoubtedly would have exaggerated the exploits of his youth just as he did those of his old age. His account of the outing to Gadshill tells us that much. Did Sir John Fastolf employ similar elaborations when he sat with William Worcester in the Winter Hall of Caister beneath the tapestry of the siege of Falaise to tell him of what he did at it and to relate in what terms the Duke of Exeter praised him for his captainship of the Bastille?[1] The *Acta Domini Johanni Fastolf* would have helped us formulate an answer. It would be a mistake to think that lost work might have been a sober affair. Fastolf could certainly magnify his debts, why not his military achievements? It is surely wrong also to believe that 'all he cared to remember as he . . . sank . . . into the grave were the debts . . . not paid him'.[2] His old soldier's 'sense of ill-usage' is not in question; the evidence for it is overwhelming.[3] Evidence for the old warrior's assessment of his military past is slighter. *The Book of Noblesse* may reflect (and faithfully) his views, but they are of the 'warre outward' in general, not of his part in it. In other words, we do not have the younger Fastolf (in any version), as we have Fastolf in his seventies, reduced 'to a state of querulous and unmanageable senility . . . a close-fisted, litigious and irascible old man'.[4]

There is one letter. It prompted McFarlane to comment: 'In his younger

[1] A.D. Hawkyard, 'Some Late Medieval Fortified Manor Houses: a Study of the Building Works of Sir John Fastolf, Ralph, Lord Cromwell, and Edward Stafford, Third Duke of Buckingham', unpublished MA thesis, University of Keele, 1968, pp. 23, 52, 53.

[2] K.B. McFarlane, *England in the Fifteenth Century* (London, 1981), p. 177, my italics. I should give the whole passage, as McFarlane was not saying quite what I am questioning: 'Though he owed much to the Lancastrian dynasty all he cared to remember as he and it sank together into the grave were the debts it had not paid him.'

[3] *Ibid.* [4] *Ibid.*, p. 176.

days he had not been without a measure of that *largesse* which the age expected in a knight.'[5] The letter[6] is addressed to 'Herry Inglose and John Berny escuiers' and begins,

Ryght wel belovyd cosyns, I comaund me to yow. And please you to hafe in knowlege that at whyche tyme ye were delyvered out of pryson by the moyen of ij prysonners that y delyvered yow, whyche, as ye know wel, one was Burd Vynollys and the other Johan de Seint Johan dit Dolot, and in lyke wyse I boughte anothyr prysonner clepyt Johan Villers for the delyveraunce of Mautbye Sqwyer, whych mater ye knowythe welle.

John Mautby, John Berney, Henry Inglose: when had these youthful esquires been made prisoner? Not at Baugé in March 1421, when their leader and Fastolf's, the Duke of Clarence, was killed, and *Sir* Henry Inglose was captured (for a second time).[7] Whether one of Sir Henry's brothers in arms at the siege of Rouen in 1419, Sir William Bowet of Horsford, Norfolk, was at Baugé is not clear;[8] what is, is that Henry married Sir William's widow, Ann or Amy, before 1427. Amy has the distinction of writing (possibly to William Paston) the first 'Paston Letter'.[9] Another Norfolk soldier who had shared their room at the siege of Rouen was Sir Philip Braunch, Fastolf's brother-in-law. He may have been killed at Baugé;[10] his widow Margaret lived at Caister in the 1430s, though she paid for her board.[11] Could there have been 'a Baugé generation' (as there was 'the Agincourt generation'),[12] sad and not triumphant, but committed to one another, Sir John Fastolf being chief among those who remembered and was committed? Fastolf's commitment so far as John Berney and John Mautby

[5] *Ibid.*, p. 192 and note 89.

[6] Gairdner II, no. 39. I have examined the original at Pembroke College, Cambridge (LC. 2. 230. item 3); from this I have taken the address which differs slightly from the transcription in Gairdner. The letter has been folded and sealed, and was, therefore, sent. Gairdner assigned it to 'After 1440(?)'; McFarlane (*England in the Fifteenth Century*, p. 192, note 89), on the grounds that Sir Henry was a knight by November 1435, assigned it to 1435 or earlier. As Henry was a knight by 15 November 1419 (*CCR 1419–22*, p. 65), it has to be much earlier: see note 14.

[7] C.L. Kingsford, *English Historical Literature in the Fifteenth Century* (London, 1913), p. 320: Latin Brut; the chronicle of Peter Basset and Christopher Hanson (for which see Benedicta Rowe, 'A Contemporary Account of the Hundred Years War from 1415 to 1429', *EHR*, 41 (1926), pp. 504–13), College of Arms MS 9, f. xliii v. I owe this reference to Dr Anne Curry.

[8] For the room-mates ('le logeyng felowys') at Rouen, see Worcester, *Itineraries*, p. 361. The eight of them were a distinguished Norfolk company; they included Robert, Lord Morley, Sir William Oldhall and Sir John Clifton. Another of them was Sir John Knyvett; to which of Knyvett's companions does the following passage in William Worcester (*Itineraries*, ed. John Harvey (London, 1969) p. 359) refer: 'At Baugé with the Duke of Clarence; taken prisoner in the Vale of Verberie near Senis in an action with Lord Cromwell. Sir John Knyvett was likewise taken prisoner there'?

[9] Her letter is Gairdner II, no. 2. For the marriage see p. 215; below.

[10] 'that deyde and was slayn in Fraunce', as Fastolf put it in his will: Gairdner III, p. 157.

[11] Hawkyard, 'Some Late Medieval Fortified Manor Houses', p. 4.

[12] E.F. Jacob, *Archbishop Henry Chichele* (London, 1967), pp. 96–9.

are concerned we have noticed before;[13] it seems to have begun with Fastolf, a new knight and in his late twenties, paying the ransoms of the three unlucky esquires: that was as early as 1416–19.[14] What of Fastolf's commitment to Sir Henry Inglose?

At Caister, for the building of which in the 1430s Sir Henry lent Fastolf 100 marks, a room was always kept for him in the 1440s. The room bore his name; it may have been made for him. It was comfortably appointed: a bed with arras furnishings, a green carpet on the floor, tapestry-covered benches and cushions, wall hangings, even, though it was unpainted, a chair.[15] Given such solicitude I think we can reckon Henry, seven times a knight of the shire, a justice of the peace in Norfolk for more than twenty years, as more than simply one of Fastolf's councillors and feoffees.[16] He

[13] Above, pp. 123 and 158.

[14] I have arrived at this dating in the following fashion. Henry Inglose had been knighted by 15 November 1419: *CCR 1419–22*, p. 65. If the Henry Ynglish of the Agincourt Roll *is* him (Sir N.H. Nicolas, *History of the Battle of Agincourt* (London, 1832), p. 386), he was not knighted then or after the battle. In fact, Henry was almost certainly in Gascony in 1415 in the company of Sir John Tiploft. He indented with Tiptoft on 13 May 1415 for a year's service with sixteen men at arms and eighty archers; they subsequently disagreed over the rates of pay and Henry petitioned the Duke of Bedford and the court of chivalry: BL Cotton MS, Titus CI, f. 229. Henry was an esquire when he made this petition, and was still an esquire on 6 October 1416 (*CFR 1416–22*, pp. 53–4). In the ransom letter Fastolf addresses Henry as esquire and signs himself 'chevalier'. Fastolf was knighted at Harfleur in January 1416 (Anthony Smith, 'Aspects of the Career of Sir John Fastolf, 1380–1459', unpublished DPhil. thesis, Oxford, 1982, p. 2). The letter, therefore, has to be dated to 1416–19. Its phrasing suggests the three esquires had been taken together, but only suggests it. At what engagement or engagements in these years were they taken by the enemy? Not at the seige of Caen in August 1417, at any rate, for in the successful assault on 4 September, Henry Inglose was the first to get into the town: Worcester, *Itineraries*, p. 359; J.H. Wylie and W. Waugh, *The Reign of Henry V*, III (London, 1929), p. 60. Between May 1417 and October 1419 Henry was in the retinue of the Duke of Clarence (*The Deputy Keeper of the Public Records*, Report 44, pp. 601, 612). Was he in Clarence's retinue at Baugé, or in William de la Pole's (see note 27 below)? By 1426–7 he was in the retinue of the Duke of Bedford: *DKR* 48, pp. 244, 250. I owe these references to Dr Anne Curry.

[15] Hawkyard, 'Some Late Medieval Fortified Manor Houses', pp. 11, 16, 21, 23, 25, 26, 27. The 1448 inventory is Gairdner III, no. 389; 'Inglose Chambre' is on p. 182.

[16] Sir Henry was Fastolf's proxy when Sir John received the Order of the Garter in 1426: Blomefield V, p. 1412. In the same year he was, along with William Paston, Sir John Radcliff, John Fastolf (of Oulton), and John Hartling, clerk, an attorney of Sir John's: *Norfolk Archaeology*, 4 (1855), pp. 17–18. He was 'a mounted lance in Sir John's company assembled on 13 January 1429 at Chartres in preparation for the siege of Orléans (BL Add. Ch. 11,611)', as Dr Curry has kindly informed me. Fastolf called Henry his 'ryght welbelovyd cosyn' in 1450 (as he had called him and John Berney his 'ryght wel belovyd cosyns' back in 1418 or thereabouts): Gairdner II, p. 199. In his will, among souls to be prayed for, Fastolf put that of 'Sir Henry Inglose, Knyght, of my consangwynite: Gairdner III, p. 157. Their kinship may have arisen through Henry's father's marriage to Ann, daughter of Robert Geney by Margaret, daughter and heir of John Fastolf (apparently of Fishley beside Acle): Wedgwood, *Biographies*, p. 492; Blomefield IV, p. 391; Copinger, *Manors* V, p. 4. But who was Robert Geney? (For other Geneys see note 23.) Sir Henry was also a feoffee of Humphrey, Duke of Buckingham (in 1450) and of another old but geographically distant soldier, Sir Roland Lenthall: *CCR 1447–54*, pp. 244, 312.

had, after all, a home of his own at Dilham, only a few miles north-west of Caister and not far from Paston. Despite his imprisonment in France, he seems to have had money to spare: Dilham may not have been a new house,[17] it was a new manor. It was not Sir Henry's only purchase.

Sir John Geney of Dilham made his brief testament at Dilham on 14 January 1423 and his last will on 4 February 1423.[18] In the sad beginning of the former lies the reason for most of what follows in the latter: Sir John wished to be buried in the church of the Austin Friars at Norwich beside the tomb of his son, Roger. He mentions no other children.[19] What followed was the sale of his estates to Sir Henry Inglose. Sir John's widow, Alice, was to have his manors of Dilham and Haveringland for life; they were then (within a year) to be sold to Sir Henry for £300.[20] Sir Henry was also to be sold Sir John's Rutland estate of Pickworth for 1,000 marks (to be paid within a year).

Why, one wonders, was Sir Henry favoured? His family home was Loddon, some distance to the south.[21] That his mother was a Geney seems the most likely explanation,[22] unless it was simply that Sir Henry had the money. What is clear is that Sir John Geney, as the last of the Geneys,[23] was

[17] Harry Brittain, 'Dilham Castle', *Norfolk Archaeology*, 15 (1904), pp. 190–3, describes a black flint tower. The tower is hidden among trees at Hall Farm. As I was discourteously denied access to it, I am unable to say what date it is. Rooms at Dilham where money was handed over are mentioned in the Haveringland manorial accounts of 1425–6 and 1427–8 (BL Add. Ch. 9336, 9338); one was the Baschambre, another was where dame Ann received money 'in alta camera'.

[18] NRO, NCC Reg. Hyrnyng, f. 114. Proof was made on 5 November 1423.

[19] Robert Clippesby, one of his three executors, is the only notable legatee; he was left a sword and a 'daggard argent', and Sir John's best fur-lined gown. Robert was also to have £40 out of the issues of Dilham and Haveringland for implementing the testament. It is evident from the Haveringland accounts that Robert was an important officer of Sir John Geney's (for example, BL Add. Ch. 9327; 9331; 9332: 1418–19, when Sir John observed (at a cost of just under 6s) the obit (anniversary) of Robert's sister; 9334: 1422–3 (10 Henry V–I Henry VI, the year of Sir John's (unanticipated) death, when on three occasions he was with the Augustinian canons at Norwich *and* his long sword was repaired). Another officer of Sir John's was Henry Goneld (9333, 9334); was this Henry Goneld a relative of Geoffrey Somerton, 'qwos trew surnome ys Goneld' (Davis I, p. xlii)? William Purk was Sir John's chaplain and secretary (BL Add. Ch. 9329, 9330). Sir John bequeathed 40 shillings to Dilham church 'pro le pathyng'; 3s 4d was to be distributed among the poor of his manor of Pickworth, Rutland. One of his feoffees was William Paston, whom he had fee'd as a councillor at £1 a year from 1415 (BL Add. Ch. 9329, 9330, 9331, 9332, 9333, 9334).

[20] The only reservation was of a 2-mark annuity for the truly ubiquitous – he was at the beginning of his getting about – John Linford of Stalham. John had been fee'd at this sum (as Sir John's steward) since 1415 (BL Add. Ch. 9329 etc.).

[21] Inglose manor house to the south-south-west of Loddon remains, but the family had sold this estate of Inglose Hall in the 1360s: Blomefield V, p. 1146.

[22] Wedgwood, *Biographies*, p. 492; and note 16, above.

[23] Sir John does not feature in William Worcester's list of East Anglian gentry who had no sons, as properly he should not, his son Roger having died before him. Sir Thomas Geney, however, does: NRO, MS 7197, fs. 305v–306. He was of Brandiston, Norfolk. His will is dated 5 May 1417 and was proved 18 February 1420: NRO, NCC Reg. Hyrnyng, f. 78. He

disposing of his landed estate to one man. We cannot, therefore, help having in mind Sir John Fastolf in 1459, or, when it is a matter of selling one's lands at death, Sir Henry himself in 1451, though in his case there were significant and interesting differences: he had two adult sons. Sir Henry did not have to wait until Alice Geney died before acquiring Dilham and the other two estates. He was in possession of Haveringland by 1424, Dilham by 1426, and when Alice made her last will at Norwich on 30 September 1438 all she disposed of was a tenement in the city.[24] By then Sir Henry had long been a friend of William Paston: in 1425 William had put him forward as one of his four candidates to arbitrate in the dispute with Walter Aslak.[25] The Paston–Inglose association continued after William's death: the Earl of Oxford considered John Paston could influence Sir Henry and urged him to do so;[26] Sir Henry was an ally of Paston and Fastolf in the struggle to oust Tuddenham and Heydon during 1450–1.[27] He lived long enough to see their hopes dashed, but later in that same month of May 1451 he had seisin made to feoffees of much of his property,[28] and on 20 June he made his will:

appears to have been a bachelor. According to Blomefield's somewhat scrambled pedigrees (IV, pp. 369, 391), Sir Thomas and Sir John were of different branches of the family. Sir John's father was Sir Roger Geney of Dilham, who died in 1376 (NRO, NCC Reg. Heydon, f. 125; *CIPM Edward III*, XIV, p. 263); he left £5 for the building of Dilham Church tower, and was to be buried at Dilham. Sir Thomas' father was Sir Thomas, who died between 1400 and 1403 (NRO, NCC Reg. Harsyk f. 296); his destroyed will was sealed at Wood Norton. Brandiston, or at any rate Guton in Brandiston, was purchased by Sir John Fastolf (from Marjorie, the eldest daughter of the elder Sir Thomas, in 1436: Anthony Smith, 'Sir John Fastolf', p. 17), escaped the Pastons and ended up with William Wainfleet: see Davis II, index, *sub* Brandeston. Although Davis I, p. 574, line 40 suggests the Boleyns in 1472 got this estate, which they had coveted after Fastolf's death (Davis II, p. 224), Guton became part of Wainfleet's endowment of Magdalen College: Blomefield IV, p. 369. In connection with the 1436 sale to Fastolf, it is intriguing to discover recorded in the Haveringland account for 1434–5 (BL Add. Ch. 9345) Sir Henry Inglose's expenses 'quando dominus intravet in maneriam de Guton'. Was this entry on Fastolf's behalf?

[24] Haveringland account for 1424–5, BL Add. Ch. 9335; he was called 'of Dilham' in his protection of the autumn of 1426 (*The Deputy Keeper of the Public Records*, Report 48, p. 244). Alice's will is NRO, NCC Reg. Aleyn, f. 33; she was buried beside her husband and son in the church of the Austin Friars, Norwich. Free wood for fuel was sent to her at Norwich from Haveringland in the mid-1430s: BL Add. Ch. 9346, 9347.

[25] Davis I, pp. 9–10.

[26] Davis II, p. 70. The earl and Sir Henry were also drawn into troubles between one Seggeford/ Sechforth/Sexeford and the Prior of Walsingham's tenants at Salle: Davis II, pp. 56–7, 63 (lines 46–77); Gairdner II, p. 200.

[27] Gairdner II, p. 238. Years before, in 1433–4, he had spoken with the counsel of the Earl of Suffolk at Haveringland: BL Add. Ch. 9344. And years before that, in 1422, he had served William de la Pole when he was governor of Lower Normandy: *The Deputy Keeper of the Public Records*, Report 48, p. 221.

[28] *Cal. Anc. Deeds* IV, p. 236, 29 May 1451. Among these feoffees were his executors, Robert Inglose, his son, Edmund Wytchingham, and John Parham; there were both his sons-in-law, Sir John Colville and Thomas Beaupre there was Fastolf, there was William Jenny (but not John Paston). There was also Sir Robert Conyers. Sir Robert, of Street Ellingham and Scoulton, Norfolk, was knight of the shire for the county in the parliament of 1449–50; he, like Edmund Wytchingham, was a councillor of Richard, Duke of York (*CPR 1446–52*, p.

he died on 30 June, as on 1 July Margaret Paston wrote to John from Norwich 'Ser Herry Inglose is passyd to God this nygth, hoys sowle God asoyll, and was caryid forth this day at ix of the clok to Seynt Feythis, and there shall be beryid'.[29]

Sir Henry's will is interesting, as we have already indicated, because with two mature sons he yet required that many of his lands, possibly the bulk of his landed estate, should be sold. It is also interesting for other reasons. For example, he desired to be buried (and, as we have just been told, was) beside his wife Ann in the choir of the church of the Benedictine priory at Horsham St Faiths, not (so far as one is able to tell) a fashionable house, certainly not to choose to be buried in. His choice therefore may tell us something of his regard for Ann. He left 6 marks for masses to be said for his soul there for six years. To Elizabeth, Lady Dacre, his wife's stepdaughter,[30] and to Sybille Osbern, his own stepdaughter,[31] he left merely sets of linen (and great bitterness). To Anne, the eldest daughter of his friend and executor Edmund Wytchingham, he left £10 towards her marriage.[32] He was generous to local churches: Dilham got £2 'ad emendacionem', Hickling, Bromholm Priory,

231), and was a friend of Sir John Fastolf: see for example, *CCR 1447–54*, pp. 228–9, Gairdner II, p. 240. Sir Robert's wife (according to Blomefield I, pp. 328, 347, 609, 611, 618) was Maud FitzRalph, heir to her father Sir John FitzRalph after the death of her brother John, whose soul Sir John Fastolf included among those for whom he desired prayers to be said: 'John Fitzraf Squyer, my neveu' (Gairdner III, p. 157). Sir Robert's son, John, married Eleanor, daughter of William Yelverton; this match Yelverton was so pleased with that having drunk and eaten too well he was unwise enough to boast of it, thus allowing Friar Brackley to write unforgettably of the scene at his despised enemy's expense: Davis II, pp. 332–3. One day, probably in January 1463, Sir Robert dined with Margaret Paston; his news showed how important he was reckoned to be in Norfolk society, by the government of Edward IV at any rate; 'I felle hym be hys seyyng [Margaret wrote to John] that he ys right welle disposyd to you ward': Davis I, p. 284. The next generation of Conyers and Paston were also, apparently, close: Davis I, p. 511, lines 28–30. I would like to know more about this family: for example, what, if any, were their links with the Yorkshire Conyers?

29 His last will and testament, proved on 4 July 1451, are NRO, NCC Reg. Bettyns, f. 62. William Worcester recorded the day of his death as 21 June: *Itineraries*, p. 361. The Norfolk *IPM* records 21 June, the Rutland one 1 July (PRO, C139/151/48; C139/141/9). Margaret's letter is Davis I, p. 243. Proof of the will looks suspiciously fast, though Sir Henry did die in Norwich.

30 Elizabeth was the daughter of Sir William Bowet, by his first wife, Joan Ufford. Sir William had sold her marriage to Thomas, Lord Dacre of Gilsland, who had married her to his son and heir, Sir Thomas Dacre. Sir Henry Inglose, William Paston, and William Garneys were among her feoffees for her Suffolk estates: *CIPM Henry VII*, I, pp. 86–7. Thomas, Lord Scales, John Heydon (also her chief steward with an annual fee of £3 6s 8d), and Sir William Calthorp were among those for her Norfolk ones: NRO, NRS 18533, her receiver-general's account for 1456–7. She died early in 1459: *CFR 1452–61*, p. 213. Her husband was killed at the battle of Towton. Their daughter, Joan (said to be twenty-six in 1459) carried the title to Sir Richard Fiennes (*CP* IV, pp. 8–9). For Elizabeth's problems see below.

31 She was the daughter of Sir William Bowet by his second wife, Amy (or Ann), whom Sir Henry married after Sir William's death. Sibylle had been married to Robert Osbern of Barking, Essex. For her difficulties see below, pp. 218–20.

32 For Ann Wytchingham and her sisters see chapter 5 above.

and St Martin's in Norwich £1 apiece, while six churches were to have a set of vestments each. He was open-handed to his (presumably household) servants. Twenty-two were to have their 'stipends', and mainly money or sometimes a gown besides. Especially favoured were Thomas Selers and his wife, Katherine, he having a gown lined with marten fur, she getting a silver cup, half a dozen knives and a pair of silver salt cellars. A further three servants were simply left a sum of money. Did this prosperous ex-soldier's household staff comprise twenty-five? To Henry, his eldest son, he left various items of plate, his 'chamberyng' of arras of the Nine Worthies 'and of the Egle deorum' with bed hangings of silk, all his stock and grain at Dilham, and his sheep at his manor of Ashby in Suffolk. To Robert, his second son, he bequeathed plate, a gold chain, his gold seal, sets of linen, a primer, a black gown lined with marten fur, a 'chamberyng' of green and black with bed hangings of the same, and 500 sheep. To his daughter Ann and to her husband Sir John Colville he left silken belts decorated with gold, and to Ann he also bequeathed a primer. To Margaret his daughter, married – he was her second husband – to Thomas Beaupre (to whom Sir Henry left nothing in his testament), he gave a silver-gilt cup.[33]

It is mainly in the disposal of his lands that Sir Henry surprises us. Certainly Henry and his heirs were to have the manors of Dilham, Loddon, Wassingford (in Loddon),[34] and Ashby in Suffolk; certainly, Robert and his heirs were to have the manor of Haveringland and a messuage at Eccles By The Sea. But Sir Henry's manors of Buckenham Ferry, North Walsham, Bryants in Felmingham, Rackheath, 'Hoothgate', Mauclerks in Mundham, Sco Ruston in Norfolk, his manors of Gunton and Hopton, just to the north of Lowestoft in Suffolk, and the outlying estate of Pickworth, Rutland, were to be sold to pay his debts and perform his will. Two other Norfolk manors, Hedenham and Kelling, were to go to a Lady Ilketshall – there is a blank where her Christian name ought to be – for life; then they too were to be disposed of for the carrying out of his will.[35] The five advowsons he owned (to churches in places not hitherto named) were also to be sold. The only

[33] At one point, according to Agnes, Sir Henry had been 'ryght besy a-bowt [Sir Stephen] Schrowpe fore on of his dogthteres': Davis I, p. 31. Margaret had previously been married to Simon Groos; they had had a daughter Amy: see chapter 6.

[34] Blomefield V, p. 1147.

[35] Why were they his to dispose of? According to Blomefield's account of Sir Thomas Ilketshall's will of 1417 (V, pp. 932–3, 1133; though Sir Thomas was of Horsley, Surrey, the will was proved at Norwich: NRO, NCC Reg. Hyrnyng, f. 26), these two estates were left to Isobel, his widow, for life, unless their daughter married with the approval of her kin, in which case they were to go to her on her marriage. Isobel, who had married again, was alive in 1451. There were complicated disputes about Hedenham and Kelling in the 1450s; John Heydon got a firm hold on them in the 1460s. I wonder where (if anywhere) the 'wydow in Woorstede' is to be placed in this? Thus Edmund Paston II to William Paston III *c.* 1480 (Davis I, p. 639–40): 'I hartely recomawnd me to yow. Here is lately fallyn a wydow in Woorstede whyche was wyff to on Boolt, a worstede marchant, and worth a ml li., and gaff to hys wyff a c marke in mony, stuffe of howsold and plate to the valew of an c marke, and x

qualifications to these sales were three annuities which were to be paid, the first of 5 marks to John Parham, clerk, (one of his executors) out of Buckenham Ferry, the second of 26s 8d to Robert Payn, also out of Buckenham Ferry, the third of £1 to Henry Wilton at North Walsham.

Why did Sir Henry sell so much? Was he in such a parlous financial plight that he was forced to sell more manors than he handed on to his sons? There seems nothing 'wrong' with Henry and Robert, nothing at any rate which may be readily detected now and which deterred their father from giving them more. We are bound to entertain the thought that this soldier, who once had money to spare,[36] did not, once his soldiering days were done, live frugally enough. Was his household too large, too lavish, did he over-purchase, did he (at Dilham) over-build?[37] Did he endeavour to emulate Sir

li. be yere in land. She is callyd a fayere iantylwoman. I wyll for your sake se here. She is rytht systyre of fader and modyre to Herry Ynglows. I purpose to speke wyth hym to gett hys good wyll. Thys jantylwoman is abowght xxx yeres, and has but ij chylderen whyche shalbe at the dedys charge. She was hys wyff but v yere. Yf she be eny better than I wryght fore, take it in worthe I shew the leeste. Thus lete me have knowlache of your mynde as shortly as ye can, and whan ye shall moun be in this cuntré.' The Henry Inglose mentioned here is Sir Henry's son, said to have died in 1516 (Blomefield V, p. 1147). He cannot have been forty in 1451 as his father's *inquisition post mortem* (and Wedgwood, *Biographies*, p. 493) states; his father Sir Henry did not marry Amy Bowet until 1423 or later.

[36] Apart from buying the Geney lands, he had paid the ransom of Sir William Bowes captured with him at Baugé (see references in note 7); this was 'according to an agreement between them made' (presumably as brothers-in-arms). William was still in captivity in November 1422, when Sir Henry came into Chancery to acknowledge his obligation to pay for William's release: *CCR 1422–9*, p. 54. Was this Sir William Bowes the builder of Streatlam Castle, Co. Durham? It was *not* Sir William Bowet, as Bowes came into Chancery on 5 March 1431 to acknowledge Sir Henry's payment, and Bowet had died between May 1422 and April 1423 (*CPR 1416–22*, pp. 437–8; *CCR 1422–9*, p. 204, cf. Blomefield V, p. 1357: 10 Henry V).

[37] I have in mind William Harleston's advice to the recently widowed Sir William Stonor: 'And more over, syr, for Goddes sake . . . stabill your howsehold now saddely and wisely with a convenient feleshepp so as ye may kepe yow withynne yowr lyvelode . . . And of certen thynges I wold desire you . . . that ye wolle not over wissh yow, ner owyr purches yow, ner owyr bild you': C.L. Kingsford (ed.), *The Stonor Letters and Papers*, Camden Society, Third Series, XXX (London, 1919), p. 98. Harleston's concluding shot, 'Ner medyll not with no gret materis in the lawe', Sir Henry may not have observed either. Between 1422 and 1442 he was the plaintiff in thirty-nine cases in King's Bench; thirty-three of these cases involved property. In two instances at least he settled out of court. He waived damages from all but one of the twelve Dilham tenants who had dug his turf, claiming it to be their communal right. The action had begun in Michaelmas term 1433; in Easter term 1435 Sir Henry was awarded £40 in damages; on 4 July 1438 he waived his right to damages from all of the defendants except John Linstead, who was in the Marshalsea prison; John made a 20 shillings fine in Michaelmas term 1438. This is all in Philippa Maddern, 'Violence, Crime, and Public Disorder in East Anglia 1422–1442', unpublished DPhil. thesis, Oxford, 1985, pp. 289–91. Dr Maddern comments: 'Inglose . . . appears to have taken it as a matter of routine.' Still these cases appear not to have involved 'gret materis in the lawe'.

Sir Henry came to an out of court agreement with John Topy and others who had committed trespass against him at Stalham; he halted the legal process he had begun, and undertook to pay the sheriff's fees: see BL Add. Ch. 17232 (abstracted in Gairdner II, no. 32), a public declaration which was to remain with John Topy, signed and sealed by Sir Henry at Dilham 18 August 1438, the seal cut off.

The Ingloses

Sir John Wythe of Smallborough, d. 1387 = Sibylle d. 1421 = Sir William Calthorp d. 1420

whose son

Joan Ufford = Sir William Bowet (2) d. 1422/3 = Amy (or Ann) = (1) John Calthorp d. before 1417

= (3) Sir Henry Inglose

Elizabeth = Sir Thomas Dacre

Sibylle = Robert Osbern

William Calthorp b. 1410

Henry

Robert

Margaret = (1) Simon Groos

(2) Thomas Beaupre

Ann = Sir John Colville

Amy

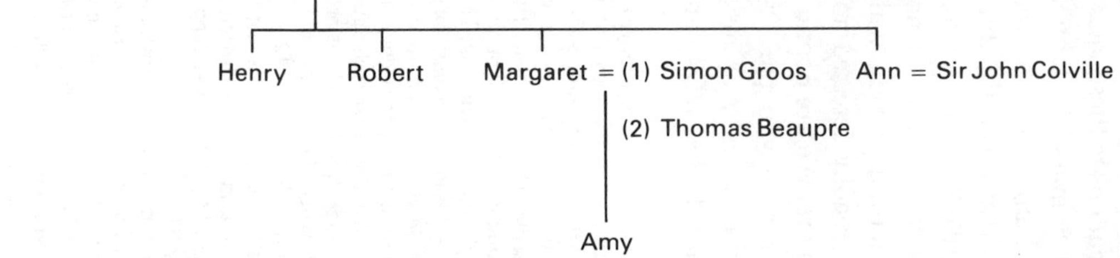

John Fastolf of Caister, or (as the great days at Caister were mostly after Sir Henry's death in 1451) did Fastolf emulate, and surpass him? Such speculation is not pointless; I have indulged in it because there is a drama here of which we are conceded a glimpse in Sir Henry's desire to, or need to, sell on such a scale at his death.

Another and altogether more revealing glimpse of the drama is revealed in proceedings in Chancery after Sir Henry's death. Sir Henry's 'family' had been a complicated one. When he married Amy (or Ann) Bowet some time between 1423 and 1427 he was her third husband. Amy was the daughter and heiress of Sir John Wythe of Smallborough (next door to Dilham), who had died in 1387.[38] Whereas (and perhaps when) her mother Sibylle married Sir William Calthorp, Amy was married to Sir William's son John Calthorp. John and Amy had a son in 1410, *the* Sir William Calthorp, who died in 1494.[39] John Calthorp died young, at Southampton of dysentery contracted at the siege of Harfleur, in October 1415;[40] soon afterwards Amy was writing her 'Paston letter' and signing herself Amy Bowet. After Sir William Calthorp died in 1420,[41] Amy and Sir William Bowet purchased from the Crown *via* Robert, Lord Willoughby, the wardship and marriage of her son, William Calthorp, for 700 marks.[42] Sir William Bowet, the son and heir of Thomas Bowet of Cumbria, had inherited three Cumbrian manors (which were held by his mother Margaret for life),[43] and had obtained three Norfolk properties and seven Suffolk ones with his first wife Joan, daughter and heir of Sir Robert Ufford. The Norfolk properties were Horsford, Burgh St Margarets, and Great Hautbois; the Suffolk ones, Wrentham, Benacre, Covehithe, Henstead, South Cove, Thorington, and Burgh by Grundisburgh.[44] But Sir William Bowet soon died, and was buried beside Joan Ufford at Langley Abbey near Loddon,[45] leaving Amy widowed for a second time. They had a daughter, named for her grandmother Sibylle, who had died in 1421. Thus, when Amy married Sir Henry Inglose between 1423 and 1427 she took to him two children: William Calthorp and Sibylle Bowet. A third child, Elizabeth, Sir William Bowet's daughter by Joan Ufford,

[38] Blomefield III, p. 718; IV, p. 1438; Sir John's will is NRO NCC Reg. Harsyk f. 90.

[39] Wedgwood, *Biographies*, p. 149. He had a daughter, named after his mother, Amy: Blomefield III, p. 718.

[40] William Worcester, *Itineraries*, p. 357.

[41] Sir William died in December 1420; William Paston and Sibylle were his executors; Sibylle died the following year: Blomefield III, p. 718.

[42] *CPR 1416–22*, p. 340; PRO C1/19/40a. This was in May 1421; the timing suggests Sir William Bowet had not been at Baugé in March.

[43] *CPR 1416–22*, pp. 437–8; *CCR 1422–9*, p. 204. Might the great Archbishop Henry Bowet (d. 1423) have been his uncle?

[44] Blomefield V, p. 1357; *CIPM Henry VII*, I, pp. 86–7; Copinger, *Manors*, II, pp. 6, 43, 165, 211.

[45] Blomefield V, p. 1357.

he had already 'sold' to Thomas, Lord Dacre.[46] She was valuable because, Sir William having had no sons by Joan Ufford, she was Joan's heir; she was also with Sibylle co-heiress to her father.

In any attempt to sort out the tangled story which follows it is simplest to take each of the aggrieved, William Calthorp, Sibylle Bowet, Elizabeth Dacre (as she became) in turn, in an ascending order of grievance. First, William Calthorp. Sir Henry Inglose had 'sold' his wardship and marriage to Reginald, Lord Grey of Ruthin, for 800 marks;[47] Lord Grey duly married William to his daughter, Elizabeth.[48] William demanded (through Friar Perys of Horsham St Faiths[49]) half of his marriage money; this he maintained his stepfather had promised him if he married 'aftre your ordenauns'. Sir Henry gave a dusty answer; having paid 600 [*sic*] marks for William's wardship he considered he had done more than enough on his behalf. There was also the question of a sheephouse at Smallborough which Sir Henry had allowed to fall down while William was his ward. It was rotten and might no longer stand, Sir Henry countered; besides, he had built a new barn which was of more use to William than the sheephouse had been. As for William's enclosure of some bondland in the parish of Dilham pertaining to the manor of Smallborough, Sir Henry was conciliatory, 'god for bede that any stryf schal be . . . I hawe gewe as much frelond to Smalborwe therfor. And yf myn sone be nowth plesyd leth hym gewe up agen this frelond and he schal hawe hys bondland a geyn.' As Friar Perys piously remarked elsewhere in the letter, 'promysse is dette [deed] in the trewe manys mowthe'.

Perhaps Sir Henry's son, Henry, was not pleased. He and William Calthorp fell out, made an agreement, could not keep it, and William on 5 September 1459 destroyed a fishhouse of Henry's at Smallborough, fished his waters there, and attacked his property elsewhere in Norfolk. By the time Henry petitioned George Nevill the chancellor in the mid-1460s it was he, 'sometime servant to your noble grandfather the earl of Salisbury and late servant to your noble father the lord of Warwick' (as he described himself), who was the injured party.[50] By then, too, the house of Calthorp was rising, that of Inglose had declined. If Henry was not the man his father had been,

[46] PRO, C1/19/40a, Robert and Sybille Osbern vs Henry's executors; cf. *CCR 1422–9*, p. 204.
[47] PRO, C1/19/40a.
[48] R.I. Jack, *The Grey of Ruthin Valor 1467–8*, Bedfordshire Historical Record Society, XLVI (London, 1965), pp. 52, 139.
[49] This is NRO, Le Strange MS P.20, no. 10 of the 'Calthorp Letters'. As also in the case of no. 7 used below, only an unhelpful summary of this fascinating letter is given in HMC, *Eleventh Report*, Appendix VII, p. 95. Its date must be fairly early, about 1430. It was addressed to William Calthorp esquire dwelling at Great Yarmouth. William made proof of his age, or rather Robert, Lord Willoughby, and Amy Bowet made it on his behalf, in spring 1431: the writ is dated 27 March 1431: PRO, C139/52/66.
[50] PRO, C1/31/509.

might not his father's failure to hand on to him the greater part of the Inglose property have also contributed to the family's social descent?

Secondly, Elizabeth Dacre. Sir Henry had been meaner to her than to his ward. Dispatched by Sir William Bowet to the Dacres of Gilsland with whom as she said 'she was in household by many years' before returning to Norfolk, she was married to Sir Thomas Dacre *c.* 1430. Elizabeth, of course, should have had her mother, Joan Ufford's East Anglian inheritance (as well as her half of her father's Cumbrian manors). Sir Henry thought otherwise:

So by his myght havyng alle thvidences in his hand kept the seid maner [of Great Hautbois] and the maners of Horsford and Burgh [St Margarets] and toke the profites thereof claymyng to have them duryng the lyve of the seid dame Amye and never wold shewe non evidences to the seid Elisabeth but wordes and wold not suffre the seid Elisabeth to have nor take ne profites of the seid manoirs but only the profites of the seid manoir of Hauteboys.

After Amy's death he claimed them in fee simple, saying he might give or sell them as he pleased. Elizabeth (in order to head off so outrageous a claim) was obliged to agree to Henry's having Horsford and Burgh St Margarets for life for an annual rent of a mere 40 marks, whereas Burgh alone was worth that and Horsford was worth £50.[51] She continued to enjoy only Great Hautbois. Of the enfeoffment Sir Henry made of this manor (to her and her heirs, *not* to Robert Osbern and Sibylle for their lives as Robert claimed) she was not aware ('she at that tyme not ther'); only 'upon his dede bed lying' did Sir Henry and his executors inform Elizabeth of what had been done. She was told that Master Henry Bowet (from Lincolnshire) was enfeoffed on her behalf; Henry Bowet duly entered and she enfeoffed Robert, Lord Willoughby, Thomas, Lord Scales, and others to her use. Then Sibylle (whose worse case we shall encounter shortly) was stirred up (by Henry Wilton) to challenge Elizabeth's title, and when Elizabeth got Henry Bowet to come to demonstrate the rightness of her possession 'in his retornyng ayen towards London [he] was fully [foully] murdered'.[52]

The manner in which Sir Henry defrauded Elizabeth of the Suffolk parts of her Ufford inheritance was equally bare-faced (though she did not complain about it, perhaps because the 'fraud' ended before Sir Henry's death). What Sir Henry did, as the principal feoffee of a group of feoffees, who were, one presumes, Sir William Bowet's, was to settle the Suffolk estates on Amy for life and for 'ten years over'. In the first place Amy was no more entitled after

[51] She said, correctly, one is sure, that she was 'rewled by' Sir Henry and also that one of those who induced her to accept this arrangement was Henry Wilton at that time one of *her* 'counceill'; it is interesting to observe that Henry Wilton was one of the three persons left a pension by Sir Henry Inglose (see above, p. 213) in 1451. He was a feoffee of Sir Henry's in May 1451: *Cal. Anc. Deeds*, IV, p. 236; cf. Davis II, p. 193, lines 11–13.

[52] PRO, C1/21/47, for which see note 54, below.

the death of Sir William to this Suffolk part of the Ufford property than she was to the Norfolk part: Elizabeth was not *her* daughter. In the second, what undisguised robbery that extraordinary 'ten years over' clause was, for the beneficiaries can only have been the feoffees, headed (of course) by Sir Henry. It was, therefore, only early in 1447 that the estates were settled on Sir Thomas Dacre and Elizabeth, ten years after Amy's death.[53] Thus, in one way or another, Elizabeth was denied her substantial Ufford inheritance for about twenty-five years. I do not understand why her father-in-law, Thomas, Lord Dacre, did not protest. He had bought Elizabeth from Sir William Bowet because she was an heiress; he must have paid handsomely for her.

Elizabeth Dacre's battle in Chancery with her half-sister Sybille (in which so much came to light) took place in 1453–5.[54] In September 1456 the new chancellor, Archbishop Thomas Bourchier, wrote to John Paston to intervene in a matter of murder: Sir Nicholas Bowet had accused a Robert Ufford of Berking, Norfolk, of the murder of Henry Bowet and the Chancellor was seeking 'a convenient treetie to be taken in that behalve'.[55] As St Francis said: property leads to murder. In this case it was Sir Henry Inglose's covetousness which had deathly consequences: Master Henry Bowet was a last victim. Sir Henry's avarice was twofold: not only did he cheat his wife's stepdaughter of her inheritance, he also denied his own stepdaughter, Sybille Bowet, hers – in this he behaved as Fastolf did towards *his* stepson, Stephen Scrope.

We come to the third and most abused of this trinity of sufferers at the hands of their 'fadyr Inglose'.[56] Sybille had already been badly treated by her own father, Sir William Bowet; he had sold 'a litel before his decesse' her half of his Cumbrian patrimony to the man who had the other half, Thomas, Lord Dacre, father-in-law of Sir William's elder daughter, Elizabeth. The price Lord Dacre paid was 500 marks. He did not pay it, however, until after William's death; nor would he until Sir William's feoffees made a full release to him. This was finally done in April 1423 before Amy married Sir Henry Inglose.[57] According to Sybille, petitioning the chancellor thirty years later, Sir William 'in discharge of his soule and conscience' because he had disinherited his daughter, 'then being of tender age', wished her to have out of his and Amy's moveable goods 500 marks towards her marriage.

[53] This is all to be discovered in *CIPM Henry VII*, I, pp. 86–7, where it features without comment.

[54] The accounts in the case of Robert and Sybille Osbern vs Elizabeth Dacre are as follows: the Osberns' bill, PRO, C1/21/49 (another, damaged copy is 22/157); Elizabeth's answer 21/47; Elizabeth's response to the Osberns' missing replication, 21/45–6; writs to examine, 21/44, 48.

[55] Davis II, no. 562.

[56] NRO, Le Strange MS, P. 20, no. 10.

[57] *CCR 1422–9*, p. 204.

Once Amy had married Sir Henry, and despite the fact that Sir Henry 'hadde grete and notable money and jewelles to the valewe of m^{e} li with his seid wif dame Amye', there was nothing for Sybille. Moreover, after Sir Henry's death his executors said, perhaps truthfully, that they knew nothing about any of this.[58]

Sybille's petition of 1453 was a joint one with her husband, Robert Osbern of Barking, Essex. They appear to have married before 1436. Probably soon after the marriage Robert wrote from London a mournful letter to William Calthorp, a copy of which he despatched to 'Bryan Stapilton Squier':[59]

Plese it you to undrestande howe sooth it is that the gentilwoman your sustre whome not oonly to hir grete hurt I upon trust unwarely wedded but also to my grete hindrance and discomfort in many wise being delaied of hir dewtees by my lade Dacre hir sustre after hir promesse as it is knowen and god woteth hath grete cause of hevynesse Seeyng amonges othre thinges howe they that she is next of Kynne unto be not to hir so lovyng helping nor favoring as reson humanite and kindnesse and nature wolde but some of theym cause of hir afflicion and misery in grete party.

He asked William to talk to Elizabeth Dacre – 'and my lady [to be] felt and stirred by you in especialle whom your sustre oweth moost to trust of al her Kynne' – and undertook to abide by whatever reasonable accommodation William might be able to arrange: 'Wherefore I beseche you as ye be a verrey gentilman do me to wite in writing what ye fele therin.' William Calthorp was gentlemanly enough to do what he was asked and (as we shall see) he got Elizabeth to do one thing for her sister. For Robert Osbern it was too little; it was he who was obliged to stoop to 'ungentlemanly' tactics.

What 'dewtees' had Elizabeth promised Sibylle?[60] It seems that Sir Henry Inglose, her almost fairytale stepfather (so odious is his behaviour to her), not content with denying her nine-tenths of her Ufford inheritance, now endeavoured to get her to give the profits of the remaining tenth, Great Hautbois, to the young couple. Robert Osbern maintained Sir Henry had (once again) prevailed; Great Hautbois was settled on him and Sybille for life; moreover, Elizabeth was to give them £10 per annum until they had received £100. None of this, however, had happened. Elizabeth said in Chancery in the early 1450s that she knew about Sybille's marriage only when it 'wer fully fynysshed excepte only the solempnysyng'; Robert asked her to come to the wedding; she came, but he did not pay her costs. The wedding was held in Norfolk while Amy was alive. It was after Amy's death that Elizabeth, under (renewed) pressure from Sir Henry, who sent Henry

[58] This is all PRO, C1/19/40a/b.

[59] The letter is NRO, Le Strange MS, P. 20, no. 7. Brian Stapleton was knighted in 1436: Wedgwood, *Biographies*, p. 804.

[60] For all that follows see PRO C1/21/45–46, 47, 49.

Wilton to her in Sussex, and because William Calthorp entreated her to give 'sumwhat to here mariage', granted Robert and Sybille the profits of Great Hautbois *but* for one year only as 'here lyvelod was smale and she myght not departe therfrom', and in addition £20, 'so that he wold labour for her and be frendely to her and to alle her maters'. The £10 that was the year's income out of Great Hautbois, Elizabeth maintained, was paid; the £20 was not, because Robert had sued for it, had arrested her servants and had defamed her. After Sir Henry Inglose's death, Robert and Sybille challenged her title; Henry Bowet's murder, as we have seen, was a consequence of that challenge. It was not the first killing. At Elizabeth's entry of Great Hautbois, presumably after Sir Henry's death, Robert Osbern had sent along some men to whom, Elizabeth said, she had paid 5 nobles; they were, she continued, 'mis govned men and ded moch harme . . . and one of them kylled an other to the grete slaundre of the seid Elizabeth'.

Elizabeth had already been slandered after another fashion. Robert Osbern said that she and her husband Sir Thomas Dacre no longer cohabited, and (in his replication to her reply) hinted at worse. Elizabeth protested. She had always been obedient to her husband and his kin, both the Earl and Countess of Salisbury and her father- and mother-in-law, and since she came to Norfolk 'she reporteth hir to alle the gentelez of this contre'; moreover, at all times she had and would be 'demeaned by here seid husbond as lowly as any lady owe to be', and whether she and her husband came together or not, Robert Osbern had 'not to do with it'. As Thomas and Elizabeth's two daughters, Joan and Philippa, had been born as long before as the early and mid 1430s, it looks as if there was a fire beneath all the smoke. None the less, so far as Great Hautbois is concerned Elizabeth is to be believed, when William Calthorp (after all Sybille's brother) was examined, he claimed that Elizabeth had only given Robert and Sybille a year's profits of the manor 'in the name of x li'.

If Robert and Sybille Osbern resorted to lying and defamation of character who will blame them? William Calthorp's troubles were relatively and ultimately minor ones, while Elizabeth Dacre, whatever her marital disappointments, was a lady of property. Sybille, on the other hand, out of her enforced association with Sir Henry Inglose had got nothing – she truly had been robbed.

Sir Henry is hard to understand. Evidently he had no feeling for his extended family, and little for his nuclear one, as he sold more estates than he left to his sons, was not conspicuously generous to his daughters, and omitted to leave anything at all to one of his two sons-in-law. He is almost to be thought of as an ogre, until one remembers John Wyndham's willingness to sell his own son in order to tempt a propertied widow into marrying him, or John Paston's treatment of his brothers and sisters. Sir John Fastolf's discourtesy to his stepson, Sir Stephen Scrope, has also been noted. Many other examples, I am sure, might easily be gathered. They illustrate McFarlane's view of the fifteenth-century landed classes as shamelessly competitive. Still, even among hard men, Sir Henry Inglose was a hard man. How, then, is his paying of Sir William Bowes' ransom in 1422[61] or Sir John Fastolf's paying of his, John Berney's, and John Mautby's ransoms in the previous decade to be seen? Was the way brothers-in-arms behaved towards each other one thing, how such warriors behaved towards those defenceless and often very young men and women, who became dependent on them, entirely another? Would it be correct to contrast the 'good' ethic of the camp with the 'bad' of the family?

There is a need for greater precision here. It is almost as if, in Inglose's and Fastolf's cases at least, those children whom a man received into his household as a result of his wife's previous marriages were not 'his' and therefore might be abused. And yet John Hopton did not behave like that to the children of Thomasin.[62] There are invariably exceptions. None the less, one is struck by the 'drivenness' of the landlord of the fifteenth century. Just as King John's barons got themselves into debt at the Exchequer because they were ready to pay almost any price for heirs and heiresses to advance their 'lineages', so perhaps were fifteenth-century landowners ready to 'do anything' to enhance theirs. John's barons over-reached themselves because they had to pay inflationary prices. Were fifteenth-century landowners so cruel to their stepchildren because they could not be nasty to their tenants? Was that landlordly urge to get every penny diverted after 1381 from successfully resistant tenants to exploitable kin or half-kin? If one was unable to make war on one's tenants, one could at least be aggressive towards one's almost nearest but not dearest. I expect not: it sounds too neat, too like a Marxist pamphlet: landlords thwarted by the peasantry turn on the weakest members of their own class.

But what of the riddle of Sir Henry Inglose? If there is one. His case might be simple. In (or about) 1423, despite having been taken prisoner at Baugé (his second capture by the French), he had money because he had married it in the person of Amy Bowet, widow of his old comrade in arms, Sir William Bowet. With Amy, as we have seen, he got £1,000 in cash and jewels, 500 marks she had recently received from Thomas, Lord Dacre, for Sybille Bowet's inheritance which Sir William had sold him, and William Calthorp, whose wardship and marriage Sir Henry may have had to pay Robert, Lord Willoughby, 600 marks for (as he claimed), but which he fairly promptly sold to Reginald, Lord Grey of Ruthin, for 800 marks (as Elizabeth Dacre claimed). It was undoubtedly out of this windfall that he purchased the

[61] See above, note 36. [62] *Hopton*, p. 117 ff.

Geney inheritance and paid for Sir William Bowes' ransom. Was this 'over-purchasing'? And, despite his clinging to profitable property not his own – Elizabeth Dacre's (and possibly Isobel Ilketshall's) – did he never recover from it? He does not make much of his debts in his will; moreover, his enfeoffment of a month previously does not suggest he was caught unawares by death and thus had no time to make a reckoning.[63] None the less, he had contrived to leave things in turmoil. The hostility his greed had engendered between Elizabeth Dacre, Sybille Osbern, and William Calthorp blazed out in Chancery and in Norfolk, leaving two men dead. The bitterness of soul he had caused is incalculable.[64]

[63] His will is unhurried and knowledgeable. Contrast, for example, that of John Fastolf of Oulton, Suffolk, of 1445, which is the opposite: John does not know whether his lands will suffice to pay his debts and provide for the marriage of his two daughters; the reversions of land left to his widow, Katherine, might have to be sold by his executors, Ralph Lampet and Alexander Kingston (NRO, NCC Reg. Wylbey f. 64). The reversion of his single manor of Oulton was indeed sold, eventually to none other than James Hobart for £240 (PRO, C1/53/87), but not before there had been broken promises and sharp practice on the part of William Jenny: Davis II, no. 658, which relates the difficulties and vulnerabilities of executors in such a case; the writer is likely to be the husband of John Fastolf's daughter, Joan, rather than of his other daughter, Margaret, as Joan was to inherit after her mother, Katherine's death and was to pay Margaret 100 marks towards her marriage. William Jenny was the supervisor of Katherine Fastolf's will of 1478 (NRO, NCC Reg. Gelour, f. 221). Neither the manor of Oulton nor Joan or Margaret are mentioned in Katherine's will; it is the children of her second marriage to John Sampson who are (at length); one of them, Eleanor, married William Jenny after the death of her first husband, Robert Inglose: see below, note 71. Katherine had much (non-manorial) property in and around Oulton and elsewhere in Suffolk, including that bought by John Fastolf, beside whom she chose to be buried in Oulton church. Their 'magnificent brasses' were stolen in 1857: H. Munro Cautley, *Suffolk Churches and their Treasures* (third edition, London, 1954), p. 300.

[64] Or perhaps measurable into the next generation. Sir Thomas Dacre and Sir Roger Fiennes agreed on a double marriage: Thomas and Elizabeth's daughters, Joan and Philippa, were to be married to Sir Roger's sons, Joan to Richard, his eldest son, and Philippa to Robert. Sir Roger paid Sir Thomas 1,800 marks for these heiresses (to both Dacre and Ufford properties). Her own property, at least the three Norfolk estates we are more familiar with than she may have been, Elizabeth, none the less attempted to set aside for the performance of her will in the late 1450s by means of an assize of novel disseisin taken 'prively' against herself by her feoffees (see PRO, C1/29/354 and her receiver-general's accounts of 1456–7, NRO, NRS 18533: it cost her £10 5s 8d). When Joan and Richard married, the three estates had been settled on Elizabeth with remainder to them. Richard and Joan, after Elizabeth's death, battled in Chancery against her executors: one of them, Thomas Cryne, a Norwich gentleman, they put in prison (PRO C1/29/350); Thomas was released to explain in Chancery on 9 November 1461 that as a result of an award made in that court in Richard and Joan's favour (see dorse of PRO, C1/29/501), he had fully granted the estates to them (PRO, C1/29/349). Thomas was alive and well twenty years later: he wrote Davis II, no. 794 to John Paston III in April 1482. Poor Elizabeth: even in death she was overborne by her 'family'; so much for the power of the unwidowed woman in fifteenth-century England. The double marriage-making occurred in 1446, when the Suffolk manors were settled on Thomas and Elizabeth with remainder to Robert and Philippa; that was, no doubt, part of the deal: the Dacre lands (or some of them) and the three Norfolk manors to Richard and Joan, the Suffolk lands to Robert and Philippa (*CIPM Henry VII*, I, pp. 86–7; *CP* IV, pp. 8–9; Copinger, *Manors*, II, p. 6). Philippa died before leaving Robert any children; brother then fought brother, and brother sister-in-law; their unseemly disputes do not concern us. Robert was unruly. He was anti-Paston in the Paston–Poynings dispute: Davis I, pp. 198–9, 207–9. He lived in Suffolk in the 1470s and 1480s: Wedgwood, *Biographies*, p. 325.

Not only that: Sir Henry's sons (as one might expect) were not satisfied with his desire to sell so much. Nothing seems to have gone smoothly. Henry Inglose's flaring up against the men of Tunstead (leaving another two dead) may have been part of his frustration.[65] Indeed, Henry had gone behind his father's back over the Rutland manor of Pickworth even before Sir Henry's last enfeoffment of May 1451.[66] As a result, the sale of Pickworth proved troublesome, for there were (it seems) two buyers, Robert Danvers and John Browe, to fight it out.[67] Ashby may have been another contentious property; according to his father's will, this Suffolk manor should have descended to Henry: by 1458 or 1460 his brother Robert had it.[68] Robert also got the manor of Gunton.[69] Presumably Gunton, like Buckenham Ferry, the executors (of whom he was one) sold him: Buckenham Ferry was settled on him and his heirs on 29 October 1456.[70] He may have 'bought' other estates.[71] One estate Robert did not get was Rackheath. He offered it to Sir John Fastolf; Sir John thought he would have it; he told Thomas Howes to undertake the necessary explorations:[72]

[65] Eighteen months after Sir Henry's death Margaret wrote to John from Norwich (Davis I, pp. 252–3): 'As for tydyngys in this contré, Harry Ingloses men have slayn ij men of Tonsted on Thursday last past, as it is seyd, and all that contré is sore trobelid therwith; and if he had abedyn at hom he had be lyke to have be fechid owte of his owyn hows, for the peple therabowgth is sore mevod [moved] with hym. And on Saterday last past he come ryding thorow this town toward Framyngham, and if he had abedyn in this town he shuld have ben arestyd; for men of Tonsted and of the contré pusewid after hym in-to this town and made a grett noyse of hym and required the mayre and sheryves that he ne his men shuld not pas the town but that they shuld do as it longed to here parte to do, and told hem the cause why. And as it is seyd, the sergeantys were fals and lete hym have knowleche ther-of and he hythid hym hens in hast &c.' Presumably Henry was on his way to the Duke of Norfolk at Framlingham: cf. (though it is many years afterwards) Davis II, p. 380.

[66] Davis I, pp. 104–5.

[67] PRO, C1/26/618; *CCR 1454–61*, pp. 301–2; *CCR 1461–8*, p. 439.

[68] Copinger, *Manors*, V, pp. 4–5, citing Bodleian Library, Suffolk Charter 738.

[69] Copinger, *Manors* V, p. 40. [70] *Cal. Anc. Deeds*, IV, p. 241.

[71] PRO, C1/26/135 shows Sir Henry's feoffees reluctant to make estate to the buyers, or so the executors (Robert among them) complained. Robert lived at Gunton beside Lowestoft; he dated his will there on 31 July 1475, and wished to be buried in the chancel of St Peter's church at Gunton. Haveringland (which he had been given by his father, and where money was delivered to him in the accounting year 1450–1: BL Add. Ch. 9355) he left to his wife Eleanor and her heirs in perpetuity. Gunton, Hopton, and Ashby he left to her for life, with remainder to their daughter Katherine. Eleanor was to have all his moveable goods. She was his sole executor. The will (NRO, NCC Reg. Gelour, f. 111) was proved on 24 January 1476. Clearly, Robert regarded Eleanor highly. No wonder, therefore, she was speedily married by the elderly and grand William Jenny (Wedgwood, *Biographies*, p. 500, has her husbands in the wrong order). Eleanor's will of 14 September 1494 is NRO NCC Reg. Typpes, f. 19: she left money for prayers for the soul of both her husbands. Eleanor was the daughter of John Sampson and Katherine, the widow of John Fastolf of Oulton (see note 63). To the heirs male of Katherine, her daughter by Robert Inglose, who had married Richard Bloomvill, Eleanor bequeathed a silver-gilt basin with the arms of Inglose on it, a silver cup decorated with an image of St Martin, and a silver-gilt goblet. Priests were to sing for her soul and the souls of her husbands, Katherine and Richard's souls, and all their children's souls at Gunton, Oulton, and Rome. Her rosary of gold she left to Master John Jenny, master of Brundish college in Suffolk, one of her two executors. The will was proved 9 January 1497.

[72] Gairdner II, pp. 326–7.

Item, Robert Inglose hath spoke wyth me and hath offred me to by lond to satisfye my dewtee that lyeth in Rakhyth, and y am avysed to by it, if ye can send thedre som trusty man that can telle whate it ys worth cleerly, and off whome it ys halde, and also yf it be sure lyvelode, and your avice wythall.

In the end, Sir John did not buy. Rackheath, which had been bought by Sir Henry from one branch of the Yelvertons, returned to another, stronger one.[73]

Sir Henry Inglose's moveable goods were also up for sale. After Margaret Paston had informed John on 1 July 1451 of Sir Henry's death the night before, she added: 'If ye deseyer to bey any of hys stuff I pray you send me word ther-of in hast, and I shall speke to Robert Inglose and to Wychyngham ther-of. I suppose thei ben executorys.'[74] Why should 'hys stuff' have been open to purchasers? Was that not abnormal in the same way the expeditious proving of his will on 4 July was unusual? Was it not odd also that the three executors included Robert but not Henry, and that Henry was not one of the feoffees, though Robert was, when their father made his unusual enfeoffment of 26 May 1451, a month or so before his death? It was unusual not simply because of its late date; the lands enfeoffed were all those that (in his will) Sir Henry wanted sold. It looks as though Sir Henry believed Henry was an unsuitable heir. It was, after all, Henry who was two-thirds disinherited even if, as I think we may assume, the manors Sir Henry wished sold were ones he had bought. Moreover, Henry, in the ordinary course of things, might have expected to have had the bulk of his widower father's household gear. If we conclude that antipathy between Sir Henry and his heir was as important, possibly more important, than debts as the cause of his selling up, is that not, knowing what we know of Sir Henry, entirely understandable? He may have alienated his eldest son as he alienated so many others.[75] Sir Henry seems not unlike his friend Sir John Fastolf, save that Sir John had no son and heir to alienate.

[73] Blomefield V, p. 1365.

[74] Davis I, p. 243. Margaret believed John had bought something, probably wood and hay as appears from her letter to him of 6 July (Davis I, p. 244, lines 2–7), although later she wrote, 'And as for stuff of howsold, I can non bye at Inglos' (Davis I, p. 246, lines 18–19).

[75] He seems to have been tough in the usual ways fifteenth-century gentlemen were tough: Davis II, no. 476 and note 37 above. In his youth he had been reckless, rioting against the parson of Stockton (PRO, C1/16/101), and as an esquire, in France with Sir William Bowet and Sir George Felbrigg purloining (and keeping) from a wrecked ship valuables and armour belonging to the Earls of March and Dorset, Robert, Lord Willoughby, and (of all people) Sir Roger Swillington – which puts this unbrotherly-in-arms incident before August 1417, when Sir Roger died (PRO, C1/6/311). In 1426 he was poaching Duchy of Lancaster hares with his greyhounds: Mark Bailey, 'The Rabbit and the Medieval East Anglian Economy', *Agricultural History Review* 36 (1988), p. 17, note 115. One would like to know what the abbot of St Benet's at Holm was suing Sir Henry for in 1439 (*CCR 1435–41*, p. 274); it is fitting that two doughty warriors were Sir Henry's mainpernors, Sir John Radcliff and Sir William Oldhall: there certainly was a 'military community' in East Anglia in the years 1415–55: I take the phrase from Philip Morgan, *War and Society in Medieval Cheshire 1277–1403*, Cheetham Society, third series, XXXIV (London, 1987), chapter 4.

Thanks to Bruce McFarlane,[76] Anthony Smith,[77] and the Fastolf papers at Magdalen College, Oxford, we know a great deal more about Sir John Fastolf than we do about Sir Henry Inglose. Not all that is knowable; far from it. Sir John's letters, even those in the British Library, have not been published in their entirety, the riches of the Fastolf papers at Magdalen College, Oxford, have not been fully exposed. Dr Smith, we must hope, will show more of Sir John to us than yet stands revealed. Moreover, Smith's Fastolf may not exactly be McFarlane's; is not already, where Sir John and his lands are concerned.[78] Meanwhile, we are still far from knowing the John Fastolf Sir Henry Inglose knew.

Our business is with the Pastons, currently the Pastons and Sir John Fastolf. Moreover, while they and he had been associated from before John Paston's time,[79] while John's brother William also gave Fastolf 'devoted service',[80] it is the quality of the association of Sir John Fastolf and John Paston which has to occupy us, because all lines of vision converge on 5 November 1459 (another – *the* – deathbed). The truth of Fastolf's intentions will never be known, were not (if the truth could be told) known then to his associates, servants, and friends. By 5 November Fastolf himself may not have had any: he had been ill, according to William Worcester, since 1 June 1459.[81] He made a will two weeks later, on 14 June. The intentions it embodied were radically other than those John Paston claimed Fastolf gave expression to later. Any attempt to assess the truth of these claims must include an inquiry into the relationship of John Paston and Sir John Fastolf. If Sir John, in the end, did intend to leave John everything he had, in order that John should do everything he wanted done, he must have trusted him. Absolutely, we are prepared to add. Did he? An examination of their association may not tell us; it will give us a clearer idea of what to suppose.

We may divide the Fastolf–Paston relationship into three phases; these three phases are arrived at (necessarily) by the way in which Fastolf's own letters, or we ought to say, his surviving letters, fall into three clearly defined groups; but these clusters are not artificial: his letters bunch because of the pressure of business and of events. The first phase is from March 1450 to

[76] Particularly his exhilarating paper, 'The Investment of Sir John Fastolf's Profits of War', collected in *England in the Fifteenth Century*, pp. 175–97.

[77] 'Litigation and Politics: Sir John Fastolf's Defence of his English Property', in A.J. Pollard (ed.), *Property and Politics* (Gloucester, 1984), pp. 59–75. This is no more than a taste of his unpublished thesis, 'Aspects of the Career of Sir John Fastolf'.

[78] Where Fastolf and his land are concerned Dr Peter Lewis' impeccable paper, 'Sir John Fastolf's Lawsuit over Titchwell 1448-55', *The Historical Journal*, 1 (1985), pp. 1–20, has to be gratefully acknowledged. With Dr Smith's work done it has its influential and proper context.

[79] By 1436 (at the latest) William Paston was Sir John's legal advisor: Anthony Smith, 'Sir John Fastolf', p. 28.

[80] The phrase is Anthony Smith's, *ibid.*, p. 65; his evidence, Davis II no. 925.

[81] BL Sloane MS 4, f. 38v: ill for 158 days.

September 1451, when the pressing business was Sir John's unsuccessful attempt to gain redress for injuries done to him by the Duke of Suffolk and his followers, and to get some of the duke's collaborators punished by commissioners of oyer et terminer. The second phase is from June 1454 to November 1456, when political circumstances once again (and once again temporarily) favoured Fastolf and put his opponents at a disadvantage. Fastolf's chief opponent was Sir Philip Wentworth; the vital issue was Wentworth's spurious claim to the manors of Beighton and Bradwell, but their competition for the wardship of Thomas Fastolf, a subsidiary battle in the main campaign over the two manors, claimed much of Sir John and his advisors' attention during this stage, not least John Paston's, for at one point John thought of Thomas Fastolf as a husband for one of his daughters – Margery presumably – and Sir John was happy at the thought.[82] The third phase is the last phase, Fastolf's last days, 1458–9, when the spurt of letter writing was occasioned by the old man's impending end.

Most of Fastolf's letters remain unpublished in the British Library: James Gairdner usually gave only an abstract.[83] Until all his letters are both readily accessible and in their complete form any 'reading' of the last decade of Sir John Fastolf's life must be an interim and impartial one. Dr Anthony Smith has read those letters, so have I. Put simply (too simply, of course) we like Fastolf more than McFarlane (in print) did. This is a tricky matter, being one of impressions, and Dr Smith must (and one day will) speak for himself. For my part I have neither the presumption nor the temerity to say I know better than McFarlane, that I know Fastolf better than he knew him. I do not believe I do. Yet I 'read' him differently, more precisely my study of Sir John's letters in the British Library has made me (even against my will) think better of Fastolf than McFarlane did in 1957. In his last decade Fastolf does not strike me as an 'irascible old man . . . [reduced] . . . to a state of querulous and unmanageable senility'.

By the time we make Sir John's acquaintance in the *Paston Letters* he had become a close-fisted, litigious and irascible old man. With one or two trifling exceptions the letters from, to and about him begin in 1450 when he was already seventy years of age; his active military career had ended a full decade before. Thenceforward until his death after a long illness in December [*sic*: November] 1459 the material

[82] Davis II, p. 105; Davis I, p. lxii.

[83] An extreme example of how misleading a Gairdner 'abstract' can be is his no. 144. This is BL Add. MS 34888, f. 49. It is a very long, carefully paragraphed or 'itemized' letter, probably written by William Worcester. There are ten 'items' in the main body of the letter, dated (as Gairdner has dated his abstract) London, 15 October 1450, and signed by Fastolf. There is then a postscript of five 'items', one of which concerns 'Hygham' place; it is this paragraph alone that appears as Gairdner's no. 144. Fastolf also signed the postscript. The address on the dorse should be amended from Gairdner's 'in haste, at Castre Yn, by Jermuth' to 'in haste. Item Castre is by Jermuth'. The letter is a splendid example of Fastolf's grasp of the dozen or so matters occupying him in autumn 1450.

consequences of the English defeat in France and the steady collapse of public order at home combined with the evidence of his own declining physical powers to reduce him to a state of querulous and unmanageable senility. Though he owed much to the Lancastrian dynasty all he cared to remember as he and it sank together into the grave were the debts it had not paid him.[84]

That is not my impression. In the first phase, 1450–1, though he is concerned with redress and revenge and reasonably so considering the gross actions and expensive wrongs done to him by the Duke of Suffolk, Sir John is not ill-tempered and not vindictive. Professor Storey and Dr Smith, in revealing the depth of the Suffolk regime's disregard for the rights of others in the 1440s have made us better understand Fastolf's justified sense of injury and outrage, which at last he could freely express in 1450–1. We might almost go so far as to admire Fastolf's restraint. To the Duke of Suffolk, his vendetta against Fastolf, and the impact on John Paston of observing it at close quarters, we will come shortly. First, what is there to say about Paston and Fastolf in this first phase of 1450–1?

During this period Sir John wrote Paston only one letter, *all* his other two dozen or so letters are addressed to Thomas Howes, to Thomas Howes and John Berney, or to Thomas Howes and others of his officers at Caister or Norwich. There is a straightforward reason for this: throughout this time Fastolf was living in his house at Southwark,[85] John Paston lodged close by in London just across and up river at the 'Innere In of the Temple'.[86] John, as well as helping to wage Fastolf's battles, had his own to fight: against Lord Moleyns for Gresham. The single letter written to Paston, of 14 September 1450, is the exception which proves our rule; it is addressed to John Berney, John Paston, and Thomas Howes, in that order, and was written from London; they were, as is clear from what Fastolf has to say to them, in Norfolk preparing for oyer et terminer sessions at Norwich.[87] It is possible John did not keep the letters Fastolf wrote him, whereas Fastolf's officers were careful to keep in the archives at Caister all he wrote to them, hence the

[84] *England in the Fifteenth Century*, pp. 176–7.

[85] Smith, 'Sir John Fastolf', p. 159. He spent £1,225 improving his substantial holdings there; acquired between 1439 and 1446 for £1,227 13s 4d were fifty-one messuages, including the Boar's Head and the Hart's Head, two watermills, seven gardens, lands, meadows, and wharves worth £102 per annum: *ibid.*, p. 12. It was, one feels, a mistake for William Wainfleet to have exchanged much of this urban property for the advowsons of Findon, Sussex, and Slimbridge, Glos., in 1484. For Fastolf's house, see Martha Carlin, 'Fastolf Place, Southwark: the Home of the Duke of York's Family, 1460', in J. Petre (ed.), *Richard III, Crown and People* (London, 1985), pp. 44–7. A visit to where Fastolf's house once was with David Morgan on 11 June 1986 brought vividly to life Davis II, no. 692: Sir John Fastolf and Cade's revolt. The topography of lines 44–50 had not been grasped by us previously: the Tower was a five-minute row away almost directly across the Thames.

[86] See the sequence of Agnes' letters addressed to him there between 'probably' February 1450 and 'probably' November 1452: Davis I nos. 19, 20, 23, 24, 25.

[87] Davis II, no. 457. William Worcester wrote the letter.

survival of the letter of 14 September 1450, but I think it more likely that Fastolf talked rather than wrote to Paston in 1450–1.[88]

Fastolf's officers also kept copies of their letters to him, or were meant to. On one occasion Howes proceeded without Fastolf's authorization, or so Fastolf thought,

as to that [Fastolf wrote to Howes] I can weel agree me therto with that ye wole sende me the dowble of myn writing sent to you in that behalf. And if hit so be that myn writing be forseyd sent you for that cause be generall for what so ever ye dede for me werhit with the lawe or ayenst the lawe then hit is Reson be my feith that I bere you ought what so ever hit cost me notwithstonding I am not avised that ther passed any suche letter in myn name but your letter wole shewe the trought of the mater. Wheche I pray yow may be sent me in alle hast goodly and of whos hande the seyd letters ben etc.[89]

At the end of the letter he commanded Howes to send 'alle the dowbles of your letters' concerning this matter and concluded 'I pray yow wryte no thing to me but as ye wole abide by upon your worschip.' This seems to me an important letter for an assessment of Sir John Fastolf: his willingness to stand by Howes whatever Howes has done, if he has done it with Fastolf's authorization, should be contrasted with what he said (possibly a week earlier) when he believed Howes had acted without such authorization:

And know for certeyn, there passed no such warauntis undre my sele; nothyr I comaunded you not for to labour ne do thyng that shuld be ayenst the law, nether unlawfully ayenst ryght and trouth. And therfor y ought not ne wolle not pay for yow.[90]

If these two statements concern the same matter, as seems likely,[91] then Fastolf's discovery that he may have been responsible for what Howes had done led him to that almost stirring declaration of support. What comes first is a hasty and unconsidered judgement: it was your fault, you can pay for it. What follows (after further information received, after reflection) is the opposite: maybe it was my fault, count on me. Howes knew which of these

[88] John kept the letters others wrote him at this time, those from William Wayte and James Gresham, for example.

[89] BL Add. MS 39848, f.19. This is the passage which appears in Gairdner as 'but if there was any letter to that effect F. will bear him out': II, no. 202. They, of course, kept copies of other documents, including those concerning Fastolf's commercial dealings; when he wanted indentures sent to him at London relating to wheat and malt delivered to Cornelys Florysson *and* Cornelys Heynsson at Norwich for shipping to London, he urged Berney, Howes, and Walter Shipdam to 'kepe ye a double of hem wyth yow'. Things had gone wrong: Fastolf had arrested both the ship *and* Cornelys Heynsson. It is noteworthy that Fastolf's officers had been careful: there were *two* indentures with Florysson and Heynsson, for the delivery of the grain. This is all BL Add. MS 39848, f. 20, abstracted in Gairdner II, no. 203 as 'Bids them send *an* indenture of Cornelys Floryson about wheat and malt.'

[90] Gairdner II, no. 251, dated 12 July 1454.

[91] I suspect Gairdner II, no. 202 might be 20 July 1454 rather than 1451.

Fastolfs was the true one, the master who had written to him once before in similar vein:

trusty and welbelovyd frende . . . I pray you sende me word who darre be so hardy to keck agen you in my ryght. And sey hem on my half that they shall be qwyt as ferre as law and reson wolle. And yff they wolle not dredde, ne obey that, then they shall be quyt by Blackberd or Whyteberd; that ys to sey, by God or the Devyll.[92]

Sir John Fastolf was not a monster to his servants. He could be critical, but there seems to have been good cause:

Item I hafe grete merveylle that ye ne none othyr of my servauntz beyng of long tyme wyth me hafe not ne can not sende me severell and particuler declaration after the trouth ys or was of the grete damages and hurtes don to me in especiall and to dyvers of my tenaunts thys x or xij yeer day by meyntenaunce of myne adversaryes etc. as I hafe sondry tymys wryt unto you.[93]

He worried about his wine at Caister and his rabbits at Hellesdon,[94] but as any absent landlord might, and that his revenues were being too freely spent by his servants, as any good landlord ought.[95] He was a hard employer, even a harsh one; Henry Windsor's 'Hit is not unknoon that cruell and vengible he hath byn ever, and for the most parte with aute pité and mercy', cannot be denied: McFarlane reckoned that as 'a judgement on Fastolf's character [it] was true enough'.[96] I am less certain. For instance, its context should be carefully considered. Henry's letter to John Paston was on a delicate and complicated issue. He was making an appeal with dignity, yet also conspiratorially: Paston was going to reveal in court some illegality in which Henry had been involved over the matter of the wardship of Thomas Fastolf; be forgiving, wrote Henry, citing Matthew 18, verses 15–17, 21–2; we know what Fastolf is like, you should be otherwise.[97] Thus, that condemnatory 'ever' is written (I think) for contrasting effect, not in unremitting bitterness. Alongside it, at any rate, we should remember that William Worcester was repeating what was intended as a joke – even if a heavy, Fastolfian one – when in a light-hearted letter he told John Paston his

[92] *Ibid.*, no. 125.

[93] BL Add. MS 39848, f. 5 (abstracted in Gairdner II, no. 122). Cf. f. 6: 'And there as it hath been by negligence of yow there or of my servauntz here moo of my grevaunces and extorcions don to me left out unremembered as I doubt nott there ys as myne officers can sey etc. I pray yow doo ye putt and ingroose hem amonges the othyr' (abstracted in Gairdner II, no. 130). [94] Gairdner II, no. 125.

[95] 'And that they make lyvereez of money uppon her charges beter than I vele they doo, for and myne auditores had such officers undre hem they wolde be ryght wroth but they had moo lyverees of her charge and office then I have. I sey allwey a comyn sawe. Shew me the meete but show me not the man etc.': BL Add. MS 39848, f. 10 (abstracted in Gairdner II, no. 158).

[96] K.B. McFarlane, *The Nobility of Later Medieval England* (London, 1973), p. 50. I have not examined John Bocking's petition, Magdalen College, FP. 98, also referred to by McFarlane. For Fastolf as the driver of a hard bargain, see Davis II, no. 713. [97] Davis II, no. 550.

master had said he wished the married Worcester had been a priest so his salary might be a benefice given him by someone else, like the bishop. 'And so I endure *inter egenos ut servus ad aratrum*' is followed at once by 'Foryefe me, I wryte to make yow laugh.'[98] Moreover, as McFarlane himself pointed out, William was an employee who remained loyal to his master even after his death, trying to carry out at his own expense and against stiff opposition Fastolf's intentions.[99] Still, even plough horses rest, but one Christmas William was not allowed to get away for a holiday:

> I asked licence to ryde yn-to my contree, and my maistre dyd not graunt it; he seyd hys wille was for to make, &c. Y aunsuerd it syt not me to know it. God gefe hym grace of holsom councell and of a gode disposicion. Non est opus unius diei nec unius septimane.[100]

But I have run on too far: William Worcester's missed vacation was in January 1456, Henry Windsor's letter dates from the following May. By then undoubtedly Fastolf was deteriorating.[101]

In 1450–1 there is no indication that he had grown tetchy and unreasonable. One letter, of January 1451, shows, I think, just how reasonable a man he was. This long letter also demonstrates the enormous limitations of an abstract.[102] We begin quietly enough. Hugh Acton, Master of the Hospital of St Giles, to whom Fastolf had sold the manor of Mundham, had been with him;[103] they had talked about the sale of other lands of Fastolf, called Rees,

[98] *Ibid.*, p. 102. When Paston replied he perhaps did so facetiously. Through Thomas Howes Worcester told him to forget it; what is the tone of that: 'He preyth yow foryete it': Davis II, p. 103, lines 12–16?

[99] *England in the Fifteenth Century*, pp. 204–5.

[100] Davis II, p. 129.

[101] The question of Sir John Fastolf as harsh stepfather ought also to be discussed; I shall not discuss it here. He was less harsh than Sir Henry Inglose, but perhaps only because he had less opportunity to be. The evidence for the sad story of Stephen Scrope is set out by G. Poulett Scrope, *History of the Manor and Ancient Barony of . . . Castle Combe* (London, 1852), chapter 8, especially pp. 264–88. Interesting in this context is the remarkable autograph postscript of a letter from Thomas, Lord Scales, to Fastolf. The letter (Magdalen College, Oxford, Hickling 104) is abstracted in Gairdner, where the postscript has been completely misunderstood, its meaning turned upon its head: II, p. 82. The letter is discussed by Dr Smith ('Sir John Fastolf', p. 195). Dr Smith does not mention that the letter is addressed 'To my Right worshipfull Fader John Fastolff knyght' and that Lord Scales opens the postscript, 'Fadre'. The postscript reads: 'Fadre and ye had be to me as feythful and kend eyr I cam in to Ynglond as ye were in Fraunsse by myn trewtheh ther had been non man of yowr astat that so moche I wold do for.'

[102] This is Gairdner II, no. 174: BL Add. MS 39848, f. 16.

[103] See Gairdner II, no. 156, p. 192. This letter of Fastolf's, like no. 174, was in Blomefield's possession, and he quotes from it (II, p. 762, note): 'I was not avysed to sell yt, except it goth to a good use . . . and he [Hugh Acton] wolde I shoulde hafe do Almesse on hem and relesse hem som money, but ye may sey hem the untrouth of the Pryour of Hykelyng drawyth awey my devocion to such causes.' In no. 174 Fastolf comments again, 'And were it nought bought for the use of the said place of Seint Gylys I wold not have sold it yhgt.' Gairdner, no. 156 was a Paston letter McFarlane owned: P.S. Lewis, 'Sir John Fastolf's Lawsuit over Titchwell', p. 17, note.

but we coude not accord of price, for I wolle not sylle it lesse then after the value of xx yeere, as it makyth clerlye in value now at thys day, or in value at the yer late before I purchased the said place. It lyeth nere to Mundham, and therefore it ys better worth to hym by agrete money then to onye othyr. Notwythstandyng in acqyuytyng me to my Cosyn Sir William Chambyrleyn I wold ye wete of hym before yff he wolle chaunge wyth me for that place asmoch lond in value lyeng off hys in Corton and Newton by my maners in Lodylond, then I wold well he have Rees, for such a chaunge suffisiauntlye made as ye and my councell shall well avyse for my most proffyt and avaylle. I have undrestand well a letter of you wryten uppon the value of the said Rees but I desyre to see the accompts of it wythall.

Later, Fastolf turns to another topic, reduced by Gairdner to the unrevealing 'Fastolf's audit books':

Item as to myn audit I undrestand that the bokes he almoste made upp and engroced but abydyth William Cole ys examinacion and visityng of hem, praying you in ony wyse that in all your allouance of Reparacions or othyr causes that Requyrith maundments that ye the Auditors clepe you to wytnesse the work or the deede or that ell ye se that my lyfelode be not minisshed by nedelese allouances or male werkes were ne nede ys. I woll my lyvelode there were as well approwed and aunsuerd no wors then my wyffes londz that lyeth ferre from me or onye of my surveyors or servauntz about hem. At the reverence of God tendyr ye thys mater for it ys the substaunce of my wellfare and of you all. And myne auditors ought not take straungelie none mater that ye or my servauntz meoffe or wryte on my behalf or by my commaundment, and I desyre to have my bokes valued in the end of the rolle, as the old maner ys, and also the greyernyg and aunsueryng of my officers in the mergyn upon every title to be set out. I doubt they can do it, they remembre it not, byt yhyt esyth my spiryts so sey my conceyt wyth them, and to be corrected and amended for the better.

And towards the end he mentions another,

And whereas he [John Berney] wrytith to me that the respyt and sufferaunce of hys entree in the maner of Rokelond Toftes at my Request doon, ys lyke to preiudice hys title, as to that I were ryht loth that he shuld be damaged in hys ryght and yff it myght lye in my power I wold gladlye sett it in a gode wey, as hys rygt were saved, and both parties contented; nevertheless I kepe not ne wold not but that he doo hys avauntage lawfullie to ryght hys ryght yff he have onye, and that he doo by councell that it preiudice hym not hereafter.

None of this is conclusive. All I have sought to do, and it is only a preliminary report, is to redress the balance: Sir John Fastolf was not as grim as all that, not until 1456 at any rate.

By then he had come to rely on, if he had not become reliant on, John Paston. In 1450–1 this was not yet the case. Undoubtedly, Paston and William Jenny were foremost among his legal counsellors,[104] but there is no

[104] Cf. Gairdner II, p. 193; 'To speak to Paston and Jenny about various matters', and the postscript to BL Add. MS 39848, f. 8, missing from Gairdner II, no. 138: 'And speke wyth my councell William Jenney Paston and Thomas Greene for her avice.' See also the last paragraph of William Yelverton's letter to Fastolf of November 1450: Davis II, no. 877.

real indication that Fastolf looked more to one than the other at this time.[105] Paston did, however, do one notable service. In September 1450 Sir John urged Thomas Howes to 'make such diligence forth to the Jury [at the forthcoming sessions of oyer et terminer] or to such as shall hafe rule yn such causes for the remedie off etc',[106] so that, as he wrote in another letter but in the same context, those causes 'may take a worschypfull eende on my syde'.[107] One of those whom he thought would have such 'rule' was the Duke of Norfolk,

> Item such maters as ye shall nede be labour or meoffe unto my lord of Norffolk that hys goode lordshyp mey help etc. Ye, sir parson, or John Bernay or onye othyr of my lerned councell may meoffe unto hym and I doubt not but he wolle gefe you audience. And I pray you Recommaund me to my Lord ys gode grace and ye may sey hym I shall be ther yn short tyme and awayt uppon hys gode lordshyp.[108]

The member of Fastolf's learned counsel who went with Thomas Howes to urge the right course on the duke was John Paston.[109] He was, I think we may say, valuable to Fastolf, his family's firmly established connection with the Duke of Norfolk particularly valuable perhaps, but he was not invaluable. John's influence with Sir John, by the later years of the decade said to be very great indeed, is not yet noticeable. It was probably negligible.

One of the singular aspects of this sequence of Fastolf's letters in 1450–1 is that there is not a word about politics in them. In all that hectic time Sir John does not refer to the loss of Normandy, the Duke of York's return from Ireland, the parliament of November 1450, the government's recovery the following spring. When he writes it is about the measures to undo the wrongs the Suffolk regime had perpetrated upon him. What are we to make of this? Not, I am sure, that he was uninterested in politics: we know that he was passionately interested.[110] We can be sure too that he was discussing each event, as each followed hard upon the heels of another,[111] nor was he merely talking about events: he was participant in them.[112] But there was

105 It is true that at the end of this phase, in April 1451, on one matter Paston's advice alone was to be sought 'as ye remembre me', wrote Fastolf to Thomas Howes: BL Add. MS 39848, f. 17 (abstracted in Gairdner II, no. 186); on the other hand, in the previous December, Fastolf was prepared to go ahead to initiate a legal action without the dilatory Paston: Gairdner II, p. 199.

106 BL Add. MS 39848, f. 8 (Gairdner II, no. 138).

107 BL Add. MS 39848, f. 9 (Gairdner II, no. 153).

108 BL Add. MS 39848, f. 8, the omitted postscript to Gairdner II, no. 138.

109 Gairdner II, no. 153.

110 See, for instance, C.A.J. Armstrong, 'Politics and the Battle of St Albans, 1455' *BIHR*, 33 (1960), pp. 1–72.

111 For example, the first paragraph of John Bocking's letter to William Wayte, Gairdner II, no. 169, or William Wayte's to John Paston, Davis II, no. 460.

112 I have in mind his slightly earlier involvement with the Duke of York when, apparently after a discussion over breakfast at 'The Mermaid', on 3 July 1445, Fastolf, Sir Andrew

no cause to write to his officers in Norfolk about such matters; it was hardly for him to keep them informed.

What, however, his preoccupation with getting local miscarriages of justice set straight does show is, on the one hand, just how far justice had miscarried in East Anglia in the 1440s, and on the other that he saw his efforts as part of a co-operative, communal exercise[113] to restore a political, a social fabric thoroughly rent during that decade. He was not simply settling his own old scores. He wrote to Thomas Howes (and thus there is no public striking of attitudes[114]) in December 1450,[115]

> and yt is lyke that grete labour and speciall pursute shall be made to the Lord Scalys that he wolle meynteyn the said Tuddenham and Heydon in all he can or may, and thus I have herd say. Wherfor such persones as have founde hem soore greved by extorcion as I have ben, and have processe or wolle hafe processe before the Commissioners, they most effectuelly labour to my Lord Oxford, and to my brothyr Zelverton, Justice, that they wolle as ferre as justice, reason, and concience do that justice may [be] egallie mynistred, and not to wythdrawe theyr couragez well sett from the pore pople; for and they hald not the hand well and stedfast yn thys mater from hens forth whyle it shall dure, they hve herebefore, the pore peple and all the grete part of both shyres of Norffolk and Suffolk be destroyed. For it shewyth well by what manyfold undewe menys of extorcion they have lyved yn myserie and grete pouverte by manye yeers contynewed that the moste part of the comyners have litill or nought to meynteyn their menage and housold, ne to pay the Kyngs taskys, nothyr theyr rents and services to the Lordz they be tenants un too, as it shewyth daylie to all the world, whych ys overe a grete pitie to thynk. And when he said pore peple have be by such injuries overladd and so undoon, nedz most the gentlemen that have they porer lyvelode amongs hem be gretely minisshed and hyndered of their increse and levyng.

We may notice, and it is altogether as we would expect, that while Fastolf's view of society was traditional, conservative – which is why he had been so scandalized by Suffolk's radically anti-social behaviour – he was genuinely concerned for the well-being of society.[116] When the defeat of the East

Ogard, and Sir William (Ap) Thomas ordered a copy of the agreement between John of Gaunt and John, son of Henry of Trastamare, to be made for the duke: BL Egerton Roll 8782. And, of course, there was Cade's revolt: for Fastolf's part in which see Davis II, no. 692. As that letter shows, the government regarded him as a political opponent and in 1453 charged him, Ralph, Lord Cromwell, and Edmund, Lord Grey of Ruthin, with treasonable plotting. As Anthony Smith points out, Fastolf came close to losing his estates to the Duke of Somerset and the king's Tudor half-brothers, just as Sir William Oldhall did for the moment lose his: 'Sir John Fastolf', pp. 153–5, citing Davis no. 529; *CCR 1447–54*, p. 398; and Roger Virgoe, 'William Tailboys and Lord Cromwell: Crime and Politics in Lancastrian England', *Bulletin of the John Rylands Library*, 55 (1972–3), pp. 459–82.

[113] Anthony Smith, 'Sir John Fastolf', pp. 142–5. [114] *Ibid.*, pp. 146–7.

[115] Gairdner II, pp. 196–7.

[116] Cf. Anthony Smith, 'Sir John Fastolf', pp. 167–8: 'The sense of regional identity expressed in 1450 was similar to, though not as pronounced as, that displayed by "county communities" in the 17th century.' Cf. also my comment on fifteenth-century Derbyshire in *Medieval Prosopography*, 6 (1985), p. 116.

Anglian movement came in May 1451 Fastolf's active political career, as Anthony Smith has pointed out, ended also.[117] Was it disillusion with this defeat which began the deterioration to be observed in 1456? There were, of course, more, though probably not greater, disillusionments still to come.[118] We will turn to those in a moment.

The impact of all this on John Paston, one may infer, was considerable. In 1450 he was deeply involved in the measures to indict the chief members of the Duke of Suffolk's regime in East Anglia. He was particularly and intimately concerned with drawing up the list of damages on behalf of Fastolf, the regime's foremost victim. He will have known of the bitter antagonism of William de la Pole towards Sir John Fastolf and, from 1437 onwards, its disastrous consequences for Sir John. Detailing those consequences and summing them in 1450 at 5,000 marks – 'certainly the right order of magnitude', according to Dr Smith[119] – not only may have brought home to him the seriousness of Fastolf's charges against the duke, but also may have implanted in him (for it is not evidenced hitherto[120]) a distaste for the de la Poles which was confirmed by the hostility of the duke's widow and her son towards him and his family in the 1460s and 1470s. By inheriting (or rather claiming to inherit) Fastolf's lands, he inherited the animosity of Alice and John de la Pole, for they continued the duke's fight, which he had conducted entirely by foul and not at all by fair means, to get back estates he had been obliged to sell to Fastolf and others he had simply attempted to wrest from him. But long before the 1460s, it is my contention, John Paston's anti-de la Pole stance had been determined; it had been determined

[117] 'Sir John Fastolf', pp. 151–2.

[118] Although Fastolf had been prudent at the battle of the Herrings, one cannot imagine him being like the lords of 1450 or 1454, whose prudence in running away from their political responsibilities amounted to downright cowardice: see my comments in 'After McFarlane', *History*, 68 (1983), pp. 47–8, subsequently reinforced by the discovery of Ralph A. Griffiths, published by him in 'The King's Council and the first Protectorate of the Duke of York, 1453–4', *EHR*, 99 (1984), pp. 69–82. Such cowardly conduct can only have deepened Fastolf's dissatisfaction with contemporary English politics and politicians.

[119] 'Sir John Fastolf', p. 164.

[120] When Margaret wrote to him, probably as late as 1449, as she did in Davis I, no. 135, lines 27–36, one's impression is that she was not writing to a man who could not or would not become the duke's man. Once upon a time, in 1438–9, he may have been. He was then a yeoman of the stable in the royal household. He had ceased to be so by (at the latest) 1441: D.A.L. Morgan, 'The House of Policy: the Political Role of the Late Plantagenet Household, 1422–1485', in David Starkey (ed.), *The English Court from the Wars of the Roses to the Civil War* (London, 1987), p. 57, note 89. The Duke of Suffolk was steward of the household from 1433 to 1447. John Paston was barely eighteen years old; this raises the question of when he was at Cambridge: before or after his brief sojourn in the king's household? Perhaps he was at Trinity Hall before 1438 (Davis II, no. 438), and at Peterhouse after 1440 (Davis I, no. 124). It seems unlikely that it was marriage to Margaret which got him 'out of court'. Did his father have second thoughts, or did the Duke of Suffolk? John must have enjoyed and valued the experience, as he sent both his sons to Edward IV's household.

by his general experience as an East Anglian of the 1440s, by his particular experience in his own person at East Beckham and Gresham, and as a servant of Fastolf, most abused of all by 'the system', that systematic and illegal exploitation of his position by the Duke of Suffolk.

Whatever the nature of the relationship of Fastolf and the de la Poles before 1437,[121] from that year, because of William de la Pole's sharp practice with regard to the wardship of Fastolf's niece Anne Harling, he and the Duke of Suffolk were downright enemies.[122] There were two estates which were at the heart of their enmity: Cotton in Suffolk, Dedham in Essex. Both were Fastolf's; both the Duke of Suffolk thought were his and ought to be his. They were not so legally; that did not deter him.

First, Cotton: William de la Pole sold Cotton to Sir John Fastolf in 1434 for £933 6s 8d. It was worth £35 per annum. William was in financial difficulties over the payment of his ransom; he had owned this estate since the fourteenth century.[123] More importantly, William had been born and

[121] Was the twenty-five-year-old John Fastolf in service with Michael de la Pole, Earl of Suffolk, in 1405–6? In BL Egerton Roll 8778, which is a fragment of the earl's expenses for a naval expedition ('presumably', as the BL catalogue says, that of summer 1405, which attacked Sluys), 16d was charged for a horse of John Fastolf's at Sandwich. David Morgan also comments in a letter: 'You will have looked at those other Egerton pieces – with the doublet bought for John Fastolf while in Michael I's keeping?' So far we cannot discover the doublet (only the horse). Egerton Roll 8776, however, discloses that John Fastolf lent the new earl, William himself, 113s 4d on 19 January 1417: in this complicated set of receiver-general's accounts for 1416–17 – complex because of the complications of two earls dying in two months in autumn 1415 – under 'Creancia' appears the receipt of the sum from John Fastolf on that date. It is interesting and significant that in 1435–6, just, that is, before Fastolf and William de la Pole fell out, Sir Henry Inglose was with Thomas Tuddenham, John Roys, and other de la Pole counsellors at the holding of the Costessey courts: Staffs. RO, Stafford Collection (Jerningham papers), D641/3, packet 5, Costessey estate accounts 1435–6. (For Inglose's other de la Pole connections, see note 27, above.) When there was a parting of the ways in the late 1430s, Sir Henry clearly chose to travel with Fastolf: a courageous choice. John Roys may have been saved having to make such a choice, by his death (probably) in 1437. He was a councillor of Fastolf's, being his auditor in 1435–6 (Smith, 'Sir John Fastolf', pp. 28, 63), as well as of William de la Pole, by whom he was retained as 'custodiens placitorum domini in curiam Regis'. In 1430–1 he and another councillor of William de la Pole's, Sir John Shardelow, were particularly busy when the men of Gayton broke one of the earl's foldcourses at Gaytonthorp: Staffs. RO, D641/3, packet 5, Costessey estate accounts, 1431–2. For Roys, recorder of Norwich and MP for Norfolk in 1433–4, see above, chapter 3: it was none other than he and his heirs whom William Paston cheated out of Baxter's Place in Walsham. For Sir John Shardelow, MP for Norfolk in 1432, who died in 1433, see *Hopton*, pp. 80–1. Fastolf bought the manor of Hainford near Norwich from Ela Shardelow, Sir John's mother, in 1434 (Smith, 'Sir John Fastolf', pp. 17, 28): her son had been the last of the direct male line. She sold the reversion of Easton Bavents to John Hopton in the following year (*Hopton*, p. 78 ff.). To set the record straight: it was Sir John Fastolf himself who, having bought Cockfield Hall from the executors of John Norwich in 1430 (annual value £13 6s 8d; purchase price £233 6s 8d), sold it to John Hopton in 1440 (Smith, 'Sir John Fastolf', p. 27, and table II corrects *Hopton*, pp. 26–7).

[122] Smith, 'Litigation and Politics', pp. 65–6; 'Sir John Fastolf', pp. 136–140.

[123] Smith, 'Sir John Fastolf', p. 25 and table I.

baptized there in 1396;[124] it is clear that he never reconciled himself to the loss of his birthplace. Although Sir John had paid the purchase price in full, the duke accused him of defaulting on the payments for this and the neighbouring estate of Wickham Skeith, which Sir John had also bought from him: his officers distrained on both properties. This was in 1441–3.

In 1457 the tenants at Cotton were treated leniently over their arrears by Fastolf, and in the following year William Worcester, having been there with John Paston, reported 'there nedyth grete reparacion or the jnner court and the barnys wylle falle doune'.[125] Was this because William's widow, Duchess Alice, as sentimentally attached to her late husband[126] as he seems to have been to Cotton, would not let it go either? For, in 1453–4 she had a farmer there, who was no Suffolk yokel but the loyal and urbane de la Pole retainer Jaquet Blondell esquire. He accounted for nearly £37, £15 of arrears, and his current farm of £22.[127] How long had he been there? How long was he to be there? It looks as though there may have been a competition for Cotton *c.* 1453–*c.* 1457 which has escaped mention in the Paston letters and Fastolf papers. It was for the consequences of this that the tenants there were to be treated leniently in 1457. It was probably the government's attack on Fastolf in 1453 which rendered him vulnerable to attack by its supporters, Alice herself at Cotton and (over the wardship of

[124] H.A. Napier, *Swyncombe and Ewelme* (Oxford, 1858), pp. 64–5. Ought one to assume that the grand church at Cotton, where William was christened, owes its grandeur to the de la Poles of the fourteenth and fifteenth centuries? Money was delivered to William at Cotton in 1416–17: BL Egerton Roll 8776.

[125] Davis II, p. 531; and Smith, 'Sir John Fastolf', pp. 138–9, 'Litigation and Politics', p. 66.

[126] The extravagant tower of Eye church remains as testimony to that sentiment. In 1453–4 Alice gave 20 marks to the churchwardens towards its construction 'pro perpetuo memoriale habendum inter tenentes domine ibidem pro anima . . . [William] . . . ac pro bono statu ducisse et Johanni filii eorundam': BL, Egerton Roll 8779. We might, however, compare her 20 marks with the £40 collected by the churchwardens in one year, 1470, 'chiefly of the franke and devowte hartes of the people': cited in *Hopton*, p. 175, note 71. The lengthening of the chancel at the collegiate church of Wingfield was altogether more her work. So Hawe [Hugh?], mason of Occold's estimate suggests; it (Bodleian Library, Ewelme MSS, A37) deserves to be better known. It is printed without its heading in HMC *Eighth Report*, appendix part I, section III, 627b. I cite the heading and conclusion (incompletely printed in HMC) here:

[heading]

Hawe mason of Ocotte estemed the werkes and stuff undernethe specified at such value as herafter apereth.

[conclusion]

For the whiche werke to be made of my ladies stuff redy caryed to the churche and with all suche othere stuff specified in this bille to be ordeyned redy at my ladies cost the seid Hawe Estemed shulde stonde my lady the werkmanship in 1. markes.

[127] BL, Egerton Roll 8779, the duchess' receiver-general's accounts of 1453–4. For Blondell, a serviceable (and mendacious) Norman, who made his career in England after 1450, see the all too brief passage in D.A.L. Morgan, 'The King's Affinity in the Polity of Yorkist England', *TRHS*, fifth series, 23 (1973), p. 14. We may note that the farm was preferential, being well below £35, the Fastolf valuation.

Thomas Fastolf) her retainer Sir Philip Wentworth.[128] Alice's attack was premature. It was not variable and unreliable politics but that dependable old standby, a disputed deathbed, which was to give her the opportunity to 'recover' Cotton permanently. After Sir John Fastolf's death Cotton was a property which John Paston never looked like keeping. Sir Gilbert Debenham and the Duke of Norfolk were after it as well as Alice. It was Alice who triumphed. In 1469 she was granted Cotton and Wickham Skeith by the Fastolf executors opposed to the Pastons. In 1470 Sir John Paston acknowledged that these two estates (among others) had been lost.[129] In 1475 Cotton was one of the properties whose revenues Alice set aside for the performance of her will.[130] Sir John Fastolf must have turned in his grave: if she had paid anything for it in 1469, that money, such as it was (if it was anything), is unlikely to have done much for the good of his soul. The de la Poles were unworthy winners.[131]

Second, Dedham: this valuable estate had been granted by Richard II to Michael the first de la Pole earl; he had lost it in 1388. Fastolf's purchase had been entirely legitimate; his title was thoroughly sound. The Duke of Suffolk's officers occupied the two manors (Overhall and Netherhall) in 1447. They were not removed until Suffolk had fallen from power early in 1450, and after arbitration by the Archbishop of Canterbury, the Bishop of Norwich, and others. They did much damage before they went; Fastolf

[128] Anthony Smith, 'Sir John Fastolf', p. 155; and below, p. 241.

[129] BL Harleian Charter 43 G 36; Davis I, p. 426; for this story, see a later volume. In 1470–1 Alice seems to have been dismantling the manor house at Cotton ['detectacionis']; the roof tiles were carted to Westhorpe (Westhorpe bailiff's account 1470–1, SRO, 4373/411 (Ph 26487); I owe this reference to the kindness of Dr Steven Gunn). So much for sentiment. I wonder if John Dorman, carpenter of Bury St Edmunds, took 1,200 oak trees from Cotton at this time (Worcester, *Itineraries*, p. 161). If so, they may have been for the repair of the burned roof of the abbey: J.H. Harvey, *English Medieval Architects* (London, 1954), p. 85.

[130] *CCR 1476–85*, p. 29.

[131] There is one earlier and small mystery concerning Cotton. Why was Dame Ela Shardelow's household moved there in 1431–2 (*Hopton*, p. 80)? The fragmentary estate accounts for Cotton at the PRO (SC6/933/16, 17, and SC6/994/24, 25, 26) are helpful only in one respect: Henry Holm, the bailiff, handed over to her nearly £35 in two payments in 1433–4: *sub* arrears, 1434–5 account (SC6/933/16), and 1435–6 account (SC6/994/24). Thus, presumably, she left when the duke sold to Fastolf in 1434. She may have moved to Bury St Edmunds; there she lived at the end of her life and worshipped in St Mary's, where in 1457 she desired to be buried (Samuel Tymms (ed.), *Wills and Inventories from the Registers of the Commissary of Bury St Edmunds and the Archdeacon of Sudbury*, Camden Society, XLIX (London, 1850), p. 13). We know exactly where she worshipped from a remarkable passage in the remarkable will of John Baret of 1463 (*ibid.* p. 15): 'And my body to be beryed by the awter of Seynt Marteyn, namyd also our Ladyes awter, in Seynt Marye chirche at Bury, under the parcloos of the retourne of the candilbeem, be fore the ymage of oure Savyour, and no stoon to be steryd of my grave, but a pet to be maad under the ground sille ther my lady Schardelowe was wont to sitte.' The tomb remains. Cotton may not have had many tenants in the 1430s: Fastolf had 300 or 400 sheep there in 1435–6 (SC6/994/24, dorse) and in the same year created a park (Smith, 'Sir John Fastolf', pp. 34–5).

never got any compensation; that was one of the disappointments of 1451.[132] Moreover, in Duchess Alice's receiver-general's account of 1453–4, against Dedham stands the entry: nothing received 'eo quod Sir John Fastolf miles dictum manerium occupat'.[133] Was the appearance of Dedham in the account solely due to bureaucratic inertia? I think not. The manor had been Ufford property in the fourteenth century: did not William regard it as 'going with' the earldom? Of course, the late date of his occupation suggests opportunism, yet I fancy the duke thought of Dedham as 'his'. Where William had been, Alice sentimentally followed. Hence the 1453–4 entry.

At Dedham Fastolf may never have felt secure; in his last surviving letter to John Paston of July 1459 Dedham is the first item in what is more a memorandum than a letter:[134]

> Hyt ys to remembre my cosyn John Paston that where as he desyred to hafe the namys of the newe feffement of the maner of Dedham that William Geney myght see to grounde such mater uppon as myght be for the seurtee of the seyd maner, I sent a copy of the seyd feffement by John Daunson the last weke.

It is evident that William Jenny and John were worried; Fastolf had also sent them 'the principal evidenses of Dedham . . . wyth the copies of iij relesses of the auncetrie of Poles, and also wyth a copy of the warde late made by the Archebysshop of Caunterbury, the Bysshop of Norwich, Ser John Forscue and William Yelverton, Justices.' From the sequel they had cause to be. Such 'evidenses', rendered fairly useless by the dispute over Fastolf's will, which shifted the struggle into a new battle-zone, were all that the Pastons were to see of Dedham.[135] It seems to have gone quickly; it went to John, Duke of Suffolk, who was William and Alice's son and the new king's brother-in-law.[136] William Jenny and William Yelverton after 1459 had no further reason to be antagonistic to the de la Poles: rather, the duke should have Dedham than their implacable opponent John Paston. They may have been right – so long as he paid the full purchase price. One suspects (one knows) he did no such thing.[137] Thus, dead as well as alive Sir John Falstolf was cheated by the de la Poles.[138]

[132] Smith, 'Litigation and Politics', pp. 10–13 and 16; 'Sir John Fastolf', pp. 126–8.

[133] BL Egerton Roll 8779. [134] Davis II, p. 180.

[135] Davis I, p. 445; II, pp. 576–7.

[136] Davis I, pp. 390–1, would suggest by summer 1461; certainly the duke held it by 1465: p. 134, lines 65–6.

[137] Davis II, pp. 576–7, shows (I think) that Jenny and Yelverton had never been in possession either. It looks as though John de la Pole, or more likely Alice, mounted a successful *coup* at Dedham *c.* 1460.

[138] On Dedham I owe much to Colin Swift, 'Fastolf versus de la Pole: the Dispute over the Manors of Dedham, Hellesdon and Drayton', unpublished BA dissertation, Keele University, 1978, chapter 1.

Third, Drayton and Hellesdon, for, although these two Norfolk estates were not as central to the Fastolf–de la Pole conflict as were Cotton and Dedham, they became in the later 1440s part of it. Also, their later history is the same as that of Cotton and Dedham: Alice was as intent on obtaining them as she was on 'getting back' Cotton and Dedham. In the 1440s her husband had claimed both estates, and at both his officers had caused Fastolf financial losses. Only (Anthony Smith maintains) the duke's fall saved Fastolf from losing Hellesdon, a property to which Suffolk had no title whatsoever; he claimed by descent; the claim was fictitious.[139] An indignant John Paston writing in 1465 was absolutely right:[140]

the Dewk of Suffolk that last dijd wold have bough it of Fastolf, and for he mygth not have it so he claymyd the maner, seying it was on Polis, and for his name was Poole, he claymid to be eyr. He was ansueryid that he com nothing of that stok, and how somever were kyn to the Polis that owth it, it hurt not for it was laufully bowth and sold.

In this instance no case can convincingly be made for William de la Pole believing these manors ought to have been his.[141] He simply coveted them, as Anthony Smith points out, because of 'their high annual values, which Fastolf had enhanced by spending considerable sums on improvements'.[142]

Another reason, I think, was strategic: across the river Yare opposite, and, because of the river's bend, almost between Hellesdon and Drayton, lay the duke's own valuable estate of Costessey.[143] Like Fastolf across the river,

[139] 'Litigation and Politics', p. 12.

[140] Davis I, pp. 132–3. For Fastolf's purchase and Suffolk's counterfeit claim see Smith, 'Sir John Fastolf', pp. 17 and 133–5 and Colin Swift, 'Fastolf versus de la Pole', chapter 2.

[141] The suspicious nature of his acquisition of Geldeston and Stockton has been noted above: chapter 5, pp. 147–8.

[142] 'Litigation and Politics', p. 12. Fastolf's Norwich house was at Hellesdon; he built a brick lodge at Drayton, the shell of which survives: Smith, 'Sir John Fastolf', p. 35. He also built at Earlham, a mile or two to the south, but on a small scale: 10s 4d was paid to a wright for 'part of ye newe hows makyng', 5s 6d to two masons, and there were similar payments for thatching, for plaster, for work on the bakehouse and well, and for building a 30-foot wall by 'ye weye-syde'. These (and other) payments appear in a brief, undated account headed 'these arne ye costys qwiche that John Stucleye hath done at Erlham for my mayster Fastolf be ye comawndement of mayster Thomas Howes', which is NRO, DCN 59/11. I owe my knowledge of this document to the unfailing courtesy of Mr Paul Rutledge.

[143] Liveries of cash in 1442–3 were over £100: NRO, Jerningham 55/2, item 4, account of Richard Wood, bailiff for 1442–3. (In 1453–4, however, only £68 was delivered: BM Egerton Roll 8779.) The four accounts at Staffs. RO (not all of them complete), for 1425–6, 1431–2, 1435–6, and 1450–1 (D641/3, packet 5) show that that £100 was (very roughly) what Costessey's clear annual value ought to have been. Receipts less arrears were about £150, charges were about £50, including, as in 1431–2, a number of fees and annuities like that of Thomas Hoo, the chief steward, of £20. Sir John Clifton's £10 life retainer, however, was charged on the Suffolk estate of Haughley in 1419–20, when he was still an esquire; this, one of the two surviving Haughley estate accounts tells us: Staffs. RO, D641/4, unnumbered bundle 3. Haughley was another profitable property: liveries in 1419–20 amounted to £79, and in 1463–4 (the date of the other account) they were £69.

the duke was making improvements: in 1442–3, for instance, he spent £16 on repairing one of the three mills, the watermill called Grystmill.[144] One of the other mills was a fulling mill. He had more than 1,200 sheep here; their wool was sold in Norwich.[145] The steward of its profitable court in 1442–3 was John Fastolf esquire of Oulton, though he was not paid his fee; he had been superseded in 1450–1 by John Heydon.[146] Perhaps this was a sign of the times; if it was they had changed again: when in November 1451 Robert Wood was finally allowed his 8s 8d expenses for having ridden on the orders of the lord's council to the Tower to consult with the duke in February 1450 and for having attended on him for two weeks at Westhorpe after his release,[147] his master had been dead for eighteen months and John Heydon was fighting a tactical retreat against an all but literally up-in-arms county.

Duchess Alice was one of the first to recover from the débâcle of 1450.[148] But Hellesdon and Drayton do not feature, as Dedham and Cotton do, on her receiver-general's accounts of 1453–4. They had never been the duke's – he had not been in power quite long enough to have filched them from Fastolf. Nevertheless, it is clear, from her determination to have them when the opportunity arose after Sir John's death, that she coveted them as much as her late husband had, even if she may have coveted them for his sake. Her or her son's success in wresting them from the Pastons in the 1460s is part of another story. Sir John Paston struggled hard to get them back; he was still struggling in 1478;[149] there was, however, nothing he or William Wainfleet could do to get the de la Poles out: 'And the Duchesse of Suffolkes men sey

[144] NRO, Jerningham 55/2, item 4. Capital investment continued despite William de la Pole's murder: in July 1451 Richard Dogget, the supervisor, and Andrew Grigges, the receiver-general, consulted with a carpenter of Norwich about the building of a mill at the de la Pole estate of Cawston. They claimed and got their expenses: voucher attached to SRO D641/4, packet 5, Costessey account of 1450–1.

[145] Compare NRO, Jerningham 55/2, item 4 (1442–3) and the 1431–2 account at Stafford. In 1431–2, 92 stones of wool were sold to Richard Baxter of Norwich at 2s a stone; this suggests either that the wool was not up to the usual East Anglian standard (of 3s a stone: *Hopton*, p. 94) or that Richard was getting a bargain. There were only half a dozen cows at Costessey; in 1442–3 these were farmed out for £1. If things had not changed in seventy years then the de la Pole's main dairy farm was at Wingfield; in 1378–9 the first earl had more than fifty cows in his 'dayar' there: Wingfield estate accounts 1378–9, Staffs. RO, D641/4, unnumbered bundle 13. (There were also over 800 sheep.)

[146] NRO, Jerningham 55/2, item 4; Staffs. RO, D641/3, packet 5. John Fastolf had died in 1445: see note 63.

[147] Staffs. RO, D641/3, packet 5, the 1450–1 accounts. These with other Norfolk estate accounts were determined at Norwich in November 1451 by the supervisor, receiver-general, William Harleston, and others of what was now the lady's council. They also discussed other matters, and allowed themselves 40s 6d expenses: despite such a crisis as the disgrace and brutal murder of their lord, unrestrained luxury continued.

[148] Carole A. Metcalfe, 'Alice Chaucer, Duchess of Suffolk *c.* 1404–1475', unpublished BA dissertation, Keele University, 1970, pp. 37–8.

[149] See, for example, Davis I, pp. 509, 510.

that she wull not departe from Heylesdon ner Drayton, she wuld rathere departe from money.'[150] That was in 1472; Alice died in 1475.

Geoffrey Chaucer's grand-daughter had come a long way, far enough to get the better of Sir John Fastolf as well as the Pastons. Her attachment to her third and final husband had been fierce and fiercely successful. She had got from Sir John Fastolf dead more than her husband, the most powerful man in the realm, had got from him alive. Firmness of purpose on her part and the multiplying divisions among those who pretended to be pursuing the wishes and interests of their former patron saw to that. Like a lioness she scattered the vultures and had her pick of the carcase. John Paston never learnt how to cope with her: conciliation not confrontation was the only way to deal with one both so great and so determined. Fastolf had been prepared to compromise with the duke over Dedham,[151] John was too pig-headed, too greedy, or too blinkered to do the same with the dowager duchess in the 1460s. He might have lost one or two manors, but kept one or two; as it was he lost all. Yet, he had long enough in which to learn how to handle her. As far back as the mid-1450s,[152] when he and Fastolf had been fighting her retainer Sir Philip Wentworth over the wardship of Thomas Fastolf, he had experience of her. To this second phase of the Fastolf–Paston relationship we must now turn.

The struggle between Sir John Fastolf and Sir Philip Wentworth over the wardship of Thomas Fastolf, son and heir of John Fastolf of Oulton, itself part of the greater battle between them for the manors of Bradwell and Beighton does not need reciting at length here.[153] Wentworth's claims to those two estates were, as Dr Smith authoritatively states, 'groundless'; Sir John had bought them from Sir Hugh Fastolf, 'a close relative and comrade in arms', Thomas Fastolf's grandfather. Wentworth, courtier and member of the queen's household as well as de la Pole retainer, first got the wardship granted by the crown to his brother-in-law, Robert Constable, in November 1447,[154] though John Fastolf had desired that Sir John should be his son's guardian and that he should use the inheritance for the 'most advayle' of

[150] *Ibid.*, p. 366, lines 12–14. [151] Smith, 'Litigation and Politics', p. 11.

[152] Or 1451? How active was Alice in foiling the attempts of the county community to get justice done on Sir Thomas Tuddenham and John Heydon? The town of Swaffham, for instance, complained of the sixteen-year oppression of their steward and farmer, Thomas Tuddenham, 'a comon extorcioner' (John Paston had helped draft the townspeople's petition: Davis II, pp. 528–30). Swaffham was a de la Pole manor and Tuddenham was still the farmer in 1453–4: BL Egerton Roll 8779.

[153] For what follows see Anthony Smith, 'Litigation and Politics', *passim*, esp. pp. 7–8, 14–17; I quote from it (pp. 1, 3, 8, 15), and from Dr Smith's 'Sir John Fastolf', pp. 204–5, 207.

[154] *CFR 1445–52*, p. 79. One of Constable's mainpernors was John Hopton; for his connection with the Duke of Suffolk and with the Wentworths, see *Hopton*, pp. 103–4, 106–11. The other mainpernor was John Ulveston, for whom see *ibid.*, pp. 198–201.

Thomas' mother and Thomas' sister's marriage.[155] Then in the summer of 1449 Wentworth had two of his de la Pole colleagues, John Ulveston and John Andrew,[156] engineer false inquisitions finding that Beighton and Bradwell were of the inheritance of Thomas Fastolf. 'By traversing the inquests Fastolf prevented the manors from entering Wentworth's hands, but he was obliged to farm them from the crown for three and five years respectively, thereby incurring substantial legal expenses and losses of revenue.' In 1453, with the revival of the government's confidence, this traverse of Fastolf's 'was rejected and the manor [of Bradwell] was awarded to the King'.

Fastolf's vulnerability[157] was, like the government's revival, ended by Henry VI's collapse, the subsequent protectorship of the Duke of York in 1454, and the outcome of the first battle of St Albans in 1455. From early 1454 until the second recovery of the government in the summer of 1456 'politics' favoured Fastolf. He took on his opponents with a new-found vigour, Sir Philip Wentworth among them. In 1454 technical irregularities were discovered in Wentworth's grant of Thomas Fastolf's wardship of 1447 (he had not, for example, paid for it[158]); this enabled its restoration to the Crown and Sir John's purchase of it for himself. Wentworth did not take this lying down: he attempted to abduct Thomas Fastolf. There was competitive court holding and competing farmers. But particularly after St Albans, in which battle Wentworth was reported to have taken a most inglorious part, Fastolf, with access to the victorious Yorkists, was clearly getting the upper hand. Beighton, for instance, was recovered and recovered for good. And in February 1456 Wentworth agreed to arbitration. 'This satisfying progress', as Dr Smith terms it, was halted by Queen Margaret's ousting of the Duke of York later that year. Wentworth may not

[155] John himself had been a royal ward; his marriage had been sold to two London businessmen: *CFR 1413–22*, p. 280.

[156] For John Ulveston see the reference in note 154. For John Andrew see Wedgwood, *Biographies*, p. 11; for his father, see Roger Virgoe, 'The Murder of James Andrew: Suffolk Faction in the 1430s', *Proceedings of the Suffolk Institute of Archaeology and History*, 34, part 4 (1980), pp. 263–8. For his daughters and heirs, see 'The Sulyard Papers', in Daniel Williams (ed.), *England in the Fifteenth Century* (Woodbridge, 1987), pp. 205–6, 208, 210, 214–18.

[157] Smith, 'Sir John Fastolf', pp. 154–5.

[158] Fastolf did not pay either (not for two years anyway); see, for example, Davis II, pp. 160, 161, 162, lines 29–32.

[159] Fastolf sold Thomas Fastolf to Sir Thomas Fulthorpe for 300 marks (or more): Smith, 'Sir John Fastolf', p. 216, citing Davis II, p. 181, Sir John's last written words (that survive) to John Paston. He had been sold by October 1456: Davis II, p. 162, lines 30–2. Thomas Fastolf came of age in 1466: *Cal. IPM*, 6 Edward IV, no. 64, though this seems too late considering he was a mainpernor in 1462 (*CFR 1461–71*, p. 69) and his mother was ready to swear he was over twenty-one in November 1461 (Davis I, p. 272). He had a room and bed at Caister in 1448 – can he have used them? (Hawkyard, 'Some Late Medieval Fortified Manor Houses', pp. 18, 21 and Gairdner III, p. 184). Alasdair Hawkyard cites (p.

have got Thomas Fastolf;[159] on the other hand Fastolf did not get Bradwell back.[160]

What concerns us in this 1454–6 phase of the saga is the impact it had on the relationship of Fastolf and Paston. Dr Anthony Smith tells us:

> Paston's influence on Fastolf grew markedly as the dispute progressed. In May 1455 Fastolf allowed him the freedom to take whatever steps he desired; he guaranteed that he would meet Paston's costs.[161] Paston struggled hard against Wentworth, motivated by the hope of gaining the wardship profits for himself and marrying his daughter to the ward: Fastolf approved of this plan, which was recommended by those of his servants, notably Thomas Howes, who were now deliberately cultivating Paston's friendship.[162]

All that needs to be done is to gloss that passage. Certainly it is substantiated by the dramatic increase in the number of letters Fastolf wrote to John. It is true that they were no longer within walking distance (or a short boat ride) of each other in London; both were, however, in Norfolk, Sir John at Caister, fairly permanently from the summer of 1454, John Paston usually at Norwich,[163] or perhaps sometimes at Gresham or Mautby. John was often in London on business, Fastolf's business mainly,[164] but he no longer lived there. He lived at home: there are *no* letters to him from Margaret between

250) BL Add. Ch. 17258, which 'records a plea by Thomas Fastolf concerning transgressions of his guardian and confirms Scrope's remarks'; but BL Add. Ch. 17258 is nothing of the kind. It is no surprise, given his childhood and adolescent experience (whatever his treatment by Sir John Fastolf), that, long before 1466, Thomas had joined John Paston's opponents (Davis I, p. 248, lines 20–1; II, p. 240), though his mother sought a reconciliation (Davis I, p. 272, lines 52–7). He was married by 1458 (but not by Sir John Fastolf's means) to Ela, daughter of John Wyndham (Davis I, p. 588, lines 14–15; Davis II, pp. 177, 189, 240; H.A. Wyndham, *A Family History 1410–1688. The Wyndhams of Norfolk and Somerset* (London, 1939), pp. 15–16). It is also ironic, as Mandy Kuijvehoven has pointed out ('Sir John Fastolf: the Rights of Wardship', unpublished BA dissertation, Keele University, 1972, p. 54), that Thomas should make a claim to Caister itself (Davis I, p. 334; II, p. 240). He may have pestered the long-suffering William Worcester most: '. . . and Thomas Fastolf, Milicent Fastolf, and manye othyrs that make me noyed and werye': Davis II, p. 586. As the principal estate of Oulton was sold out of the family (as we have seen in note 63, above) no doubt Thomas too was 'noyed and werye'.

[160] Although John Clerke's testimony (Gairdner IV, p. 144) seems to suggest he did, his own will suggests he did not (Gairdner III, p. 154); and Bradwell does not feature in Wainfleet's release to Sir John Paston of January 1468 (Gairdner IV, p. 292). See also John Bocking, 8 October 1456 (Davis II, p. 161, lines 21–3), and Fastolf himself in November 1456 (*ibid.*, pp. 167, 169, lines 39–40).

[161] Davis II, no. 520. [162] 'Sir John Fastolf', pp. 215–16.

[163] From where he wrote Davis I, nos. 49, 50 and 52; and where William Worcester wrote to him, Davis II, nos. 498 and 572; the Countess of Oxford, *ibid.*, nos. 502 and 503; James Gresham, *ibid.*, no. 534; Hugh Fenn, *ibid.*, nos. 543 and 546; and John Bocking, *ibid.*, no. 552.

[164] Davis II, nos. 510 (cf. 509, 511), 538, 569 (cf. 568), 570 were addressed to him at London and others are clearly sent to him there, for example no. 526, postscript. In June 1455, during the post-St Albans excitement, Fastolf urged him to get up to London: *ibid.*, pp. 119, 124 (no. 532, lines 4–7). Thomas Playter's no. 573 is addressed to him at London, 'elles sent to hym to Norwich'. He continued to lodge at the Temple when in town: *ibid.*, nos. 569, 570, 578.

early 1454 and late 1459, nor any from Agnes between July 1453 and December 1461. If he wrote to either, neither of them kept his letters. It is a passage of William Paston's which sets this phase of the Fastolf–Paston association in context; he in London is writing to John in Norfolk in July 1454:[165]

Syr Jon Fastolf recomande hjm to yow &c. He wyll ryde jn-to Norfolke ward as on Trusday, and he wyll dwelle at Caster, and Skrop wyth hym. He saythe ye are the hartyest kynsman and frynd that he knowyt. He wulde have yow at Mawdeby dwellyng.

Even though they were not very far from each other Fastolf wrote to John a good deal, and wrote to him a good deal more than he had done previously because they had drawn closer. Being at Caister he had no need to write to Howes or Bocking, Berney or Worcester, as he had done so frequently in 1450–1 from London.[166] 1454–6 is 1450–1 in reverse; then he wrote two dozen letters to Howes and the others, but only once to Paston, now he writes more than two dozen letters to John[167] and not once to Howes and the rest. John (of course) wrote to him,[168] as well as talked with him.[169] There were many tactical conferences, as, given the number of issues of law Fastolf was involved in, there had to be. These usually included William Jenny and William Yelverton, Fastolf's other legal advisers. The Wentworth affair was not Fastolf's sole matter of business, John Paston was not his only lawyer. William Worcester in a breathless, irate letter, spoke of his own and Fastolf's ignorance of the law,[170]

I bare nevere my maister purs, ne condyt nevere chargeable mater alone of hys yn lawe, for my discrecion me counyng know not whate such materes menyth. I knew nevere of oyer ne terminer, ne rad nevere patent before, ne my maister knew nevere the condyt of such thynges; and when he wrote of hys grevonse to hys frendys he commaunded no man to be endyted for he wyst not whate belonged to such thynges, ne the parson [Thomas Howes] neyther, but remitted it to hys councell lerned.

William's anger or anguish, I think, makes him a truth-teller: he, Howes, and their master were legal innocents very much in the hands of Paston, Jenny, and Yelverton.[171]

[165] Davis I, p. 154.

[166] Three times in four days to Thomas Howes in December 1450, for instance (Gairdner II, nos. 158, 160, 161).

[167] Sometimes almost bombarding him with batches of letters: as in January–February 1456 (Davis II, nos. 538, 539, 541, 542), and June–July 1455 (*ibid.*, nos. 525, 526, 530), while in June 1456 he wrote three times in six days, twice on one day, 24 June (*ibid.*, nos. 553, 554, 555), and in November 1456 three times in a week (*ibid.*, nos. 568, 569, 570).

[168] See, for example, *ibid.*, pp. 102–3, 136, lines 21–2. And to Bocking, *ibid.*, p. 141.

[169] See, for instance, *ibid.*, p. 111, lines 6–9; p. 121, lines 6–7, 12; p. 123, lines 25–6; p. 141, lines 31–3.

[170] *Ibid.*, p. 163.

[171] William especially, as at Caister he was far from what property he had: *ibid.*, p. 134, lines 27–34.

Keeping Thomas Howes out of prison was one of the other pieces of business which occupied them.[172] *Them* we stress. William Jenny and William Yelverton were as important as John Paston in determining the battle plans of Fastolf's cases.[173]

At reverence of God [wrote Worcester to Paston[174]], beyth assone as ye may wyth my maister, to ease hys spyryttes. He questioneth and desputyth wyth hys servantes here, and wolle not be aunsuerd ne satisfyed som tyme but after hys wylfullnesse, for hyt suffysyth not our simple wyttes to appease hys soule. But when he spekyth wyth Maister Yelverton, yow, or wyth William Geney, and such othyrs as be autorised yn the law and wyth haboundaunce of godes, he ys content and haldeth hym pleased wyth your aunsuers and mocions, as reson ys that he be. So wold Jesus one of yow iij or som such othyr yn your stede mygt hang at hys gyrdyll dayly to aunsuer hys materes.

Even if John Paston did oversee the Yorkshire West Riding manors, Fastolf retained the lawyer Henry Sotell there.[175] Sir John Fastolf did not (in this phase) crumble into a dodderer who was in Paston's pocket. Very far from it.

This is by no means to deny all that Paston did. He was doing so much one wonders whether he was not the used – as he was certainly not the user. He was, one is tempted to think, a dogsbody, save that he kept his dignity, as the letters of others who sought to make use of him show. Dame Alice Ogard, for instance, though she was asking a favour, wrote prettily,[176]

And, jentyll cosyn, have me excusid thowh I wryte thus brefly and homly to yow, for in trouth I do it of a syngulere trust and affeccion the wheche I have in yow, consideryng the goode name and fame of trouth, wysdom, and goode conducte the which I here of you.

And Thomas, Lord Scales, Fastolf's most committed opponent, wrote equally gracefully to his 'Right trusty and enterly welbeloved frend', thanking John for the 'grete gentilnesse and benyvolence' he had shown to Brian Stapleton.[177] It is a pity we have no letters of John's to show how he stood the strain. Evidently his letters were not filed away at Caister as Fastolf's of 1450–1 had been. Fastolf undoubtedly valued him for his connection with the Duke of Norfolk – his continuing connection; John here was (as they say) a channel of communication. In a memorandum probably of August 1454, which he sent as a letter to Thomas Green, Fastolf recorded, 'Item upon the motion of my cousin Paston my lord Norfolk may take upon him the suit of the attaint and to maintain the sewers as his men at the said

[172] *Ibid.*, pp. 102–3, 106, 107, 111, 112, 121; Gairdner II, p. 326; III, pp. 6–7, 20–21.
[173] Davis II, pp. 106, 107, 111, 129–30. [174] *Ibid.*, pp. 156–7.
[175] *Ibid.*, pp. 93, 134, 166, cf. Davis I, pp. 85–6. But as Fastolf only 'officially' appointed Paston supervisor of the Yorkshire estates on 1 May 1458, presumably in anticipation of his visit (NRO, Phillipps MS 612/2), was this his only trip North? Paston's list of expenses of 1457–8 covers (and dates) the visit of May 1458: Add. Ch. 17246 (see Gairdner III, p. 135, and Davis I, p. 85, headnote). For Henry Sotell, see *Hopton*, pp. 183–6. [176] Davis II, p. 139.
[177] *Ibid.*, pp. 158, 159.

Fastolf's costs.'[178] Possibly, the inducement was a loan: 'as to the 1,000 marks', Fastolf went on, 'I will that he [the duke] have it for 2 year day if be will none otherwise etc. with sufficient surety.' Certainly the duke borrowed £100 from Fastolf.[179] Paston's association with the Earl of Oxford Fastolf may also have valued,[180] but there is no evidence that he cultivated the earl's patronage (at this stage) as he did the duke's. Oxford was, after all, not as anti-Lancastrian as he had been anti-Suffolk; he was certainly not as 'Yorkist' as (at this stage) Norfolk was.

Still, we do not need to invent reasons: Fastolf valued Paston for himself. John was an efficient perhaps even a tireless (or relentless), man of business. He was also a kinsman. And there is more than this. The tone of Fastolf's compliments is not formal courtesy. Sometimes he is apologetic: 'And I pray yow foryeve me that I noye yow somech wyth my materys.'[181] Sometimes unapologetic: 'And all though my writyngges put yow many tymes to gret labour and besynesses I pray yow to take it that I do it for the synguler affiaunce and feythfull trust un-to yow.'[182] Once (at least) he is fulsome:

Worshipfull ser and right trusty cosyn, I comaunde me to yow and hertilie thank yowe as I can or maye for the gret labour and peyn that ye daylie take upon yow for the goode spede and avauncement of my chargeable maters, as I knowe and fele right wele. And I fele wele that I was never holde so moche to any kynnesman of myn as I am to yowe, which tendreth so moche my worship and my profyte.[183]

Mainly he is brisk and affectionate. It may not seem the right word, but William Worcester used it,

Worshypfull ser, aftyr dew recommendacion please your gode maistershyp to wete that where-as my maister wrytith to yow so homelye of so manye materes to yow of hys, to be remembred unto hys councell lerned by mene of yow and of hys frends and servaunts there, y pray yow and requyre yow not to wyte it me that I am the causer of it that my seyd maister noyeth yow with so manye materes; for, be God, hym-sylf remembryth the moste part of hem, albe it the particular rehersell of tho materes be fressher yn my remembraunce than yn hys. And, ser, yn trouth he boldyth hym to wryte to yow for the grete lofe and singuler affeccion he hath yn yow before all othyr yn hys causes spedyng, and that ye wille moste tendyrlye of ony othyr remembre hys servauntes aswell as othyrs to whom belongyth to spede thos materes.[184]

[178] Magdalen College, Oxford, FP 102/33. This related to the Thomas Howes affair (see note 172), especially Thomas Howes' postscript to his letter of 2 September (1454): Davis II, p. 103. But William Jenny (we should note) was also expected to speak to the duke: Davis II, p. 107, lines 8–12. Fastolf's unprecedentedly obsequious letter to the duke of 2 April 1455 is also relevant: Gairdner III, no. 278.

[179] Gairdner III, p. 7.

[180] Davis II, p. 102, lines 1–3.

[181] *Ibid.*, p. 190, line 17.

[182] *Ibid.*, p. 141, lines 26–8.

[183] *Ibid.*, p. 128 (no. 536).

[184] *Ibid.*, pp. 133–4. John Paston as 'go-between' is neatly shown in a passage of a letter of Fastolf's to Nicholas Molyneux (BL Add. MS 39848, f. 32) omitted from the abstract in Gairdner III, no. 304: 'And I pray yow comyun wyth my cosyn Paston of thys mater that he may the better enforme me of your laboure at hys comyng yn to thys contrée.'

It is a revealing passage. Dr Smith is right: Paston's commitment over the wardship of Thomas Fastolf and Sir John's awareness of it was a turning point.

That is clear from Fastolf's first letter to John in this sequence, in November 1454.

And where as I have understand late by certeyn well-willers to you warde whych have meoved me that yn case the seyd warde myght be had, that ye desyre an alliaunce shulde take atwyx a doughter of yourys and the seyd waard, of whych mocion y was ryght glad to hyre off and wylle be ryght well-wyllyng and helpyng that your blode and myne myght increse yn alliaunce . . . I ensure you ye and y shuld appoynt and accorde yn such wyse as ye shuld hald you ryght well plesed both for the encresyng of your lynage and also of myne . . . And yff y had knowe rathyr of your entent it shuld hafe cost me more of my gode before thys, to hafe com to a gode conclusion, whych y promysse yhyt shall bee, and the mater take, by the fayth of my bodye.[185]

It was Thomas Howes who had told him, as Thomas explained to John in a letter written two days after Fastolf's,

I meovyd to hym upon myn hed that encas be the child were wyse that thanne it were a good maryage be-twen my wyffe youre doutir and hym; and, ser, my maistyr was glad when he herd that moyan, consertheryng that youre doutyr is descendyd of hym be the modyr syde.[186]

The deepening of trust that the older man had in the younger (seventy-four to thirty-three) is displayed the following February in that famous letter in which Sir John demanded a written report of a dinner John had attended in Norwich where 'skornefull' and I suspect tipsy 'language' was bandied about Sir John's meanness. Names he particularly required. There is no hint that Fastolf thought Paston might have been among the culprits.[187]

By May 1455, as Dr Smith has told us,[188] John was given *carte blanche* in the matter of the wardship. This developed, rather than developing friendship, unequal though it may have been (that is, flowing more strongly in one direction than another), is evident in Fastolf's buoyant letters of June and July 1455.[189] For example: 'Hyt ys hard to put a man ys trust yn one man to labour, for the moo the better; for your presence shall be worth half a doseyn of the best lerned men that shall be there yn thys cause.'[190] Even his criticism is tentative and muted: 'And therefor, savyng your better avice, I had lever ye were at London a weke the rather and tymelyer than a weke to late. I pray yow doth somwhate aftyr my councell as I wolle do by youres.'[191]

[185] Davis II, p. 105.

[186] *Ibid.*, p. 106. We dare not say he had 'a soft spot' for Margaret, but he did give her a 'dormant [beam]': Davis I, p. 253, lines 1–6.

[187] Davis II, pp. 109–10.

[188] See above, p. 243, and Davis II, no. 520.

[189] Davis II, nos. 523, 525, 526, 530.

[190] *Ibid.*, p. 118.

[191] *Ibid.*, p. 124, no. 531, lines 4–7.

Yet we must be careful and distinguish: John Paston by summer 1455 was Fastolf's most influential councillor; there was, however, no dependency. I have said Fastolf was brisk: vigorous is another word one might use of him in 1455 and 1456, whether he is thinking of a canal between Caister and Mautby,[192] or continuing to send advice and give directions in the Wentworth affair, getting partial repayment of loans made to the Duke of Suffolk,[193] or planning the college at Caister.[194] He remains authoritative. On the one hand, Henry Windsor can say, though we must remember he is seeking to flatter, 'My maister can do no thing the which shall comme in opon audience at thise deise but it shalbe called your dede';[195] on the other (as we have just seen), William Worcester testifies to Fastolf's sound memory, 'for, be God, hym-sylf remembryth the moste party of hem [so manye materes]'. There was no loss of grip: the two letters he dictated to William on 24 June 1456 witness to that;[196] or the three he dictated to John Bocking the following November.[197] Once, and most untypically, he felt sorry for himself;[198] six days later after the de la Poleites, Sir Miles Stapleton, Simon Brayles, Andrew Grigges, and Edward Grimston,[199] had visited him

[192] *Ibid.*, p. 141. [193] *Ibid.*, pp. 150, 151–2.

[194] *Ibid.*, pp. 167–8, 168–9; cf. Gairdner III, no. 340 [195] Davis II, p. 145, lines 35–6.

[196] *Ibid.*, nos. 554, 555. [197] *Ibid.*, nos. 568, 569, 570. [198] *Ibid.*, no. 553, esp. lines 7–10.

[199] They were all either officers of the dowager duchess or 'followers' of hers. Sir Miles Stapleton and his de la Pole wife we have encountered in chapter 2; Simon Brayles was her chaplain and household treasurer (BL Egerton Roll 8779); Andrew Grigges was her receiver-general (as Fastolf said: Davis II, p. 150, line 3; cf Egerton Roll 8779); for Edward Grimston, see M.J. Constantine, 'Edward Grimston', unpublished BA dissertation, Keele University, 1973. Grimston is interesting because we know what he looked like; he was painted by Petrus Christus, probably at Brussels in 1446, and may be looked at in the National Gallery, London. His first wife, Alice, was close to the duchess, possibly her companion in 1453–4 (BL Egerton Roll 8779: William Harleston reimbursed her £14 she had spent on behalf of the duchess). Apparently Alice had been a gentlewoman of Queen Margaret; she died and was buried at Eye in 1456: A.W. Franks, 'Notes on Edward Grimston, Esq., Ambassador to the Duchess of Burgundy', *Archaeologia* 40, part II, p. 465. I wonder if she was French. Yet 'de la Poleites' is a misleading appellation: it means something to us because we have to simplify, it is a term which, I am sure, would have puzzled contemporaries. The social–political role of these gentlemen was too dense, and too complex for such clumsy definitions. Take the feoffees of John Timperley, squire, when he made a settlement of Hintlesham, Suffolk, in March 1454 (*CPR 1452–61*, p. 150). Undoubtedly a 'Mowbrayite', Timperley was friendly to John Paston over the Gresham affair in 1451 (Davis II, pp. 71, 73–4), unfriendly in the business of the Thomas Fastolf wardship in 1454 (*ibid.*, p. 94), and still in 1461 over Cotton (*ibid.*, pp. 248–9). It would be tempting to regard 1452–3, when Paston and others were opposed to the outrages perpetrated by thuggish followers of the Duke of Norfolk, as a turning point: 'Itt is to remembre undere hos rule that the gode lord [Norfolk] is at this day, and whiche be of his new cownseyll. Item, that Debenham, Lee, Tymperlé, and his old cownseyl and attendans, as well as the gode ladijs servawntys, be avoydyd, and Tymperlé of malys, apelyd of treson' (Davis I, p. 72). Or, seeing that his mother was a Wentworth, we might want to make that a sufficient cause of his change: yet John Paston is among Timperley's feoffees of March 1454. Among John's fellow-feoffees it is not at all surprising to discover Richard Southwell, Gilbert Debenham, John Jermy, and John Wyndham (except to find John Paston in their company); but it is something of a shock that Sir Thomas Tuddenham and Reginald Rous

at Caister he was as spirited as ever: full of news and complaints of old grievances.[200] Once, Worcester reports him different:

> And my maister wille comyn wyth yow for the moyens of a chauntuarye to be founded of the place ye wote off. Y seyd hym such chargeable maters wold be doo betyme to know the certeyntee. And a gret lak ys yn hym, he taryeth so long to put all thynges off charge yn a sure wey; hyt ys for lak of sad councell to meove hym.[201]

Significantly, Fastolf's uncharacteristic temporizing is on a matter which is to do with death, his own death: the prospect of departure from this world must have come hard to so active a man. Worcester's letter is not dated; 'perhaps 1456' is all Davis allows himself; a later date is not absolutely ruled out. All in all, there is no sign of a decline, no indication of narrowed interests, atrophied faculties. Powerful as Paston had become, and (given the work he did) deservedly so, his influence was not *over* his patron, only with him, with a man who knew his affairs and directed their conduct.

If there was a falling away it may have been among Fastolf's officers. They were the ones who felt the pressure. On 12 October 'perhaps 1456', William Worcester in a not always comprehensible outburst expressed some of the burden of being Fastolf's secretary. As good natured as he was mercurial, at the close of the letter he wrote 'I am eased of my spyrytes now that I hafe expressed my leude menyng because of my felow Barker, as of such othyr berkers ayenst the mone, to make wysemen laugh at her folye', and at the end of the postscript 'Foryefe me of my leude lettre wrytyng, and I pray you laugh at it.'[202] It probably was a storm in a teacup. As had been Thomas Howes' demonstration of lost temper on 6 October 'probably 1456'. This, at first sight, may seem more important, as Howes was outraged at his ill-usage by Fastolf.[203] So incensed was he that, for the only time we are aware of, he picked up a pen himself and his hand shaking began abruptly, 'Reverent ser &c.'[204] Yet at the end, having closed with 'Wretyn brevely at

are of their number. For Rous see above, chapter 2, note 91. Wedgwood (*Biographies*, p. 727) has him as a 'Norfolk servant'; he was misled by Gairdner (II, no. 37) misreading Norfolk for Suffolk in Davis II, p. 518. For Debenham and Timperley see Wedgwood, *Biographies*, pp. 264–5, 856–7; for John Jermy the elder see *Hopton*, pp. 249–50. Hintlesham had been purchased by Sir John Fortescue in 1448 for 1,000 marks; he sold it to John Timperley in 1454 (for how much?): G.H. Ryan and Lilian J. Redstone, *Tymperley of Hintlesham: a Study of a Suffolk Family* (London, 1931), p. 117.

200 See, for the latter, the postscript of Davis II, no. 555: he was harking back twenty years to the wrong Suffolk had done him over the wardship of Anne Harling.

201 *Ibid.*, p. 155.

202 *Ibid.*, pp. 163, 164. His ending is the same as that of his earlier letter about how ill-paid he was: 'Foryefe me I wryte to make yow laugh': *ibid.*, p. 102. But there was apparently no reconciliation with William Barker: *ibid.*, p. 355, lines 19–22; p. 356, lines 48–9.

203 Fastolf seems (temporarily at least) to have gone back on earlier promises to support Howes, even financially: see above pp. 228–9 and Davis II, p. 107, lines 22–5.

204 Davis II, no. 564: 'the hand is surprisingly crude' remarks Davis, as the notes demonstrate. Contrast the form of his address to John Paston in nos. 507, 510, 511, and 516. No. 564 was the last letter (we know of) that he wrote to John Paston before Fastolf's death, though he had never written to him much.

Horseydown',[205] he added a postscript: 'I shal nowt leve this mater to serve the most enemy that he hat in Inglond. I wele non of his good. I have lever other men go to the dvele for his good than I, &c.' He was almost incoherent, but can we not detect two things? One, that he would not leave his master; two, that who was to get Fastolf's property after his death was discussed (naturally enough) by his servants. Howes was too heated to be circumspect; he discloses what was at the back of all their minds: how to behave in these latter days in order to get something for the years of ill-rewarded, ill-regarded service. We may ponder why he stuck.

One other thing is clearer. Thomas Howes, John Paston, and William Worcester did stick: together. Howes was not (and Fastolf I am sure knew it) the most efficient of his officers;[206] Howes too by the mid-1450s may have realized his own limitations.[207] He grew closer to Paston in these years. William Worcester (as he told John Berney just after Fastolf's death, not one suspects without a certain enlarging of his own role in order to enhance it) was the one who had made them Fastolf's first team: 'Yff I caused Maister Paston and myne oncle the parson that they hafe such autorité as they hafe, they ought be the fayner and desyrouse of the contynaunce of myne autorité, that ys as grete as theyrs or gretter.'[208] William is referring to the authority they had been given (or had taken) in Sir John's nuncupative will, but it is clear from the way he speaks of his own authority that he is thinking generally of Fastolf's last years. This trio was the old man's support. How they, and especially John Paston, responded in 1457–9 to Hugh Fenn's appeal we must try to discover,

> Now ser, for Goddis sake, as I have meved you a-fore, help to sette my maister [Fastolf] in a worchepful dyreccion of his maters to his honour, his profyte, and his hertis ease, the whuch so doon he shall have the better leysour to dysspose hym-self godly and be-sette his londe and his goodys to the plesour of God and the wele of his sowle, that all men may sey he deyeth a wyse man and a worchepfull.[209]

Thus, we arrive at the third and last phase – these 'phases' are artificial, of course. It may be that the trio of Paston, Howes, and Worcester as an inner

[205] Presumably he had ridden away from Caister in some heat. If Horseydown is (or was) Horsey, he rode ten or so miles north of Caister before stopping to compose himself sufficiently to write.

[206] See above, pp. 228–9. Cf. William Worcester's passage in *ibid.*, p. 163, lines 34–7.

[207] Richard Calle reported to John Paston 'probably' in 1455: 'He seithe as for any thyng that he hathe do wythoute your advice it schal no more be soo, &c.': *ibid.*, no. 519, lines 15–6.

[208] *Ibid.*, p. 539, lines 9–11. Cf. lines 42–6, and lines 27–8 of Worcester's letter copied by Richard Calle for Margaret to send to John Paston (*ibid.*, no. 604); and his 'I enformyd yow for trouth and as I will prefe, that I was the principall doer and cause that both Majster Paston and myne oncle came fyrst yn the testament viij yeer goon, to a gode entent': *ibid.*, p. 553, lines 15–17. Davis II no. 604 might also be to John Berney if 'as I tolde you' means as I wrote to you.

[209] *Ibid.*, p. 137.

group upon whom Fastolf had come to rely is also more invention than fact. We have more of them than we have of John Bocking, or William Barker, or William Jenny or (a new name in these last days) Thomas Playter,[210] who by the summer of 1459 if he was not 'Fastolf's chief legal adviser' had become his principal legal agent.[211] John Berney, it is true, does not feature after 1454, but what about those arch-enemies Friar Brackley and John Russe? Letters are slippery documents: correspondents too often tell each other what they want to hear. Besides, William Worcester's recollections of before 5 November 1459 were those of a disillusioned as well as a disappointed man. William is to be trusted, yet a natural self-esteem makes all of us exaggerate, to ourselves but especially to others, our role in stirring times past. Yet, of the twenty-eight letters of Sir John Fastolf in Davis' edition written between November 1454 and July 1459 John Bocking wrote five, William Barker three, John Russe one, William Worcester eleven. Who, one wonders, wrote the unidentified hands of the other eight? Do such figures have any meaning, other than to tell us (what we already knew) that William Worcester was Sir John's principal secretary? Let us stick to that: what we know.

In this last phase William Jenny continued to be important. In April 1459, when Fastolf sent his signet to Paston and Howes at London to seal letters to 'such lordes and other my frendes as yowr wisedomes can and shall seme best and most profitable to myn use', it was 'my right trusty frend William Jenneye' who was to be associated with them in the task.[212] In July and August Jenny and Paston were again in harness and still in harmony.[213] The 'newe feffement of the maner of Dedham', with which they were concerned, had occupied them in 1457. William Worcester had to ride

[210] Thomas Playter seems to make his first appearance at the close of Friar Brackley's letter to John Paston of 29 June, 'probably 1456' (*ibid.*, no. 557). It is an interesting passage. I use Mary Harris' translation: 'Commend me to my master William Paston, your brother, and to Thomas Playter my kinsman, telling him that he may win William Jenny's favour, since Sampson, the son and heir of John Sampson, the former husband of Katherine Fastolf has died at Oulton, and there are two widows – the greater and the lesser, elder and younger. Let him choose the one who pleases him better . . . Master Thomas Howes [he added in a postscript] your very good friend most cordially commends himself to you. Also, William Worcester commends himself to you with all his heart.' There is no doubt where Brackley stood: perhaps the trio was really a quartet, or, bearing in mind Thomas Playter, a quintet. William Jenny chose neither of these ladies, but later (after 1475) he did marry Eleanor, daughter of John Sampson and Katherine Fastolf, widow of Robert Inglose: see note 71, above.

[211] I am quoting 'The Expenses of Thomas Playter of Sotterley, 1459–60', *Proceedings of the Suffolk Institute of Archaeology and History*, 35 (1981), p. 41. This seems an odd statement, then as now. What about John Paston? 'Principal legal agent' is intended to put Thomas at the lowest level of a three-tier operational structure for legal combat: command (Fastolf); technical policy-making (Paston); mechanic, signaller, runner, stretcher-bearer, infantry man (Playter).' [212] Davis II, p. 178.

[213] *Ibid.*, p. 180, lines 1–5; *ibid.*, no. 580.

first into Gloucestershire and then to Coventry, where they were with the king, in pursuit of Ralph, Lord Sudeley, and John, Lord Beauchamp of Powick, feoffees of Fastolf, and again from London to York to see another, Nicholas Girlington;[214] Sudeley and Girlington were bowing out as feoffees, Beauchamp (with Paston and the chancellor, William Wainfleet) was stepping in. Licence for enfeoffment was granted on 18 October 1457.[215] They had been efficient: Worcester had told John only on the previous 20 April of the need for a new enfeoffment,

> seth my maister ys fully yn wille to renew hys feffment, that it may be do be-tyme by the surest grounde that may be had, for be it nevyr so suerly doon hyt shall be thought lytille ynowgh to kepe hys lond owte of trouble; and spare for no councell ne cost to make it sure, for a peny yn seson spent wille safe a pounde. I comyned wyth my brothere Spyrlyng, whych seyth he will do hys attendaunce and to kepe it rygt close of the namys. Taryeng drawyth parell.[216]

Efficiency, energy: there was no lack of this, it seems to me, in these last years.

John Paston was kept busy: successfully, according to William Worcester, at London in March 1458,[217] less than successfully, according to his own report, in Yorkshire in May, 'but we shall do the best that we may'. The 'we' was the trio: Paston, Howes, Worcester.[218] The manor of Bentley had not been well-managed – 'yn the shrewdest reule and governaunce that ever I sawe', said Paston, who went on to spell out the details. Is this mismanagement at a distance significant? In conjunction with two oft-quoted letters of Worcester's to Paston of a year previously[219] it has been seen so: evidence of Fastolf losing what had once been so firm a grip on the administration of his estates, the running of his household, and his officers' conduct of his financial affairs. It had been Paston himself who had raised with the two other members of the trio the need for Fastolf's income and expenditure to be clearly set out,

> And ye meved a gode matere to the parson and to me at your last beyng at Castre, that my maister shuld be lerned whate hys housold standyth uppon yerlye seth he kept it holye to-ghedre at one place, and that don, then to see by the revenues of hys yeerly lyfelode whate may be leyd and assigned owte for that cause to meynteyn hys seyd housold, and over that whate may be assigned to beere owte hys plees and also to pay for hys foreyn charges and dedes of almes to a convenyent somme.

[214] Magdalen College, FP 72, a list of William Worcester's expenses, m.7.

[215] *CPR 1452–61*, p. 386.

[216] Davis II, p. 170. If Worcester is anticipating the 'great enfeoffments of May 1457' (see *ibid.*, pp. 558–9, the phrase is Anthony Smith's), then surely his letter is more likely to be dated 1456 than 1457. Dedham was separately enfeoffed.

[217] *Ibid.*, no. 884, lines 24–7.

[218] William wrote the report: Davis I, p. 86, lines 12–13.

[219] Davis II, nos. 571, 572.

Particularly, the auditing of Fastolf's household accounts had not been properly done since he had come to live at Caister: the fault lay with his officers not with their master,

> And seth the grettist ordynarye charge most be hys housold kepyng, hyt were moste exspedyent that ye wold note well to remembre specially my maister to do hys audytours cast and make rollys of hys accomptes concernyng the seyd housold seth he came yn-to Norffolk thys ij yere and half, whych was nevyr so long to doo thys xl wyntere as ys now. And it ys pytee that hys audyt ys none othyrwyse yn that entended. Ye must nedys, yff ye wille my maister know how hyt stand wyth hym yerly of hys charges, that thys be do fyrst, as it was allwey acustomed. My maister wille acord it to be don, but it ys foryete throwgh negligence of men yoven to sensualité, as Thomas Upton, me, and othyrs. My maister can not know whethere he go backward or forward till thys be doon.

So Worcester wrote on 20 April 1457.[220]

The matter weighed on him. On 1 May he wrote again,[221] a letter (apart from its political postscript) entirely on this theme,

> Shypdam and Spyrlyng ought to labour fyrst of onye thyng that belongyth to audyt the accomptes of the resseyt and despenses of my maister housold at Castre seth he come last in-to Norffolk, whych aswell for the provisyons that ys had of hys oune growyng as in money payd. For till the seyd accomptes be made ordynatlye, whych be of a grete charge yeerlye, wete ye for certeyn my maister shall nevere know whethyr he goth bakward or forward.

So far as household budgeting was concerned it had been better done in those now distant years when Fastolf had been away and his household divided between one place and another,

> And seth it hath be kept ordynarylye seth my maister began to kepe house thys l yeere almoste, and when he hath be absent beyond see, &c., hyt ought be more redelyere be doon and made upp whyle he ys present, and well the rathere that hys housold menye were not so hole to-ghedre thys xl yere as be now at Castre.

But it was not only at Caister that things required reformation. Hellesdon could be more efficiently managed, Fastolf's shipping and commercial interests were unprofitable, and maintaining a house at Yarmouth was too expensive. He was no longer putting money by as he had been wont to do,

> He shall never be monyed, ne be aunsuerd clerly of hys revenues yeerly, but those thynges abofeseyd be amended be-tyme. Yn Lowys days xij yeere to-ghedre my maister was wont to ley upp money yeerly at London and Castre, and now the contrarye.

For the moment this was to be only between the two (or three) of them, but Paston was to discover what others thought and he was, William urged, to endeavour to get Fastolf (and the others) to do something:

[220] *Ibid.*, no. 571, p. 170. [221] *Ibid.*, no. 572, pp. 171–2.

I dar not be know of thys bille, but ye may question and vele of the disposicion of thys maters of otheres, and then undrestand yff I wryt justlye or no; and ye, as of your mocion for my maister worshyp and proffyt, exortyng hym, the stuard, Shypdam, and Spyrlyng to take a labour and a peyn that thys be reformed . . . I pray yow and require yow kepe thys mater to your-sylf.

The conspiratorial air is to be noted. The reasons for it are obvious. This was a delicate issue to bring out into the open, the criticism of one group of officers by another. If such a matter was to be raised and was to encounter the minimum resentment it had best be done by someone less on the inside: hence Paston, the most inside outsider. That is significant: Fastolf listened to (might listen to) Paston, acted on (might act on) his advice.[222] But this we know already.

More important, is Fastolf, that tough old nut, cracking? Are his affairs actually in such a bad state? Had he lost his once fearsome drive, capacity for decisions, initiative? Undoubtedly Worcester thought that Fastolf's affairs had previously been better managed than they were being managed in 1457. He, if anyone, ought to have, could have, might have, known. And we trust him, even though he was an emotional man, liable to latch onto an idea and get carried away with it. The estate account of Loundhall in Saxthorpe for 1457–8 corroborates William's testimony.[223] It is unfinished: charge and discharge are not summed, save in a second hand in the margin; in the same or another hand there are additions, for example, of the omitted bailiff's wages and of cash delivered to Thomas Howes at the audit. As, however, there is (also in that hand) a valor note at the foot, all was not completely chaotic. We have to accept, I think, that those who were responsible for the management of Fastolf's estate, household, and business affairs were failing in that responsibility. Things had not fallen apart, but these men were not being kept up to the mark. Which brings us back to Sir John himself.

His last letters do not show him as anything other than the Fastolf we have always observed. Only once in the 1450s have we seen him out of sorts,[224] and although illness supposedly kept him from meetings of the Order of the Garter after 1452,[225] there is little or no sign of illness in his letters or the letters of others. Indeed, on one occasion he is caught laughing[226] – a precious moment (to set against others) – and on 24 June 1459 William Barker reported him 'as freshe as ever he was this ij yere, thanked be God'.[227] Which takes us back to William Worcester, who said

[222] Cf. Henry Windsor, 27 August, 'probably' 1458: *ibid.*, p. 175, lines 33–41.
[223] NRO, NRS 19687. Davis I, p. 273, lines 21–4, also indicates slovenliness, and see also chapter 2, note 16 for further, extended comment. [224] Davis II, no. 553, lines 7–10.
[225] Anthony Smith, 'Sir John Fastolf', p. 115. [226] Davis II, no. 581, lines 34–6.
[227] *Ibid.*, p. 179, line 17.

Fastolf's last illness began on 1 June 1459.[228] There is a riddle here which must remain: Fastolf's letters are not in the least feverish. In October 1457 he wrote earnestly on Thomas Howes' behalf to those who were to sit in judgement in the suit John Andrew had brought against him. To one of them, his old friend William Yelverton, he expressed himself eloquently: 'it were a full blessed deede that it myght be reformed in your dayes by your autorite and grete descrecion and that ye myght be the fadyr of the chastysyng of the seyd periure, for ye coude never do a more meritable deede'.[229] Eloquence returns us to William Worcester again: he wrote that letter.

The possibility that the continuing vigour of these last letters is the secretary's, not Fastolf's, has to be voiced,[230] if only to be dismissed: Fastolf's last letters are like almost all his earlier ones, whoever is the scribe. Thus, in April 1459 he sends his signet to London for Howes, Paston, and Jenny to seal letters with because they will know which lords are in London to be written or spoken to: he is too busy (not too feeble).[231] Take care, he says, to keep copies and that Howes brings them home with him. In July 1459 his last letter is one of businesslike memoranda, barely a letter at all. One can observe him ticking off the items which John Paston needs to be reminded of: Dedham (three distinct matters); the Southwark beerhouses (with a reference to a release, 'Trinité terme A° xxix r. r. Hvj'); the patent for Ralph Alygh's fee ('I have do wrote it and enseled it and sendyth it now upp to London to yow'); the iniquities of Laurence Donne at Southwark; Richard Philip, 'grocer uppon London Bryg', Donne's 'grettist mayntenour'; some affair of Stephen Scrope's; a postscript on the money owing from Lady Fulthorp for the wardship of Thomas Fastolf; 'And that it please yow thynk uppon all othyr maters that I can not wryte esylye now.'[232] There the authentic voice ceases. Until that moment, 3 July 1459, it has continued strong. Only in the very last phase, as Fastolf sinks, do we hear it no longer. Not until then was Paston urged to come to Caister. It would not be a brief visit, wrote Friar Brackley; and bring William Yelverton with you if you can, 'Ryhte reverent mayster, &c., as sone as ye may goodly comyth to Castre, and Yelverton wyth yow and ye think it be to don; and sendyth home your men and hors tyl ye haf do here, &c . . . it is hey tyme.'[233] That should make us pause: 'and Yelverton wyth yow'. Fastolf may have been asking daily for

[228] BL Sloane MS 4, f. 38v.

[229] BL Add. MS 39848, f. 44, abstracted in Gairdner III, no. 359.

[230] I was thinking here of Worcester's plea to John Paston in January 1456: Davis II, p. 134, lines 4–8. How did this Fastolf–Worcester partnership work in practice – how, above all, did the letters get composed?

[231] *Ibid.*, p. 178, line 21: 'for lakke of leysar'.

[232] *Ibid.*, pp. 180–1.

[233] *Ibid.*, p. 186.

John Paston, 'a feythful man and ever on man',[234] but Brackley (of all people, as we, who know what will happen, are allowed to add) wants William Yelverton at the deathbed.

On the one hand, therefore, Sir John Fastolf, who was hale and hearty after midsummer 1459, did not sink slowly into a dithering senility, and on the other, John Paston was not the only man he trusted, was not single and supreme in his thoughts about the college at Caister and its endowment.[235] The college had occupied his thinking over many years; here, now, at the last, it was his major preoccupation.[236] Paston had been involved with the project from the beginning (or from an early stage). There had been obstacles to a decision, the high price of a royal licence to allow Fastolf to alienate land in mortmain being among the most daunting to a man never readily parted from his money,[237] or so it seems to us at this distance. It may be, however, that in waiting for the right opportunity to approach the great – for who could get near the king after 1456? – all opportunity was lost. Politics and politicians changed and the great after 1457 had war on their minds. It may be that Chancellor Wainfleet, whom retrospectively one thinks of as both sympathetic and able to pull strings, had schemes of his own for the Fastolf inheritance. There were, at any rate, obstructions not all or only of Fastolf's making. In these circumstances indecision was natural; death was too; it caught up with him before decision and action had been taken. Even in those dying days it was not clear what was the best course; as Brackley's letter shows, the involvement of St Benet's at Holm had not been ruled out.[238]

There is no reason, therefore, to reject out of hand John Paston's account of what happened at the very end:

the final appeal of Sir John Fastolf in concluding hastily with John Paston was that viscount Beaumont, the Duke of Somerset, the Earl of Warwick wished to buy [Caister], and that he considered that his executors desired to sell and not to establish a college, which was completely contrary to the intention of him, the said John Fastolf. And he considered that a sure means for the permission of the King and of the lords had not been provided, and so the whole foundation of the college hung in doubt. And, therefore, for the fulfilment of his intention he wished to make the said bargain with John Paston, hoping that he would have a genuine wish to complete the said college and would remain there so that it should not fall into the hands of the Lords.[239]

[234] *Ibid.*, lines 19–23.

[235] Later testimony, like Geoffrey Boleyn's (*ibid.*, pp. 224–5) and Ralph Lampet's (*ibid.*, p. 543) is not (for various reasons) to be trusted.

[236] *Ibid.*, p. 186, lines 8–16.

[237] See especially Gairdner III, p. 98; Davis II, pp. 174–5; and Fastolf himself: *ibid.*, pp. 168–9.

[238] If I am not misinterpreting Friar Brackley here: Davis II, p. 186, lines 8–16.

[239] Davis I, p. 103 (Mary Harris' translation). Compare the (Paston) account in John's *IPM* of 1466: Davis II, no. 900, line 49ff. For the *IPM*'s 'Pastonness' see *ibid.*, p. 554–6 and 'The Expenses of Thomas Playter', p. 42. Because the *inquisition post mortem* account is partisan

John also mentions the disagreements and differences of opinion among the executors. These seem more credible than an unwillingness on their part to found the college at all. Which of the executors were there at the end? Did John know all their minds on the subject? Doubt should be cast on this deathbed scene, given William Worcester's reaction in 1460 and Thomas Howes' volte-face in 1468, yet John's account is not impossible. Fastolf may well have come round to the idea, perhaps first broached to him only after he had made his will on 14 June 1459. William Barker wrote to John on 24 June: 'And youre mater that ye have meved of to Ser Thomas for the purchase, &c., myn mayster is weel agreed therto, but fyrst hit was taken strangely, &c.'[240] The college was the heart of the matter. While William Yelverton and William Jenny were not the evil men they later became in Paston myth-making, John *was* a relative, he had been trustworthy, he got things done, and one cook might indeed save the broth where many had been known to spoil it. Manipulation of the durable old man seems to me unlikely, even if his endurance was at its end, even though (even because) he may still from time to time have regarded the idea 'strangely'.[241]

What convinces me that Fastolf did want to commit Caister (and everything else) to John Paston (and Thomas Howes) is his outright, sealed grant to the two of them of all his moveable goods on 2 October, over a month before his death.[242] Perhaps he then did not have time to alter, because he became incapable of altering, his will. Perhaps he changed his mind (again).[243] None the less, I am more rather than less certain that Sir John Fastolf intended to leave all his lands to John on condition that he

its chronology of the following is suspect: (1) Fastolf deciding to make John his heir and to give him the responsibility for founding the college; (2) John desiring new feoffees who would be favourable to him; (3) those feoffees being appointed and new enfeoffments made (which they were in May 1457): Davis II, pp. 557–9. It is not only suspect. Fastolf's will of June 1459 contradicts it: at that date he was still wanting his executors to sell. Moreover, if the new enfeoffments were John's idea it is distinctly odd that William Worcester urged him to make them *after* reporting that Fastolf was 'fully yn wille to renew hys feffment': *ibid.*, p. 170, lines 5–6.

[240] Davis II, p. 179, lines 18–20: Geoffrey Spirling's letter of 6 January 1460 would suggest Fastolf had already had the idea in the autumn of 1457 ('Halwemasse was twelmoneth'), but Geoffrey was writing what Paston wished to be told: *ibid.*, pp. 202–3.

[241] Neither Thomas Howes nor Friar Brackley had recently reminded Fastolf of it when Brackley wrote in the autumn for Paston to hurry to Caister: 'Sire Thomas the parson, yowr owne most trewe, &c., by myn trewthe, and I your bedeman and yowrys at your comaundment in yowr letter, haf no more towchid of the mater, &c., to my mayster &c.' (*ibid.*, p. 186, lines 17–19). The resort to 'etc.' shows that this, if not a secret matter (William Barker knew of it), was a delicate one.

[242] NRO, Phillipps MS 612/3. There are slits for the seal tag, but no seal remains.

[243] William Worcester (*Itineraries*, p. 246) noted in 1479 that on Tuesday 22 November 1463 Thomas Howes said that Fastolf had told him, 'I pray God sende hym vengeance that wolle chaunge my testament and last wylle that I hafe made late aboute mydsomer.' One wonders what spiritual advice Fastolf was getting as he sank towards the pains of purgatory – 'whos soule God hafe pytie on and bryng hym owte of peyn', wrote William

brought Caister college into being.[244] John Paston, against my instinct and almost against my better judgement, gets the benefit of the doubt. I have a powerful mental picture: John *knows* Sir John wishes to leave him everything, but the old warhorse is either too feeble, or too much out of this world and into the next, to make a will which says so. John Paston tormented: it is a consolatory vision.

Worcester in the late 1460s, believing him (with good reason) still to be there: Davis II, p. 553. And who gave it him, as all the evidence suggests that the advice that Friar Brackley, Thomas Howes, and Master John Smyth, the Bishop of Norwich's chancellor, were offering him was secular. Master John Smyth, William Worcester recalled, 'Thomas Howys seyd to me was none holsom counceller yn the reformacion of the last testament made but ij executours to hafe the rule allone. I wold he had nevyr medled of yt; that councell made moch trouble': *ibid.*, pp. 355–6.

[244] That is, as John's *IPM* (Davis II, no. 900) has it, but less categorically: 'idem Johannes Fastolf pubplicavit et ore proprio pronunciavit' (line 128), and 'it was fully agreed, accorded, determynde, and concluded' (line 138).

CONCLUSION

What happened on the day Sir John Fastolf died we shall never know; there are too many conflicting and contradictory statements from too many interested parties for the truth to be disentangled. What happened after 5 November 1459 will have to be told in another volume. It is a sad story.

In his corrected working copy of the book Sir Stephen Scrope had translated for Sir John Fastolf, *The Dicts and Sayings of the Philosophers*, William Worcester, making his corrections in March 1473, could not resist annotating those 'dicts and sayings' which had particular, personal meaning for himself.[1] Against 'women be snares' he (a married gentleman) wrote 'nota';[2] against 'he is free that is free of honesty' he put his other name (he used two), 'Botoner', presumably in a moment of self-pity; against a passage on 'villainous speaking' he could not resist entering 'Botoner nota bene'; and against 'hevynes is a pasion touching thingis passed and sorowe is a fere of thingis for to come' he wrote, with touching self-justification 'pro Botoner'.[3]

More specific were his recollections of what we might properly call 'The Tragedy of Sir John Fastolf'. Against the 'dict' that one should not make great buildings which others will inherit he wrote, with feeling, 'pro Johannes Fastolff milite ditissimo qui egit contra istud concilium'; and alongside 'whi old peple enforceth theym to kepe theire Ritchesse and he aunswerd theyme bicause that after theire dethe thei had lever leve it to

[1] This is Emmanuel College, Cambridge, MS 1. 2. 10. See Curt F. Bühler (ed.), *The Dicts and Sayings of the Philosophers*, EETS, OS 211 (London, 1941), pp. xxi–xxiv, xli–xlii; M.R. James, *The Western Manuscripts in the Library of Emmanuel College* (Cambridge, 1904), pp. 29–30; and especially K.B. McFarlane, *England in the Fifteenth Century* (London, 1981), pp. 211, 218.

[2] Cf. his 'and yn especyalle to be not conversaunt ne neere amonges wommen, as I was kept froo her company xxx yeres or ony such were of my councelle, I thank God of yt': Davis II, p. 424, lines 13–15.

[3] Fs. 11v, 14v, 19v, 30v. The note on f. 30v I saw for myself; the three others I have taken from Bühler, *Dicts and Sayings*, p. xxiv. I would like to thank the staff of the MSS department of Cambridge University Library for allowing me to look at the Emmanuel MS, which was temporarily deposited there in summer 1986.

their ennemyes than to be in daunger of theire freendes' he put simply (and, as it were, with all passion spent), 'pro J. Fastolff'.[4]

Sir John had been an old friend; William also had his old enemy on his mind. I am fairly sure that as he wrote 'Note weele' beside 'whan ye wilt do eny thing folowe not aloonly thi wille but seke counsaille for by counsaile thou shalt knowe the trouthe of thinges' he had the John Paston of after 5 November 1459 in mind, as I expect he did when against 'whi a wise man askid counsail he aunswerd bicause he doubted that his will in som wise be medled with his witt' he wrote 'Nota optime'. I am certain John Paston was the target for 'Nota' beside 'And he saithe all evyll is in delite of money'.[5] In two instances there is no doubt William had John Paston in mind, for he named him: 'J.P.' They are interesting cases because they are not trite. Alongside 'And he saithe to be suspiciouse makithe man to be evil condicioned and to lyve evill', he wrote what I translate as 'J.P. extra suspicious'. Secondly, beside 'And he saithe who so trustith in this worlde is deceyved', he entered what I think may be translated as 'this happened to J.P.'[6]

What happened to John Paston – prison, an early death – William may have been thinking was deserved, not because John had fabricated Fastolf's nuncupative will, but because he had behaved so selfishly in endeavouring to carry it out; John behaved negligently towards William himself,[7] arrogantly where Fastolf's other old and faithful servants were concerned,[8] and above all indecently with regard to Fastolf's soul – not only was the funeral misconducted,[9] the college was not founded at Caister. William's own conscience was clear: 'As I support me to alle the world, I put nevyr

[4] Fs. 13v, 46v. Both these annotations are recorded by M.R. James, *Western Manuscripts*, p. 30. Worcester's marginalia occupy the earlier folios; they tend to die away after f. 54.

[5] Fs. 7v. 9, 29v.

[6] Fs. 26v., 36v. These Latin jottings of Worcester's are not easy to decipher. The 'J.P.' is clear enough; on the remainder I am ready to be corrected. In a 1480 notebook (*Itineraries*, pp. 322, 324) William wrote 'Nota J. Paston' and the quotation (I use Harvey's translation of the Latin), 'A monstrous and wretched infamy that the new comer should force the old inhabitants to plough', clearly having the 1450s in mind, as on the previous page he had had the 1460s when he wrote 'Nota pro J. Fastolf' and the quotation 'Rarely or never has an Emperor left a son in succession but has had either enemies or the unknown for heirs.'

[7] The nub of the matter was the 'liffelode' Fastolf promised Worcester, a promise John Paston was reluctant to fulfil (Davis II, p. 205, lines 54–60), and never did (*ibid.*, p. 584, lines 46–50). This is not to overlook the fact that Fastolf himself was negligent in not getting everything properly settled during his lifetime, but that is a forgivable failing in the elderly. John Paston's failure was wilful – clearly this was William's perception.

[8] See, for example, *ibid.*, pp. 585–6, lines 31–41. Thomas Howes' faithfulness is demonstrated by the window he put up in the church of Pulham Market, of which he became rector in 1465: the window was of the kneeling figures of Sir John Fastolf and his wife Milicent, with their arms: Blomefield III, p. 265. The inscription contained a phrase about Sir John – 'qui multa bona fecit in tempore vita' – which is ironic only to us twentieth-century ironists.

[9] See, particularly, William's scandalized humiliation in Davis II, pp. 204, 539–40.

maner ne lyfelode of my maister Fastolf yn trouble', he wrote in a letter of reconciliation to Margaret Paston after John's death.[10] He had done the right thing in promoting John Paston to first place. John Paston had let him down.

We share his disenchantment; his, ours, finds expression in a poem of a thirteenth-century Dominican of Florence, Remigio de' Girolami:[11]

> Everyone does well except me . . .
> I turn over books, read many of them, try to make
> my mind rule me, cover my shame,
> think and rethink.

William's intellectual curiosity – thinking, rethinking, looking, looking again – prevented his disenchantment deteriorating into despair, as it prevented Remigio's, and as it must do ours.

[10] *Ibid.*, no. 727, lines 55–6; he stressed the point (as he was bound to do in such emotional circumstances), for here he is repeating in the postscript what he had already said in the body of the letter, *and* told the bearer of the letter to Margaret to repeat to her: 'And now ye may opynly ondrestond the sothe, and your son Ser John also. And yhyt for all that I put never my maister Fastolf lyfelode yn trouble, for alle the unkyndnesse and covetise that was shewed me, as I hafe declared to the berer heroff that I know ye trust well, to whom yn thys ye may gefe credence at thys tyme.' The last letter of William to John, or perhaps the last John kept, was of 1458 (*ibid.*, no. 576); none the less, William and John met more than once in London during the autumn of 1461; William told Margaret at Christmas that he hoped John would 'be hys good master': Davis I, p. 281.

[11] George Holmes, *Florence, Rome and the Origins of the Renaissance* (Oxford, 1986), p. 83.

INDEX

None of the Pastons appears in the index. A small number of persons who are mentioned throughout the book (e.g. Sir John Fastolf) are indexed selectively.